To Trust the People with Arms

# To Trust the People with Arms

## THE SUPREME COURT AND THE SECOND AMENDMENT

Robert J. Cottrol

and

Brannon P. Denning

University Press of Kansas

© 2023 by the University Press of Kansas

Published by the University Press of Kansas (Lawrence, Kansas 66045), which
was organized by the Kansas Board of Regents and is operated and funded by
Emporia State University, Fort Hays State University, Kansas State University,
Pittsburg State University, the University of Kansas, and Wichita State
University.

Library of Congress Cataloging-in-Publication Data

Names: Cottrol, Robert J., author. | Denning, Brannon P., author.
Title: To trust the people with arms : the Supreme Court and the Second
    Amendment / Robert J. Cottrol, Brannon P. Denning.
Description: Lawrence : University Press of Kansas, 2023. | Includes
    bibliographical references and index.
Identifiers: LCCN 2023001557 (print) | LCCN 2023001558 (ebook)
    ISBN 9780700635719 (cloth)
    ISBN 9780700635726 (ebook)
Subjects: LCSH: Firearms—Law and legislation—United States. | United
    States. Constitution. 2nd Amendment. | United States. Supreme Court.
Classification: LCC KF3941 .C68 2023  (print) | LCC KF3941  (ebook) | DDC
    344.7305/33—dc23/eng/20230719
LC record available at https://lccn.loc.gov/2023001557.
LC ebook record available at https://lccn.loc.gov/2023001558.

British Library Cataloguing-in-Publication Data is available.

Printed in the United States of America

10  9  8  7  6  5  4  3  2  1

The paper used in this publication is acid free and meets the minimum
requirements of the American National Standard for Permanence of Paper for
Printed Library Materials Z39.48-1992.

# Contents

*Notwithstanding the military establishments in the several kingdoms of Europe, which are carried as far as the public resources will bear, the governments are afraid to trust the people with arms.*

—James Madison, *Federalist,* no. 46

# Acknowledgments

During the writing of this volume, we have benefited to a great degree from the consideration, counsel, and criticism of a number of different friends and colleagues from a variety of different disciplines and backgrounds—legal scholars, historians, political scientists, and practicing attorneys—who have either read portions of the manuscript at various stages of its writing or been willing to listen to and give thoughtful responses to ideas that we have developed during the course of this project. We gratefully acknowledge the critical readings and valuable suggestions of, in no particular order, Raymond T. Diamond, Nelson Lund, Kenneth Kersch, Joyce Malcolm, Jonathan Bush, Stephen Halbrook, Peter Hoffer, Renée Lerner, Naomi Schoenbaum, David Hardy, Alice Beard, Jean Yarborough, James Ely, Paul Kens, David O'Brien, Anthony Peacock, Kristen Goss, David Bernstein, Catherine Ross, Earl Maltz, Robert Dowlut, Burlette Carter, Gary Lawson, Art Wilmarth, and Alex Tsesis. We would like to especially acknowledge the helpful suggestions and encouragement of the late Dmitry Karshtedt, our good colleague and friend who passed away before the publication of this volume.

Our work was made better, and our thinking became clearer, through working with two superb editors at the University Press of Kansas: Michael J. Briggs, with whom we began the project; and David Congdon, our editor for the completion of the volume. Scott Pagel, director of the Jacob Burns Law Library at George Washington, and Iris Lee of the law library staff provided critical bibliographic support that greatly aided in the completion of this project. We would also like to thank George Washington University Law School students Clay Katsky, Scott Neall, Courtland Ingraham, José Rodriguez, and Tahminah Dehbozorgi, and Samford University, Cumberland School of Law student Trent Mansfield for valuable research assistance. A sabbatical provided by the George Washington University Law School to Robert Cottrol played a critical role in the writing and completion of this volume.

# Introduction

On Tuesday, November 20, 2007, the United States Supreme Court did something it had not done for nearly seventy years: it agreed to hear a case involving the Second Amendment. The case brought by Richard Heller would result in a landmark decision, the 2008 case known as *District of Columbia v. Heller*. *Heller* would declare unconstitutional the District of Columbia's ban on handguns, a ban that was some three decades old when the Court agreed to examine Richard Heller's case. *Heller* was the first time the Supreme Court declared a firearms restriction invalid on the grounds that the Second Amendment made the restriction unconstitutional. The case involving the District of Columbia would be followed two years later by the 2010 case *McDonald v. City of Chicago*, which invalidated a similar ban on handguns in Chicago. Both cases were decided by narrow 5 to 4 majorities. These two cases and the often curious and at times tortured history behind them are the subject of this book.[1]

*Heller* and *McDonald* are the focus of this volume, but we found ourselves in a somewhat curious position as the editorial process unfolded. By January 2022 we had finished the manuscript, having received the readers' comments and suggestions from our editor David Congdon. We were ready to go. But sometimes the writing of history can, like history itself, be untidy. As we were putting the finishing touches to this volume, we realized the looming case of *New York State Rifle and Pistol Association v. Bruen* belonged in any volume discussing the twenty-first century revitalization of the Second Amendment. *Bruen*, which involved the question of whether the Second Amendment protects a right to carry firearms outside the home for protection, had been argued before the Supreme Court on November 3, 2021, after we had submitted the manuscript to the press for reader evaluation. We saw from the amicus briefs that were filed, the oral arguments that were made, and the questions that were asked by the justices that *Bruen* was likely to be a significant case in the still slim history of the Supreme Court's Second Amendment jurisprudence. Our intuitive hunch in January 2022 has been borne out. The Court's decision, delivered on June 23 of that same year in *New York State Rifle and Pistol Association v. Bruen*, was far reaching, controversial, and consequential. We decided that we would treat *Bruen* at the end of this volume in a discussion we have titled "An Unanticipated Epilogue," wherein we look at the case and its ramifications for the future direction of Second Amendment jurisprudence and firearms policy.

But the core of this volume, our original intentions as it were, is devoted to tracing the Court's and the nation's path to *Heller* and *McDonald*. The road to *Heller* and *McDonald* was an uncertain one. The Second Amendment reads, "A well-regulated Militia, being necessary to the security of a free State, the right of the people to keep and bear Arms, shall not be infringed." Prior to the Court's decision to hear *Heller*, the constitutional provision had only had rather limited contact with the nation's highest court. The right to bear arms had been discussed briefly by the Court in the nineteenth century—we will examine those cases later in this volume. The Court had heard one case on the Second Amendment in the twentieth century, the curious 1939 case of *United States v. Miller*, which we will also discuss at some length later in the book. But otherwise, the right to bear arms and the meaning and scope of the Second Amendment remained largely unexamined by the high court. There had been, to be sure, a history in the twentieth century of dicta or judicial musings concerning the right to bear arms. These dicta usually appeared in cases unrelated to arms or firearms regulation. The Second Amendment had also from time to time been the subject of out-of-court statements or writings by justices, but again, apart from *Miller*, there had been nothing in the way of judicial opinions in cases involving regulation of firearms and claims that Second Amendment rights had been violated.[2]

In a very real sense, the Second Amendment had sort of missed the constitutional bus, or a series of constitutional buses that had driven by in the twentieth century. The Bill of Rights, as we all know from our high school history texts, was adopted in 1791. The first ten amendments were passed by Congress in 1789 as a kind of codicil to the new constitution. They were ratified by the states two years later. They were part of the Constitution, indeed probably best thought of as part of the original Constitution. These amendments were occasionally referenced in judicial opinion and more frequently discussed by constitutional commentators in the nineteenth century. But the great business of examining statutes and the practices of government agencies to see if those statutes and practices violated specific provisions of the Bill of Rights really began in earnest in the twentieth century. The First Amendment would get its first serious examinations during and immediately after the First World War as the Supreme Court began the process of weighing that constitutional provision's protection for freedom of expression against government claims that restrictions on some speech and expression were essential to public safety and national security. The high court would not actually invalidate a statute on the grounds that it violated the Constitution's guarantee of freedom of the press until the 1931 case of *Near v. Minnesota ex. Rel., Olson*, some 140 years after the adoption of the First Amendment. The Bill of Rights would further come alive over the course of the twentieth century as the Supreme Court increasingly came to recognize that American notions of liberty and individual rights demanded that the protections of the Bill of Rights had to shield the citizen not only from the actions of the federal government but from restrictions that came from state and local authorities as well.[3]

The Supreme Court's lack of engagement with the Second Amendment in the twentieth century would prove critical. The Bill of Rights, like similar proclamations of rights in the constitutions of other nations, expresses grand principles concerning the rights of individuals. But these principles are not self-defining. At best they only suggest how those principles are going to be or should be applied when actual individuals claim that a particular governmental policy violates a right, and when the government makes a countervailing claim that the policy is required by the public interest. We saw this process throughout the twentieth century with respect to different provisions of the Bill of Rights. Does the First Amendment's guarantee of freedom of speech protect speech that arguably libels or incites hatred against racial or religious groups? Does the same amendment's guarantee of freedom of religion or its prohibition on the establishment of religion mean that nondenominational prayers cannot be part of a public school's morning ritual? Is the Fourth Amendment's prohibition on unreasonable searches and seizures best enforced by the exclusionary rule, a rule that mandates that illegally seized evidence must be excluded at trial, even if it means a clearly guilty defendant might go free? Should the Eighth Amendment's prohibition of cruel and unusual punishment be interpreted as prohibiting the execution of juveniles or people with severe mental disabilities?

Throughout the twentieth century, and indeed now into the twenty-first century, the Supreme Court would wrestle with these and other difficult questions, hearing the arguments of those who claimed violations of their rights and the counterarguments of governmental representatives arguing public necessity. The latter would usually urge that the courts would take the wiser path if they deferred to legislatures that reflected the will of the people or state or federal agencies familiar with the practical problems of administering policies in difficult and complex areas. Through this process of hearing and trying to resolve the competing claims, the courts would make the grand pronouncements of the Bill of Rights confront the practical problems of governing a complex nation. It would also force the nation's judges to resolve or attempt to resolve the difficult question of how to apply the principles in the first ten amendments to a nation that had witnessed significant social, political, and technological change since the late eighteenth century. That process is only in its infancy with the Second Amendment.

If the Court had largely maintained an institutional silence on the subject of the Second Amendment before *Heller*, the four decades before the Supreme Court's decision to hear the case had produced a lively polemical and later academic debate over the exact meaning of the constitutional provision. That debate was part of the often-acrimonious national fight over gun control, a political controversy that has been a staple of the nation's politics since the 1960s. The gun-control movement that emerged out of the 1960s was something new in American culture and politics. While there had long been limited efforts to control firearms—local ordinances regulating how firearms might or might not be carried, or prohibitions on the ownership of weapons that were believed to be peculiarly suited to criminal use—a new set of sentiments began to emerge or gain increased currency toward the end of the 1960s. That decade of turbulence and tragedy—the assassinations of John F. Kennedy, Martin Luther King Jr., and Robert F. Kennedy, and urban riots that at times bordered on large-scale insurrection, brought about a national reassessment of the place of firearms in American life. If previous efforts at firearms regulation had been largely local and limited, a new set of commentators were beginning to see the widespread ownership of firearms by the American public as symptomatic of a national sickness, a bit of American atavism that could only be cured by radical measures, such as national restrictions on firearms ownership. Some of the more exuberant advocates for national gun control, in the movement's salad days of the late 1960s and early 1970s, openly expressed the hope that initially modest control measures would later ripen into outright prohibitions. The handgun bans in the District of Columbia and Chicago were part of a larger, generally unsuccessful effort to ban or severely restrict handgun ownership nationwide. This new sentiment would help produce a new interpretation, or perhaps more accurately fortify what had previously been a minority interpretation of the meaning of the constitutional guarantee of the right to keep and bear arms. That new or revised interpretation would produce the modern debate over the Second Amendment, a debate unlike the interpretive debates over other parts of the Constitution. It would be a debate over basic meaning.[4]

Broadly speaking, two interpretations of the amendment have emerged from the decades-old controversy. Some students of the constitutional provision have stressed the amendment's militia clause, arguing either that the amendment was only meant to ensure that state militias would be maintained against potential federal encroachment or that the individual's right to keep and bear arms was meant to be protected only within the context of a highly regulated, regularly drilling state militia. Adherents of both variants of what might be called the collective rights view argue that the Second Amendment poses little in the way of an impediment to strict, even prohibitory, gun-control measures given the fact that most Americans in the late twentieth century and now early twenty-first century are not regularly engaged in the business of militia training.[5]

Their opponents, supporters of an individual rights reading of the amendment, stress the Second Amendment's second clause, arguing that the framers of the constitutional provision intended to make possible a militia of the whole population, or at the very least a militia consisting of the entire population of able-bodied White men. They argue that this militia of the whole was expected to perform its duties with privately owned weapons. Advocates of this view go further. They argue that the advocates of various versions of the collective rights view have in fact misconstrued the relationship between the right to have arms and the well-regulated militia. The well-regulated militia is dependent on the right of the people to keep and bear arms, not the other way around. Advocates of an individualist reading also urge that the amendment's militia clause should be read as an amplifying rather than a qualifying clause—that is, while protecting a "well-regulated militia" was a major reason for including the Second Amendment in the Bill of Rights, it should not be viewed as a sole or limiting reason. The framers, according to this view, also had other reason for proposing or adopting this amendment, including protecting the individual's right to self-defense.[6]

We believe that those who argue for the individualist view of the amendment have the better of the argument. Only a highly strained, and indeed artificial, reading of the relevant sources could produce an interpretation that read the individual right to have arms out of the Constitution. The history of the right to have arms at English law, the history of the drafting of the Second

Amendment, and examination of the late eighteenth-century and early nineteenth-century commentators discussing the constitutional provision all support an individualist reading of the Second Amendment. The history of the Fourteenth Amendment and the clearly expressed intentions of the drafters of that amendment to protect the newly freed Black population from state-imposed racial restrictions on the right to bear arms also must be taken into account in our constitutional history. When that is done, the idea that the Constitution was not meant to afford protection for a private right to have arms becomes, in our view, totally untenable.[7]

Our views on the history of the Second and Fourteenth Amendments, coupled with the controversy over the Second Amendment's meaning, caused us to wonder how we should proceed with this volume. We decided against making Chapter 1, which examines, among other things, the history of the Second and Fourteenth Amendments, an occasion to revisit the individual versus collective rights debate. We will not use it as the occasion to do a point/counterpoint on each aspect or potential aspect of the controversy. Instead, we decided that in the first chapter we would present the histories of the Second and Fourteenth Amendments and how they were understood by those who proposed and accepted those constitutional provisions, according to what we see as the best evidence available.

A discussion of the history of the Second Amendment and its intended original meaning is actually a rather small part of this volume's concern. Both *Heller* and *McDonald* are valuable as case studies on the influence of social movements on constitutional interpretation. Two quite different social movements supported the differing interpretations of the Second Amendment. The first, the gun-control movement in the 1960s–1980s, captured the allegiances of the nation's elites, the national press, the American Bar Association, most university professors who expressed a public opinion on the topic, and national commissions studying crime and violence, among others. Most importantly, the gun-control movement captured the allegiances of the judiciary—many who considered themselves conservative, as well as those who saw themselves as liberal: Gun control—indeed, severe restrictions on ownership of guns, and perhaps even prohibitions—was seen as common sense and good policy. The Second Amendment, after all, did speak of a well-regulated militia; wouldn't the more prudent interpretation be one that confined whatever right that that anachronistic constitutional provision was meant to protect to state militias, the National Guard, or some such body? The lower federal courts, particularly after the passage of the Gun Control Act of 1968, would often accept this interpretation, generally diminishing, as a matter of positive law, or what the courts would enforce: the idea of an individual right to arms in the Constitution.[8]

Still, constitutional sensibilities are not simply confined to the nation's elites and the judiciary and their notions of good policy and good interpretation. Ordinary people also read the Constitution and come to their own conclusions as to the meaning of the document and its different provisions. If elite opinion makers were arguing that the language protecting the right to keep and bear arms was essentially meaningless as far as the individual was concerned, large segments of the public disagreed. Before the advent of the great gun-control movement of the 1960s, before the heating up of the bitter culture wars of which that movement was but one manifestation, the idea that the rights of American citizens included a right to be armed, even armed against a potentially tyrannical government, had been part of the common culture and, indeed, part of the common curriculum taught in the nation's schools. It was mentioned in grade school and high school civics texts, and even in a Boy Scout publication. If these were not the kind of writings likely to impress a court, they would remain part of the folk memory of many Americans, particularly, but by no means exclusively, in vast stretches of rural America where gun ownership was common and part of the cultural heritage of many families. If the polls are to be believed, the individualist interpretation of the Second Amendment remained popular with a majority of the American public, even among people who favored stricter gun-control measures, at a time when elite opinion including that of the judiciary largely favored the collective rights view of the constitutional provision.[9]

But the Second Amendment or its individualistic interpretation would not simply remain a bit of retained folklore, cherished by the masses but safely ignored by the more sophisticated. One result of the development of a national gun-control movement was the transformation of the National Rifle Association (NRA) from what had once been a largely apolitical organization of hunters and target shooters into a political force, indeed a mass movement. One consequence of that transformation was that individuals affiliated with the NRA—and, it should be added, others who were skeptical of the gun-control movement—began to explore the Second Amendment and its implications for gun control. It was an area that historians and law professors had, for a variety of reasons, largely overlooked. At first the research of this new group of scholars had little impact on the thinking of most scholars or the courts. The researchers by and large lacked the credentials normally associated with scholarship of this sort. Few individuals with PhDs. in history or allied disciplines examined the issue, at least not initially. Some of the individuals examining the history of the right to bear arms were practicing attorneys, but many were individuals who simply had an interest in firearms and an antiquarian interest in history. Published at first in the NRA's *American Rifleman* and other gun magazines, these researchers produced a body of scholarship that could safely be ignored, even sneered at by readers of journals with more respectable intellectual pedigrees. And yet, the insurgent scholars were raising uncomfortable questions, questions about the founding era and what late eighteenth-century Americans were actually saying about arms and the rights of the citizen. What they were uncovering was often in direct contradiction to the new conventional wisdom that the right to have arms had little to do with the rights of the citizen. By the 1980s this new insurrectionary scholarship was migrating from the gun magazines and beginning to enter the nation's law reviews and other academic journals.[10] More and more historians and legal scholars were also beginning to reexamine the issue. By the 1990s a full-fledged academic reconsideration of the Second Amendment was being conducted by many scholars, ourselves included. That reconsideration helped produce a narrative that made a strong case for the individual rights reading of the right to keep and bear arms. It is part of the story of how *Heller* and *McDonald* came about.[11]

*Heller* and *McDonald* involve more than the debate over the meaning of the Second Amendment. The constitutional history of the right to keep and bear arms is also in large part the story of the Fourteenth Amendment and what has come to be called the incorporation doctrine. The Fourteenth Amendment, passed by Congress in 1866 and ratified by the states in 1868, had two broad goals. The first has been generally acknowledged: the amendment was intended to bring equality before the law to people of different races. That was the clear meaning of the amendment's equal protection clause. It was, to be sure, an underenforced constitutional norm for much of the twentieth century, but few disputed that racial equality under the law was the intended purpose and understanding of those who proposed and ratified the clause. The framers of the Fourteenth Amendment also had another aim: to make the states respect the rights found in the Bill of Rights. The best evidence indicates that those who proposed the Fourteenth Amendment intended for the amendment's privileges or immunities clause to prevent state governments from infringing on the guarantees found in the Bill of Rights, including the right to keep and bear arms. The Supreme Court, in cases decided soon after the enactment of the Fourteenth Amendment, severely limited the privileges or immunities clause as a vehicle for protecting citizens from actions by state governments. The Court would then spend a good deal of the twentieth century rediscovering the principle that the states could not infringe on fundamental rights through the process of selective incorporation, applying parts of the Bill of Rights to the states through the Fourteenth Amendment's due process clause.[12]

Selective incorporation was a controversial process. It was more intellectually haphazard and less straightforward than full incorporation through the privileges or immunities clause. It was opposed by many political and judicial conservatives, many of whom saw the application of constitutional rights by federal courts against state legislation or state officials as a violation of states' rights or an unwarranted interference with democracy on the local level. Those who hoped for judicial enforcement of the Second Amendment faced two formidable hurdles when contemplating potential litigation. Judicial liberals, and quite a few conservatives as well, tended to support the collective rights reading of the Second Amendment because it would further gun control, a policy objective with which they agreed. Those judicial conservatives who might have been skeptical of many gun-control measures and who might have been sympathetic to an individualist reading of the amendment would nonetheless be reluctant to interfere with state or local legislation and further extend what they believed to be the unwise or illegitimate doctrine of incorporation. Part of the story of *McDonald,* and to a lesser extent *Heller* as well, is the story of how conservative legal thinkers and conservative jurists came to accept the evidence from the Reconstruction era, both the Fourteenth Amendment and federal statutes enacted at the time, that indicated that the framers of the Fourteenth Amendment also saw the right to keep and bear arms as one of the fundamental rights of citizens.

Discussions of the Second and Fourteenth Amendments and the intentions and understandings of the framers of those constitutional provisions inevitably raise the question of originalism and its place in constitutional litigation and decision making. The questions of original intent and original meaning played an outsize role in the *Heller* and *McDonald* litigations. Because there was little in the way of Supreme Court Second Amendment precedent—the somewhat odd 1939 case of *United States v. Miller* was claimed by both sides of the debate—the Court was free to look at the Second Amendment as a matter of first principles. What was it intended to do in 1789 when it was drafted, or in 1791 when it was ratified? The Court is always free to, and to some extent usually does, return to the late eighteenth-century roots of the Bill of Rights when examining a claim of alleged violation of constitutional rights, but *Heller* was something different. It was a case of alleged infringement where the Court could consider the original meaning of a constitutional provision on a blank or virtually blank canvas, uncluttered by precedents—precedents that almost inevitably expand or contract the original scope of a constitutional provision. It is significant that the individualist majorities and the dissenting minorities in both cases claimed that their views better represented the intentions and understandings of those who drafted and ratified the Second and Fourteenth Amendments.

The questions of original intentions and original understandings in *Heller* and *McDonald* do not end with the simple question of who got closer to the historical mark, the individual rights–leaning majorities or the collective rights–leaning dissenters. Both cases raise critical questions concerning the applications of original intentions and original understandings even when they are properly understood. There is, of course, an ongoing debate over whether jurists should be bound by the late eighteenth-century sensibilities that gave rise to the Bill of Rights or the post–Civil War sentiments that helped create the Fourteenth Amendment. Many argue that jurists should look to modern needs or felt needs in crafting their decisions, shaping constitutional doctrine to contemporary requirements. There was certainly an undercurrent— indeed, more than an undercurrent of this—in the Second Amendment debate, with some commentators arguing that the amendment was an anachronism and that its idea of a universally armed population acting as a militia at large was a dangerous invitation to anarchy and insurrection. But assuming that the original purposes of the Second Amendment cannot be lightly discarded, and assuming that the individualist reading better reflects the amendment's history and text, the question of how to apply the right to keep and bear arms in the modern age is still a complex one. If the framers intended a population that would be armed with the military weapons of the day—the single-shot "Brown Bess" musket or "Kentucky Long Rifle" come readily to mind—can that principle be applied today when each soldier, regardless of specialty or assignment, is expected to be proficient with fully automatic weapons and grenade launchers? Justice Scalia had to wrestle with this issue in his majority opinion in *Heller*. We will assess his opinion in Chapter 7 and use that discussion to examine the difficulties of doing an intellectually rigorous jurisprudence that remains faithful to original intentions and understandings while also translating those understandings into a form that is workable in the modern age.

Chapter 8 also causes us to look again at the difficult issue of original understanding. Justice Thomas's opinion in *McDonald* invited the Court to consider anew its jurisprudence of incorporation or applying the Bill of Rights to the states. The Court had severely curtailed the Fourteenth Amendment's privileges or immunities clause, the intended vehicle for incorporation, soon after the enactment of the amendment in the *Slaughter-House Cases* of 1873. Over the course of the twentieth century, particularly after the Second World War, the Supreme Court had redeveloped incorporation through the Fourteenth Amendment's due process clause. By the time *McDonald* was heard, most of the provisions of the Bill of Rights had been applied to the states through that clause. The easiest way to indicate that the Second Amendment limited the actions of state governments as well as the federal government was to use the Court's existing due process jurisprudence to incorporate the right to have arms as it had done with the other provisions of the Bill of Rights. Four justices—Roberts, Scalia, Kennedy, and Alito—signed onto an opinion that did just that. Justice Thomas wrote an opinion urging the Court to reconsider incorporation this time through the all-but-forgotten privileges or immunities clause. Indeed, Justice Thomas's concurrence in *McDonald* has been something of a catalyst for an early twenty-first century reconsideration of the clause. The differing opinions of Thomas and the due process plurality produced a strange result in which an opinion stressing precedent battled with an opinion stressing original intent to produce the same substantive result.

The opinions in *Heller* and *McDonald*, like the opinions in most cases, were reactions to the arguments presented by the opposing parties. The story of the litigation that produced the briefs and oral arguments that the justices considered is a story of conflicts and tensions often on the part of allies seeking the same ends. There were often sharp divisions within the individual rights camp. Richard Heller's case was filed by his attorneys Robert Levy, Alan Gura, and Clark Neily. The NRA was initially skeptical of the DC litigation, fearing that it was premature and that it could lead to disastrous results—a definitive ruling from the Supreme Court holding that the Second Amendment was a collective right that did not apply to individuals, at least not in any practical sense. Part of the story of the *Heller* litigation is the story of the conflict between the NRA and Heller's attorneys, how they initially fought each other eventually came together as uneasy allies in the *Heller* case. But the individual rights camp was not alone in experiencing intramural conflict. Many gun-control supporters were also somewhat wary of the litigation. The stakes were high. A ruling from the high court that the constitutional provision discussing "the right of the people to keep and bear arms" did indeed protect the right of the people to keep and bear arms, would cast into doubt existing and potentially future gun-control measures. As the litigation progressed, a number of activists in the gun-control movement became increasingly concerned about the prospect of the government of the District of Columbia defending its gun-control statute before the Supreme Court. The law not only prohibited the ownership of pistols but also proscribed the use of rifles and shotguns for home defense. An extreme statute might be more likely to push the Court to accept an individualist reading of the amendment. Better to let the Second Amendment and gun control have their day in court on another occasion with a statute that gave the case for gun control a surer footing.[13]

If *Heller* produced internecine conflict in both camps, *McDonald* created something of an ideological and methodological free-for-all on all sides. The NRA and Alan Gura, who represented petitioner Otis McDonald, quarreled over whether the argument for incorporation was best made through a conservative due process claim, as the NRA argued, or a privileges or immunities claim, which Gura believed more appropriate. They were joined by others. A number of interest groups from the right to the left, with agendas quite far afield from the gun issue, saw the privileges or immunities argument as a vehicle through which they could argue for an expanded view of constitutional protection for unenumerated rights. A group that believed the privileges or immunities clause would protect and expand sexual privacy in areas like same-sex marriage signed on. A conservative group that believed a proper reading of the privileges or immunities clause would revive freedom of contract as it had been interpreted by the Supreme Court in the 1905 case *Lochner v. New York*, which declared legislation limiting the number of hours an employee could work during the day unconstitutional, joined in. These and other groups signed on to amicus briefs urging the Court to incorporate the Second Amendment through the Fourteenth Amendment's privileges or immunities clause and thus expand the possibilities for greater consideration of unenumerated rights. In contrast, the National Association for the Advancement of Colored People (NAACP), which had filed an amicus brief in support of the

District of Columbia and the constitutionality of gun control in *Heller,* filed a brief asking for due process incorporation in *McDonald.* The NAACP brief expressed the fear that incorporation through the Fourteenth Amendment's privileges or immunities clause would call into question previous civil rights rulings that had been based on the due process clause. Unlike *Heller,* the *McDonald* litigation ignited hopes and fears that went far beyond the concerns of the firearms community and its opponents.

*Heller* and *McDonald* were decided. In the first decade of the twenty-first century an amendment that was adopted in the last decade of the eighteenth had finally come to life in the nation's courts. The decisions were controversial and remain so. Some commentators condemned the decisions as monstrous examples of judicial overreach. Other observers criticized the decisions as far too modest. The reactions of the lower federal courts and the state courts to the Second Amendment decisions were varied. Most judges in the first decade after *McDonald* only gave a grudging acknowledgment of the significance of the cases and the principle that the constitution protects the right to have arms. Other jurists embraced the cases and overturned restrictive legislation recognizing in a few cases the idea that the Second Amendment protected a right not only to have arms in the home for defense of self and family, but also a right to carry weapons outside the home for protection. The differing approaches to *Heller* and *McDonald,* where some courts took only a minimalist view of the scope of the Second Amendment while other courts adopted more robust views of the protections afforded by the constitutional provision, has already begun to change in the wake of the Court's decision in *Bruen.* That case clearly calls for a robust view of the right protected by the Second Amendment. The decision will undoubtedly sweep away some of the more conservative methodologies that have been developed in a number of the lower federal courts and state courts on the issue.

We are finishing this volume a little more than two months after the Court's decision in *Bruen.* We will discuss some of the early changes that have occurred in *Bruen*'s immediate aftermath in Chapter 9. The decision promises a new judicial skepticism concerning the constitutionality of many firearms regulations and the likelihood that governmental entities will bear a significant burden in proving the constitutionality of such regulations. In the last chapter we also want to discuss our view that the effort to eliminate or minimize the idea that the Constitution provides protection for the citizen's right to have arms has been counterproductive and has been a major impediment to the effort to develop firearms policies that protect public safety while preserving the right of the people to keep and bear arms.

AUTHOR NOTE

We would like to add a two-part postscript—if postscripts are still possible in this age of word processing and endless possibilities for seemingly seamless editing. The first part of this postscript has to do with terminology. You, the reader, will find that in the course of this volume we spend a good deal of time discussing the nation's racial history and the linkages between that history and the history of the right to keep and bear arms. The connections between these two themes in the nation's history have been strong. The Second Amendment debate is, to a great degree, a debate about force and whether or not the state should have a monopoly of force. That debate is an important one for society in general, but it is particularly salient for members of groups who have not been able to consistently rely on the state for protection, and who indeed have often found the state to be actively hostile. There is a new literature that has emerged within the past two decades indicating that the ability of Black people to have arms for self-defense played a significant role in mitigating the racial violence that plagued the Jim Crow South in the first six decades of the twentieth century.[14] We will include some of the insights of this literature in our overall discussion of the evolution of the right to keep and bear arms in American law, politics, and culture.

Part of our discussion of the right to bear arms is going to engage our nation's racial history. There has been a tendency in recent decades for historians and other writers when discussing race to feel compelled to take often strenuous efforts to either avoid using the term *Negro* or to preface their use of the term with an apology or perhaps to bracket the word with quotation marks when usage was unavoidable. That will not be our practice in this volume. Negro was the term that most Black people used to describe themselves for a good portion of American history. It was used with pride by some of the most courageous people in the history of the United States, including the parents of one of the coauthors of this volume. Ida B. Wells would so describe herself when she was an outspoken newspaper editor taking a brave and physically dangerous stand against lynching and mob rule in late nineteenth-century America. Carter Woodson would use the term when he founded the Association for the

Study of Negro Life and History in 1915 at a time when American apartheid, Jim Crow, was becoming even harsher, when the American historical profession was dominated by proslavery apologists, and when the best scientific minds of the day proclaimed the doctrine of White supremacy. Woodson's efforts and those of his associates and successors would, over time, change the way the nation and the world viewed people of African descent. Thurgood Marshall and Constance Baker Motley and their colleagues, White and Black, used the term in *Brown v. Board of Education* when they asked the Supreme Court why Negroes, of all the people in the American nation, were singled out for separate and stigmatizing treatment in segregated schools. Martin Luther King Jr. would use the word *Negro* throughout his inspiring career, most notably when he stirred and forever changed the nation with his "I Have a Dream" speech during the 1963 March on Washington. *Negro* requires neither avoidance nor apology. It will be used in this volume with respect, along with other names Americans of African descent have proudly called themselves and fought to make terms of honor.

The second part of this postscript involves a brief word about us and our perspective. Even before we began work on this volume, our reading of the relevant history and law had led us to the view that the right to bear arms was an important but underenforced civil right. That belief in turn had caused us to lend our support to amicus briefs and other efforts designed to vindicate the right to bear arms in the courts. We provided this support without compensation. We did so in part because of our concern for fidelity to the constitutional and historical record. We did so also because of our belief that the debate over the Second Amendment is a debate over the most fundamental of rights, the right of ordinary people to defend their lives. In this discussion we won't claim to be neutral commentators; few scholars approach this issue, or indeed other issues involving modern history, without prior opinions. Nonetheless, if we cannot be neutral commentators, we will strive to be fair ones.

# 1. Constitutional Predicates

By the time the Supreme Court had decided to hear Richard Heller's case, the Second Amendment had been the subject of a fierce controversy for the better part of four decades. This had not always been the case. For much of American history the right to keep and bear arms, at least as an ideal, had been extolled as a precious right, a symbol of the freedom and independence of the American people. This widespread agreement was in part a product of the nation's history. The frontier conditions that existed in colonial America and persisted well into the nineteenth century had contributed to this consensus. Arms—private arms—were important at the nation's founding. The ragtag bands that served as militia were, more often than not, equipped with the members' own weapons. These often-ill-equipped formations played an important role in achieving the nation's independence. They had played an especially critical part in the early rebellions that would ultimately become the American Revolution. That history contributed to the widespread agreement that a right to arms was among the important rights of the citizen. The often-violent nature of early American society including a significant amount of racial conflict and racial violence also helped contribute to the widespread view that the right to possess arms for self-defense was critical.

But the Second Amendment and the right to keep and bear arms cannot be understood solely through an examination of American history. Like a number of other provisions of the Bill of Rights, the Second Amendment was an attempt to secure what was believed to be an already existing right. To a large extent, the framers of the Bill of Rights did not see themselves as the creators of new rights. Instead, they were attempting to assuage the fears of those who believed that a strengthened federal government, fortified by the new, proposed constitution, might encroach on rights already considered part of the English, or perhaps better put, Anglo-American constitutional heritage.

To understand the Second Amendment, it is necessary to understand the framers' world and their view of the right to bear arms as one of the traditional "rights of Englishmen." This requires a few words of explanation. There were other groups who were also part of the American nation at the time of the drafting of the Constitution. Nearly 20 percent were people of African descent, of which over 90 percent of these were enslaved and a little less than 9 percent were free. Among the White population there were people of English, Scottish, Scots-Irish, Irish, Dutch, German, and French descent, among others. But the English predominated, constituting some 60 percent of the White population.[1] By way of contrast, the second-largest group, the Scots-Irish, constituted a little over 10 percent of the White population. Of equal or, indeed, probably greater importance, the English were by far the dominant group culturally. Their language would become the lingua franca for the British colonies that would become the United States. And it was their notions of law and governance that dominated the courts and legislatures of the different colonies before the Revolution. These notions would continue to dominate the political and judicial institutions of the new states and the national government after independence. Any discussion of the Constitution and its roots in European history must take into account the overwhelming importance of the history of English law and culture to that enterprise.[2]

The English settlers who began to populate North America in the seventeenth century were heirs to a tradition over five centuries old governing both the right and duty to be armed. Part of the right to be armed stemmed from traditional notions of the individual's right to security in his home. England's ancient maxim that "a man's home was his castle and that even the King could not enter without permission" came with a corollary. The individual, however noble or base, had the right to defend his home, his inviolable castle. To better understand this view, it may be helpful to turn to the writings of seventeenth-century English jurist Sir Edward Coke. Coke was a strong advocate of the view that the common law, as developed by English judges, was a reflection of natural law, a product of the superior ability of English jurists to discern that which was right and reasonable. In Coke's opinion the King, like his subjects, was bound by the common law. The seventeenth-century jurist and commentator also believed that Parliament was also subject to the common law as well and that statutes that ran contrary to common law and good reason should be considered void or at the very least interpreted quite narrowly.[3]

In his Institutes, which summarized English law—or at least Coke's view of English law—the jurist discussed the problems of arms and crime in early modern England. In commenting on a sixteenth-century statute that prohibited the carrying of arms in search of illegal confrontations, Coke cautioned that the statute should not be interpreted in a way that would prohibit defense of the home:

> And yet in some cases a man may not onely use force and armes, but assemble company also. As any may assemble his friends and neighbours, to keep his house against those that come to rob, or kill him, or to offer him violence in it, and is by construction excepted out of this act: and the sheriff, and company ought not to deal with him upon this act: for a mans house is his castle . . . for where shall a man be safe, if it be not in his house.[4]

The English roots of the right to have arms extended beyond this traditional concern for the right to protect one's home and family. There was a long-standing English distrust for professional armies and police forces. In English law the idea of an armed citizenry responsible for the security of the community had long coexisted, admittedly somewhat uneasily, with regulation of the ownership of arms, particularly along class lines. The Assize of Arms of 1181 required the arming of all free men. Later statutes would require even villeins, people who had a status somewhat similar to serfs in Continental Europe, to have arms in order to be prepared to participate in the defense of their communities. Lacking both professional police forces and a standing army, English law and custom dictated that the citizenry as a whole, equipped with their own weapons, assist in both law enforcement and military defense. By law all men between the ages of sixteen and sixty were liable to be summoned into the sheriff's posse comitatus. All persons were expected to participate in the hot pursuit of criminal suspects, the "hue and cry," supplying their own arms for the occasion. There were legal penalties for failure to participate. The maintenance of law and order was a community affair, a duty of all the King's subjects.[5]

All able-bodied men were considered part of the militia and were required, at least in theory, to be prepared to assist in military defense. The law required citizens to possess arms. Towns and villages were required to provide target ranges in order to maintain the martial proficiency of the yeomanry. Despite this, the English discovered that the militia as a whole maintained a rather indifferent proficiency and motivation. As early as the fourteenth century, English authorities made efforts to promote archery as a sport and to legally restrict other forms of recreation that might compete with the militarily useful art. Authorities did so in the hope that public proficiency with arms gained through recreational activity would produce a better-trained militia at large. The efforts appeared to be largely unsuccessful. By the sixteenth century, English authorities increasingly came to rely on select bodies of men intensively trained for militia duty rather than to rely on the population at large.[6]

Although English law recognized a duty and a right to be armed, both were highly circumscribed by English class structure. The common people were expected to participate in the defense of their communities, to be sure. But the law regarded the common people with due wariness. They might be useful in defense of shire and realm, but they were also capable of mischief with their weapons—mischief toward each other, toward their betters, and toward their betters' game. Restrictions on the type of arms deemed suitable for the yeomanry, or at least on the type that they could carry, had also long been part of English law and custom. Game laws had been one tool used to limit the arms available to commoners. The fourteenth-century Statute of Northampton restricted the ability of people to carry weapons in public places. The sixteenth-century statute that caused Coke to note the right to have arms for defense of the home was a crime-control measure that prohibited the carrying of handguns and crossbows by those with incomes of less than 100 pounds a year. At times Catholics were also subject to being disarmed as potential subversives after the English Reformation. Although historical research indicates that the various class and religious discriminations did not rise to the level of total prohibition of arms ownership, the idea of qualifying the right to own and carry arms by social condition coexisted with the English notion of arming the population at large.[7]

The need to provide for community security, and the security of the kingdom as well, had produced the traditional duty to be armed at English law. But it would take the religious and political turmoil of seventeenth-century England to help transform that duty into the modern notion of a political right to have arms. Attempts by the Stuart kings Charles II and James II to disarm large portions of the population, particularly Protestants and other suspected political opponents, met with popular resistance. Their efforts helped implant into English and later American constitutional sensibilities the idea that the right to possess arms was a right not only of personal importance, but political significance as well. James II encountered strong opposition and ultimately a revolution in 1688 from the Whigs, the name given to those who opposed his reign.[8] Among the complaints listed against James II was that he was guilty of "causing several good subjects being Protestants to be disarmed at the same time when Papists were both armed and employed contrary to law."[9] The Whig opposition proposed a Bill of Rights, which was adopted into law in 1689. It included a number of measures that would influence eighteenth-century American constitutional thinking, including a recognition of the right to petition and prohibitions on cruel and unusual punishment and on excessive bail and excessive fines. Among the other measures found in the document was a seventh provision: "That the subjects which are Protestants may have arms for their defence suitable to their conditions and as allowed by law."[10]

By the eighteenth century, the right to possess arms, both for personal protection and as a counterbalance against potentially oppressive state power, had come to be viewed as one of the fundamental rights of Englishmen on both sides of the Atlantic. Sir William Blackstone and his writings are important to an understanding of this way of thinking. Blackstone's *Commentaries on the Laws of England*, written between 1765 and 1769, greatly influenced American legal thought both during the American Revolution and well into the nineteenth century. For much of the latter part of the eighteenth century and well into the early decades of the nineteenth, case reporters, the staple of a common law lawyer's training and practice, were rare on the American continent. Blackstone's *Commentaries* served as summaries of the common law for many a fledgling and veteran American attorney. His writings were not only important to the generation that fought the American Revolution and adopted the original Constitution but also played a critical part in the legal training of the generation that fought the Civil War and later adopted the Fourteenth Amendment.[11]

Blackstone listed the right to possess arms as one of the five auxiliary rights of English subjects without which their primary rights could not be maintained:

> The fifth and last auxiliary right of the subject, that I shall at present mention, is that of having arms for their defence, suitable to their condition and degree and such as are allowed by law. Which is also declared by the same statute . . . and is indeed a public allowance, under due restrictions, of the natural right of resistance and self-preservation, when the sanctions of society and laws are found insufficient to restrain the violence of oppression.[12]

So, what was the importance of the seventh provision of the English Bill of Rights and Blackstone's "Fifth Auxiliary Right" to our discussion of the

Second Amendment and the meaning of the right to keep and bear arms in the American Constitution? To answer this question, we have to understand what both of those documents from England's legal history were, and perhaps more importantly what they were not. First, they were not constitutional documents, at least not as that term might be used in the United States. England, quite famously, did not have a written Constitution, a fundamental charter against which the statutes and governmental practices of the day could be deemed constitutional or unconstitutional. England did have custom, tradition, and the common law. These often formed strong and long-standing notions of the rights of the subject. But these could be modified—and even swept aside by acts of Parliament. Sir Edward Coke early in the seventeenth century had made an effort to develop the notion of what today we would call judicial review. He wanted to assert that acts of Parliament in fundamental contradiction to the common law could be declared void, or unconstitutional, if we might somewhat anachronistically use modern American terminology. But ultimately that strain of judicial thinking reached a dead end in English jurisprudence. It is fair to say that by the eighteenth century the reigning doctrine in English law was an acceptance of Parliamentary supremacy. While the common law would govern in the absence of a statute, once Parliament had spoken and a statute was properly enacted—with the consent of the House of Commons, the House of Lords, and the King—that was the law of the land whether or not it violated tradition, the common law, or even previous statutes.[13]

The seventh provision of the English Bill of Rights, the one protecting the right of Protestants to have arms, was part of a statute that became law in 1689. We are spending a very brief amount of time pointing this out because the presence of a right to arms provision in a document labeled the "English Bill of Rights" has created some amount of confusion in the debate over the American right to keep and bear arms. How, some ask, can the English provision be said to protect a right to have arms when the English have enacted very strict, indeed essentially prohibitory, gun-control measures in the twentieth century? If the English provision is the ancestor of the American Second Amendment, it must mean that the Bill of Rights of 1689 was not intended to protect the individual's right to have arms and that the American Second Amendment of 1791 was not intended to do so either. The answer to this is simple. As part of a statute, the seventh provision of the Bill of Rights of 1689 was not meant to restrict Parliament but rather to ensure that the Crown—specifically, the incoming sovereigns King William and Queen Mary of Orange—would not curtail the right of English Protestants to have arms, as James II had done. It was not meant to limit the ability of future Parliaments to legislate on the subject of arms or anything else for that matter. As a piece of legislation, it provides evidence that Englishmen in the late seventeenth century had a belief that the right to arms was important, that it should be protected from undue restrictions by the Crown, but such a belief formalized in a written statute, unlike a constitutional provision, could not be thought of as limiting the actions of future Parliaments.[14]

Blackstone's discussion of the English right to arms has also brought about some degree of misinterpretation. Some students of the subject have argued that because Blackstone called the right to have arms an "auxiliary right," he deemed the right to arms as being a right of lesser importance. In one sense this is correct. For Blackstone the three primary or absolute rights of the individual (or perhaps more properly put, the English subject), were the rights to life, liberty, and property. But these rights needed to be guarded. In Blackstone's words:

> But in vain would these rights be declared . . . if the constitution had provided no other method to secure their actual enjoyment. It has, therefore, established certain other auxiliary rights of the subject, which serve principally as outworks or barriers, to protect and maintain inviolate the three great and primary rights of personal security, personal liberty and private property.[15]

Blackstone went on to list the power of Parliament and limitations on the King's prerogative or powers as auxiliary or subordinate rights. Both a well-functioning Parliament and limitations on the King's power were seen as safeguards against arbitrary or oppressive rule. Blackstone also listed the right to petition the courts for redress of grievances as the subject's third auxiliary right. He further noted a fourth auxiliary right: to petition the King or either House of Parliament. The fifth auxiliary right, the right to have arms, should be seen not as part of a set of rights that were deemed inconsequential because they were labeled subordinate or auxiliary, but instead as essential guarantees that enabled the individual to defend his primary rights. Indeed, the auxiliary rights, as Blackstone defined them, would find their way into the American Constitution in Article 1 defining the powers of Congress, the First Amendment's guarantee of the right to petition Congress, and the Fifth Amendment's requirement for due process of law before a person could be deprived of life, liberty, or property, as well as the Second Amendment's protection for the right to keep and bear arms, among other provisions of the Constitution.[16]

The arms provision in the English Bill of Rights and Blackstone's discussion of arms give evidence that the right to have arms was a part of English law and political philosophy, and yet, as the documents themselves indicate, the right was limited by both religion and by England's class structure. Blackstone was quite aware of the limitations on the English right to arms. He noted that England's game laws also frequently served as a device to limit the right of common people to have arms or at least their ability to carry them outside the home. The English recognized a right to arms, but even in the seventeenth and eighteenth centuries when it was explicitly discussed as part of the law of the realm, it was recognized as a right with significant limitations both social and legal. How did that change in the American context?[17]

## THE PALLADIUM OF LIBERTY

The English experience had been one in which the right to have arms for defense of the home and the duty to be armed for the common defense had been transformed during the turmoil that was England in the seventeenth century into the notion of a right to be armed partly as a means to resist political oppression. A similar evolution in thinking would occur or reoccur in the British colonies that would become the United States between the earliest seventeenth-century settlements and the American Revolution. Early English settlement in North America had a quasi-military character, an obvious response to often perilous frontier conditions. Leaders of settlements often held the title of militia captain, reflecting both the civil and military nature of their office. In order to provide for the defense of often isolated colonies, special efforts were made to ensure that White men, capable of bearing arms, were brought into the colonies.[18]

Far from the security of Britain, often bordering on the colonies of other frequently hostile European powers, colonial governments viewed the arming of able-bodied White men and the requirement that they perform militia service as essential to a colony's survival. The right and duty to be armed broadened in colonial America. If English law qualified the right to own arms by religion and class, those considerations were significantly less important in the often-insecure colonies of early America. If by the seventeenth century the concept of the militia of the whole had become largely theoretical in England, in contemporary America it was often the chief instrument of a colony's defense. While the English upper classes sought to restrict the ownership of arms on the part of the lower classes as a means of helping to enforce game laws, any significant effort to restrict hunting in North America with its small population and abundant game would have been hard to sustain. From the beginning, conditions in colonial America created a very different attitude toward arms and the people.

Race provided another reason for the renewed emphasis on the right and duty to be armed in America. Britain's American colonies were home to three often antagonistic races: the indigenous population and the White and Black newcomers. These indigenous so-called Indian populations, the English and other European settlers who would come to dominate British North America, and the enslaved African populations found themselves in often shifting patterns of alliances and antagonisms. Enslaved Africans and their Afro-American slave children at times ran away seeking freedom by joining ranks with the Indian tribes that lived beyond the boundaries of White settlements. Other Blacks, some slave, some free, helped guard European settlements from Indian attacks. Some Indian tribes helped capture and return fugitive slaves to bondage with their White owners. Free Negroes, slaves, and some Indians tribes found themselves aligned with British colonists in territorial wars with France and Spain. Others sided with the French and Spanish either to regain territory or to gain freedom.[19]

The threat from the indigenous population, fear of warfare with French and Spanish colonies, and the need to maintain control over the enslaved Black population ensured that settlers in British North America would recognize the need for an armed and universally deputized White population. This experience helped to broaden the right of White people to have arms. The need for White men not only to act in the traditional militia and posse capacities but also to keep order over the slave population helped lessen the importance of class, religious, and ethnic distinctions among Whites in colonial America. That need also helped extend the right to bear arms to classes traditionally viewed with suspicion in England, including indentured servants. In most colonies all White men were expected to possess and bear arms to defend their commonwealths from both external and internal threats. The statutes of many colonies specified that White men be armed at public expense. In most colonies all White men between the ages of sixteen and sixty, often with the exception of clergy and in some cases religious objectors, were considered part of the militia and were required to be armed. Not only were White men required to perform traditional militia and posse duties, in colonies with large slave populations they were often required to serve as patrollers, a specialized posse dedicated to keeping order among the slave populations. This broadening of the right and responsibility to keep and bear arms reflected a more general lessening of class, religious, and ethnic distinctions among Whites in colonial America.[20]

In some cases, and at some times, that broadening of the right and responsibility to be armed would even extend to elements of the African American population. In Virginia in the early eighteenth-century, free Negroes who owned their own homes were permitted to keep one gun in their house for home defense. In that colony, Blacks, both enslaved and free, who lived on frontier plantations were able to keep guns to help defend isolated plantations. Massachusetts had no laws prohibiting Blacks from owning guns, although free Negroes were not permitted to participate in militia drills. Other northern colonies also permitted free Afro-Americans to own guns, although they generally did not permit Blacks to perform militia service; some free Afro-Americans undoubtedly served as members of posses. South Carolina in the early eighteenth century permitted free Black men to become members of the militia and to own firearms. As Whites were then a minority of South Carolina's population, the arming of free Black men was considered necessary as a security measure to ward off rebellion from the majority of the population, which was enslaved. It was also a security measure that helped to prevent attack from the Spanish colony of Florida.[21]

The colonial experience, which included significant fear of and experience with racial conflict, helped strengthen the appreciation of early Americans for the virtues of an armed citizenry. The experience of the American Revolution, of course, would further strengthen that appreciation. The Revolution began with acts of rebellion by armed citizens. Though sober historical analysis reveals that it was actually American and French regulars who ultimately defeated the British and established American independence, the image of the ragtag privately equipped militia successfully challenging the British Empire has earned an enduring place in American thought and folklore. It also helped shape the new nation's political philosophy. For the generation that authored the Constitution, it reinforced the lessons their English ancestors had learned a century earlier. It helped revitalize Whiggish notions that standing armies were dangerous to liberty. The lessons of the Revolution helped transform the idea that the people should be armed, and that security should be provided by a militia of the whole body of the people from a matter of military necessity, into a political notion—and one that would find its way into the new Constitution.

This view that an armed population contributed to political liberty as well as community security found its way into the debates over the Constitution and can help us understand the thinking behind the Second Amendment. Like other provisions of the Constitution, the clause that gave Congress the power to provide for the organizing, arming, and disciplining of the militia excited fears among those who believed that the proposed Constitution could be used to destroy both state power and individual rights. This fear of the proposed Constitution, the desire of those known as anti-Federalists to maintain the Articles of Confederation or the weak federal government that the Articles had created, led to fierce debates between Federalists and anti-Federalists. The anti-Federalist argument that a fortified federal government would be destructive of individual liberty was met by the Federalist response that the key structural features of the new constitution—separation of powers and specified limitations on the authority of the national government—would be the best mechanism for ensuring that the federal government would not usurp its authority and destroy individual liberties. The anti-Federalists were skeptical. They demanded a Bill of Rights specifying rights that the new government could not infringe. James Madison, who would draft the Bill of Rights, was initially among those who believed that such a listing of rights was unnecessary and would only provide a weak set of "parchment barriers" against infringements of individual liberty. Like a number of other Federalists, Madison believed that protection of individual rights lay not in a formal enumeration of rights, but instead in the structural features of the Constitution that strictly limited the federal government to clearly specified powers and each branch of the federal government to well-defined and limited spheres of influence. Nonetheless, Madison and other advocates of the proposed Constitution recognized that ratification required the support of at least some of those who were skeptical of it. They recognized that a Bill of Rights could help build that support.[22]

Many of those who were critics of the proposed Constitution feared that the clause that gave Congress the power to arm and discipline the militia could be used both to do away with the state's control over the militia and to disarm the population. It is interesting in light of our modern debates over the meaning of the Second Amendment that both the Federalist champions of the new Constitution and its anti-Federalist critics assumed that the militia included all White men between the ages of sixteen and sixty, presuming a universal arming of the White population. Yet some critics expressed grave concerns that Congress would use its new power to establish a select militia, a body of men chosen from the population at large who would receive special military training and would essentially preempt all the duties of the militia. Many commentators viewed a select militia with as much apprehension as they did a standing army. The English experience of the seventeenth century had shown that a select militia could be used as an excuse to disarm the population at large. A letter dated January 25, 1788, and traditionally attributed to Richard Henry Lee of Virginia argued for a broad-based militia and against the enlistment of a select militia. His letter reiterated the notion that a select militia would be as dangerous to individual liberty as a standing army and that arming the population at large was essential to the prevention of tyranny:

> A militia when properly formed, are in fact the people themselves, and render regular troops unnecessary. . . . The constitution ought to secure a genuine militia and guard against a select militia by providing that the militia shall always be kept well organized, armed and disciplined, and include, . . . all men capable of bearing arms; and that all regulations tending to render this general militia useless and defenseless, by establishing select corps of militia, . . . be avoided. . . . These corps, not much unlike regular troops, will ever produce an inattention to the general militia; and the consequence has ever been, and always must be, that the substantial men, having families and property, will generally be without arms, without knowing the use of them, and defenseless; whereas, to preserve liberty, it is essential that the whole body of the people always possess arms, and be taught alike, . . . how to use them; nor does it follow from this, that all promiscuously must go into actual service on every occasion. The mind that aims at a select militia, must be influenced by a truly anti-republican principle.[23]

In their efforts to answer critics of the Constitution, Alexander Hamilton and James Madison addressed the charges of those critics who argued that the new Constitution could both destroy the independence of the militia and deny arms to the population. Hamilton's responses are particularly interesting because he wrote as someone who was openly skeptical concerning the military value of the militia of the whole. Militia units had had a mixed record during the War for Independence. It is probably fair to say that a number of militia units performed well in what military analysts might call a home guard role, defending their own communities while close to home. Other units performed reasonably well as partisan or guerilla forces that were able to harass British formations as they attempted to move through difficult terrain in remote locations. But militia formations proved to be generally unequal to the task of fighting regular British troops in the pitched set piece battles that characterized regular eighteenth-century warfare.[24]

Hamilton, the former Revolutionary War artillery officer and aide to George Washington, conceded that the militia had fought bravely enough during the conflict, but he argued it proved no match when pitted against regular troops. Hamilton urged the creation of a select militia that would be more amenable to military training and discipline than the population as a whole. Despite this, he recognized that there was strong sentiment in favor of arming the whole militia, that is, the free citizenry. As a concession to that sentiment, he expressed a somewhat grudging support for arming the people as a whole in what is frequently termed a sedentary militia but might more accurately be described as an inchoate militia—one that was armed and could be summoned in an emergency, but that nonetheless received no training beyond an annual check to ensure that it was in fact equipped: "Little more can be reasonably be aimed at, with respect to the people at large, than to have them properly armed and equipped, and in order to see that this be not neglected, it will be necessary to assemble them once or twice in the course of the year."[25]

But if Hamilton made only a grudging, tactical concession to the concept of the militia of the whole, Madison, the author of the Second Amendment, was a much more vigorous defender of the concept. In the *Federalist,* no. 46 he left little doubt that he saw the armed population as a potential counterweight to tyranny:

> Let a regular army, fully equal to the resources of the country, be formed; and let
> it be entirely at the devotion of the federal government: still it would not be going
> too far to say that the State governments with the people on their side would
> be able to repel the danger. . . . This proportion would not yield, in the United
> States an army of more than twenty-five or thirty thousand men. To these would
> be opposed a militia amounting to near half a million citizens with arms in their

hands, officered by men chosen among themselves, fighting for their common liberties and united and conducted by governments possessing their affections and confidence. It may well be doubted whether a militia thus circumstanced could ever be conquered by such a proportion of regular troops. . . . Besides the advantage of being armed, which the Americans possess over the people of almost every other nation, the existence of subordinate governments, to which the people are attached and by which the militia officers are appointed, forms a barrier against the enterprises of ambition. . . . Notwithstanding the military establishments in the several kingdoms of Europe, which are carried as far as the public resources will bear, the governments are afraid to trust the people with arms.[26]

Madison's estimate of a militia of half a million citizens is of particular significance. The census of 1790 listed the White male population over the age of sixteen as 813,298. It did not indicate how many White men were over sixty and would be beyond the contemplated age for militia service.[27] But a militia of 500,000 out of a population of some 800,000 would indicate the near universality of the contemplated militia. This desire to maintain a universal militia, and an armed population that would support it, played a critical part in the adoption of the Second Amendment. It is also important to remember that firearm ownership, for self-defense and hunting, was widespread, with few restrictions, at least for the White population. Our best estimates indicate that well over 60 percent of free White men owned guns in the late eighteenth century.[28] The Second Amendment, like other provisions of the Bill of Rights, was designed to prevent the newly created federal government from encroaching on rights that were then enjoyed. It is significant that the universally accepted view of the militia, at the time, was that militiamen would supply their own arms. One year after the ratification of the Bill of Rights, Congress passed legislation reaffirming the notion of a privately equipped militia of the whole. The act, titled "An Act more effectually to provide for the National Defence by establishing an Uniform Militia throughout the United States," called for the enrollment of every free, able-bodied White male citizen between the ages of eighteen and forty-five into the militia. The act required every militia member to provide himself with a musket or firelock, a bayonet, and ammunition. The statute also exempted the military equipment owned by militiamen from lawsuits for debt or payment of taxes.[29]

How might we attempt to assess what Madison and his colleagues were doing or believed that they were doing with the proposal and adoption of what ultimately became the Second Amendment? We can start by briefly considering the history of the drafting of the amendment. Madison was presented with an array of proposals concerning the related but distinguishable issues of the right to have arms and the militia. Some proposals, like that of Roger Sherman of Connecticut, were designed to ensure the state's control over the militia. A proposal supported by anti-Federalists from Pennsylvania reflected the strong right-to-arms provision in that state's Constitution of 1776, which protected the right to arms for individual defense, defense of the state, and the right to hunt. An omnibus Virginia resolution sought to protect the right to keep and bear arms, show support for a well-regulated militia, and prevent the establishment of a standing army.[30]

Which of these proposals or sets of concerns ultimately influenced Madison and his contemporaries? Did Madison see the amendment as protecting an individual's right to arms or as a provision that would preserve the militia? As a number of historians have observed, in many ways this question sets up something of a false dichotomy, an anachronistic view of the amendment dictated more by the modern gun-control debate than by the world as Madison and his contemporaries probably saw it. For the generation that debated and ultimately ratified the Bill of Rights, there was no bright line distinction between the armed people and the militia. The world they inhabited was one in which the citizen was armed with his own weapons. It was a world in which professional police forces were nonexistent. The armed citizen was expected to protect himself, his family, and his property and also to protect the community when summoned to do so. The citizen would bring his own arms if summoned and would be familiar with their use in part because of his familiarity with weapons gained from his private pursuits.[31]

This link between the citizen's ordinary pursuits, the familiarity with weapons that would be gained from such pursuits, and the efficacy of the citizen as a member of the militia stands out in somewhat sharper relief when the militia is considered more as a vehicle for law enforcement than as a military instrument. The text of the Constitution defines the mission of the militia in both police and military terms: the militia may be employed to enforce the law, a police mission; it could also be used to suppress insurrections and repel invasions—ergo, military missions.[32] With the Constitution's envisioning of a militia with dual functions, the distinction between the militia, even the broad-based militia envisioned during the debates over the Constitution and the posse comitatus, which could enlist all members of the community on short notice in the task of fighting crime, seems highly tenuous. Considering also that Blackstone regarded the posse comitatus as not only a vehicle for law enforcement but also a body that could aid the sheriff in assisting the Crown to resist invasions, the distinction becomes even more tenuous. All of this fleshes out or reinforces the idea of a community where a familiarity with arms gained from private activities might be readily converted to public defense.[33]

Madison's initial treatment of the draft that would ultimately evolve into the Second Amendment reflected this general understanding. We are now accustomed to the Bill of Rights as the first ten amendments, a distinct addition to the original Constitution. However, this scheme with which we are all familiar was not part of Madison's original drafting design. Madison instead initially proposed that the provisions would be added to the Constitution as guarantees of individual rights or clarifications on the limitations of governmental power, placed in those sections of the Constitution that either protected individual liberties or outlined the powers of the different branches of the federal government. Thus, in Madison's initial draft of what would ultimately become parts of the Fifth, Sixth, and Seventh Amendments, he proposed placing the guarantees of the right to a hearing by a grand jury and the right to jury trials in criminal and civil cases as additions to Article 3, Section 2 modifying the provision in the original Constitution outlining the power of the judiciary. Madison's initial proposal for what would become the Tenth Amendment, reserving powers not delegated to the federal government to the states, was placed after Article 6, which, among other provisions, contains the supremacy clause indicating the supremacy of federal laws made pursuant to the Constitution. What would become the Second Amendment, along with other key provisions of the Bill of Rights—the First Amendment's guarantees of freedom of religion, protection for the right of peaceable assembly, prohibition on the establishment of religion, the Third Amendment's injunction against the quartering of soldiers in private homes, the Fifth Amendment's prohibition against double jeopardy and self-incrimination and that amendment's guarantee of due process, the Sixth Amendment's requirement for a speedy trial, and the Eighth Amendment's prohibition on cruel or unusual punishment—were all placed in Article 9, Sections 3 and 4 of the original Constitution. Had Madison's initial draft been followed, Article 9 would have included Section 2, which protects habeas corpus, Section 3 prohibiting bills of attainder (a statute outlawing a particular individual), and ex post facto laws. There would also have been subsequent sections protecting freedom of assembly and religion,[34] the right to keep and bear arms,[35] the rights of conscientious objectors,[36] and provisions prohibiting the quartering of soldiers,[37] double jeopardy,[38] and the other familiar guarantees of individual rights.[39]

Madison's suggested placement of what would become the Second Amendment and other key provisions of what we now know as the Bill of Rights suggests that he saw those provisions as having the primary aim of extending or amplifying a section of the Constitution that was specifying the rights of individuals. Had he seen the proposed provision concerning the right to arms as having the primary purpose of clarifying or modifying Congress's power over the militia, he would have been more likely to suggest its inclusion in Section 8, which specifies Congress's power over the arming and disciplining of the militia. Madison's proposed language can help us to understand what he was intending to achieve: "The right of the people to keep and bear arms shall not be infringed, a well-armed, and well- regulated militia being the best security of a free country, but no person scrupulous of bearing arms, shall be compelled to render military service in person."[40]

This initial draft indicates an intention to protect two rights: the right to keep and bear arms, and the right of religious objectors not to be compelled to perform military service. The right to keep and bear arms is linked to the preservation of the militia, but the language here suggests that the militia is dependent on maintaining the right of the people to keep and bear arms, not the other way around. The militia is extolled as the best defense of a free society, but nothing in the language, unlike the language concerning the right to arms and the protection for what we today might term conscientious objectors, suggests a legally enforceable claim for a state to have additional powers over the militia or for an individual to serve or participate in the militia.

The language of the Second Amendment, as it was ultimately adopted, tracked that of Madison's initial proposal in one important respect. The protection for conscientious objectors was dropped during the course of the debates. But the idea that the operative language—the language providing that a legally enforceable guarantee would be confined to the right to keep and bear arms—remained. The final product, like Madison's initial proposal, left the injunction, the imperative, of the constitutional provision confined to the right to keep and bear arms. The clause discussing the militia can properly be seen as declaratory, a statement of principle, but not as a modification or limitation on the right to have arms. Indeed, such a principle had been suggested by a draft passed by the House of Representatives that would have protected the right to keep and bear arms for "the common defence," but that limitation was taken out in the Senate.[41]

So why did the First Congress pass on to the states an amendment that protected the right to have arms and did little more than reiterate the importance of the militia? It did so in part because the right to have arms was one point that Federalists and anti-Federalists could generally agree on. Some historians have tried to argue for a Federalist–anti-Federalist split over the right to have arms. They further argue that Shays' Rebellion, which occurred in Massachusetts in 1786 and 1787, made Federalists even more leery of the concept of an individual right to arms.[42] The historical record does not support this view. Control of the militia was controversial. The right to have arms was not. Arch Federalist Alexander Hamilton in *Federalist*, no. 29 gave his support to the idea of arming all citizens, not because he believed doing so would have much military value, but because he recognized that agreeing to this was a necessary concession to popular sentiment. James Wilson of Pennsylvania had been a delegate to the Constitutional Convention and would later be appointed as an associate justice of the Supreme Court by George Washington. Wilson extolled the virtues of the provision protecting the right to arms in the Pennsylvania Constitution. In expressing his approval, Wilson quoted Coke's discussion of the subject's duty and right to defend his own home. He also noted that the right stemmed from the traditional English duty to be armed both for "the preservation of the kingdom, and of their own persons."[43]

William Rawle was another committed Federalist. He served as US district attorney for Pennsylvania under both Washington and John Adams. In that capacity he prosecuted John Fries for his participation in an anti-tax rebellion in western Pennsylvania. In his treatise *A View of the Constitution of the United States of America*, Rawle would express the view that the Bill of Rights protected citizens from infringements by state and federal governments. His discussion of the Second Amendment analyzed the militia and right to bear arms clauses separately. Rawle acknowledged that in wartime, regular troops were more valuable than militia formations but that the militia was an important security force in times of peace and at the early stages of a conflict before a regular army could be raised. In discussing the right to keep and bear arms, Rawle noted that the right was far more robust in the United States than in England, where the right was restricted to Protestants. He also argued that the

Second Amendment would protect people from disarmament by the actions of state legislatures as well as Congress.[44]

No contemporary observer of the framing generation can give us a better sense of how the Constitution was viewed as a legal document, how it specified the allocation and limitation of governmental powers and the rights that were protected in the American constitutional system, than St. George Tucker. Tucker, a Virginia jurist, had been a professor of law at the College of William and Mary from 1790 to 1804, when he was appointed to Virginia's Supreme Court of Appeals. Despite some earlier misgivings about the proposed Constitution, he had by 1788 become a firm supporter of the successor to the Articles of Confederation. Undoubtedly Tucker's greatest contribution to American law was his work in producing an edited and annotated American version of Blackstone's *Commentaries*. In his observations on the English jurist's commentaries, and in his earlier lectures on American law at William and Mary, Tucker had much to say on the American Constitution, including the Second Amendment's protection for the right to have arms. Tucker described the right to arms as "the palladium of liberty," noting that "self-defense is the first law of nature." He would also note, in contrasting Blackstone's discussion of the right to have arms in England with the American Second Amendment, that the American right was far more robust than that of England. Tucker would attribute the relatively truncated nature of the right to arms in England in part to British game laws, which he saw as having "effectually taken [the right to have arms] away from the people of England." Tucker's observations reflected a belief common at the beginning of the nineteenth century that the Constitution protected a robust right of the citizen to own and use arms.[45]

If Tucker would extol the right to bear as the palladium of American liberty, the decades between his 1803 publication of *Blackstone's Commentaries with Notes of Reference to the Constitution and Laws of the United States* [ . . . ] and the Civil War would produce almost no federal jurisprudence on the subject of arms and the Second Amendment. Massachusetts born–Supreme Court Justice Joseph Story in his 1833 *Commentaries on the Constitution of the United States* would echo Tucker's sentiment on the subject, writing: "The right of the citizens to keep, and bear arms has been justly considered, as the palladium of the liberties of a republic; since it offers a strong moral check against the usurpation and arbitrary power of rulers; and will generally, even if they are successful in the first instance, enable the people to resist, and triumph over them."[46]

But with the exception of the *Dred Scott* case, which we will discuss shortly, antebellum federal jurists did not discuss the right to arms in actual cases. There were a number of reasons for this judicial silence. Probably first among these was that before the Civil War most jurists and commentators would have agreed that the Bill of Rights did not restrict the actions of the states, only those of the federal government. During the drafting of what would become the Bill of Rights, Madison had suggested that the Constitution should include protection from state violations of basic rights, including protection for the freedom of conscience, speech, and press and the right to trial by jury in criminal cases. But these proposals did not succeed. The principle that the Bill of Rights only limited the federal and not the state governments was reiterated by the Supreme Court in 1833 in *Barron v. Baltimore*, a case involving a landowner's claim that the city of Baltimore had taken his property without just compensation, in violation of the Fifth Amendment.[47] Because regulation of firearms in antebellum America was almost exclusively a matter of state and local law, the federal judiciary remained silent on the subject.

## A HOUSE DIVIDED

There was, if the commentators and state court opinions are representative, a general consensus in antebellum America that the right to have arms was one of the badges of American citizenship. To the extent that there was serious infringement of the right to have arms before the Civil War, the infringements were largely linked to restrictions brought about by the reinvigoration and extension of slavery in the nineteenth-century South. That reinvigoration of American slavery brought with it a new sentiment, one that had not been present, or not present to the same degree during the establishment of the nation and the drafting of the Constitution. The sentiment that was gaining increased support in the nineteenth century was that the United States was to be a republic for White people, with others, particularly the Afro-American population, denied any possibility of citizenship. The late eighteenth century—the era of the drafting of the Constitution and its Bill of Rights—had been a time of relative embarrassment concerning slavery and relative silence concerning race or racial restrictions. There were racial restrictions, to be sure. Federal law had placed a racial limitation on militia membership in the 1792 legislation defining the militia. Some communities prohibited settlement by free Blacks. But the era of the Constitution's formation was a time that had considerably less in the way of racial restrictions than the nineteenth century that would follow. Strong antislavery sentiment had developed in the wake of the Revolution. The late eighteenth century was a time when the northern states began the process of ending slavery. In the Upper South, states like Delaware, Maryland, Virginia, and North Carolina, a number of masters were making arrangements to privately manumit their slaves, and the laws were being changed to facilitate this generosity. Most interestingly, the initial tendency of the law was to recognize the free Negro as a citizen. Most states, including Delaware, Maryland, North Carolina, and Tennessee, where slavery would persist until the passage of the Thirteenth Amendment after the Civil War, allowed free Black men to vote—if they met the requisite property qualifications. Indeed, the only states in the late eighteenth century that absolutely restricted the vote to White men were Virginia, South Carolina, and Georgia.[48]

The relatively liberal racial atmosphere of the late eighteenth century would not last. Slavery in the nineteenth century would become more important to the South as new developments—the cotton gin and the opening of western states to cotton cultivation, among others—would give a new profitability to slavery. With that new profitability would come a greater determination to maintain what would come to be known as "the peculiar institution." That determination would bring about a more muscular defense of slavery and a new emphasis on race and racial restriction. The fear of slave rebellion intensified in the nineteenth century, stoked by slavery's increased importance and the fear that the rebellion that ended slavery in Haiti would serve as an example for American slaves. New legislation reflected these new fears. The era after the War of 1812 was a time of hardening racial attitudes and increased restriction on the rights of free Afro-Americans. These restrictions became especially acute in the slaveholding South. Southern legislatures were particularly afraid that free Blacks would make common cause with slaves and foment or facilitate slave rebellion. Fears of slave revolts were heightened by actual slave rebellions that occurred on American soil, including the revolt led by a free Black man, Denmark Vesey, in South Carolina in 1822, and the rebellion led by slave Nat Turner in Virginia a decade later. Responding to the new, more restrictive racial atmosphere of the nineteenth century, Southern states began eliminating rights that some free Afro-Americans had previously enjoyed. North Carolina and Tennessee disenfranchised free Black men in their state constitutional conventions in 1835 and 1836 respectively. And to emphasize that Blacks were not citizens, throughout the South new legislation in the nineteenth century curtailed the rights of free Negroes to have firearms. Very often the new legislation was more concerned with disarming free African Americans than slaves. This was on the theory that a slave under the control of his master might be entrusted with a firearm, but that an armed free Black person was a danger to the social order. In 1831 Maryland and Virginia passed legislation restricting the ownership of weapons by free Blacks. Research by historian Martha Jones indicates that the free Black residents of Baltimore greatly valued the right to have arms both as a means of self-protection and as a badge of citizenship. They actively sought and were frequently successful in getting permits to have guns. No permit was required for White residents. Delaware, a slave state, passed legislation in 1831 requiring, for the first time, that free Afro-Americans who wanted to carry firearms had to obtain a special license from a Justice of the Peace. Georgia passed legislation in 1833 declaring that "it shall not be lawful for any free person of colour in this state, to own, use or carry fire-arms of any description whatever." In 1834 the Tennessee Constitution was amended to restrict the right to keep and bear arms to free White men. The previous constitution adopted in 1796 had granted the right to all freemen. Other Southern states would adopt similar racial restrictions on the right to have arms in statutes or in constitutional provisions during the antebellum era. Outside of the slave states, the right to own guns was generally not impaired for free Negroes.[49]

If the right of White citizens to have arms was generally respected throughout the nation, and the right of free Blacks to own guns was recognized in the free states, the right to have arms was not totally unregulated. There were state regulations that could probably not reasonably be called infringements or at least not serious infringements. Local ordinances regulated the storage of gun powder as a safety measure. State statutes, particularly in a number of states of the South and the old Southwest (Tennessee, Arkansas, and Louisiana), among others, prohibited the carrying of weapons considered peculiarly suitable for criminal purposes; the colorful and deadly Bowie knife was frequently on the list of prohibited weapons. Cases involving these restrictions played an important part in developing a jurisprudence on the right to bear arms, one that would develop in state and not federal courts. By the early nineteenth century, most state constitutions recognized the principle of the people's right to bear arms, but state courts and legislatures realized that principle alone did not settle every question that might arise with respect to the possession and use of weapons.

Cases in two slave states, Arkansas and Tennessee, illustrate early attempts to balance the right to have arms with notions of public safety. These cases also illustrate the relationships between citizenship and race and arms and the militia as these concepts were viewed in the antebellum South. The two cases, *Aymette v. State*, an 1840 case from Tennessee, and *State v. Buzzard*, decided by the Arkansas Supreme Court in 1842, started with state constitutional provisions protecting the right of "free White men to keep and bear arms for the common defense.[50] The wording of the two state constitutional provisions was revealing. The right to bear arms had a clear racial restriction. And to modern eyes the relevant provisions of the Arkansas and Tennessee constitutions might appear at first reading to support a right to bear arms only for very restricted militia purposes. Such a reading would miss an important social reality of life in the slave states before the Civil War. The constant need to monitor and discipline the slave population, to prevent runaways and to ensure that free Negroes were kept subservient, had greatly expanded the notion of the militia or the idea of the citizen as a participant in the state's defense in the antebellum South. The militia of the whole, the inchoate militia, or the idea that every male citizen should be armed to defend the community had by the 1840s become a largely theoretical concept in many northern states. This was not the case in the South. The need for racial control ensured the continued deputization of all White men. They might be formally organized into militia companies or slave patrol formations. Even if not formally organized, White men had to be ready to respond to new versions of the hue and cry should the possibility of runaways or the dreaded slave rebellion occur. And even during normal times White men were expected to enforce the slave code, to ensure that a slave off the plantation had a pass or other evidence of his master's permission. The provisions of the Arkansas and Tennessee Constitutions reflected the reality of a state and a society that expected all White men to have their own arms.[51]

The latter case, *State v. Buzzard*, gives us the chance to see how three jurists approached the issue of weapons control in light of state and federal guarantees protecting the right to have arms. The case involved a challenge to an Arkansas statute that forbade the concealed carrying of pistols, dirks, butcher knives, or other large knives. The case was presided over by the state's first chief justice, Daniel Ringo, who wrote an opinion upholding the statute. Ringo's opinion acknowledged the basic principle of the right to have arms but also argued for what modern jurists might call a balancing test: the need to weigh the right in question against the interests of public safety and security. Ringo was joined by his colleague Justice Townsend Dickinson, who wrote an opinion that stressed that the right to arms in the Arkansas statute was enacted for the preservation of the militia. His opinion emphasized that the statute regulated the carrying of weapons and focused on weapons that would not ordinarily be considered military equipment. The carrying of such weapons was not, in Dickinson's view, protected, although presumably the owning of arms useful for the common defense was. A third justice, Thomas J. Lacy, dissented on the grounds that the state statute infringed on the right to keep and bear arms.[52]

In the earlier case, *Aymette v. State*, the Supreme Court of Tennessee heard the appeal of William Aymette, who had been convicted under a state statute prohibiting the carrying of concealed Bowie knives. The court opinion by Justice Nathan Green rejected Aymette's contention that the right to bear arms gave an unlimited right to carry any weapon and that it prevented all legislation on the subject. The state high court held that the open carrying of weapons was protected by the right to bear arms and made a distinction between arms useful for the common defense and those weapons that were essentially the tools of criminals.[53]

Two important ideas were developed in *Aymette*. The first of these was the distinction between bearing arms openly and carrying concealed weapons. The second idea was that some weapons were protected under a constitutional right to keep and bear arms, and others were not. The Tennessee Supreme Court focused on the idea that arms that were useful for the common defense were protected by the state constitution whereas weapons such as the Bowie knife, which seemed to be more the tool of criminals, were beyond the scope of the state constitution's guarantee. This view, similar to the Dickinson opinion in *Buzzard*, would come to be known as "the civilized warfare test" and would go on to play a role in state court jurisprudence on the right to bear arms in the nineteenth century; it would also play a limited role in the United States Supreme Court's jurisprudence on the subject in the twentieth century.

*Aymette* was important because it revealed some of the practical difficulties that would inevitably occur as a court tried to wrestle with the problem of balancing a right to have arms with the need for a legislature to pass laws designed to improve public safety and control crime. The first issue before the Tennessee Court seems unproblematic enough. The state statute prohibited the carrying of concealed weapons. The argument can certainly be made that a legislature might reasonably decide that requiring people to carry their weapons openly puts everyone on notice that an individual is armed. One can avoid that individual or at least be aware that one is dealing with an armed person. There is less likelihood under such circumstances, assuming of course the law is obeyed, of a surprise armed confrontation. The distinction between a right to bear arms openly and the carrying of concealed weapons was an important one for many nineteenth-century state courts.

But the second part of the *Aymette* decision, the distinction between protected arms and unprotected weapons, was less clear. The notion that some weapons are inherently useful only for crime and not for legitimate purposes, including self-defense and the common defense, seems somewhat more problematic. If a weapon would be an effective weapon for criminals, it seems logical, at least at first blush, that it could also be useful for self-defense, for police and military purposes, and for citizen assistance to police and military forces, that is, the militia. Why were Bowie knives singled out by the legislature? Why did the Tennessee Supreme Court say that the prohibition was constitutional? Bowie knives enjoyed a colorful and dangerous reputation in the old southwestern frontier. These "Arkansas toothpicks" had a reputation as the "weapon of choice" for brawlers and ruffians. But Bowie knives were in fact no more dangerous than many other knives commonly carried at the time. The original Militia Act of 1792 required designated citizens to equip themselves with bayonets in addition to rifles or muskets. Could it be reasonable to prohibit Bowie knives when the law, at least in theory, required all White men to own bayonets? The Court gave no clear reason for the distinction, indeed no reason at all. Nonetheless, *Aymette* was an early example of a line of judicial inquiry and reasoning that would have far-reaching consequences for the right to have arms. It is a question courts are still grappling with today: Recognizing a constitutional right to have arms, and also recognizing that that right is protected in order to protect the serious—indeed, often deadly—business of personal self-defense and citizen participation in the defense of the community, which arms are protected? What are the limits of a right to have arms? Can legislatures and courts make distinctions and, perhaps most importantly, principled distinctions between those arms that fall within the ambit of constitutional protection and those that do not? *Aymette* raised these questions but did not give particularly clear guidelines on how they might be answered.

Another case from a slaveholding state, *Nunn v. Georgia*, was intriguing though less far-reaching. *Nunn* also involved the concealed carrying of a weapon, in this case a pistol. The intriguing aspect of *Nunn* was Georgia jurist Judge Joseph Henry Lumpkin's opinion that the Second Amendment of the US Constitution was binding on the state of Georgia. Lumpkin held this even though that view ran counter to the US Supreme Court's decision in *Barron v. Baltimore* and to generally held notions of constitutional jurisprudence at the time. Of perhaps special significance was Lumpkin's view that the right extended beyond militia purposes:

> The right of the whole people, old and young, men, women and boys, and not militia only, to keep and bear arms of every description, and not such merely as are used by the militia, shall not be infringed, curtailed or broken in upon, in the smallest degree; and all this for the important end to be attained: the rearing up and qualifying a well-regulated militia, so vitally necessary to the security of a free state. Our opinion is, that any law, state or federal is repugnant to the Constitution, and void, which contravenes this right, originally belonging to our forefathers, trampled under foot by Charles I and his two wicked sons and successors, re-established by the revolution of 1688.[54]

Both *Aymette* and *Nunn* provide strong evidence of the agreement among jurists in antebellum America concerning the purposes and importance of the right to bear arms. Justice Green of the Tennessee court and Judge Lumpkin of Georgia saw the right to bear arms as descending from the English experience of a need for an armed citizenry capable of resisting the excesses of the Crown. They saw the right as one that would enable the population to maintain freedom against potential governmental domination. Essentially their view was that it was one of the more important prerogatives of a free people.

The only antebellum discussion of the subject in the Supreme Court came in Chief Justice Roger B. Taney's opinion in *Dred Scott v. Sanford*. Taney indicated that Afro-Americans, enslaved or free, could be denied the right to possess arms just as they could be denied freedom of speech, assembly, and travel. The Taney opinion invites interesting speculation concerning antebellum views on the scope of the Second Amendment. The principal restrictions on the ownership or carrying of weapons by Blacks were state statutes. There was no general federal prohibition, and outside of the South most states permitted free Negroes to own and carry arms on the same basis as Whites. Was Taney saying that the kind of restrictions enacted by Southern states limiting the right of Blacks to own arms would have been unconstitutional if applied to

Whites? Was Taney echoing the views of William Rawle and Joseph Lumpkins that the Constitution limited the ability of state governments to restrict the right of citizens to have arms? Too much might be made of this, but Taney's opinion does invite such questions.[55]

Slavery was at the heart of the *Dred Scott* case, and the conflict over the peculiar institution would ultimately lead to civil war. The War of the Rebellion would bring with it a number of developments relevant to our discussion of the Second Amendment and the right to have arms. The first of these was an 1862 congressional alteration of the Militia Act. The original legislation of 1792 had confined militia membership to White men. The new statute eliminated the racial restriction. The 1792 racial restriction had enjoyed a history of somewhat uneven enforcement. As a rule, Black men were not formally enrolled in the state militia, although they often participated in state military formations in times of war and invasion. But even this statement has to be qualified. When New Orleans was facing British invasion in 1814, Governor William C. C. Clairborne formally enrolled free Francophonic mulattoes, Louisiana's *gens de couleur libre*, into the state militia, even formally giving officers' commissions to some members of this community. Peter Caulder, a free Black man, served as a substitute for Alexander Lane, a White man, in the South Carolina militia during the War of 1812. North Carolina and Tennessee enrolled free Black men in their militias as musicians and drummers until the mid-1830s, when both states disenfranchised Black men and struck them from the militia rolls. The Whig-dominated government of Rhode Island supplied state arms to a private African American militia company in the 1840s in part because the state's Black men had supported the Whigs during the state's Dorr Rebellion in the early part of the decade. Were these antebellum examples valid examples of Black participation in state militias? Should the 1792 Militia Act be read as imposing a rigid categorical exclusion of Black men from the militia, or only an indication that White men were compelled to be enrolled in the militia while states might allow free Negroes to serve at their discretion? The point might be debated, but the 1862 legislation was clear: there were no longer racial restrictions on militia membership. It was, at least theoretically, a privilege and responsibility of men of all races.[56]

Another issue highlighted by the Civil War also relates to the question of the militia and how broadly or narrowly the term might be interpreted. Much has been written about the failure of the militia system and how it proved ineffective in wartime. The failure of militia units particularly as part of expeditionary units invading Canada during the War of 1812 has been frequently noted.[57] Less attention has been paid to the militia as a home guard force, one that guarded communities during wartime while regular forces, including mobilized units of the organized militia, were away and unavailable for local defense. In that capacity the participation of armed citizens in defense of their communities was frequently broader than the statutory boundaries of militia membership, often involving men outside the statutory ages for militia service and free Black men. The Civil War would be the occasion for widespread use of civilians as members of home guard forces, particularly in the border states. Some of these forces had Unionist sympathies. Others were pro-Confederate. Some were successful in helping to guard their communities, particularly against irregular forces; others were not. But successful or not, they give something of an illustration of the use of broad-based militia forces in one capacity during the Civil War. A somewhat sentimentalized version of the use of this kind of hastily assembled militia as home guard can be seen in the 1956 film *Friendly Persuasion,* in which actor Gary Cooper portrayed a Quaker pacifist who reluctantly joined a home guard militia to help protect his community from Confederate attack.[58]

The connection between private arms and military affairs was not confined to hastily formed home guard units. It was also revealed in the relative skill of the opposing armies. Confederate forces fought to leave the Union and to preserve slavery. Union forces fought to preserve the nation and ultimately to end slavery. Billy Yank had the better cause. Johnny Reb was the better shot. Northern forces were recruited from men who were more urban. The Union Army also had more men who were foreign born. And the federal forces enlisted large numbers of former slaves, nearly 100,000 according to the official records. The men from cities, the foreign born, and the former slaves were less likely to have experience with firearms than the men who enlisted in the Confederate forces. Southern recruits were more likely to have lived in rural areas, likely to have participated in slave patrols and informal posses, and more likely to have had experience with firearms. The experience of having fought Southern men who were more skilled with firearms during the conflict would lead former Union generals to form the National Rifle Association in 1871. The purpose of the organization would be, in part, to improve the public's proficiency with firearms in order to ensure that recruits in future conflicts would be better riflemen.

A REVOLUTION DELAYED

The most important contribution made by the Civil War to the Second Amendment came not in how that conflict expanded or altered the scope of the militia, or in the linkages that it showed between civilian experience with firearms and military marksmanship. Instead, the most important developments came with the constitutional change that would follow in the wake of the conflict. The end of the War of the Rebellion brought about a new debate over the status of the former slaves and the power of the states. The defeated White South sought to preserve as much of the antebellum Southern social order as could survive Northern victory and constitutional amendment. In the immediate aftermath of the war and the enactment of the Thirteenth Amendment, which abolished slavery, the former states of the Confederacy were not prepared to accord the general liberties to the newly emancipated Black population that White citizens enjoyed. Indeed, the Southern states were not prepared to grant the former slaves the rights that Northern states had long given their free Afro-American populations. In 1865 and 1866, Southern states passed a series of statutes known as the Black Codes. These statutes were designed, in part, to ensure that traditional Southern labor arrangements would be preserved. They often required Blacks to sign labor contracts that bound Black agricultural workers to their employers for a year. Blacks were forbidden from serving on juries and could not testify or act as parties against Whites. Vagrancy laws were used to force Blacks into labor contracts and to limit freedom of movement.[59] And as further indication that the former slaves had not yet joined the ranks of free citizens, Southern states passed legislation prohibiting Blacks from carrying firearms without licenses, a requirement to which Whites were not subjected. A Mississippi statute provides a typical example of restrictions of this kind:

> *Be it enacted*, . . . that no freedman, free Negro or mulatto, not in the military
> service of the United States government, and not licensed so to do by the
> board of police of his or her county, shall keep or carry firearms of any kind,
> or any ammunition, dirk or Bowie knife, and on conviction thereof in the
> county court shall be punished by fine, not exceeding ten dollars, and pay the
> cost of such proceedings and all such arms or ammunition shall be forfeited
> to the informer; and it shall be the duty of every civil or military officer to
> arrest any such freedman, free Negro or mulatto found with any such arms or

ammunition, and shall cause him or her to be committed to trial in default of bail.[60]

Such measures caused strong concerns on the part of many northern Republicans. Many Republicans in Congress charged that the South was trying to reinstitute slavery and deny former slaves those rights long considered essential to a free people. The news that the freedmen were being deprived of the right to keep and bear arms was of particular concern to the champions of Negro citizenship. For them the right of the Black population to possess weapons went beyond symbolic importance. It was seen as important both as a means of maintaining the recently reunited union and as a means of insuring against the virtual reenslavement of those formerly in bondage. Faced with a hostile, often recalcitrant South, and determined, by legal and extra-legal means, to preserve the antebellum social order, northern Republicans were particularly alarmed at provisions that in effect preserved the right to keep and bear arms for former Confederates while disarming Blacks, the one group in the South with clear unionist sympathies. Kansas Republican Sidney Clarke expressed the outrage and fear of many northern Republicans when he argued in support of the Civil Rights Act of 1866 and his hope that the proposed legislation would prevent the South from disarming the freedmen:

> Who, sir, were those men? Not the present militia, but the brave black soldiers of the Union, disarmed and robbed by this wicked and despotic order. Nearly every white man in [Mississippi] that could bear arms was in the rebel ranks. Nearly all of their able-bodied colored men who could reach our lines enlisted under the old flag. Many of these brave defenders of the nation paid for their arms with which they went into battle. And I regret sir, that justice compels me to say, to the disgrace of the Federal Government, that the "reconstructed" state authorities of Mississippi were allowed to rob and disarm our veteran soldiers and arm the rebels fresh from the field of treasonable strife. Sir, the disarmed loyalists of Alabama, Mississippi, and Louisiana are powerless today, and oppressed by the pardoned and encouraged rebels of those States.[61]

Such concerns helped feed the determination of many northern Republicans to provide for national enforcement for the Bill of Rights. To understand this determination, it may be useful to consider two propositions concerning the Fourteenth Amendment specifically and indeed the Civil War amendments more generally. The first of these propositions is that the Civil War amendments were intended primarily to give Congress the authority to legislate to protect the civil rights of American citizens. It is no accident that the Thirteenth, Fourteenth, and Fifteenth Amendments all include language granting Congress the authority to enforce the new additions to the Constitution with legislation. Two aspects of the nation's recent history had convinced Republicans in the Thirty-Ninth Congress that they needed this legislative authority in the Fourteenth Amendment: first, Andrew Johnson's unwillingness as president to protect the civil rights of the newly freed Black population, and second, the memory of the antebellum decision in *Dred Scott*—the belief that the Supreme Court had gotten that case fundamentally and tragically wrong. With the passage of the Civil Rights Act of 1866, Republican supporters of equal rights indicated early on that they viewed the Thirteenth Amendment as a constitutional change that gave Congress a preeminent role in protecting the civil rights of American citizens. The passage of the Fourteenth Amendment was designed to further bolster congressional authority in this regard and to remove any doubts concerning Congress's ability to enact protective legislation.[62]

The second proposition is that proponents of the Fourteenth Amendment saw the principles of equality before the law, embodied in the amendment's equal protection clause, and the application of the Bill of Rights to the states as related but nonetheless distinguishable concepts. The latter principle was intended to be protected through the amendment's privileges or immunities clause. These two principles could be seen both in the floor debates over the Fourteenth Amendment and in the discussions of the rights of citizens during the debates on civil rights legislation. Supporters of Section 1 of the amendment, which included the new amendment's privileges or immunities clause, indicated that the clause was intended to make the states respect what they saw as the basic rights of free Americans. On February 28, 1866, during House debates on a proposed amendment that would later become part of Section 1 of the Fourteenth Amendment, John Bingham, a Republican from Ohio, specifically expressed his disagreement with the Supreme Court's decision in *Barron v. Baltimore*. He further expressed his views that the federal courts had failed in their responsibility to protect citizens from violations of their constitutional rights. Bingham went on to note that the proposed privileges or immunities clause would authorize Congress to protect the rights of citizens through the enactment of statutes that would provide criminal penalties for civil rights violations.[63]

In the Senate, Jacob Howard of Michigan introduced the privileges or immunities clause by reading the first eight amendments to the Constitution and indicating that the rights found in those amendments would be protected from violations by state officials. Howard specifically spelled out the amendments, including a discussion of the Second Amendment, in individualistic terms, that is, as the right to keep and bear arms without any mention of the militia. Howard indicated his belief that the primary vehicle for enforcing the privileges or immunities clause would be legislation enacted by Congress and authorized by Section 5 of the new amendment. The Southern efforts to disarm the freedmen and to deny other basic rights to former slaves played an important role in convincing the Thirty-Ninth Congress that traditional notions concerning federalism and individual rights needed to change. The generation that had authored the original US Constitution and Bill of Rights had been concerned with dangers from a potentially tyrannical federal government. The authors of the Fourteenth Amendment were concerned with oppression that could come from state authorities.[64]

If the Black Codes had persuaded the Thirty-Ninth Congress of the need for applying the Bill of Rights to the states, the US Supreme Court in its earliest decisions on the Fourteenth Amendment moved to maintain as much of the antebellum federal structure as could survive the Civil War and the Civil War amendments. The Fourteenth Amendment had multiple purposes. Its equal protection clause was designed to prevent the kind of unequal treatment of Blacks that prevailed throughout the nation before the Civil War and was especially acute in the Southern states after the end of the Rebellion. The amendment's citizenship clause made all persons born in the United States citizens of the nation and was clearly meant to overturn Justice Taney's opinion in *Dred Scott* that argued Negroes could not be citizens. The due process clause was meant to ensure that the states would provide due process—fair trials—before subjecting individuals to criminal or civil penalties. And the privileges or immunities clause was, according to its major proponents, meant to apply the Bill of Rights to the states. That latter intention met with an immediate hostile reaction from the Supreme Court. It contradicted the old federalism that had existed before the Civil War. That old federalism held that the national Constitution had little to say concerning state governments and how those governments treated the citizen. For vindication of individual rights, the adherents of the old federalism argued, the citizen would have to look at state constitutions and state constitutional provisions, not the guarantees in the federal Bill of Rights.

The first case to examine the privileges or immunities clause and the limits that it might impose on state action had nothing to do with the right to bear arms or the militia or indeed any right specifically mentioned in the Constitution's first eight amendments. That case would nonetheless have an important impact on the course of Second Amendment jurisprudence for well over a century. A group of cases collectively known as the *Slaughter-House Cases* involved state-granted monopolies on the slaughterhouse business in Louisiana. The monopolies were challenged in part on the grounds that the right to pursue a profession was one of the privileges or immunities of citizenship protected by the new amendment. The Supreme Court denied the claim, and it did so in a way that indicated that the Fourteenth Amendment's privileges or immunities clause provided little protection against the actions of state governments, certainly not the robust application of the Bill of Rights to the states envisioned by Representative John Bingham, Senator Jacob Howard, and their supporters.[65]

The Supreme Court's first direct examinations of the Second Amendment came about after the enactment of the Fourteenth Amendment and concerned the question of the extent to which the amendment empowered the federal government to protect the right to keep and bear arms. It is one of the ironies of our constitutional history that although the Second Amendment was originally meant to constrain the power of the national government, the first party to bring a claim before the federal courts alleging a violation of the right to keep and bear arms was in fact the federal government. As Bingham and Howard had predicted, Congress used its authority under Section 5 of the Fourteenth Amendment to pass civil rights legislation to protect the newly emancipated Black population and White unionists in the South. One such piece of legislation, the Enforcement Act of 1870, contained language that made it a felony to "injure, oppress, threaten or intimidate any citizen with intent to prevent or hinder his free exercise and enjoyment of any right or privilege granted or secured to him by the Constitution or laws of the United States."[66]

The racial violence that plagued the South in the Reconstruction era would bring the Enforcement Act and the Second Amendment to the Supreme Court in the 1876 case *United States v. Cruikshank.* In Colfax, Louisiana, in 1873 an armed body of White men set upon and massacred some 100 Black men who were going to the polls. The Black men, anticipating an attack, had gone to the polls armed. Federal authorities brought charges against William Cruikshank and others under the Enforcement Act. The charges included violating the rights of two of the Black men, Levi Nelson and Alexander Tillman. Cruikshank was convicted of violating the rights of the two men to peaceably assemble and with interfering with their right to bear arms. Cruikshank and his associates appealed to the Supreme Court. The Court in a majority opinion authored by Chief Justice Morrison R. Waite held that the federal government had no power to protect citizens against private actions that deprived them of their constitutional rights. The opinion held that the First and Second Amendments were limitations on Congress, not on private individuals. It also declared that Congress could not protect individuals against actions by private parties that deprived them of civil rights; for such protection, individuals would be forced to rely on state governments. It was a case that would give a green light to the kind of racial violence that would play a major role in suppressing the rights of the Afro-American population of the Southern states.[67]

The next case in which the Court examined the Second Amendment, *Presser v. Illinois*, more directly involved the question of whether the Fourteenth Amendment made the Second Amendment applicable to state action, thereby protecting citizens from state infringements on the right to bear arms. *Presser* involved a challenge to an Illinois statute that prohibited individuals who were not members of the organized militia from parading with arms. Although Justice William Woods, author of the Supreme Court's unanimous opinion, noted that the statute did not infringe on the right to keep and bear arms, he nonetheless used the case to pronounce his view that the Second Amendment was a limitation only on the federal government, not on the states. Although much of the Woods opinion might be viewed as dicta extraneous to the central issue in *Presser*, the decision in that case would remain the major precedent that allowed state firearms restrictions to avoid review in federal courts until *McDonald* in 2010. Interestingly enough, the Woods opinion, despite declaring that the Second Amendment did not protect the individual from the actions of state authorities, nonetheless endorsed the view that the people at large constituted an inchoate militia and were a military resource for the federal government and that state governments could not disarm their populations:

> It is undoubtedly true that all citizens capable of bearing arms constitute the
> reserved military force of the United States as well as of the States, and, in view
> of this prerogative of the general government, as well as of its general powers, the

states cannot, even laying the constitutional provision in question out of view, prohibit the people from keeping and bearing arms so as to deprive the United States of their rightful resource for maintaining the public security and disable the people form performing their duty to the general government.[68]

In the decades after the Civil War, the Supreme Court contributed little toward the development of a jurisprudence of the Second Amendment, except to use claims involving the right to bear arms as occasion to limit the scope of federal authority under the Fourteenth Amendment. The Court's jurisprudence in this regard might be seen as part of a broader reaction against the Fourteenth Amendment and the revolution in the federal structure that that amendment represented. In this regard one could regard the Court's decision in *Cruikshank* as similar in aim as its 1883 decision in the *Civil Rights Cases*. With the Civil Rights Act of 1875, Congress had passed far-reaching legislation prohibiting racial discrimination in what today we would call public accommodations. The Supreme Court struck the legislation down, declaring that the new amendments did not empower Congress to regulate the conduct of private businesses that were engaging in racial discrimination.[69] If the Congresses that enacted the Civil War amendments and contemporaneous civil rights legislation believed they had enabled the national legislature to take far-reaching measures to protect the rights of citizens, the Supreme Court would insist on a far more modest view of the powers of the national legislature. The Second Amendment and other parts of the Bill of Rights would suffer as a result.

The Supreme Court was not inclined to enforce the Second Amendment against state authorities. It was also inclined to limit Congress's role as an enforcer of the amendment. Nonetheless, state courts interpreting state constitutional provisions wrestled with the vexing problem of developing a body of legal doctrine that balanced the right to keep and bear arms with notions of public safety and state police power. One of the more significant of these cases, *Andrews v. State*, was decided by the Tennessee Supreme Court in 1871. The decision in *Andrews* made several potential contributions to the still underdeveloped but growing field of a jurisprudence of the right to keep and bear arms. The case's principal holding was that the right to keep arms and the right to bear arms are separate; that the former belongs to the individual in his private capacity while the latter is incidental to militia service. *Andrews* also analyzed the very modern issue of the importance and relevance of the right to keep and bear arms in the absence of a system of universal militia training.

Judge Freeman's opinion reflects traditional thinking on the subject, namely that the right of the people to own military weapons helped ensure that citizens summoned into militia service would be better able to perform such service because of their familiarity with military weapons and their ability to provide such weapons for the occasion. The need, of course, for a citizenry that could be rapidly mobilized into impromptu militia or home guard forces with relatively little training was a matter of recent memory to citizens of Tennessee, who had fought on both sides during the Civil War.[70]

If the question of the right to arms occupied state courts, it also attracted the attention of constitutional commentators in the late nineteenth century. One of the more prominent of these was conservative Michigan Supreme Court Justice Thomas M. Cooley. The Michigan jurist viewed the right in traditional political terms: as a right that would enable the people to resist potential tyranny. His analysis also anticipated and answered the modern view that the right only extended to members of the militia:

> The Right is General.—It may be supposed from the phraseology of this provision that the right to keep and bear arms was only guaranteed to the militia; but this would be an interpretation not warranted by the intent. The militia, as has been elsewhere explained, consists of those persons who, under the law, are liable to the performance of military duty, and are officered and enrolled for service when called upon. But the law may make provision for the enrolment of all who are fit to perform military duty, or of a small number only, or it may wholly omit to make any provision at all; and if the right were limited to those enrolled, the purpose of this guaranty might be defeated altogether by the action or neglect to act of the government it was meant to hold in check. The meaning of the provision undoubtedly is, that the people, from whom the militia must be taken, shall have the right to keep and bear arms, and they need no permission or regulation of law for the purpose. But this enables the government to have a well-regulated militia; for to bear arms implies something more than the mere keeping; it implies the learning to handle and use them in a way that makes those who keep them ready for their efficient use; in other words, it implies the right to meet for voluntary discipline in arms, observing in doing so the laws of public order.[71]

It is fair to say that the nineteenth century ended with little disagreement that the right to keep and bear arms was a fundamental right of Americans.

Although there was little in the way of federal court jurisprudence concerning the Second Amendment, a number of state courts had begun the difficult task of reconciling concerns for public safety with the risks inherent in a right to bear arms. Federal courts remained largely silent on the question in part because of the prevailing doctrine that the Bill of Rights, despite the history of the Fourteenth Amendment, only constrained the federal government, not the states. It should be added that this viewpoint led to a great deal of silence on the part of the federal judiciary concerning other provisions of the Bill of Rights as well. The nineteenth century was a time when many states passed legislation or engaged in practices that might have been deemed highly questionable if they had been rigorously examined through the lens of the Bill of Rights. And state and federal courts were often not inclined to engage in rigorous examinations of state legislation and governmental practices. Most jurists were inclined to defer to state authorities under the doctrine that the police power gave states broad authority to regulate in the interests of the health, safety, and morals of the public. Individual rights, particularly the rights of individuals from unpopular groups, were routinely violated. Restrictions on speech existed in a number of states. It was not uncommon in a number of states for police to routinely beat confessions out of suspects in criminal cases. Individuals were tried for felonies without lawyers. Towns put up signs warning Negroes not to be caught within municipal boundaries after dark. To an extent that would probably amaze most Americans today, the protections of the Bill of Rights were largely theoretical, symbolic, and in many ways illusory in the nineteenth century, certainly from the point of view of any meaningful federal judicial enforcement. Despite the intentions of the Thirty-Ninth Congress, the Supreme Court would not begin the process of applying the Bill of Rights to the states until well into the twentieth century. For that reason, most provisions of the Bill of Rights would not get rigorous Supreme Court scrutiny until the twentieth century.[72]

And yet, even in the absence of judicial protection, restrictions on the ownership of arms were relatively rare in late nineteenth-century America. There was more of a tendency on the part of state and local governments to regulate the carrying of arms. A number of western towns restricted the carrying of weapons, but these ordinances were usually aimed at disarming itinerant strangers, wild cowboys, and suspicious drifters, not the good citizens of the town. Firearms were still very much a part of the national culture at the end of the nineteenth century, a reflection of the fact that the American population was still predominately rural, that much of the nation was still a frontier, or at the very least that the frontier was still a recent memory for many. It was also at least in part a reflection of the fact that the nation had fought a devastating war on its own soil. For many, the still-fresh memory of that conflict and its aftermath helped produce a new appreciation of the need to be armed for both personal and the common defense. Firearms ownership was widespread. If the original vision of the militia of the whole in its military incarnation remained elusive and theoretical, there were still large sections of the country with few professional police officers and frequent resort to the posse comitatus to aid in law enforcement.

With widespread ownership of firearms and the judicial doctrine that the Bill of Rights applied only to the largely distant federal government and not to the state and local governments that directly impacted most peoples' lives, the Second Amendment would remain more the concern of the legal commentator than the working jurist. The latter could extol the right to bear arms as an essential tool for preserving the people's liberty while the former would have relatively little to say about actual restrictions imposed at the local level. It would take social changes partly brought about by urbanization and increased racial and ethnic conflict in twentieth-century America to bring about increased regulation and new attitudes concerning the right to keep and bear arms.

# 2. "Negro Laborers," "Low-Browed Foreigners," and the "Efficiency of a Well-Regulated Militia"

The new century would bring changes—changes that were a strengthening of developments that were already well underway in post–Civil War America. Guns had changed. Both Billy Yank and Johnny Reb began the great conflict with muzzle-loading muskets or rifles not too different from the weapons their great-grandfathers had used to win independence in the 1770s. To be sure, officers and cavalrymen carried revolvers, but even these were relatively slow and clumsy devices, with powder and ball loaded separately into each chamber. During the course of the war, soldiers in a few Union companies privately equipped themselves with what was then the cutting edge of firearms technology, the Henry rifle. It used modern ammunition: powder and bullet in a single metal cartridge. The Henry could hold sixteen such cartridges. Spent cartridges were expelled from the weapon, and new rounds were placed in the rifle's chamber by the action of a lever. It was one of the most rapid-firing small arms of its day. Confederates called it "that damned Yankee rifle that you load on Sunday and shoot all week." The conservative War Department would not make the Henry a standard-issue weapon for federal troops, fearing that the new technology would cause soldiers to waste ammunition.[1]

But luddites in the Ordnance Department notwithstanding, the Henry was a harbinger of things to come. After the Civil War, the cartridge with powder and bullet housed in a single metal capsule would increasingly replace the venerable cap-and-ball muzzle loader. Repeating rifles and pistols, usually six-shot revolvers, became more common. And the technology would continue to improve. It is not an overstatement to say that modern firearms as we know them today are largely the products of developments that occurred between the American Civil War and 1914, the year the world became engulfed in what was once called "The Great War." Bolt- and lever-action repeating rifles, revolvers, and even semiautomatic pistols, rifles, and shotguns came to be more and more familiar. Fully automatic weapons—weapons that continue to fire as long as the trigger is depressed and ammunition is available—had also made their debut even before the beginning of the new century. Firearms technology had changed, and it had changed significantly.[2]

The law too was changing, but less dramatically. The right to bear arms was still an honored principle, in principle. Of the forty-five states that were part of the American Union in 1900, thirty had provisions protecting the right to have arms in their state constitutions.[3] Most constitutional commentators would probably have agreed with Thomas Cooley's views expressed in 1883 that the Second Amendment's right to keep and bear arms belonged to all citizens and not just those who had been selected for extensive militia training. The principle that the citizenry at large constituted an inchoate militia of the whole had been reaffirmed by Congress with the passage of the Dick Act in 1903. The Dick Act was the start of a process by which Congress, over the course of the twentieth century, would transform the organized militia of the nineteenth century into the National Guard. Although it would retain its designation as the organized militia of the various states and territories, the National Guard would increasingly come under the control of the US Army, and after World War II, under the Army and the US Air Force. Over time, the Guard took on more the character of a reserve component of the two services and less and less the character of a state militia. The Dick Act declared that the National Guard constituted the organized militia of the several states and the United States, and that men between the ages of seventeen and forty-five constituted the unorganized militia.[4]

The idea that the population at large constituted a reserve or inchoate militia was still recognized by statute, and the federal and most state constitutions contained provisions intended to safeguard the individual's right to have arms. But new pressures were beginning to strain these traditional American principles, at least around the edges, at the beginning of the twentieth century. Some of these pressures were the result of the increased racial conflict that had come with the new century. In the immediate wake of the Civil War, Congress had passed the Thirteenth, Fourteenth, and Fifteenth Amendments and a significant body of civil rights legislation. The primary purpose of this new body of laws had been to protect the rights of former slaves in the South. Along with the new constitutional amendments and federal legislation came enforcement in the form of federal troops and a proactive Justice Department. The new laws, the protection provided by federal troops, the enforcement efforts of the Justice Department, and the enfranchisement of hundreds of thousands of

Black men throughout the South had brought a measure of racial equality to
the former slave states in the 1870s and 1880s.[5]

By the beginning of the twentieth century that egalitarian era was rapidly
becoming a fading memory in much of the South. The withdrawal of federal
troops from the South, coupled with new legislation and extra-legal violence—
terrorism administered by the Ku Klux Klan and similar White supremacist
organizations—had driven large numbers of Negroes from state voting rolls,
paving the way for new legislation that either openly discriminated against
Afro-Americans or seemingly fair legislation that could be enforced with great
discrimination. This would occur in legislation governing firearms possession,
as well as other areas. A number of Southern states in the late nineteenth or
early twentieth century passed legislation restricting the carrying of firearms.
The statutes were framed in racially neutral terms, as a law prohibiting African Americans from carrying firearms but allowing Whites to do so would
have been a clear violation of the Fourteenth Amendment's equal protection
clause. It probably would have been recognized as such even by the racially
conservative courts of the day. But the laws could be enforced in a discriminatory manner, with Blacks subject to criminal penalties for violations while
illegal carrying by Whites might be ignored.[6]

One law ripe for discriminatory enforcement appears to have been a statute passed by the Florida legislature in 1893. In 1941 a majority of the Florida Supreme Court voted to overturn the conviction of a White man for violating the statute that prohibited the carrying of pistols without a license.
Justice Rivers H. Buford wrote an opinion concurring with the majority. He
began his opinion by expressing the view that the statute violated the Second
Amendment and an analogous provision of the Florida Constitution. Buford's
concurrence continued with a discussion that indicated the racial motivations
behind the legislation and the likelihood that there was considerable discrimination in enforcement of the legislation:

> I know something of the history of this legislation. The original Act of 1893 was
> passed when there was a great influx of negro laborers in this State drawn here
> for the purpose of working in turpentine and lumber camps. . . . The Act was
> passed for the purpose of disarming the negro laborers and to thereby reduce
> the unlawful homicides that were prevalent in turpentine and saw-mill camps
> and to give the white citizens in sparsely settled areas a better feeling of security.
> *The statute was never intended to be applied to the white population.* . . . It is a

safe guess to assume that more than 80% of the white men living in the rural sections of Florida have violated this statute. . . . There has never been, within my knowledge, any effort to enforce the provisions of this statute as to white people, because it has been generally conceded to be in contravention of the Constitution and non-enforceable if contested.[7]

Legislation like the Florida statute reflected changes in attitudes concerning the right to have arms in the South and other regions. Traditional beliefs concerning the importance of arms in the American scheme of rights were increasingly being tempered by the view that whole classes of people were unfit to exercise this traditional American prerogative. A number of Southern states passed legislation that, like the Florida statute discussed by Justice Buford, appear to have been designed to restrict the access of Blacks and in some cases probably poor Whites as well, to firearms. In 1892 Alabama passed legislation imposing an expensive licensing fee on businesses that sold handguns. The Texas legislature enacted a statute in 1907 charging merchants a 50 percent tax on the sale of handguns. Restrictions on sales could be circumvented through mail-order purchases, but they indicated a legislative desire in several states to restrict firearms purchases to "the better classes" of the population—"better classes" who met turn-of-the-century standards of respectability as shown by their ability to pay higher prices. Some states, including states outside of the South, enacted legislation requiring licenses to purchase pistols or revolvers. The Oregon legislature passed such a statute in 1913.[8]

These new restrictions were in part prompted by traditional fears of marginal groups and marginal men. Poor laborers without property, the itinerant cowboys in the cattle towns of the West, or the recently freed Blacks of the plantation South, these were peoples who were feared, even if their labor was needed. Viewed as part of the dangerous classes, their presence in different regions had long prompted efforts to control guns—at least, guns in the hands of those deemed a threat to the social order. But toward the end of the nineteenth century, a new group of people was adding to the concerns of respectable citizens afraid of the perils that might emanate from the hands of the dangerous poor. The hands or pockets of that dangerous poor class too often seemed to be filled with the abundant array of inexpensive, often low-powered revolvers readily available in hardware stores, pawnshops, general stores, and the ubiquitous Sears and Roebuck catalog.

The nation was becoming more urban and, to many of the old-line inhabitants of Northern European ancestry who dominated the nation's culture and politics and legislatures and courts, less American. From the point of view of many who could proudly trace their family trees to early English, Scottish, Scots-Irish, Welsh, or Dutch settlers—what we today would call the ethnic composition of the nation but what many at the end of the nineteenth century would insist was the nation's *racial* composition—was becoming more and more disturbing. The ships that delivered new European settlers to American shores were carrying immigrants from Southern and Eastern Europe. These new residents were crowding the nation's cities and spoke languages largely unknown in the United States. Their physical appearances were frequently quite different from those of old-line White Americans, even different from the more recently arrived Irish. The new immigrants, like others before and since, met with often hostile receptions. They were associated with crime and anarchy. In an age that was the apex of scientific racism in the United States, they were stereotyped as lazy, criminally inclined, and mentally unfit. Many native-born Americans feared the immigrants would contribute to labor unrest and would also bring anarchist-inspired crime from Europe, including politically motivated armed robberies.[9]

Such fears would lead the New York State legislature in 1911 to pass what was then the most restrictive and far-reaching gun control measure of the time, New York's Sullivan Law. The law went far beyond typical weapons control measures of the day. It prohibited the unlicensed carrying of concealed weapons and required a permit not only for the carrying but also for the ownership or purchase of pistols. Violation of the statute was a felony. The statute was aimed at New York City, a place whose large foreign-born— particularly Italian—immigrant population was believed to be peculiarly susceptible to crime and vice. The *New York Times*, which was a particularly energetic supporter of the legislation, frequently emphasized the need to control crime on the part of Italian immigrants. During 1911 as the legislation was being debated and ultimately adopted, the *Times*'s pages were replete with discussions of the dangers of "The Black Hand" and crime in Italian sections of town. In noting the rush to buy pistols before the law went into effect, the *Times* complained that "low-browed foreigners bargained for weapons" at pawn shops.[10] In commenting on the constitutional aspects of the restrictive Sullivan Law, it is interesting to note that while the New York paper was an advocate for the Sullivan legislation, it nonetheless recognized the Second Amendment in traditional individualistic terms. An article in the

*Times* published in August 1911 noted that the legislation did not violate the Second Amendment because while the measure required licenses for pistols, it did not regulate rifles and shotguns. The article further noted, "The second amendment does not restrict the right of the states, in the exercise of their police power, to regulate the manner in which arms shall be kept or borne." New York did not have a provision in its state constitution protecting the right to keep and bear arms.[11]

The editorial writers who argued in favor of the new statute played on the ethnic prejudices of the day to help pass the restrictive legislation. Once the new law was in effect, New York City authorities worked to ensure that the statute was enforced in a way that would provide a significant financial hurdle for poor and working-class people who sought to obtain permits. The initial fee for obtaining a permit was $2. It was quickly raised to $10 by the New York City authorities. The $10 fee would represent the equivalent of $292 in 2021 dollars, according to one economic website's calculations. Probably the best way to gauge the burden that the latter fee imposed would be to judge the $10 fee against the wages of an unskilled laborer in 1911. According to the website MeasuringWorth, maintained by University of Illinois economic historian Samuel H. Williamson, the average annual wage for an unskilled laborer in 1911 would have been approximately $170 a year. New York's $10 fee would have represented nearly three weeks' income. For a poor laborer, getting the license would be a substantial burden, indeed more of a financial burden than the cost of a number of the revolvers listed in the 1912 Sears and Roebuck catalog for $5 or less.[12]

The dynamics of the Sullivan Law and the later actions of New York City authorities in making pistol permits prohibitively expensive for many of the city's poorer residences provides an illustration of a policy dilemma that would frequently be revisited in the history of the gun-control debate. We can probably agree that the editorial writers and police officials who argued that there was a higher crime rate in New York's Italian immigrant communities were essentially accurate. These communities had large numbers of poor people and relatively large numbers of single young men. Many of the residences of these communities were less likely to speak English and thus less able to inform the police when they had been victims of crime. Many of the immigrants came from communities in Italy where there had long been a tradition of distrust of the police and little desire to cooperate with the authorities. And they were often victims of fierce ethnic or racial prejudice on the part of the authorities. All of this could have contributed to greater crime rates in Italian immigrant communities.[13]

And yet these very dynamics would have also meant that Italian immigrants were disproportionately victims of crime and perhaps more in need of the means of self-protection than many of the middle-class reformers who pressed for more restricted access to pistols and revolvers, particularly on the part of members of poor immigrant communities. It was, as we have noted, a policy dilemma that would be frequently revisited in the gun-control debate. Communities with high crime rates are also frequently communities with high rates of victimization. In New York in 1911, state and local authorities chose the path of trying to restrict access to firearms in those communities that were the least well protected. In doing so they made no distinction between hard-working laborers who sought to defend themselves and the predators who often ruled the streets of their neighborhoods.

The concern that the disreputable poor from an inferior race were causing uncontrolled mayhem through their carrying of pistols would later inform Tennessee senator John Knight Shield's efforts. Shields introduced a measure in 1924 that would restrict the delivery of firearms through the mails. The measure, which would ultimately become law in 1927, was designed to aid state authorities in enforcing licensing requirements. These requirements were easily circumvented by customers who simply purchased pistols through the mail. Shields stated that these circumventions had a particularly bad effect on the Afro-American population:

> How clearly the record localizes the canker on the community. Eighty-three percent of 75 homicides were negroes killed by negroes. If the record showed a greater percentage of whites killed by whites, or if it showed a pregnant danger of racial conflict, the situation would be far more appalling and difficult of solution. Cannot we, the dominant race, upon whom depends the enforcement of the law, so enforce the law that we will prevent the colored people from preying upon each other? Does the fault not rest squarely on our shoulders? But we can make no progress until we begin respecting and obeying the law much more than we do now and set the example for these colored persons to obey and respect the law also.[14]

The *New York Times* editorial writers who argued for pistol licensing maintained that the gun-control measure was consistent with the Second

Amendment as it had been traditionally understood. Others in the early part of the twentieth century were beginning to rethink the right to arms altogether and how the right might be reinterpreted to better suit the objective of keeping guns out of the hands of the dangerous classes, particularly in public spaces. It was in this early twentieth-century atmosphere that the notion that constitutional provisions guaranteeing the right to have arms protected a collective right and not a right of the individual began attracting support from some jurists. In the 1905 case *Salina v. Blaksley*, Associate Justice Adrian Greene of the Kansas Supreme Court wrote an opinion holding that the state constitution's provision protecting the right to bear arms only applied to members of the militia performing state military service and not for individual purposes. Several points should be noted about the decision in *Blaksley*. The case originated with the conviction of James Blaksley for carrying a pistol in violation of a city ordinance. Blaksley was drunk at the time of his arrest. The Kansas state constitutional provision guaranteed a right to bear arms but was silent on the question of a right to possess or keep arms. Greene's opinion focused on the issue of bearing arms. The Kansas jurist went out of his way to express his view that constitutional provisions protecting the right to bear arms should be interpreted as protecting that right solely in the context of the organized militia. His opinion included dicta that the federal Second Amendment was also restricted to the organized militia. Nonetheless, the Greene opinion had nothing to say on the subject of keeping or possessing arms, which was not at issue in Blaksley's case.[15]

Other jurists at the time were pondering the implications of the right to have arms for the increasingly felt need to regulate firearms. In 1911 Lucillius A. Emery, chief justice of the Supreme Court of Maine, published the essay "The Constitutional Right to Keep and Bear Arms" in the *Harvard Law Review*. Emery began by expressing his concern that the then new twentieth century had produced a class of professional gunmen armed with the small, easily concealed pistols of the era. These gunmen, Emery informed his readers, were responsible for dramatic increases in homicide. That increase required action by the state legislatures. In his discussion, following what had been the jurisprudence in a number of state courts, Emery urged that the right to keep arms and the right to bear arms should be viewed as distinguishable issues. He argued that the right to bear or carry arms should be viewed as a right limited to those performing state-sponsored militia service. Emery also noted that state legislatures probably could not restrict the ownership of arms or presumably their use for home defense. But in his view, restrictions on carrying arms in public spaces should be viewed as constitutional.[16]

Justice Greene's opinion in *Salina* and Chief Justice Emery's essay in the *Harvard Law Review* might be seen as part of a school or, perhaps better put, a style of legal thinking that was becoming increasingly influential among lawyers, judges, and legal scholars in the early decades of the twentieth century. Called *legal realism* by historians of early twentieth-century law, it is a style of legal thinking for which it is somewhat difficult to give a precise definition. Perhaps the best way to think of legal realism is to think of judicial decision-making, opinions in cases, as involving something of a balancing between formal sources of law and a jurist's sense of what makes good policy. Formal sources of law presumably come from sources of authority that have been established and agreed upon before a judge hears a case. These sources may include the text of a constitutional or statutory provision, the history of the adoption of particular provision, prior decisions interpreting a constitutional or statutory provision, previous legislation on the subject, or precedent developed from common law. Jurists have long had to balance at times competing sources of law, notions of what constitutes good or bad policy and sometimes even deeply felt notions of right or wrong, justice, or the equities of particular cases, in deciding cases.

But something new was occurring or perhaps gaining emphasis among some American jurists at the start of the twentieth century: a belief that jurists should be more openly taking policy considerations into account when deciding cases, and that the balance between formal sources of law and policy considerations should be weighted more heavily in favor of the policy considerations. There were several reasons for this. The newly developing social science disciplines were promising to deliver a more measurable and predictable portrait of human nature and human behavior. The pioneers of the new social sciences were modeling their disciplines after what was then, among university-educated elites, the highly renowned discipline of biology, with its Darwinian emphasis on evolution and the survival of the fittest. Judges wanted the law to reflect this best thinking of the new day that was the twentieth century. The boundaries of what were considered acceptable legal argument and proper judicial decision-making were changing. Future Supreme Court justice Louis Brandeis helped expand the boundaries of proper legal argument by presenting empirical evidence from the health and social sciences in his brief before the Supreme Court in *Mueller v. Oregon,* a case involving legislation that limited the maximum number of hours a woman could work. Previously that kind of marshaling of empirical evidence had largely been confined to legislatures. The Supreme Court responded with a favorable decision.[17]

The scientific wisdom of the day was weighted toward a worldview that challenged the tradition of rights formally written into federal and state constitutions. The strongest example of this was the judiciary's narrow view of the Fourteenth Amendment's equal protection clause and the Fifteenth Amendment's requirement that the right to vote would be extended to all American men regardless of race or color. The equal protection clause was, at best, minimally enforced with respect to its original purpose, equal treatment of people of different races. The Fifteenth Amendment had become a virtual constitutional dead letter by the beginning of the twentieth century. Minimal enforcement of both constitutional norms reflected the national judiciary's general agreement with the thinking of the scientific racists and Social Darwinists whose views indicated that the egalitarian premises of the Civil War amendments were unsound and better left unenforced. State and federal courts played a key role in facilitating the Jim Crow regime that took root in the South at the beginning of the twentieth century. The judiciary largely ignored the equal protection clause of the Fourteenth Amendment and the Fifteenth Amendment, thereby allowing apartheid-like segregation and large-scale disenfranchisement of African Americans. No less an advocate of a realist jurisprudence than Supreme Court Justice Oliver Wendell Holmes participated in this process of gutting the Civil War amendments. When confronted with the 1903 case of *Giles v. Harris*, a case wherein a registrar of voters in Alabama simply refused to register Negroes, Holmes wrote an opinion acknowledging that while the registrar's actions were a violation of the Fifteenth Amendment, correcting his actions were beyond the equitable or supervisory power of the Supreme Court. The right of Afro-Americans to vote was a right the Court would simply not enforce. The Court's actions would instead reflect the thinking of the new age, that it should not interfere with certain types of racial discrimination by local officials. This history is frequently overlooked or understated in discussions of legal realism, and yet it should be included as a part of the history of that style of legal reasoning.[18]

Leading scholars also suggested that some of the dangerous classes were dangerous not because poverty or their environments might have produced greater tendencies toward criminal behavior, but because some types of people were simply prone to vice and crime. The Negroes had long been considered mentally and morally inferior, a hazard to a well-ordered society. The more recently arrived Irish, Italians, Slavs, and Eastern European Jews crowding the cities seemed little better. There were scientists who could and did produce learned treatises proving beyond any doubt that the position of these foreign peoples' brows, the shape of their skulls, or the bumps on their heads proved to any reasonable man with an ounce of education that these were peoples unfit for traditional American concepts of individual rights—and certainly not fit for a right to carry arms in American cities. Greene's opinion in *Salina* and Emery's essay seem to reflect less the prior jurisprudence or constitutional texts on the right to keep and bear arms and more their policy predilections in the face of a troubling new (or seemingly new) world of urban crime and vice.[19]

Greene's opinion and Emery's essay took place within the context of interpreting state constitutions. That context gives us perhaps further evidence that their writings are probably better seen as efforts at instrumental interpretation designed to further what the two jurists regarded as desirable policy results and less as accurate renditions of the relevant constitutional histories and text. Both jurists were advocating a militia-centered—or, better put, militia-only—view of state provisions regarding the right to keep and bear arms. The arguments put forward by both Greene and Emery provided little in the way of historical, textual, or precedential support. Emery's essay was more frankly policy oriented, arguing that it was simply the better policy to interpret state constitutional provisions as protecting only the right to keep arms in the home, not to carry them in public. Emery was offering this method as a way of interpreting constitutions in all the states that had provisions protecting the right to bear arms, regardless of the wording or history of the particular constitutional provisions. Greene's focus was, of course, on the Kansas Constitution. The Midwestern jurist argued that the state constitutional provision had been adopted to safeguard the militia, what he termed "the people's army." Greene rejected Cooley's idea that one element of militia service was individual or private ownership and training with arms in order to maintain proficiency for militia service. The Kansas jurist instead argued that such training was the exclusive province of the organized militia.[20]

And yet the militia-only view of state constitutional provisions designed to protect the right to keep and bear arms seems highly problematic, at least from the point of view of why so many states would believe it to be necessary to include such a provision in their state constitutions. One might make a plausible argument for reading the Second Amendment in such a manner. We indicated in Chapter 1 our views as to why such a reading is flawed, but the idea that the federal constitution might contain a provision protecting state militias from federal encroachment is not inherently implausible. But why would a state constitution have a provision preventing the state government from disarming the state militia, and why would such a provision be termed a "right of the people"? Is this a right to serve in the militia? Service in militias and posses historically had been a duty of the people. There was no reason to frame this duty as a right. Emery and to a greater extent Greene were confining the right to bear arms to the organized militia, a body that was always selective as to membership. Greene's rejection of the notion that militia training included or was facilitated by private practice in marksmanship seemed to leave the right available to only the select few that the state included in the organized militia. If those were the people whose right was protected by the Kansas Constitution and presumably analogous provisions in other constitutions, the question arises, why was there a felt need for such a constitutional provision? Why would there be any fear that the state would disarm its own militia? The answer seems to lie less in constitutional interpretation than in Greene's notion of good public policy.[21]

Greene's opinion and Emery's commentary notwithstanding, early twentieth-century efforts at gun control usually took place in a framework where advocates of stricter firearms regulation generally recognized that the right to have arms was among the general rights of the American public. Their view was that the right to keep and bear arms and the regulations that they proposed were not in conflict. There were several reasons for this. First, the doctrine that the federal Bill of Rights did not limit state action allowed advocates of stricter regulation to feel quite confident that the measures that they were proposing would not be judged unconstitutional on federal constitutional grounds. Second, the measures that they were proposing, with a few exceptions, like the New York Sullivan Law, regulated the carrying of firearms, not their ownership. There had been a long history of regulating the carrying of weapons, and even in the majority of states that had provisions on the right to keep and bear arms in their constitutions, regulation of the manner of carrying had long been considered within the police power of state authorities. There was little likelihood of review of proposed legislation on Second Amendment grounds. State courts were likely to give broad deference to legislatures and their claims that laws regulating the carrying of firearms were necessary public safety measures. There was little felt need on the part of early twentieth-century gun-control advocates to reassess or reinterpret the meaning of either the Second Amendment or similar provisions in state constitutions.

Federalism and constitutional restrictions on Congress's ability to legislate, as these issues were viewed in the early decades of the twentieth century, also probably contributed to the willingness of those who believed in stricter regulation of firearms to nonetheless concede that the Second Amendment protected a right of individuals to have arms. Today, at the start of the third decade of the twenty-first century, we are accustomed to a federal government that is acknowledged to have broad powers to regulate for the health, safety, and welfare of the nation as a whole. That power can still generate a fair amount of controversy in some quarters, but the federal courts have generally held that Congress's power to regulate commerce and to tax extends to such far-flung areas as regulation of agriculture, food and drugs, wages, civil rights, and firearms control, among many other areas. Indeed, it would be accurate to say that, for most practical purposes, Congress today has the kind of broad police powers once thought to be the exclusive province of state governments. This was not the view of the courts and most students of the subject in the early part of the twentieth century, and indeed, it would not become the dominant view of the American judiciary until after the Second World War. There was no attempt to reexamine the Second Amendment and see what obstacles it might or might not pose for national gun control, because most jurists and commentators would have agreed that such a project, even putting the Second Amendment to one side, would have been beyond the scope of Congress's power. Regulation of guns, like most other matters having to do with criminal justice, was by and large the concern of state legislatures and not Congress. Outside of violations of the law on federal enclaves—the District of Columbia, or the territories or Indian reservations—crime was a state affair.[22]

But if early twentieth-century notions of federalism placed significant restraints on Congress's ability to legislate, there were other avenues for legal reformers who wanted to bring more uniformity to the law and their notions of good governance and good policy to state legislatures. The Uniform Law Commission (ULC, also known as the National Conference of Commissioners on Uniform State Laws), in conjunction with the American Bar Association began in the latter part of the nineteenth century and beginning of the twentieth century an effort to bring a greater degree of uniformity to American law. While acknowledging that for the most part, criminal law and other regulatory measures were largely the province of state legislatures and state courts, the members of the Uniform Law Commission believed that research and proposals sponsored by the institute and written by the most eminent practicing attorneys and legal scholars of the day could go a long way toward bringing a fair degree of uniformity and predictability to law and the legal profession. This effort to achieve greater uniformity in American law was in part a recognition that commerce was becoming more of a national phenomenon, and with the nationalization of commerce came a greater desire for businesses and the lawyers who would advise them to be able to predict the legal consequences of business decisions. Law that remained purely local, little influenced by broader trends in legal or economic thinking, would pose problems for businesses who might want to operate nationally. The uniform law movement sought to bring a measure of predictability by proposing model laws that state legislatures would hopefully adopt, bringing modern legal thinking in such areas as commercial relations, industrial liability, insurance, and the rules of evidence, among other areas.[23]

The idea of model legislation also came to the area of firearms regulation. The United States Revolver Association, an organization that sponsored postal matches for target shooters, helped draft the Uniform Pistol Act between 1919 and 1922. It was adopted by the National Conference of Commissioners on Uniform State Laws in 1926 and would later be supplemented by the Uniform Firearms Act, which was drafted in the 1930s. The Uniform Firearms Act had five main provisions: First, it called for increased penalties for crimes of violence committed with a pistol; second, it prohibited possession of pistols by persons convicted of crimes of violence; third, it called for a requirement for licensing of individuals who wanted to carry concealed pistols; fourth, it called for vendors selling pistols to be licensed; and fifth, it called for a legal presumption that an individual carrying an unlicensed pistol intended to commit a crime of violence.[24]

The proposals made by the drafters of the Uniform Firearms Act were in line with traditional notions concerning firearms regulation in most states. Gun regulation had traditionally encompassed prohibitions on carrying concealed weapons, and a number of states already had such provisions or adopted them, perhaps influenced by the suggested uniform legislation or perhaps simply following trends in other jurisdictions. The model legislation did not suggest that licensing should be a requirement for the ownership of pistols; instead, the proposed laws were directed at carrying. Some commentators who supported the suggested legislation expressed the view that firearms legislation should protect the rights of target shooters, particularly those who practiced with the Army's new pistol the M1911 ("the 45"), on the grounds that such activity contributed to the national defense. The proposal for uniform firearms legislation took place within a framework that recognized that regulations on guns had clear constitutional limitations.[25]

Proposed uniform statutes and discussions on which sorts of regulations were constitutional and which were constitutionally suspect affected relatively few Americans in the early decades of the twentieth century, when the nation's population was still largely rural. The 1920 census was the first to show America's population as more urban than rural, but even that enumeration had to be taken with a grain of salt. An inhabitant of a village with a scant three thousand souls would be counted among the nation's urban dwellers according to the census's lights. In this atmosphere, firearms ownership for both hunting and self-defense was commonplace. Statutes regulating firearms ownership were still relatively rare and unobtrusive. Even those proposing uniform firearms legislation were not questioning the basic right to own guns and the notion that the Constitution protected that right. Instead, the advocates of the uniform legislation were only proposing relatively limited measures to combat the use of guns in crimes. For most citizens, access to firearms was largely unimpaired, and there was not too much occasion for either courts or constitutional commentators to say much about the Second Amendment or analogous provisions in state constitutions, for that matter. They simply acknowledged their existence, seeing little inconsistency between the principle of the right to bear arms and the need for firearms regulation.[26]

World War I would help spur some rethinking about arms and public order. The "War to End All Wars" would introduce large numbers of men, the four million or so who served in the armed forces during the conflict, to firearms. Some, like Tennessee sharpshooter Alvin York, needed little introduction to the art of marksmanship. Others, particularly many men from the nation's rapidly growing cities, found themselves handling rifles and pistols for the first time. The newly formed National Guard, somewhat better trained than the nineteenth-century state militia units that preceded it, was activated for Army service, with many of its companies and regiments joining the American Expeditionary Force in France.

The First World War would also serve to reiterate the idea that community and national defense extended beyond those who were in the regular armed forces, the National Guard, or even men between the ages of seventeen and forty-five—those formally designated as the unorganized militia. State and local authorities certainly saw the general population as a force that could be mobilized, particularly given the absence or scarcity of regular police and military forces during the national emergency. Faced with incursions from revolutionaries and bandits caught up in the bloody Mexican Revolution of 1910–1920, sheriffs and their posses in the American Southwest occasionally joined soldiers from the US Army or acted alone to fight off invaders from south of the border. After the United States declared war on Germany and while the Army, including the National Guard, was either overseas or in training camps, states formed home guard companies to guard bridges, power plants, and other potential targets for sabotage. Some of these potential targets for enemy attack might have seemed a tad farfetched given that the East Coast of the United States was more than three thousand miles from the killing fields of France. Nonetheless, there were incidents of German sabotage or suspected German sabotage in the United States during the war. Some installations probably did warrant a security force, and it was probably better that that force was made up of home guard volunteers, thus freeing regular troops for more pressing duties. The people mobilized for these efforts were typically men older than the statutory age for military service, or men who were physically unfit, and, in some cases in a break with traditional sex restrictions, women. As was the case with the enlistment of free Black men in defense of communities under siege before the Civil War, the militia in practice proved to be broader than the militia's statutory definition.[27]

But it was not the fact that four million men served in the regular armed forces, nor was it the fact that a large and probably somewhat hard to quantify number of civilians acted in some sort of home-guard capacity during the war that made that conflict important to the history of guns and the desire to regulate guns in American life. An equivalent number of regular troops had been mobilized by the Union and Confederate forces during the Civil War. That conflict had also seen much more extensive and active use of home guard forces. What was different about World War I was the weaponry that had developed. The standard weapons of the American doughboy—the M1903 Springfield rifle and its fraternal twin, the M1917 American Enfield—were bolt-action five-shot rifles, little different from hunting and target rifles generally available to the public. Indeed, even before America's entry into the war, the Army and the National Rifle Association had already begun joint civilian-military marksmanship competitions with the Springfield rifle, legendary for its accuracy and a favorite of military and civilian competitors alike. The American Expeditionary Force also used a set of .45-caliber pistols. One of these was the M1911, a semiautomatic pistol adopted by the Army and Navy in 1911. Known to some five generations of American doughboys and GIs simply as "the 45," the pistol, with minor variations, would remain the official sidearm of the US Armed Forces until 1991 and continues in use with some American military units to the present day. "The 45" was augmented by the M1917 revolver, adopted the year the United States declared war on Imperial Germany. Neither the M1911 nor the M1917 represented anything particularly new or frightening in the way of firearms technology, and both were generally available on the civilian market as well as in military armories.[28]

## NEW WEAPONS, NATIONAL LAW, AND
## A CURIOUS CASE CALLED *MILLER*

But the First World War did bring a new innovation to firearms technology: the automatic weapon, which could be carried in the form of a rifle or carbine (short rifle). The automatic rifle and the submachine gun would both be developed during "The War to End All Wars." The American version of the automatic rifle, the Browning Automatic Rifle, or BAR, was developed in time to play a minor role with the American Expeditionary Forces in the last two months of the war. It was heavy, some twenty pounds unloaded, and carried a twenty-round magazine of powerful 30–06 ammunition (the same round used in the Springfield and American Enfield). It was accurate out to about a thousand yards. The BAR's field manual indicated that it had a rate of fire of some five hundred rounds per minute, but considering that the weapon only held a twenty-round magazine and that the barrel would overheat after firing a hundred rounds on fully automatic fire, its actual rate of fire was considerably less. Still, in an age of bolt-action rifles, it was far faster than most rifles then available, civilian or military. The US Army and Navy officially added the weapon to their arsenals in 1918.[29]

The submachine gun was also developed during World War I. The Thompson submachine gun, or "tommy gun," made its appearance in the United States in the 1920s. The Army and Navy would officially adopt the weapon in 1928, giving it the designation "M1928." It weighed approximately ten pounds unloaded. The tommy gun fired .45-caliber pistol ammunition. The ammunition for the earlier models was placed in a round drum magazine that contained fifty bullets. The maximum accurate range of the Thompson was usually less than fifty yards. Like the BAR, the tommy gun had an official rate of fire of better than five hundred rounds per minute, but again the practical business of actually firing the weapon made the actual rate of fire considerably more modest. The presence of easily portable automatic rifles and carbines would bring a new dimension to the traditional discussion about arms and rights and firearms and regulation.[30]

The BAR and the Thompson might have remained mere curiosities as far as the general public was concerned had it not been for the turbulence of the 1920s, the decade in which they were introduced. The Thompson sold for about $200 in 1921, when it was first made available for public sale. According to one economic index, that was the equivalent of $3,000 in 2021 dollars, but this comparison doesn't measure the relative cost for a potential purchaser in the early 1920s. To better appreciate the cost, we should bear in mind that the average factory worker would have earned about $388 a year in 1921. A Model T Ford cost $290 in 1925. Two hundred dollars for a Thompson would have represented a substantial portion of the average worker's annual wage. This was at a time when an ordinary citizen could buy a conventional rifle or shotgun for hunting or target shooting for under $20 and a pistol or revolver for protection for under $10. The Thompson's short range and pistol ammunition made it improbable as a hunting weapon. Its ability to fire in the fully automatic mode was a bit beyond what most people were looking for home or personal defense. Still, the Thompson Auto Ordinance Company, the weapon's manufacturer, ran advertisements in adventure magazines with a cowboy defending his ranch from rustlers with a tommy gun. Even so, the weapon's prohibitive price probably discouraged all but the wealthiest collectors and shooting enthusiasts from buying it for the sheer novelty and fun of firing an automatic weapon. A few Thompsons found their way into the hands of private security firms, but generally the demand on the private market was limited.[31]

Limited perhaps, but not nonexistent. The 1920s was the decade of that "Noble Experiment," Prohibition: the national ban on the manufacture, sale, and purchase of alcohol. Prohibition would change the face of crime in America, bringing about the rise of organized gangs engaged in the sale of bootlegged alcohol. Territorial rivalries among the gangs led to open warfare on the streets of the nation's major cities, made even more terrifying by the tommy gun. Used by violent criminals in their wars on each other, the Thompson also claimed the lives of some police officers and members of the general public as well.[32]

The end of the 1920s and the end of Prohibition did not bring a halt to the notorious misuse of automatic weapons. In the early 1930s such twentieth-century desperadoes as John Dillinger, Charles Arthur "Pretty Boy" Floyd, Donnie "Ma" Barker, George "Machine Gun" Kelly, and Bonnie Parker and Clyde Barrow became a part of American folklore. Bonnie and Clyde actually brought a bit more oomph to the firepower they employed in their criminal exploits: they used BARs stolen from National Guard armories in their bank robberies and other criminal misadventures.[33] The exploits of such criminals were made more vivid and terrifying by the then new medium of talking motion pictures. For the price of a movie ticket, thirty-five cents in the early 1930s, audiences could be thrilled and frightened by the likes of James Cagney in *Public Enemy*, Edward G. Robinson in *Little Caesar*, and Paul Muni in *Scarface*. The villains were deadly, the crimes vicious, the Thompsons loud. The horrors of criminal misuse of automatic weapons and handguns were forcibly brought home to the public.[34]

The movies, and perhaps more importantly, the newspapers in their reporting of terrifying events like the St. Valentine's Day Massacre and the chronicling of the dubious exploits of the Dillingers and Barrows of the nation helped bring about the first major federal efforts in the field of gun control. The time was ripe for such an effort. Public fears were heightened by the growth of organized criminal gangs, an increased homicide rate, and the perception that the traditional reliance on state and local law enforcement to fight crime was inadequate in an age when criminals could easily cross state lines in their automobiles and could hatch conspiracies over the telephone. The Roosevelt administration was prodded and encouraged to seek a greater role for Washington in the nation's crime-fighting efforts by its attorney general, former Connecticut prosecutor Homer Cummings, and by an ambitious young government attorney named John Edgar Hoover. Hoover was about the business of transforming a previously overlooked bureaucratic backwater, the Bureau of Investigation, into what would become the five-star final, banner-headline-grabbing FBI.[35]

The Roosevelt administration began looking at increased federal regulation of firearms in 1933. Franklin Roosevelt had been a supporter of gun-control legislation, including his home state's Sullivan Law as governor of New York. His attorney general, Homer Cummings, was a proponent of far-reaching gun-control legislation, including the registration of pistols and revolvers. In April 1934 the Justice Department presented a national firearms bill before Congress. The bill as originally drafted would have placed a tax of $200 and required the registration of "machine guns," defined to include both automatic and semiautomatic firearms. Short-barreled or sawed-off rifles and shotguns and silencers would also have been registered with a $200 tax. The proposed legislation would also have required registration and a $1 tax on pistols and revolvers. The bill was subject to hearings before the House Committee on Ways and Means. Cummings and Assistant Attorney General Joseph B. Keenan represented the Justice Department's position before the committee. Although most of their testimony focused on why they believed the proposed legislation was good policy, both had to answer questions concerning what was constitutionally problematic about the proposed bill. Most of this discussion focused on the issue of congressional authority to regulate firearms. Both Cummings and Keenan agreed that Congress did not have the police power to regulate firearms but argued instead that the taxing power would allow Congress to regulate the sale of weapons.[36]

The Second Amendment played something of a secondary role in the committee's deliberations on the measure. One witness, Charles V. Imlay, an attorney from Washington, DC, who had worked with the American Bar Association on drafting uniform firearms legislation, discussed the Second Amendment issue in traditional terms of the armed citizenry at large as a resource for the community's defense:

> But you are legislating for citizens and when you take the history of firearms and their legitimate use in the history of this country, what do you find? You find that law and order has always been enforced by the citizen body and you can go now into some of our rural sections and you can find it is still true, as it was in the early part of the Republic, that when the sheriff goes after a gangster he can go from house to house and he can be sure there is a householder with a weapon. It was once a shotgun or rifle, but is now a pistol.[37]

Congressman David John Lewis of Maryland raised the issue of the constitutional right to carry arms and asked Cummings "how we escaped that provision in the Constitution?" Cummings replied that the Justice Department was not attempting to escape it but was using the taxing power and the commerce clause to reach the regulation of firearms. Cummings's answer might be interpreted as not addressing the meaning of the Second Amendment but simply going to the question of congressional power to regulate. It is nonetheless important to note that neither Cummings nor Keenan attempted to contradict statements from members of the committee that argued that the Constitution protected the right to have arms. Both stressed that they were not seeking to deprive ordinary citizens of regular firearms but were instead trying to ensure that the most dangerous weapons stayed out of the hands of gangsters.[38]

The provisions requiring the registration of pistols and revolvers generated the most controversy. A number of congressmen expressed the fear that such measures would cause ordinary citizens to potentially become criminals simply for having failed to register their pistols. A few representatives noted that the measure could become a second Volstead Act, the federal statute that implemented Prohibition and that large numbers of otherwise law-abiding citizens violated. The Justice Department's case for that measure was undoubtedly weakened when both Cummings and Keenan admitted that the measure would not stop criminals from getting handguns, although they argued it would provide a basis for prosecuting criminals who failed to register their weapons.[39]

The National Rifle Association played a key role in modifying the legislation. Milton A. Reckord, the adjutant general of Maryland and executive vice president of the shooter's association, and Karl T. Frederick, the organization's president, argued for changes to the proposed bill. Frederick, who had won a gold medal for pistol shooting in the 1920 Olympics, was an attorney who had been active in the American Bar Association's efforts to craft uniform firearms legislation. Reckord had risen through the ranks in the Maryland National Guard and had commanded a National Guard regiment in the Meuse Argonne offensive during World War I. At the time of his testimony, he commanded the Maryland National Guard and had the previous year played a role in the passage of legislation making the National Guard a permanent reserve of the US Army. Both men brought considerable standing and prestige to their testimony and, it should be added, quite a few letters and telegrams from sportsmen to Congress supporting their position. They were successful in modifying two key provisions of the proposed legislation. First, they had the provision requiring the registration and taxation of pistols dropped from the legislation. Second, they insured the section discussing machine guns included only automatic weapons, not automatic and semiautomatic weapons as originally proposed. With those modifications the NRA supported the bill, which ultimately became the National Firearms Act.[40]

The hearings before the House Committee provided something of a preview of the shape the gun-control debate would take in future decades. The hearings revealed the already existing split between rural and urban America on the gun issue. They also revealed what had already become two contrasting views of citizenship and the citizen's capabilities. Charles Imlay's vision of the self-reliant rural citizen with rifle or pistol at the ready, capable of aiding the sheriff in search of desperadoes, was a vision that harkened back to the militias and posses of the founding era. It was a vision that still resonated with much of rural and small-town America. By way of contrast, J. Weston Allen, former attorney general of Massachusetts and a spokesman for the National Crime Commission, expressed skepticism that private citizens would be capable of defending themselves at all with pistols or revolvers.[41]

A subcommittee of the Senate Commerce Committee also held hearings on the proposed legislation. The testimony of two of the witnesses, Frederick L. Hoffman, a statistician who had worked for the insurance industry, and Karl Frederick of the NRA, revealed that, in part, the debate over the 1934 legislation was more than a quarrel over whether the proposed measure would reduce crime. It was, as well, an encounter between clashing views over the place of force in a civilized society. Hoffman brought to his testimony statistical data concerning the incidence of homicide in the United States. His presentation also included data from the United Kingdom and other European nations that had adopted stricter gun control legislation after World War I. But Hoffman's testimony did not rest on his empirical presentation. He went further, arguing that the disarming of the population was essential to the development of civilization: "For it is not the business of the citizen to protect himself against robbers and gunmen, but for the Government to provide adequate protection for lives and property, be the cost of such protection what it may."[42]

Hoffman's Senate testimony took the hearings beyond the routine back-and-forth debate over the likely effectiveness of the proposed legislation, or even the question of whether the new firearms regulations might ensnare more law-abiding citizens than criminals. His testimony framed the gun-control debate as a clash of culture and civilization. Hoffman was presenting the idea that force was the business, indeed the exclusive business of the state, not individuals acting in self-defense and certainly not citizens acting as a loose and informally deputized militia or posse at large. The German-born statistician was presenting an idea that had long gained acceptance among European policymakers and social theorists. German sociologist Max Weber had indicated that one of the key hallmarks of a modern state was the ability of the state to have a monopoly on violence.[43] Regular police forces, large standing armies, and tightly controlled reserve forces, combined with large-scale legal or de facto disarmament of civilian populations, had long been a reality in much of Europe. The tendency to disarm or strictly control weapons available to civilian populations in Europe had intensified in the wake of World War I and the Bolshevik Revolution in Russia. These events had heightened European political leaders' fear of revolution and the desire to limit arms available to civilian populations.[44]

For better and worse, the notion that the state should have a monopoly of force had significantly less resonance in the United States than in Europe. Dutch historian Pieter Spierenburg has advanced the thesis that from the colonial era and onward, Americans had developed a culture of self-reliance that equated democracy with the right of armed self-defense and that that equation became an enduring part of American culture. Certainly, the criticism of the 1934 legislation as originally proposed—criticism that articulated the need for private arms for home defense and for assistance to law enforcement—pointed to a very different conception of the respective roles of citizen and state than the views outlined by Frederick Hoffman. This clash of views concerning the citizen, civilization, and culture would remain a subtext in the gun-control debate as it would reemerge decades later.[45]

If Hoffman had a broader vision of where the gun-control effort should lead, the testimony by Assistant Attorney General Keenan revealed that he, Cummings, and other officials in the Justice Department wanted more than the measures proposed in the 1934 bill. Keenan indicated that he would like to see a ban on pistols, wanted to significantly reduce the number of gun sellers, and stated that "it may take many, many years before we make real headway in the control of firearms." It is significant that Keenan, while agreeing that Congress lacked the power to ban pistols, had nothing explicit to say about the Second Amendment and its possible impact on his projected agenda. This was at a time when the general consensus was that the constitutional provision protected the right of individuals. Political scientist Edward Corwin, probably the leading constitutional commentator of the day, in his 1924 treatise, *The Constitution and What It Means Today*, described the right to bear arms as "the right to bear them openly, not in concealment." He also noted that the term "free state" in the Second Amendment should be interpreted as meaning the whole of the United States and not particular states. Corwin indicated that the right was a right of citizens and could be denied to aliens on reasonable grounds.[46]

But Corwin notwithstanding, it is probably fair to say that Cummings and Keenan, like other drafters of New Deal legislation, were practical men concerned more with passing and implementing what they saw as good public policy than with pondering constitutional limitations. The makers of the New Deal were well aware that they were pushing the limits and indeed went beyond the limits of what was then deemed to be constitutionally permissible. Their hope was that the exigencies of the national emergency that was the Great Depression would give them the political power and leverage over any possible judicial obstruction to push forward new policies. This was certainly the case in the area of economic regulation, and it was also true in the field of crime fighting and firearms regulation. If Corwin represented the conventional wisdom on the meaning of the Second Amendment, that constitutional provision should not prove to be an insurmountable barrier to needed regulation any more than the Tenth Amendment and traditional notions of the scope of federal power should block other necessary measures. It should also be added that thinking about specific provisions of the Bill of Rights and the limits that they might pose on the Congress or the president was still very much in its infancy in the early 1930s. The Supreme Court had a long history of looking at the question of economic rights infusing substantive content into the seemingly procedural provisions of the due process clauses of the Fifth and Fourteenth Amendments. But the notion that the rights of ordinary citizens should be regarded seriously and that the courts were likely venues for vindication of those rights developed slowly. The underdeveloped state of thinking about rights, coupled with the fact that the agenda initially proposed in the firearms bill was far from a total prohibition, probably led to a presentation in which the Justice Department did not feel the need for elaborate constitutional defense of its agenda.

The National Firearms Act became law in June 1934 with the modifications sought by the NRA, removal of pistols and revolvers from the list of weapons to be registered, and a definition of "machine gun" that included only fully automatic weapons. It was the federal government's first significant foray into the business of gun control. An earlier act in 1927 had prohibited the shipping of handguns through the mails, but that legislation did not regulate possession of handguns, and it was easily circumvented through the use of private carriers. Attorney General Cummings would continue his efforts to require federal registration of handguns in the 1930s, but to no avail. A second statute, the Federal Firearms Act, was passed in June 1938. The later legislation required the licensing of firearms manufacturers and sellers and prohibited the transfer of firearms to people with criminal records. As was the case with the 1934 legislation, the NRA played a significant role in shaping the ultimate statute.[47]

The 1934 act gave rise to the Supreme Court's last decision on the Second Amendment before *Heller*. The case, *United States v. Miller*, would leave a curious legacy to the Second Amendment debate. Advocates of both the individualist and collective readings of the constitutional provision would, in later years, claim that the *Miller* Court vindicated their position. *Miller* would assume an outsize importance, because until *Heller*, it was the one case where the Supreme Court had come closest to addressing the issue of the meaning of the Second Amendment. The Court's previous examinations of Second Amendment claims, *Cruikshank* and *Presser*, really had more to say about the Court's view of the scope and meaning of the Fourteenth Amendment than its view of the second. In light of its importance, *Miller* was all the more curious because it was the result of a case in which the Court only heard the argument of one side, the federal government.[48]

The case began in 1938 when Jack Miller and Frank Layton were indicted for transporting between Oklahoma and Arkansas an unregistered shotgun with a barrel length of less than eighteen inches, the statutory limit under the 1934 act. Miller and Layton initially pleaded guilty, but the trial court judge, Heartsill Ragon of the US District Court for the Western District of Arkansas, refused to accept their plea. Instead, he appointed Paul Gutensohn as their defense attorney. Gutensohn filed a demurrer, a procedural motion in which a party argues that the opposing side does not have a legally sufficient basis for its case. If the court sustains a demurrer, the opposing party must lose because it has no valid legal argument. Gutensohn's demurrer contended that the National Firearms Act violated the Second Amendment's guarantee of the right to keep and bear arms and the Tenth Amendment's reservation of certain powers to the states. Judge Ragon sustained the demurrer and expressed the view that the relevant section of the 1934 statute violated the Second Amendment.[49]

Legal scholar Brian L. Frye has written that *Miller* was something of a test case from the very beginning. Far from believing that the National Firearms Act of 1934 violated the Second Amendment, Judge Ragon was a long-term supporter of restrictions on firearms ownership and hoped the case of Miller and Layton would provide an opportunity for a Supreme Court ruling declaring the gun-control measure constitutional. The opinion in the District Court seems to support Frye's analysis. Ragon's discussion of the Second Amendment claim is brief, consisting of no more than a statement saying that the 1934 act violated the constitutional provision. The opinion cited to none of the previous Supreme Court cases on the subject, nor did it discuss the state court jurisprudence on the right to bear arms. Ragon also failed to cite commentators like Cooley and Corwin, who had discussed the right to keep and bear arms as part of the body of rights that belonged to American citizens. Ragon's dismissal of the government's claim was summary, and it was done with two defendants who were unlikely to engage any court's sympathy.[50]

The United States appealed the decision to the Supreme Court. There was no representative arguing for Miller and Layton in the Supreme Court. Solicitor General Robert H. Jackson, a future associate justice of the Supreme Court, wrote the brief for the government. Gordon Dean represented the United States in oral argument. Jackson's brief offered several alternative theories as to why the National Firearms Act did not violate the Second Amendment. First, the government asserted, echoing language in *Cruikshank* and *Presser*, that the Second Amendment did not create the right to bear arms; it merely recognized the pre-existing right that had existed under common law. Because the right had always been subject to statutory restrictions in the interests of public safety, Congress was able to restrict the right to bear arms for similar reasons. Second, the Jackson brief argued that the right was a collective one that protected the people when carrying arms as members of the state militia. Finally, the government contended that in granting an individual right to bear arms, the government had a right to restrict those weapons that were peculiarly adaptable for criminal purposes and not suitable to the common defense or other legitimate purposes. The Jackson brief made much of this point, noting: "But it is also indisputable that Congress was striking not at weapons intended for legitimate use but at weapons which form the arsenal of the gangster and desperado."[51]

The Court's opinion, authored by Justice James C. McReynolds, focused on the third argument, the claim that certain weapons were not militia weapons:

> In the absence of any evidence tending to show that the possession of a [sawed-off shotgun] at this time has some reasonable relationship to the preservation or

efficiency of a well-regulated militia, we cannot say that the Second Amendment guarantees the right to keep and bear such an instrument. Certainly it is not within judicial notice that this weapon is any part of the ordinary military equipment or that its use could contribute to the common defense.[52]

Advocates of the collective rights view have emphasized the *Miller* Court's focus on the militia, claiming that it was an indication that the Court saw the Second Amendment as only being concerned with the preservation of state militia. But the *Miller* Court's discussion of the militia indicates that the Court saw a clear relationship between the individual right and the maintenance of the militia:

> The signification attributed to the term "militia" appears from the debates in the Constitutional Convention, the history and legislation of colonies and states, and the writings of approved commentators. These show plainly enough that the militia is composed of all males physically capable of acting in concert for the common defense: "A body of citizens enrolled for military discipline." Furthermore, ordinarily when called for service, these men were expected to appear bearing arms supplied by themselves and of the kind in common use at the time.[53]

Probably the most accurate way to view what the Court did in *Miller* was to see it as an updating of the nineteenth-century civilized warfare doctrine. McReynolds's decision relied on the antebellum Tennessee case *Aymette v. State*, which allowed the state to restrict the carrying of weapons not suited for the common defense. The Supreme Court reversed Ragon and remanded the case to the lower court.[54]

The case was not reheard in the lower court. Miller had been killed, and Layton pled guilty to the reinstated charges. The absence of a trial in light of the McReynolds ruling left a number of unanswered questions. The McReynolds opinion focused on the weapon, the sawed-off shotgun that Miller and Layton had been accused of carrying. McReynolds did not hold that sawed-off shotguns were not militia weapons and thus beyond the scope of the Second Amendment's protection. Instead, he stated that the Court would not take judicial notice that the weapon was part of the ordinary equipment of a militia member. Judicial notice is an evidentiary short cut that allows a court to recognize commonly accepted facts without the need for proving those facts in court. McReynolds's refusal to take judicial notice of whether the sawed-off shotgun was a militia weapon meant that that was a determination that should have been made when the case was remanded to the District Court. Factual determinations are typically made at the trial court level, not by appellate courts. Trial courts have the ability to hear witnesses and examine exhibits, all of which aid trial courts in making factual determinations. Presumably with the McReynolds ruling, prosecution and defense in a retrial of Miller and Layton would have spent much of their time trying to demonstrate that the sawed-off shotgun was or was not a suitable weapon for militia purposes. Because the retrial never occurred, that determination was never made.[55]

Even putting to one side the personal fortunes of Miller and Layton and the question of the utility of sawed-off shotguns for militia service, the opinion in *Miller* left serious Second Amendment questions unanswered—indeed, not raised, even in dicta. While McReynolds focused on the weapon and its appropriateness for militia service, the opinion in *Miller* did not provide any indication as to whether there were limitations to the principle that weapons that were ordinary militia equipment were constitutionally protected. If the World War I–era 1903 Springfield, its recently adopted but still largely unissued successor the semiautomatic eight-shot M1 Garand, and the M1911 .45-caliber pistol seemed unproblematic enough as candidates for constitutional protection, other weapons in the inventory of the regular armed forces and the National Guard raised challenges for the principle that weapons useful for members of the militia were constitutionally protected. The BAR and the Thompson submachine gun were now regularly found in the armories of the Army and Navy and their subsidiaries, the Army Air Corps, the Marine Corps, and the Coast Guard. Should the McReynolds opinion be read as extending constitutional protection to these weapons, as well as to the machine guns, flame throwers, mortars, and other heavy weapons that were by 1939 ordinary military equipment? Did advances in military technology make it impossible or highly undesirable to attempt to preserve the militia at large as an inchoate military force, leaving it only weapons that might be useful to aid civil authorities? *Miller* did not engage these questions, because they were not part of the case before the Court. Nonetheless, these questions would be part of the legacy of *United States v. Miller* and would contribute to the case's subsequent misinterpretations.

*Miller* would to a great extent close the chapter on the pre-war effort at gun control. Its peculiar posture, the fact that it was the product of an ex-parte hearing before the Supreme Court and the fact that it was never fully litigated at the district or trial court level, caused the case to raise more questions than it answered and left it open to misinterpretation. *Miller* was a case that would largely be ignored until decades later. In its immediate aftermath, the nation would turn its attention from the problems of the Great Depression and outlaw gangs to other concerns.

# 3. Arms, War, and Law in the American Century

The growing threat of a second and likely more terrible world war, coupled with a shrinking crime rate, in the late 1930s helped cool the Roosevelt administration's enthusiasm for further gun-control efforts. There were, to be sure, members of the administration who continued to advocate further restrictions on the possession and carrying of pistols.[1] Their efforts were buttressed by the influential American Law Institute, which in 1940 revised its model legislation that would require licenses to carry pistols. But by 1940 Roosevelt and his administration were increasingly concerned with events in Europe and Asia that were spinning more and more out of control. They were also concerned with an American public disillusioned by the nation's role in the First World War and determined that the country should avoid involvement in a second one. In that atmosphere the champions of the New Deal, now concerned with military preparedness, had little political capital to spend on the issue of gun control.

If fear of war and the nation's ultimate entry into World War II helped mute the concerns of those who urged stricter controls on firearms possession, the legislation passed in the 1930s would nonetheless bring the question of firearms legislation and the Constitution before the federal courts. Two cases, *United States v. Tot*[2] and *Cases v. United States*,[3] involved court examinations of convictions under the Federal Firearms Act of 1938. The act prohibited the acquisition of firearms after an individual had been convicted of a felony. Both cases involved men with criminal convictions who were arrested while in possession of pistols. The cases are interesting for what they reveal about how federal courts were going to handle Second Amendment claims in light of federal legislation and the Supreme Court's decision in *Miller. United States v. Tot* involved the conviction of Frank Tot, a New Jersey resident who was convicted in the US District Court for the District of New Jersey of violating the Federal Firearms Act of 1938. The district court found that Tot, who was also charged with possessing stolen cigarettes, had a .32-caliber semi-automatic pistol in his home.[4] Tot had previously been convicted of a violent crime and was thus ineligible to own a firearm acquired after July 30, 1938, the date of the passage of the statute. Tot appealed his conviction to the Third Circuit Court of Appeals, arguing, under several different legal theories, that his conviction was in error. One of these theories was that if the statute's prohibition applied to the weapon in question, it was a violation of Tot's rights under the Second Amendment. It was a plausible claim. The circuit court was examining Tot's claim three years after the Supreme Court's decision in *Miller*. McReynolds's opinion in *Miller* had indicated that weapons that were not useful for militia purposes were not protected by the Second Amendment. A .32-caliber semi-automatic pistol, while not identical to the .45-caliber semiautomatic used by the armed forces or the .38-caliber revolvers commonly found in police forces at the time, was a relatively common firearm among members of the general public. An individual could make a plausible claim that such a weapon could be used to assist civil or military authorities in an emergency or that it could allow an individual to gain or maintain a basic proficiency in marksmanship that would be useful for the common defense.[5]

Judge Herbert Goodrich, a recent Roosevelt appointee to the Third Circuit, dealt with the Second Amendment claim in writing the circuit court's decision. His opinion provided a mixture of what today we might call a militia-centered approach to the amendment, coupled with a recognition that law-abiding individuals might have a claim to a right to possess firearms as private citizens. Early on in his analysis, Goodrich noted that the amendment was not adopted with individual rights in mind but was "instead a protection for states against possible encroachments by federal power." The circuit court opinion went on to echo *Miller*'s requirement that a protected weapon should have the potential to be militarily useful.[6]

But Goodrich also indicated that the argument for the measure's constitutionality also rested on the grounds that the 1938 statute restricted arms possession by irresponsible individuals:

> But further the same result is definitely indicated on a broader ground and on
> this we should prefer to rest the matter. Weapon bearing was never treated
> as anything like an absolute right by the common law. . . . One could hardly
> argue seriously that a limitation upon the privilege of possessing weapons was
> unconstitutional when applied to a mental patient of the maniac type. The same
> would be true if the possessor were a child of immature years. In the situation at
> bar Congress has prohibited the receipt of weapons from interstate transactions

by persons who have previously, by due process of law, been shown to be aggressors against society. Such a classification is entirely reasonable and does not infringe upon the preservation of the well-regulated militia protected by the Second Amendment.[7]

Frank Tot's conviction would later be reversed by the US Supreme Court. The reversal came not on the grounds that the Federal Firearms Act violated the Second Amendment; indeed, Tot's attorneys did not present a Second Amendment claim in their appellate brief to the Supreme Court. Instead, Tot's brief stressed that a provision of the 1938 statute violated the Fifth Amendment. The Court agreed, holding that the law's presumption that the defendant had received the pistol after the passage of the act violated Tot's right to due process. It required him to prove that he had acquired the pistol before the passage of the legislation rather than requiring the government to prove that he had acquired the weapon after its passage. The Court was not presented with and had no reason to address Tot's Second Amendment claim.[8]

In 1942, the year that the Third Circuit Court of Appeals was considering Frank Tot's appeal, the First Circuit Court of Appeals was reviewing the conviction of Jose Cases Velazquez by the US District Court in Puerto Rico. Cases—the courts followed the Spanish practice of placing the family name in the middle—had been convicted of violating the Federal Firearms Act by illegal possession of a .38-caliber revolver. He had a previous conviction for assault and battery, making his possession of the weapon illegal under the 1938 act. Cases's possession of the revolver was discovered when he shot a patron at a social club in a suburb of San Juan.[9]

Cases appealed his conviction on a number of grounds, including the claim that convicting him under the 1938 Federal Firearms Act was a violation of his Second Amendment rights. The Court, in an opinion authored by Judge Peter Woodbury, also a recent Roosevelt appointee, sustained Cases's conviction. Woodbury's constitutional theories as to why Cases's Second Amendment claim was invalid were all over the map. They seemed less like a judge making a sure-footed pronouncement of the rule of law and more like an attorney pleading alternative legal theories on behalf of a client in the hopes that a court would accept one theory or another. The Woodbury opinion thus asked whether the Second Amendment even applied in the territories. The opinion then went on to borrow language from *Cruikshank* and *Presser* noting that the Second Amendment was not a right that was granted by the Constitution, arguing that it was only meant to restrict actions by Congress. That point was somewhat beside the point. Unlike *Cruikshank,* which involved an allegation that a private party had violated an individual's Second Amendment rights, or *Presser,* which involved a claim that a state government had violated a citizen's right to keep and bear arms, *Cases v. United States* was about the conviction of a US citizen under a federal statute in a territory governed by Congress. Woodbury then turned to an analysis of *Miller* and its implication for the case at hand. The *Miller* doctrine, that a weapon that was useful for militia purposes was eligible for constitutional protection, posed problems. Woodbury noted that applying the militia test as a categorical rule would lead to absurd results. It would produce a rule stating that Congress could not regulate machine guns, trench mortars, and other weapons that had by then become commonplace in military inventories. So, Woodbury indicated that the rule in *Miller* should not be considered a categorical rule, that is, that any weapon that might be militarily useful was constitutionally protected. Instead, Woodbury's opinion indicated that whether a weapon that was potentially useful for the common defense should receive constitutional protection would have to be decided on a case-by-case basis.[10]

But the .38-caliber revolver would surely qualify for such protection. It was found in the inventories of the armed forces and in various police departments around the nation. It was owned by many members of the general public. It did not pose the unusual dangers presented by machine guns, mortars, grenades, and other weapons designed to produce mass casualties. Woodbury recognized that the .38-revolver was capable of military use and that an individual might legitimately claim to be taking the initiative to train on his own with such a weapon to enhance his potential usefulness to the armed forces. But, as Woodbury noted, Cases in possessing and transporting the weapon, and in shooting up a social club, was "engaged in a frolic of his own," not enhancing his ability to contribute to the common defense. The opinion left unclear how close the connection between an individual's possession of a firearm and participation in a military program would have to be for the individual's possession to receive constitutional protection.[11]

*Tot* and *Cases* would begin a pattern of cases in the federal courts that would accelerate after the passage of the Gun Control Act of 1968. The pattern was simple. Federal law prohibited the possession of weapons by individuals with felony convictions. Individuals involved in criminal activities would be caught in possession of firearms. As defendants, these individuals would argue that the 1938 act or, later, the 1968 gun-control measure violated their rights under the Second Amendment. The defendants were usually not particularly sympathetic and were not likely to cause the courts to spend much time pondering their claims. In *Tot* and *Cases*, the Third and First Circuit Courts of Appeals handed down decisions that from the perspective of the modern debate over an individualist or collectivist reading of the Second Amendment seem somewhat ambiguous. The defendants' constitutional claims were denied. Both decisions stressed that the purpose of the Second Amendment was to preserve the Constitution's "well-regulated militia." But both decisions also noted the criminal activities of the defendants and stressed that the 1938 statute was not meant to restrict the rights of the law-abiding public. With a statute that only restricted the rights of people engaged in criminal activity, and with decisions that did not make overly broad claims on what the Second Amendment did or did not do, there was little reason for that relatively rare occurrence in American jurisprudence, Supreme Court review.

## OF ARMS AND ARMAGEDDON

While the defendants, prosecutors, defense attorneys, and a number of federal judges and their staffs were concerning themselves with the personal fortunes of Tot and Cases, the rest of the nation was concerning itself with the second great conflict that was engulfing the world and that would forever transform it. Even before the Japanese attack on Pearl Harbor and while the United States was engaged in a de facto naval war with the Third Reich in the North Atlantic,[12] the Roosevelt administration was making preparations, often in the face of strong isolationist opposition, for the coming conflict. A peacetime draft was instituted for the first time in 1940. That same year the National Guard was called up into the Army. Both measures were supposed to last for a year and were designed to ready a woefully unprepared nation for the coming conflict. In 1939, the year of the start of the European War, the United States had an army smaller than Portugal's.[13]

The Roosevelt administration knew that the expanded Army, Navy, and other armed forces were going to need supplies. The administration wanted the ability to requisition supplies if the ordinary processes of government procurement failed to keep the massive amount of material critical to modern warfare flowing into the hands of the War and Navy Departments, and at an agreeable price. The government's felt need for an increased power to requisition supplies would lead to new legislation, the Property Requisition Act of 1941.[14]

The new legislation would provide an occasion for Congress to weigh in on the subject of the Second Amendment. The requisition statute contained a provision restricting the government's ability to requisition personal firearms:

Nothing in this Act shall be construed—

(1) to authorize the requisitioning or require the registration of any firearms possessed by any individual for his personal protection or sport (and the possession of which is not prohibited or the registration of which is not required by existing law).

(2) to impair or infringe in any manner the right of any individual to keep and bear arms.[15]

During debates in the House on the legislation, remarks by Republican Representative Edwin Arthur Hall of Binghamton, New York, gave indication that the example of totalitarian governments in other nations was rekindling long-held American notions linking the right to bear arms with resistance to tyranny:

Before the advent of Hitler or Stalin, who took their power from the German and Russian people, measures were thrust upon the free legislatures of those countries to deprive the people of the possession and use of firearms, so that they could not resist the encroachments of such diabolical and vitriolic state police organizations as the Gestapo, the Ogpu and the Cheka. Just as sure as I am standing here today, you are going to see this measure followed by legislation sponsored by the proponents of such encroachments upon the rights of the people, which will eventually deprive the people of their constitutional liberty which provides for the possession of firearms for the protection of their homes.[16]

Even as Congressman Hall was expressing his concerns, worries about gun confiscation were yielding to another set of concerns about firearms—how to procure weapons and train the men who were beginning to be mobilized in increasing numbers in their use. World War II would be the occasion of the greatest mass mobilization of American men in the nation's history. Some fifteen-and-one-half million men, roughly 57 percent of the men listed as being between the ages of fifteen and thirty-nine in the 1940 census, would serve in the US armed forces between 1940 and 1945. Nearly 350,000 women would also enlist in the armed forces.[17] Officially the women were not supposed to be trained in the use of small arms, although that rule was occasionally broken. But the men had to be trained in firearms use regardless of service or assignment. This rule applied to Marine Corps riflemen and Air Corps mechanics, Army truck drivers, and Navy mess stewards. The need for training and arming combat soldiers was clear. But the need went beyond that. In a worldwide conflict with American forces stationed and fighting on or just off every inhabited continent, no one could be sure when an enemy breakthrough or the need for a landing or boarding party would require putting a rifle or a carbine in the hands of a man whose primary job was to repair radios or cook potatoes. Even the most improbable of combatants had to be trained. Air Corps band leader Captain Alton "Glenn" Miller took his turn on the firing line, qualifying as a marksman with the M1 carbine and the .45-caliber pistol.[18]

World War II was the beginning of not just a mass mobilization, but a mass militarization of American society that would occur between 1940 and 1973, the years of the draft in peacetime and wartime in the United States. In those three decades, more than thirty million American men would pass through the armed forces, serving in the Second World War, during the Korean and Vietnam conflicts, and during the Cold War more generally.[19] Some were eager to enlist. Others were brought in by the draft or by the decision to volunteer in the hope that enlistment would give the individual a greater possibility of choice of service and assignment. This experience would have profound effects on the nation. Immigrants served with men who grew up on Indian reservations. Men who had been raised in Irish or Italian or Polish neighborhoods in crowded industrial cities served alongside farmers and ranchers of English or Scots-Irish ancestry. The mixture wasn't complete. The US Army maintained separate and distinctly unequal units for Negro and Nisei (Japanese American) troops. Still, the experience of service during World War II and the cold and hot wars that would follow would leave an indelible mark on the American psyche.

One way it would do so would be to introduce a generation of American men to firearms and marksmanship unlike any previous event in the nation's history. As was the case in previous conflicts, some of the recruits were already accomplished marksmen before they entered the service. Audie Murphy, an impoverished teenage Army recruit of mainly Scots-Irish and Irish ancestry from Texas, had learned at an early age to shoot in order to hunt and feed his family. Doris Miller, also from Texas, had done a fair amount of squirrel hunting before he enlisted as a mess attendant, the only US Navy rating open to Negroes when he joined in 1939. He would later win the Navy Cross for shooting down four Japanese planes at Pearl Harbor. There were others like Murphy and Miller, boys and men who had learned to hunt and shoot long before they wore the Army's "O.Ds." or the Navy's dungarees. But there were others—men from cities, sons of recent immigrants, men who did not come from rural and small-town America where guns were commonplace. For many, shooting was a new experience. And even the recruits who had done some shooting in civilian life often found that they had to work with a new array of weapons, some of them quite different from the squirrel rifles and shotguns with which they were familiar.[20]

The National Rifle Association would also play a part in this effort. Since 1903 the shooters' organization had worked with the US Army's civilian marksmanship program to promote civilian familiarity with firearms, on the theory that such familiarity would prove helpful in time of mobilization. It did. With the enormous expansion of the armed forces and the proliferation of training camps, the armed forces often found themselves short of marksmanship instructors. The NRA helped set up training programs for the armed forces and in some cases even provided instructors. After the conflict, the organization would receive letters of commendation from President Harry Truman, Army Chief of Staff General George Marshall, and Chief of Naval Operations Admiral Ernest King for its contribution to wartime training.[21]

For the massive group of American men who went through the armed forces during World War II, weapons would become familiar and, for many, even commonplace. New words would also enter or be reinforced in the American lexicon reflecting this new familiarity with the small arms that were often critical to a man's chances of surviving and returning home. Few who went through the experience failed to learn the meaning of such terms as "the Garand," "M1 Thumb," "the Carbine," "the 0–3," "the .45," "the Thompson," "the BAR" or "the grease gun." Every GI knew what it meant to "bolo" on the rifle range, or what had to be done with a rifle packed in cosmoline, or what it meant to "zero in a weapon," or to use "Kentucky Windage." Many would long remember the familiar refrain from their sergeants, "Don't jerk that trigger, rookie, squeeeeeze it." Although most learned the fundamentals of marksmanship in basic training by firing the World War I–era bolt-action

0–3 Springfield, almost all US soldiers would become familiar with automatic weapons and semiautomatic rifles. The two most frequently issued weapons were semiautomatic, the M1 rifle and the M1 carbine. The M1 rifle, also known as the Garand, named for its inventor, fired the same powerful 30–06 cartridge as its predecessor, the 1903 Springfield. Like the Springfield, it was, in the hands of a skilled marksman, accurate at a range of five hundred yards. It took an eight-round clip, and its manual indicated that it could be fired at a rate of forty to fifty rounds per minute.[22] The carbine fired a light .30-caliber round, significantly less powerful than the 30–06 round used in the Garand. It was accurate out to three hundred yards, or so the manual said. The carbine was loaded with a fifteen-round detachable magazine. Its manual indicated it could fire some two hundred rounds per minute, though once again the actual, practical rate of fire was significantly less.[23] With their enhanced firepower, the M1 rifle and M1 carbine gave World War II GIs an advantage over almost every other soldier in the conflict. Other nations for the most part still used as their main battle rifles bolt-action weapons that had been developed at the end of the nineteenth century and that had been used in World War I. The American soldiers would learn to use the semiautomatic rifles that had been designed in the United States and produced at an astonishing speed by the "arsenal of democracy." Along the way many Americans also learned to use the bolt-action Lee-Enfields of their British allies as well as the bolt-action Mausers, Manlicher-Carcanos, and Ariskas of their German, Italian, and Japanese enemies. Many men would hide their government-issued weapons or captured enemy weapons in their duffle bags and bring them home upon their return to the United States. Others would buy these weapons when they became available on the surplus market after the war.[24]

And what of the concept of the militia, the notion that the population as a whole might serve as an inchoate defense force? Could that notion survive in an age of industrial warfare and mass mobilization? Surely that eighteenth-century anachronism, one that many historians have informed us failed so dismally during the War of 1812 and other nineteenth-century conflicts, played no part in and was perhaps finally put to rest during World War II, if not long before. The National Guard was mobilized for the war, but the Guard had been reorganized in the 1920s as a reserve of the US Army, with its officers and enlisted men trained under standards prescribed by the Army. With the call up of the National Guard in 1940, guardsmen received an additional year of training as part of the Army. By the time Japanese planes struck at Pearl Harbor, the units of the National Guard had been integrated into the Army and bore little or no relationship to the nineteenth-century militia, and certainly not the inchoate militia of the whole.

Still, the idea that a militia composed of people who were basically civilians with little, if any, military training or perhaps veterans whose military training was decades in the past, proved to be useful during World War II as it had in previous conflicts. The British had set the example in 1940. With the British and French armies defeated by the German blitzkrieg that had simply bypassed France's seemingly impregnable Maginot Line, nearly 340,000 British, French, and Belgian soldiers faced the prospect of annihilation or capture in the French seaport of Dunkirk. As was dramatized in the 2017 film *Dunkirk,* the allied soldiers were rescued in no small measure by private boat owners who augmented the efforts of the Royal Navy. Some seven hundred private yachts, fishing vessels, tugboats, and virtually anything else that could float, and some vessels whose claims to seaworthiness were somewhat debatable, joined some 220 ships of the British fleet. The small boats ferried allied troops from the shore to the larger vessels of the Royal Navy, which were unable to negotiate the shallow waters near the Dunkirk coastline. The owners, crews, and assorted hangers-on worked with the seamen of the Royal Navy to man the vessels. The civilians were temporarily sworn into the Royal Navy for one month or the duration of the evacuation. These mixed crews played a vital role in evacuating the surviving members of the British Expeditionary Force and quite a few French and Belgian soldiers as well. The flotilla of small boats was not, by and large, an armed militia, but it was a seagoing militia nonetheless.[25]

Perhaps closer to what we might ordinarily think of as a militia were Britain's Local Defence Volunteers, or the "Home Guard," formed in May 1940 in anticipation of a German invasion of the United Kingdom. Most of the volunteers were men who were too old for military service, along with some boys who were too young to serve. Others worked at critical occupations and would not be drafted into or even accepted as volunteers for the armed forces. There was also a Home Guard program for women.[26] Initially due to a shortage of firearms—the British Army had left many of its weapons in France and Belgium, and private firearms were in short supply in Britain—many of the recruits drilled with umbrellas, pitchforks, and the occasional venerable double-barreled shotgun. Eventually the volunteers would get Enfield rifles and uniforms, but in the late spring and early summer of 1940 there was great fear that "Dad's Army" might have to meet the well-armed Wehrmacht with little more than pitchforks, umbrellas, and a few shotguns meant to bring down doves, not Luftwaffe paratroopers. The British government asked the Roosevelt administration for assistance in getting Americans to donate private firearms in a "Rifles for Britain" program designed to furnish weapons for the Home Guard. A number of American publications, including the *New York Times* and the NRA's *American Rifleman*, ran advertisements soliciting donations of firearms for the program.[27]

The Home Guard was not designed to be a main battle force, certainly not a force that would take part in any expeditionary activities. The members of the force would continue in their civilian occupations and help guard installations and possible landing sites or help capture downed Luftwaffe pilots. They were able to free regular forces for more pressing duties in other theaters. Initially in 1940, when invasion seemed quite likely, the Home Guard was also seen as the nucleus of a people's resistance force for an occupied United Kingdom.[28]

Britain's experience with a lightly trained civilian militia that would augment the armed forces would find its counterparts in the United States and Canada after the Japanese attack on Pearl Harbor. With the mobilization of the National Guard and with many police officers either enlisted or drafted into the armed forces, several states formed state guard units to guard critical installations and to be available for civil disturbances. One state, Maryland, had not only a state guard that could be deployed throughout the state but also a reserve militia whose theater of operations was confined to the county where a particular unit was raised. As was the case in previous conflicts, men recruited for these forces were often younger than eighteen or older than forty-five and thus were beyond the militia age limits as defined by federal and state statutes. According to one student of the subject, these state guard units existed in every state except Arizona, Nevada, Montana, and Oklahoma. State governments mobilized their troops for local emergencies—some twenty-four occasions in 1943 alone. At times these state troops were issued weapons from the War Department, frequently World War I era Enfield rifles. But when the demand for weapons for federal forces made federal weapons unavailable, state forces resorted to an assortment of weapons available on the civilian market or weapons that were in private hands. Canada formed a similar militia force in British Columbia to guard against potential Japanese invasion and sabotage. The force, known as the Pacific Coast Militia Rangers, was made up largely of loggers, fishermen, and members of local Indian tribes. Their armament was a mixture of the weapons the Canadian Army could spare and various available hunting and sporting rifles.[29]

The American State Defense Forces and the Canadian Pacific Coast Militia Rangers did not encounter enemy forces. These twentieth-century militia organizations nonetheless performed important functions as force multipliers freeing regular soldiers from home security duties and making them available in critical combat zones. It should also be added that during the war, North America was home to nearly half a million Axis prisoners of war: 400,000 in the United States and 36,000 in Canada. The presence of a large number of armed civilians, whether formally organized into militia or home guard units or potentially available to assist in informal posses or search parties, should probably be seen as having augmented security in both nations.[30]

Not all militia forces escaped contact with the enemy. Any discussion of the American militia in World War II should include mention of the Civil Air Patrol and the Coast Guard Temporary Reserve. Both groups enlisted airplane and boat owners to assist in the antisubmarine effort. In 1942 German U-boats were sinking American and allied merchant ships throughout the Atlantic and Gulf Coasts. The US Navy, which in wartime also included the Coast Guard, was severely undermanned, overstretched, and not able to meet the demands of worldwide war and to also meet the considerable U-boat menace in American waters.[31]

Both the Army Air Corps and the Coast Guard enlisted civilian auxiliaries to help meet the threat. The Air Corp's Civil Air Patrol remained a force of civilians, although it was given a military mission. Owners of private planes were to act as additional eyes and ears of the Air Corps, spotting enemy submarines and occasionally dropping bombs on them when appropriate opportunities occurred. The Coast Guard went further. During the war, the Coast Guard enlisted some fifty thousand individuals as temporary reservists. Like members of other militias or militia-like organizations, they remained employed at their civilian jobs and in their spare time assisted with the war effort. While actually on duty they were temporary members of the Coast Guard, with military rank, authority, and, for Geneva Convention purposes, legal status as combatants. Those who owned boats were sent on antisubmarine missions. These yachtsmen-turned-Coast-Guard-sailors were issued machine guns, depth charges, and other weapons and given the mission to hunt, or at least harass, German U-boats. If the possibility of a duel between a Kriegsmarine U-boat manned by experienced submariners and a lightly armed yacht manned by weekend sailors seems like a mismatch, it was. But 1942 and 1943 were particularly desperate years for shipping off the East and Gulf Coasts of the United States, and in that time of desperation, the Coast Guard looked to a seagoing militia to augment its efforts. A few of the Coast Guard's Temporary Reserve boats actually made contact with the enemy. Others were enlisted in the port security effort, guarding piers, warehouses, and other installations. Still others patrolled miles of deserted beaches on horseback. The official Coast Guard history of this effort indicates that the Temporary Reserve freed over eight thousand regular Coast Guardsmen for more pressing military duties—duties that included escorting convoys in the North Atlantic and manning landing craft in the South Pacific.[32]

It should be noted that the idea of the population as a whole as an inchoate militia and the use of civilians in a militia capacity in wartime was not confined to the United States, with its large supply of civilian firearms and its Constitution's rather peculiar provision discussing "well-regulated militias" and "the right to keep and bear arms." Nor was it confined to democratic nations like Canada, which also had a large number of armed civilians, or Britain, where some commentators, including socialist essayist and Spanish Civil War veteran George Orwell, argued that the arming of the civilian population in wartime was evidence of democracy and a trust between the government and the governed.[33] World War II showed that nations with totalitarian or strongly authoritarian governments could also employ civilian militias when faced with invasion or war on the home front. The German invasion of the Soviet Union caused Joseph Stalin's government to arm civilians and turn them into partisan bands to harass the invading Wehrmacht.[34] With the final death throes of Nazi Germany as the Third Reich was being overrun by the Red Army from the east and American, British, Canadian, and French armies from the west, the Nazi government threw a desperate last-minute militia, the Volksturm, at the soon-to-be victorious allies.[35] In the summer of 1945, as Allied plans for the invasion of Japan were being finalized, the Japanese armed forces were engaged in the large-scale training of the Japanese civilian population to act as a resistance force to what would have been a largely American and British invasion. As firearms were rare in Japan, Japanese civilians, including women and children, were being trained to use sharpened bamboo sticks to meet the well-armed Allied invaders. As was the case with other militia forces on both sides of the world conflict, the Japanese civilian resistance would have supplemented, not replaced, the regular armed forces.[36]

But for the United States, it was the experience of the men in the regular armed forces that would have the deepest impact on American thinking. The nation's wartime experiences would bring a new appreciation for guns and the good that ordinary men with guns might do. The nation—indeed, the world—had been saved by that American everyman, "GI Joe." More detailed and objective historical analysis might reveal that GI Joe got quite a bit of help. The nation's industrial efforts and a providential geography that placed vast oceans between the US mainland and the nation's enemies helped. The nation's allies, including the Russians (who would become postwar adversaries), bore much of the weight of the fight against the Wehrmacht, particularly in the early stages of the conflict. Much of the Japanese army was bogged down in China. All of these circumstances contributed heavily to GI Joe's victory. But the generation that lived through the titanic struggle—the men who went to strange lands not knowing if they would come back, and the families that desperately awaited their return—might be forgiven for celebrating American heroism, heroism that indeed did help liberate a good portion of the world.[37]

And celebrate they did. If perhaps those combat veterans who had suffered the deepest wounds of war came back reluctant to talk about their experiences and wary of any celebrations, the nation as a whole seemed to view the experience as a vindication of good over evil and one that should be remembered. Any discussion of guns in American culture would be incomplete without a look at Hollywood in the postwar era. The American victory in World War II was relived in the innumerable war movies of the late 1940s, 1950s, and early 1960s. To these should be added an equally impressive outpouring of westerns, many of which told a similar story: brave armed everymen who stared down and ultimately vanquished evil. Hollywood's celebration of the common man and his rescue of the nation (and the world) would begin immediately. Film director Frank Capra, a wartime lieutenant colonel in the Signal Corps, set the tone with his first postwar movie, *It's a Wonderful Life*, detailing the wartime heroism of the ordinary men of the fictional town of Bedford Falls:

Bert the cop was wounded in North Africa, Got the Silver Star . . .

Ernie, the taxi driver, parachuted into France . . .

Marty helped capture the Remagen Bridge . . . .

Harry . . . Harry Bailey topped them all. A Navy flier, he shot down fifteen planes
. . . two of them as they were about to crash into a transport full of soldiers.[38]

Capra was not alone. Many of the stars, writers, cameramen, and directors of these cinematic epics had themselves taken part in the real and deadly drama that was World War II. Robert Pirosh, a veteran of the Battle of the Bulge, scripted the story of the 101st Airborne's epic defense of Bastogne in *Battleground*. He also directed the story of Japanese American GIs in *Go for Broke*, a film that featured many Nisei veterans. Audie Murphy, the teenage recruit, won the nation's highest award for heroism, the Medal of Honor. He became an actor after the war, starring in a number of unexceptional if entertaining westerns. He also gave two unforgettable performances, one as the troubled protagonist torn between fear and duty in John Houston's screen adaptation of Stephen Crane's Civil War novela *The Red Badge of Courage* and the other a movie where he played himself and depicted his wartime heroism, *To Hell and Back*. There were other examples, literally too numerous to mention. Former B-24 pilot James Stewart, who led daylight bombing raids over the Third Reich, refused to reference his war record in films when he returned to Hollywood. He would nonetheless play his fair share and more of courageous men facing down desperadoes and marauding Indians on the nineteenth-century frontier, or at least postwar Hollywood's depiction of the nineteenth-century frontier. On the small screen James Arness, a veteran of the Anzio landing, depicted frontier marshal Matt Dillon, beating outlaws to the draw and rescuing "Miss Kitty" for half an hour every Saturday night on *Gunsmoke* in the 1950s.[39]

The idea that the ordinary citizen, and not just those who were specially trained, had a responsibility to play a role in the defense of his community was a common theme in the westerns of the era. The men of the town were supposed to back their sheriff or marshal and not run away or cower in fear when faced with threats from outlaws. Director Fred Zinneman's 1952 western film *High Noon* depicted this traditional American ethos that the defense of the community required the willingness of all to act courageously and to lend a hand. The film's message also included the notion that a town in which the men were unwilling to aid in the common defense was, at the end of the day, a town not worth defending.[40]

In this atmosphere, there wasn't much in the way of a full-scale effort to promote national gun control. Ironically, the 1950s was a time when at least one public opinion poll taken on the subject indicated that a majority of the public might be amenable to a ban on handguns.[41] Former dean of Harvard Law School Roscoe Pound in a treatise written in 1957 acknowledged that the

Second Amendment was intended to safeguard the individual's right to keep and bear arms. But he also suggested that the courts should reinterpret the constitutional provision so that it would no longer be viewed as protecting the rights of individuals.[42]

## HUGO BLACK: THE DISSENTER AS PROPHET

From the point of view of what the Constitution might have to say concerning the citizen's right to keep and bear arms, the most important development in postwar America was not to be found in public opinion polls, nor in academic speculation concerning interpretations or reinterpretations of the Second Amendment. The most important development came from the US Supreme Court in a case having nothing to do with firearms restrictions or pronouncements on the meaning of the Second Amendment. The case that would have a major, almost fatal impact on the Second Amendment involved an appeal by a California Death Row inmate, Admiral Dewey Adamson. Adamson ("Admiral" was his given name, not a rank) had been convicted and sentenced to death for first-degree murder. He appealed his conviction to the US Supreme Court on the grounds that California law permitted prosecutors to comment and allowed juries to draw adverse inferences when a defendant refused to take the stand on his own behalf. Adamson had not testified at his trial because his taking the stand would have allowed the prosecution to bring up Adamson's other crimes on cross-examination. Adamson's argument on appeal could be boiled down to a simple proposition: the Fifth Amendment declared that a defendant could not be compelled to be a witness against himself. That rule, as Associate Justice Stanley Reed was willing to stipulate for purposes of the case in the majority opinion, prohibited federal prosecutors from making adverse comments and also prohibited juries from making adverse inferences from a defendant's refusal to testify. The question before the Court in *Adamson* was, did the Fourteenth Amendment apply that basic Fifth Amendment rule to the state of California?[43]

In posing that question, Adamson touched a constitutional nerve that had troubled the Court and the nation since the adoption of the Fourteenth Amendment, and indeed before. Doubtless the most straightforward way for the Court to have addressed the question of whether the federal Bill of Rights applied to the states would have been to have looked at the debates of the Thirty-Ninth Congress, the body that passed the Fourteenth Amendment and sent it to the states for ratification. As we have noted earlier, two of the amendment's sponsors, Ohio Representative Jonathan Bingham and New York Senator Jacob Howard, who introduced the amendment in their respective houses of Congress, said in fairly clear and simple terms that they meant through the new amendment's "privileges or immunities" clause to apply the Bill of Rights to the states.[44]

Whatever the merits of a straightforward adoption of Bingham and Howard's approach to incorporation, the Court had gotten down to the business of applying the Bill of Rights to the states by a very different and quite circuitous route. It is essentially accurate to say that the Court killed off the Fourteenth Amendment's privileges or immunities clause as a vehicle for making the states respect the Bill of Rights in the 1872 *Slaughter-House Cases*. These cases, which involved the narrow question of whether the new privileges or immunities clause prohibited state-granted monopoly licenses, were used by Justice Samuel Miller to essentially empty the recently enacted clause of any significant meaning. The Fourteenth Amendment's privileges or immunities clause, Miller informed the nation, protected a citizen's privileges or immunities, but in ways that would be found distressingly trivial to those who looked to the recently amended Constitution as a bulwark against state infringements of individual rights. Miller's majority opinion suggested that the new clause might protect a citizen's right to appear before the federal government or to have access to the seaports controlled by the federal government or the right to petition the federal government for redress of grievances. But Miller rejected the idea that the new amendment limited the traditional power of state government. Prior to the enactment of the Fourteenth Amendment, the Court's view had been that the federal Constitution had little to say concerning violations of an individual's rights by the state in which he lived. The prevailing view, and one that had been stated by the Court in the 1833 case *Barron v. Baltimore*, was that if a citizen believed his home state had violated the right to freedom of speech or trial by jury, freedom of religion, the right to have arms, or other rights long associated with Anglo-American constitutionalism, the vindication of such claims was properly in the hands of state constitutions and state courts, and the federal courts and the federal Bill of Rights could not provide relief, however severe the violations. In his opinion Miller crafted an interpretation of the Fourteenth Amendment, and particularly the privileges or immunities clause, that would preserve, to the extent possible, the antebellum federal order. Miller's majority opinion cautioned against reading the Four-teenth Amendment in such a way that would institute this Court a perpetual censor upon all the legislation of the States, on the civil rights of their own citizens, with authority to nullify such as it did not approve as consistent with those rights, as they existed at the time of the adoption of this amendment.[45]

In *Slaughter-House*, Miller would put forward a view of the Fourteenth Amendment that recognized that the new constitutional provision was meant to have far-reaching consequences for the American racial order, even while arguing that it had only modest impact on traditional notions of federalism.[46] He urged a broad reading of the Fourteenth Amendment in conjunction with the Thirteenth and Fifteenth:

> We repeat, then, in the light of this recapitulation of events, almost too
> recent to be called history, but which are familiar to us all; and on the most
> casual examination of the language of these amendments, no one can fail
> to be impressed with the one pervading purpose found in them all, lying at
> the foundation of each, and without which none of them would have even
> been suggested; we mean the freedom of the slave race, the security and firm
> establishment of that freedom, and the protection of the newly made freeman
> and citizen from the oppression of those who formerly exercised unlimited
> dominion over him. It is true that only the fifteenth amendment, in terms,
> mentions the negro by speaking of his color and his slavery. But it is just as true
> that each of the other articles was addressed to the grievances of that race, and
> designed to remedy them as the fifteenth.[47]

*Slaughter-House* would end the use of the privileges or immunities clause as a vehicle for using the Fourteenth Amendment to make claims against state action. Justice Clarence Thomas would base his concurring opinion in *Mc-Donald* on the clause, and he has led something of an effort to revive the clause (an issue we will discuss later in this volume); but aside from Justice Thom-as's efforts and academic commentary and judicial speculation on the topic, the clause effectively died in 1872, four years after it was adopted. However, the problem of whether the Constitution restrained state action against the individual would nonetheless remain, and it would continue to plague the Courts. In 1872 the *Slaughter-House* Court had declared that the privileges or immunities clause had little in the way of important meaning. Later in that decade the Court in *United States v. Cruikshank*, a case examining, among other issues, whether the First and Second Amendments provided protection against private infringements of rights, the Court provided dicta again reiterating that the Bill of Rights only limited the federal government.[48] In 1886 in *Presser v. Illinois*, the Court reaffirmed that the antebellum case of *Barron v. Baltimore* remained the law; provisions of the Bill of Rights, in this case the Second Amendment, only acted as limitations on the national government, not the states.[49]

While the Supreme Court was rejecting the notions that the privileges or immunities clause provided real restrictions on the actions of state legislatures or state officials, it also rejected the idea that specific provisions of the Bill of Rights might be applied to the states in the same way that they could be applied to the federal government. The Court by the end of the nineteenth century was increasingly starting to look at the Fourteenth Amendment's due process clause and question if state statutes and practices were consistent with its notions of due process. In doing this, the Court was engaging in an activity that many lay observers, and many lawyers and legal scholars as well, often thought of as counterintuitive. To many people, the term "due process" implies proper procedure, adequate notice, fair trials, right to counsel, and the like, rather than substantive rights. Indeed, a lay observer—and probably a fair number of legally trained observers as well—might divide the first eight amendments to the US Constitution, the federal Bill of Rights, into those provisions that apparently protect procedural rights—trial by jury in criminal and civil cases, right to counsel, protection against self-incrimination, and so forth, and those provisions that apparently protect substantive rights, freedom of speech, free exercise of religion, freedom from cruel or unusual punishment, the right to keep and bear arms, and so on. That would likely be a quick common-sense division of the various provisions of the Bill of Rights. But courts had long taken a somewhat different view of the matter. Even in antebellum America, some state courts were reading substantive property rights into the due process clauses of state constitutions. In 1857 Chief Justice Roger Taney held that the Missouri Compromise provisions that prohibited owners from bringing their slaves into free federal territory unconstitutionally deprived citizens of liberty and property. The idea of a substantive component to the term "due process" was a part of American jurisprudence before the enactment of the Fourteenth Amendment.[50]

This tendency of the courts to give a substantive reading to constitutional due process clauses would take on increased importance toward the end of the nineteenth century. Even in the *Slaughter-House Cases*, Justice Joseph Bradley in dissent had argued that not only the new amendment's privileges or immunities clause but also the Reconstruction amendment's due process clause should be seen as protecting freedom of contract. If that argument failed in *Slaughter-House*, it would take root at the end of the nineteenth century as the Supreme Court embraced classical liberal economic principles and read them as being constitutional requirements binding on the states. The Court's movement toward the constitutionalization of the classical liberal notion of freedom of contract and with what today would be called the incorporation of the Bill of Rights would begin with the 1896 case of *Allgeyer v. Louisiana*, a case involving a defendant who was penalized for purchasing insurance from an out-of-state company. *Allgeyer* in many ways set the stage for the 1905 case of *Lochner v. New York*, which held that the Fourteenth Amendment's due process clause limited the state's ability to interfere with freedom of contract, even if that interference arguably protected otherwise vulnerable workers.[51]

If disputes over economic regulations moved the Court to reconsider its initial views that the Fourteenth Amendment would not alter the traditional balance between federal and state power or the idea that the citizen should look to state constitutions and state courts to vindicate rights, developments in the world of crime and punishment would also force the Court to consider anew whether the Fourteenth Amendment and particularly the amendment's due process clause placed real limits on the ability of state governments to punish—to in effect deprive individuals of life, liberty, or property—without observing the procedural guarantees found in the Fifth Amendment's guarantee against self-incrimination or the Sixth Amendment's guarantee of a right to counsel. The Supreme Court would take up the first issue in the 1908 case *Twining and Cornell v. State of New Jersey*.[52] Justice William Henry Moody began his discussion in the majority opinion by noting that the defendants were not directly protected by the Fifth Amendment. Moody also rejected the idea that the Fourteenth Amendment's privileges or immunities clause provided a shield against self-incrimination, arguing that *Slaughter-House* had essentially cut off that line of inquiry. But Moody conceded that the due process clause of the Fourteenth Amendment might nonetheless be a vehicle for the protection of fundamental rights against the actions of state governments:

> They appeal to another clause of the 14th Amendment and insist that the self-incrimination which they allege the instruction to the jury compelled was a

denial of due process of law. This contention requires separate consideration, for it is possible that some of the personal rights safeguarded by the first eight Amendments against national action may also be safeguarded against state action, because a denial of them would be a denial of due process of law. . . . If this is so, it is not because these rights are enumerated in the first eight Amendments, but because they are of such a nature that they are included in the concept of due process of law. . . . This court has always declined to give a comprehensive definition of it [due process of law], *and has preferred that its full meaning should be gradually ascertained by the process of inclusion and exclusion in the course of discussion of cases as they arise.*[53]

Moody declined to find that the privilege against self-incrimination limited the state of New Jersey in *Twining*. But he did something more. He put forth a judicial methodology to be used by the Court in determining whether a state practice violated a fundamental right. If Bingham and Howard thought that the mere existence of a right in the Bill of Rights should settle the matter, that the Fourteenth Amendment should make the asserted right binding on the states, Moody's opinion outlined a very different methodology. Assertions of rights would have to be examined on a case-by-case basis. Never mind the presence of a prohibition against self-incrimination in the Bill of Rights. It was up to judges and not the text of the Constitution to determine if a right was so fundamental, so deeply ingrained in what the Court believed was essential to Anglo-American notions of justice, that it should limit the actions of state legislatures and state officials.[54]

*Twining* would set the framework for the Court in what has come to be called incorporation cases. Cases would arise piecemeal. The Court first looked at the extent to which the First Amendment's guarantees of freedom of speech and freedom of the press protected the citizen from the state in the 1925 case of *Gitlow v. New York*. Although the Court found that the defendant's conviction for publishing pamphlets urging the overthrow of the government was a reasonable exercise of the police power, the Court nonetheless began the case with the assumption that the First Amendment served as a limitation on state action.[55] Later, in 1931, in *Near v. Minnesota ex. Rel. Olson*, the Court would overturn a criminal conviction based on the ground that the law under which the defendant had been convicted violated the First Amendment. Chief Justice Charles Evans Hughes began the majority opinion by stating: "It is no longer open to doubt that the liberty of the press and of speech is within the liberty safeguarded by the due process clause of the Fourteenth Amendment from invasion by state action.[56]

Criminal cases would play a major role in prodding the Court to reexamine questions of due process and the limitations on state power. This would become especially true in cases in Southern states where Black defendants had been sentenced to death, convicted of crimes against White victims or complainants. In 1932 the Supreme Court reversed the conviction of a Black man convicted and sentenced to death for participating in the rape of two White women. The case *Powell v. Alabama* was one of the "Scottsboro Boys" cases. The defendants, nine Black youths, had been railroaded with essentially no legal representation. In *Powell*, the Court for the first time held that it was a violation of the Fourteenth Amendment's due process requirements to deny a defendant legal representation in a capital case.[57] Four years later, in the case of *Brown v. Mississippi*, the Court would throw out the conviction of a Black man convicted of murder solely on the basis of a confession obtained under torture.[58] These cases and others of the era would cause the Supreme Court to take a hard look at criminal justice in the Southern states. With that hard look came a new willingness to look at the due process clause of the Fourteenth Amendment and the actual behavior of state actors in criminal cases. *Powell* and *Brown* began the process of prescribing at least minimum federal standards for counsel in capital cases, in effect applying, or partially applying, the Sixth Amendment right to counsel to the states.

If the specter of racially tainted convictions would cause the Supreme Court to reconsider and broaden what was meant by due process and what constituted a fair trial under the American system of justice, the Court would nonetheless move slowly in bringing the Bill of Rights within the orbit of the Fourteenth Amendment. In 1937 the Court displayed its institutional conservatism when approaching the issue of the applicability of the Bill of Rights to the states. Frank Palko brought an appeal of his Connecticut death sentence before the Supreme Court in 1937. Palko had initially been convicted of second-degree murder by a Connecticut trial court. The prosecution successfully appealed Palko's conviction for second-degree murder on the grounds that a state statute allowed the prosecution to appeal in the event of legal error. The prosecution contended that the trial court had erred by throwing out Palko's confession. Palko was retried, convicted of first-degree murder, and sentenced to death.[59]

The Court, in a majority opinion by Justice Benjamin Cardozo, rejected

Palko's double jeopardy claim. The Cardozo opinion denied that the Fifth Amendment provision was made binding on the states through the Fourteenth Amendment. Cardozo argued that not only was double jeopardy not so fundamental a principle as to require incorporation, but the right to trial by a grand jury, and even the right to a petit jury in a criminal case, was not required in state proceedings. Justice Cardozo in *Palko* put forward what for an American jurist appears to have been an unusual standard for determining what constitutes "ordered liberty," that is, that degree of liberty that is so essential that all American jurisdictions must respect it. Cardozo noted that a number of foreign nations did not have a requirement for jury trials and the other procedural guarantees found in the Bill of Rights. While Cardozo acknowledged that the Court had moved toward an incorporation of the Sixth Amendment right to counsel in *Powell* and some of the other cases dealing with Negro defendants, he distinguished those cases on the grounds that the ignorance of the defendants made the need for legal representation more acute, while rejecting the notion that a fair trial required a full-scale adoption of the Bill of Rights for the states.[60]

So, Admiral Dewey Adamson's case came to the Supreme Court in 1946 against the background of a Court that had had a somewhat mixed and not particularly consistent jurisprudence on how to apply the provisions of the Bill of Rights to the states. *Adamson* would provide two heavyweight protagonists the opportunity to do battle over the issue of incorporation and to lay out the case for piecemeal incorporation, to in effect reconsider *Slaughter-House* and make the case for total incorporation.

Justice Reed gave the majority opinion for the Court. He indicated that neither the Court's due process precedents nor its privileges or immunities jurisprudence applied the Fifth Amendment's prohibition against forced self-incrimination to the states. He argued, echoing the concerns of Justice Miller in *Slaughter-House*, that this interpretation, this limited view of the reach of the Fourteenth Amendment, was important to federalism; it helped preserve the necessary balance between the states and the federal government. Reed also argued that due process was not designed to shield an accused from a proper conviction, that is, the conviction of an actually guilty defendant. It is important to note here that Reed in his opinion was focusing less on the nature of the privilege against self-incrimination and more on what he believed the due process guarantee was designed to do.[61]

But *Adamson* is remembered less for Reed's rendering of the Court's opinion and more for the concurring opinion of Justice Felix Frankfurter and the dissenting opinion of Justice Hugo Black. The two justices could not have been more dissimilar in background. Frankfurter, an Austrian-born Jewish immigrant, was a product of the bar's academic elite. A former Harvard Law School professor, Frankfurter had been appointed to the bench by Franklin Delano Roosevelt. On the Supreme Court he had become a strong advocate of judicial restraint and deference to state authorities. Hugo Black, also appointed to the high court by Franklin Roosevelt, was an Alabama politician who had, early in his career, joined the Ku Klux Klan to further his political ambitions. It was his familiarity with the dark side of state and local politics, according to some observers, that caused Black to be a keen advocate of civil liberties and supervision of misconduct by state officials.[62]

Frankfurter's concurrence came first. His opinion argued that the Court should keep the holding in *Twining* intact. Frankfurter's argument was that the Fifth Amendment's self-incrimination clause was, in and of itself, of dubious soundness. It would be quite proper for juries to draw a negative inference from a defendant's failure to testify. The right against self-incrimination was a dubious one that interfered with the proper administration of justice. If the federal government was saddled with this unfortunate burden, there was no need to extend it to the states through the Fourteenth Amendment's due process clause, or a somehow resurrected privileges or immunities clause—a clause that he believed was quite mischievous.[63]

Black started his dissent from an entirely different premise. *Twining* gave the Court boundless power to expand and contract constitutional rights under a vaguely defined natural law theory that made jurists and not the Constitution the arbiter of the rights of citizens. For Black, this methodology essentially gave short shrift to the Bill of Rights, which should be at the heart of any inquiry concerning the rights of the individual. Black went on to urge that the Bill of Rights had been put in the nation's charter because it consisted of a set of liberties that the American people had agreed upon in the eighteenth century.[64]

Justice Black then went on to outline the case that the Fourteenth Amendment applied the whole of the Bill of Rights to the states. For this Black looked to the history of the Thirty-Ninth Congress. He noted that the supporters of the Fourteenth Amendment in Congress were well aware of *Barron v. Baltimore* and had indicated that they meant for the new amendment to correct that decision. He accused supporters of selective incorporation, of employing a natural law methodology that left the determination of the citizen's rights to the Courts and not the Constitution. He argued that the Court's precedent in *Slaughter-House* had already rejected a natural law approach to determining individual rights. Black argued forcefully against the view that the Bill of Rights was an eighteenth-century anachronism that needed to be discarded or at least significantly modified by the modern judiciary. Finally, Black appended the legislative history of the Fourteenth Amendment to his opinion to buttress the argument that a total incorporation or application of the Bill of Rights to the states had been intended.[65]

Frankfurter, in response, argued that the very term "due process" should cause the Court to reject Black's incorporation formula. Due process, he noted, had to mean the same thing in the Fourteenth Amendment as it did in the Fifth. If that were the case, the clause in the Fourteenth Amendment should not be viewed as a vehicle for requiring the states to respect the Bill of Rights. Frankfurter's concurrence also countered Black's historical arguments. He argued that the statements of the proponents of the Fourteenth Amendment in favor of total incorporation had to be discounted because certain provisions of the Bill of Rights had not been adopted in the constitutions of a number of the ratifying states. He noted, for example, that a number of the states that ratified the Fourteenth Amendment could not have intended to apply the Bill of Rights to the states because their state constitutions and criminal law procedures did not require grand juries before criminal trials. Frankfurter's point, frequently repeated by his scholarly supporters, that a state was unlikely to ratify a constitutional amendment that granted a right the state itself did not grant is readily contradicted by the history of the Fifteenth Amendment. The Fifteenth Amendment, which prohibits race or color restrictions for voters, was ratified in 1870. Of the thirty states that ratified the amendment, only fourteen had permitted Black men to vote before the passage of the amendment. One of the difficulties inherent in trying to interpret the meaning of the Fourteenth Amendment by looking at the practices of the ratifying states is that eleven of the ratifying states, the states of the former Confederacy, were essentially compelled to ratify the new amendments as a condition of reentry into the Union. The process of ratifying a constitutional amendment under ordinary conditions might arguably involve some give and take, debate in the state legislature or ratifying convention. Those debates might ordinarily be seen as clarifying or perhaps even modifying the meaning of the proposed amendment. Because of the peculiar situation of the former Confederate states, that process would take a very different turn with

respect to the Fourteenth Amendment, giving the debates in Congress arguably greater weight than might be the case in other contexts.[66]

Frankfurter and the others who rejected total incorporation would win
the day in *Adamson*. The California inmate's appeal was denied by a 5–4 decision. The duel between Frankfurter and Black would be taken up by others
in postwar America. Generally, jurists, commentators, practicing lawyers, and
scholars considered to be liberal have argued for a robust view of incorporation while conservatives have tended to argue against the concept or to argue
for a fairly restricted view of the practice. As we shall see, the ideological divisions on the question of incorporation would shift somewhat when the Court
came to consider the question of incorporating the Second Amendment with
*McDonald vs. City of Chicago*.[67]

A decision in *Adamson* rejecting selective incorporation and agreeing instead that the Fourteenth Amendment made all provisions of the Bill of Rights
applicable to the states would probably have secured the individual rights
view of the amendment in the late 1940s. Support for the view that the Second
Amendment only protected a right of states to maintain a militia or that it protected a right that the individual could only exercise within the context of the
organized militia, one of the alternative arguments put forward by Attorney
General Cummings in *Miller*, appears to have receded in the immediate aftermath of World War II. It's probably not reading too much into the opinions
in *Adamson* to say that both Black and Frankfurter, both of whom signed on to
the unanimous decision in *Miller*, accepted the basic premise that the Second
Amendment was meant to protect a right of individuals. The case for Black's
acceptance of that view seems quite clear. Black called for an interpretation of
the Fourteenth Amendment that would apply the first eight amendments to
the states with full force. That presumably would have included the Second
Amendment. What would it mean to say that the state could not infringe on
the right guaranteed by the Second Amendment? If Black saw the right as a
right of the individual, the answer seems clear enough; at some point state
restrictions on an individual's right to have arms would be deemed unconstitutional. Whether Black would have said requirements for permits to carry
pistols, or restrictions on certain kinds of weapons or other control measures,
would or would not be considered unconstitutional cannot be known. But a
view that the right belongs to the individuals in their private capacities would,
presumably, have caused him to say that at some point, some restriction on
firearms ownership would have to be disallowed.

It would not be easy to figure out what Justice Black might have meant by making the Second Amendment applicable to the states if he saw the right as either a right of the states or a right that could only be exercised within the context of a state-run institution like the organized militia. If he saw the Second Amendment as a right of the states, the concept of incorporation of the Second Amendment becomes absurd. If he saw it as a right that could only be exercised within the context of the organized militia, then again it becomes hard to explain how it could be incorporated, how the citizen could maintain an action against the state for infringement of the right.

Frankfurter's opinion also seems to give evidence, though perhaps less directly, that he too saw the Second Amendment in individualistic terms, or at the very least that he didn't see some version of the collective rights argument as strong enough to merit mention in his concurrence. If Frankfurter wanted to make the case that the Fourteenth Amendment was not meant to apply all of the first eight amendments to the states, the argument would have been buttressed by the claim that the Second Amendment was not a right of the citizen, or only the right of the citizen in some highly restricted sense. If it was not a right of the citizen, then Black's case for total incorporation would fall of its own weight. Frankfurter made no such claim in his concurrence, nor did he do so later in a 1965 law review article restating his views on incorporation. It should be noted that Frankfurter's disciple Stanford Law professor Charles Fairman also failed to make any such argument in his scholarly writings defending Frankfurter's concurrence.[68]

That the members of the Supreme Court generally saw the Second Amendment in individualistic terms might also be seen in an opinion authored by Justice Robert Jackson in the 1950 case of *Johnson v. Eisentrager*. *Eisentrager* dealt with the issue of World War II nonresident aliens who were being imprisoned for war crimes by the US Army in Germany. The prisoners brought suit, contending that their imprisonment violated the Fifth Amendment and their rights to habeas corpus. Jackson's opinion dismissed their claims:

> But such a construction would mean that during military occupation irreconcilable enemy elements, guerilla fighters and "werewolves" could require the American Judiciary to assure the freedom of speech, press and assembly as in the First Amendment, the right to bear arms as in the Second, the Security against unreasonable search and seizure as in the Fourth Amendment, as well as the right to jury trial as in the Fifth and Sixth Amendments.[69]

Jackson's opinion indicated the acceptance of the Second Amendment as a right that might be claimed by a citizen, just as a citizen might have a claim on a right to free speech, assembly, freedom from unreasonable search or seizure, or a right to trial by jury. Nothing in the opinion indicates that the citizen's claim would have to be buttressed by some claim the citizen was performing militia service or somehow preparing to do so. Too much might be made of this. Jackson's remarks on the Second Amendment might be seen as dicta— and dicta, it should be added, in a case having nothing to do with the issue of weapons regulation. We can't say from this what Jackson might have said if confronted with a firearms regulation and a claim that that regulation was unconstitutional. Jackson in writing this opinion did not reference any of the other cases where the Supreme Court or the lower federal courts had examined Second Amendment claims. Nor did the *Eisentrager* opinion look at the state courts and how they handled analogous provisions in state constitutions. Still, in this casual reference Jackson seems to have indicated a view that the Second Amendment was not somehow set apart from the other provisions of the Bill of Rights, a provision that could only be used in a highly qualified and different manner. It was just simply a part of the Bill of Rights, one that was guaranteed the citizen but could be withheld from the enemy alien.[70]

Because Supreme Court justices in the early postwar era appear to have had little difficulty in accepting an individualistic reading of the Second Amendment, little different from other provisions of the Bill of Rights, an acceptance of total incorporation in *Adamson* would have probably led to the federal courts examining the gun-control regulations that existed in the different states. *Adamson* was decided on the eve of the great constitutional revolution that would be conducted by the Supreme Court under the leadership of Chief Justice Earl Warren. In many ways the Warren Court would bring new life to the Fourteenth Amendment. It began this revolution by strengthening the Reconstruction amendment's equal protection clause, with its 1954 school desegregation decision in *Brown v. Board of Education*.[71] Later on, the Warren Court would expand the constitutional notion of equal protection in part by requiring equal representation in state legislatures.[72] The Court under Earl Warren would take the doctrine of selective incorporation of the Bill of Rights that had been affirmed in *Adamson* and subject state legislation and state practices to an unprecedented degree of scrutiny, comparing state practices with the demands, or what the Court saw as the demands of different provisions of the Bill of Rights, particularly those provisions that governed the trials of defendants in criminal cases. The Warren Court would break new ground by applying the Fourth Amendment's restrictions on unreasonable search and seizure,[73] the Fifth Amendment's protections against self-incrimination,[74] and the Sixth Amendment's right to counsel[75] to state police and prosecutors in ways that had never been done before. In doing so it can be said that the Warren Court brought the Bill of Rights to life for many ordinary Americans. It is still true, the twentieth-century expansion of federal power notwithstanding, that it is state and local governments that have the most impact on the day-to-day lives of ordinary citizens. Certainly, in the field of criminal justice most criminal suspects are accused of violating state penal laws, are arrested by local police, are prosecuted by local prosecutors, and are tried in county courthouses. By declaring that local officials had to provide counsel to defendants in serious criminal cases, or that there were limits that would be enforced by the exclusionary rule, on how local police might conduct interrogations or search houses, the Warren Court was bringing the Bill of Rights to life, making what had once been merely a set of recitations from the nations' high school civics classes into a group of judicially enforced guarantees that protected the rights of individuals.

But this process didn't happen with the Second Amendment during the constitutional revolution that was the Warren Court. There were state and local regulations on guns, with New York's Sullivan Law probably the most well-known at the time. There were occasional challenges to state legislation in the state courts. These challenges were usually rebuffed with a reiteration of the Supreme Court's holding in *Presser* that the Second Amendment only applied to the federal government. It did not restrict the states.[76]

If the Second Amendment missed the incorporation revolution that was beginning to pick up steam with the early Warren Court, the late 1940s and 1950s seemed to be a time when most Americans had access to a broad array of firearms with little in the way of controversy. Few voices called for robust national gun control.[77] A number of states had adopted the American Law Institute's suggestion that a license should be required for individuals who wanted to carry pistols. In a number of jurisdictions these licenses were given not on the basis of some objective need but instead were doled out to political favorites, or, as was notorious with New York's Sullivan Law, supplied to individuals who were wealthy and prominent.[78] In some Southern states, pistol licenses provided one of the many occasions for racial discrimination in law enforcement. White people were rarely arrested or charged with carrying pistols without a license; those charges were usually reserved for Negroes. The ability to deny Black people pistol permits could be and often was used to make those who fought the Jim Crow system in the South vulnerable to attackers. A young pastor who feared racist violence because his home had been bombed after his participation in the Montgomery Bus Boycott found this out. He applied to the county sheriff for a permit to carry a pistol. The Reverend Martin Luther King Jr.'s application was rejected.[79]

Still, despite the requirements for licenses to carry pistols in many states, firearms were plentiful and easy to get. The surplus weapons of the armies that had taken part in the mass slaughter of 1939–1945 were brought into the post-war American surplus markets. For the most part these were the bolt-action Enfields, Mausers, and Ariskas of foreign armies, although quite a few of the semiautomatic carbines and Garands, as well as the bolt-action Springfields of the American armed forces, were also sold on the American surplus market. The appearance of millions of surplus firearms on the American civilian market reflected, in part, the Eisenhower administration's confidence that the weapons in the United States would fall into the hands of collectors, target shooters, and hunters, but these weapons, which were still in active use in armies around the world, would be a danger if they remained on the world market. They could become the tools of revolutionaries and guerrilla movements, not the toys of American shooters.[80]

This availability of surplus weapons proved to be something of a boon to the American shooter. Military surplus firearms were cheap and plentiful, making high-quality firearms available to the public at bargain prices. The British service rifle—the bolt-action Enfield—could be purchased for $14.95 in 1959 through a firearms dealer that would ship the rifle through a private carrier. The same dealer, according to an advertisement in *Guns*, a magazine for firearms enthusiasts, would also sell the British Army's Webley revolver for the same price. According to calculations made by economic historian Samuel H. Williamson and his associates, $14.95 would be roughly $138 in 2021 dollars. An advertisement in *Guns* in 1961 indicated that the semiautomatic M1 rifle and M1 carbine, weapons of the US armed forces that were being phased out in favor of the newly adopted M14 rifle, could be purchased for $80, roughly equivalent to $720 in 2021.[81]

The National Rifle Association would enjoy something of a heyday in this postwar period. The Roosevelt administration's efforts at national gun control had long since receded, and with it any significant controversy regarding the shooters' organization. In some states the NRA enjoyed a quasi-official status as the body that would certify an individual's ability to safely handle firearms for hunting licenses and pistol permit purposes. For the federal government, an organization dedicated to marksmanship training had proved that it could make a contribution to the nation's defense during World War II, and the armed forces kept up ties with it. Civilian marksmanship had a bearing on the soldier's proficiency with arms, particularly in times of mass mobilization when some recruits might get only a haphazard introduction to the use of small arms. The US Army maintained an office to promote civilian marksmanship, a continuation of a program that had started with the administration of Theodore Roosevelt. The thinking behind the program was that civilian familiarization with small arms would translate into military proficiency in times of war. All of the services participated in civilian-military marksmanship contests sponsored jointly by the Army and the NRA and held annually at Camp Perry, Ohio. The Army allowed NRA members and NRA clubs to purchase weapons at reduced rates. The M1 rifle, M1 carbine, and M1911A1 pistol were current military inventory in the 1950s and could be purchased through the NRA at significant discounts. It was a time when few publicly questioned the idea that the Constitution protected the citizen's right to have arms.

# 4. From Casual Acceptance to Virtual Desuetude

It is doubtful that the Connecticut couple who sued under the pseudonyms Paul and Pauline Poe were thinking much about the Second Amendment when they challenged their state's anticontraception statute in the US Supreme Court in 1961. It is equally unlikely that state's attorney Abraham Ullman, who defended the statute before the high court, was considering the meanings and limitations of the right to bear arms either. Nonetheless, their case became one of those instances in which a Supreme Court justice had occasion to mention the right to bear arms in a broader discussion of the rights of the American people. The majority opinion, authored by Justice Frankfurter, refused to declare the Connecticut statute unconstitutional largely because the state had had a long history of not enforcing the anticontraception law, and hence in the majority's view there was no real conflict between the state and the complaining couple. In a dissent that would be quoted in subsequent majority and concurring opinions in cases involving the right to privacy,[1] Justice John Marshall Harlan II argued that the Court should use the contraception case to reaffirm that the due process guarantees of the Fifth and Fourteenth Amendments indicated a protection for rights broader than those specified in the Constitution's first eight amendments:

> The full scope of the liberty guaranteed by the Due Process Clause cannot be found in or limited by the precise terms of the specific guarantees elsewhere provided in the Constitution. This "liberty" is not a series of isolated points pricked out in terms of the taking of property, the freedom of speech, press and religion, *the right to bear arms*, the freedom from unreasonable searches and seizures and so on.[2]

Harlan's dissent, like Jackson's majority opinion in *Eisentrager*, demonstrated a certain level of judicial comfort in referring to the right to bear arms as a right little different from the other rights protected by the first eight amendments. It was to be included among those rights that were protected by the Fourteenth Amendment's due process clause—a point also tacitly endorsed in Justice William Douglas's separate dissent in *Poe* and in his previous support for Justice Black's dissent in *Adamson*.[3] Too much and too little might be made of Harlan or Jackson's offhand inclusions of the right to bear arms among the rights of the American people, or Black or Douglas's treatment of the Second Amendment like the other provisions of the Bill of Rights, as part of the guarantee of due process safeguarded by the Fourteenth Amendment. These cases did not involve restrictions on firearms. They did not ask what might be permissible regulation of firearms in light of a constitutional provision protecting the right to have arms. Nonetheless, they seemed to reflect a general assumption among members of the postwar Court that the Second Amendment was little different from the First Amendment, or the Fourth or the Fifth, a basic right of the individual.

Harlan's listing of the right to bear arms in his discussion of the rights of the American people reflected the still largely uncontroversial nature of firearms ownership and the assumption that the Constitution protected such at the start of the 1960s. Within less than a generation, that assumption would be severely challenged. The Second Amendment as a protection for the rights of individuals would become the victim of judicial desuetude and indeed outright hostility. In this chapter we look at the journey made by the notion that the Constitution protects an individual's right to bear arms from its casual acceptance in *Poe* in 1961 to its near nullification some two decades later. That journey would take the Second Amendment and the American nation, of which it was a part, through times of turbulence, triumph, and tragedy—which would profoundly alter the nation's politics, culture, and laws and its sense of the role of law in the social order. We will discuss some of that change as the chapter unfolds.

But if we return to 1961, the year Harlan wrote his dissenting opinion in *Poe*, it was a time when there remained something of at least a public postwar consensus concerning guns and their place in American life. Hunting was, as it still is, a way of life in much of rural and small-town America. For many, it represented a way of putting food on the table. Practicing marksmanship was seen as a harmless way to have fun on the weekends and indeed one that might in the future, as it had in the recent past, contribute to the common defense. The US Army had a Directorate of Civilian Marksmanship. The colonel running the program wrote a monthly column in the NRA's magazine, the *American Rifleman*.[4] Few publicly questioned the right of individuals to have a gun in the home as a defense against possible intruders. So what if the veterans went a little overboard with their enthusiasm for Enfields and Springfields, or Mausers and carbines? They had more than earned them.

When Harlan wrote his dissenting opinion, federal firearms regulation was still quite slight. To be sure, a number of bills restricting firearms acquisition had been introduced in Congress in the postwar era. None of them met with much support.[5] Military surplus firearms were cheap and plentiful and could easily be purchased through ads in your favorite gun magazine. They could be shipped to your home via private carrier. Sporting-goods stores like Modell's sold surplus military rifles without requirements for licenses, even in New York City. Federal and state regulations on rifles were almost nonexistent. State regulations on pistols largely restricted their carrying, not their ownership. The presidential administration of Dwight David Eisenhower, the wartime supreme commander of American forces in the European theater, was yielding to a new administration led by ex-PT boat skipper John F. Kennedy. The Massachusetts Democrat had at least one quarrel with the National Rifle Association: Kennedy favored restrictions on the sale of surplus foreign weapons. He supported this restriction not out of any desire to limit gun ownership—his motive was pure protectionism. The surplus gun trade hurt the domestic firearms industry, then quite important in the Bay State.[6] Still, the new president was on good terms with the shooting community. While in the Senate, Kennedy had purchased a specially selected M1 Garand from the Army's civilian marksmanship program. He had also publicly expressed the view that the Second Amendment was put in the Constitution as a hedge against potential tyranny and that it served as a reminder that all citizens must be prepared to play a role in the national defense.[7] While president, Kennedy accepted the NRA's offer of a life membership in the organization.[8] He was part of an apparent national consensus that accepted widespread civilian ownership of firearms as a normal, indeed desirable, part of the national culture.

Three shots from a bolt-action Italian army surplus Manlicher-Carcano carbine in the hands of an unstable drifter, Lee Harvey Oswald, would begin the unraveling of that seeming consensus. Oswald, who had received an undesirable discharge from the US Marine Corps, had paid $19.95 for the rifle, which he had purchased from a mail-order house.[9] Oswald was arrested on November 22, 1963, for the murder of President Kennedy and Dallas police officer J. D. Tippit. Kennedy had been killed by rifle shots as his motorcade passed the Texas School Book Depository where Oswald worked. President

Kennedy's assassination, like the attack on Pearl Harbor for a previous generation, or the attack on the twin towers of the World Trade Center for a later one, was a moment of shared national horror. Few who lived through that moment would ever forget where they were when they heard the news. Radio and television instantly relayed the story, focusing the shocked nation's attention on Dallas and the assassination. The public's horror was further magnified when nightclub owner Jack Ruby shot Oswald in a Dallas police station in front of the whole nation, a terrible instant captured live on the black-and-white TVs of the era.[10]

An army of historians, journalists, detectives, lawyers, and just plain sensation seekers would debate, well into the present day, whether the commission headed up by Chief Justice Earl Warren was right in its conclusion that the president of the United States was killed by a lone, unstable drifter with a $20 rifle.[11] But few would dispute that the assassination brought forth a reassessment of the role of firearms in the nation's life. Whether the assassination served to rekindle support for national gun-control measures that had first surfaced during the New Deal only to be submerged during World War II and its aftermath, or whether Kennedy's death helped create new advocates for restrictions on firearms ownership, is hard to determine. What is clear is that after November 1963, new voices were being raised concerning the easy access to firearms that most Americans enjoyed. Old proposals designed to bring new restrictions concerning the sale or purchase of firearms, which had been languishing in Congress, were getting new hearings or attention.

Three days after the assassination, an article supporting legislation proposed by Senator Thomas Dodd (D-CT) appeared in the *Washington Post Times Herald*. The measure, which had been introduced the previous August, was designed, among other things, to prevent the shipment of firearms to persons under the age of eighteen and to require that purchasers get a notarized statement indicating that they had not been previously convicted of a felony. *Washington Post* reporter Ramon Germania indicated how profoundly the assassination three days earlier had affected his thinking about the question of gun control: "This was proved all too tragically Friday when a man used a mail order, foreign rifle he acquired for $12.78 to send a bullet crashing through the brain of the President, John F. Kennedy on a Dallas street."[12]

Dodd was quoted as saying on November 27, 1963, that he would use the outcry over Kennedy's assassination as a "tragic opportunity" to strengthen his gun-control bill.[13] He would not see his proposed legislation pass until some five years later, in 1968. But Dodd and Germania, the journalist, were not alone in their belief that the presidential assassination demonstrated the need for new controls on firearms. Less than a month after the assassination, a group calling itself the National Committee for the Control of Weapons was formed in New York State.[14] A Gallup Poll taken in January 1964 found 78 percent of the population favoring a hypothetical law that would require a police permit in order to purchase a gun.[15] A fear that a new antigun sentiment was sweeping the nation even caused concern on the part of the US Army. In January 1964 Colonel John K. Lee, executive officer of the National Board for the Promotion of Rifle Practice, expressed his concern that anti-firearms sentiment in the wake of the Kennedy assassination would likely lessen interest in the Army's civilian marksmanship program, a program that the Army saw as contributing to the national defense.[16]

Discontent with the nation's firearms laws and the place of guns in the national culture would become a special concern of the national press, particularly the then still young medium of television. In June 1964, *CBS Reports* aired an influential documentary, "Murder and the Right to Keep and Bear Arms." The documentary pressed the case for additional gun controls, arguing that half of what was then the nation's ten-thousand-person annual murder rate was committed by individuals with firearms. The presentation also argued that the then existing laws made it easy for criminals and the mentally unbalanced to obtain firearms. The CBS documentary, made less than a year after Kennedy's assassination, represented a new way of thinking about guns and American life.[17]

That new way of thinking was encapsulated in journalist Carl Bakal's 1966 book, *The Right to Bear Arms.* The American tradition of widespread firearms ownership was really a "plague of guns" that had, in the twentieth century, brought more American deaths than all the wars that the nation had participated in between 1900 and 1966, the year the book was published. All other Western nations had strict controls on firearms and lower rates of gun deaths. The idea that the Constitution protected an individual's right to have firearms was a wrong-headed misinterpretation. Bakal was not the first gun-control advocate to advance these arguments, nor would he be the last. His discussion nonetheless bears some examination because in many ways it came near the genesis of the modern gun-control movement, and as such, it provided something of a preview of the debate over firearms, public policy, and the Constitution that would intensify in the coming decades.[18]

Bakal's constitutional analysis would, in many ways, set the pattern for many gun-control advocates who would follow. In a chapter titled "What Right to Bear Arms?" Bakal put forward his argument against the notion that the Constitution protected an individual's right to have arms:

> Many other court decisions [referring to *Miller*] and virtually every leading legal commentator and constitutional expert in the land agree that the intent, wording and meaning of the Second Amendment, in its full context refer only to the people's collective right to bear arms as members of a well-regulated and authorized militia. It is not an individual right they agree, in the same sense as others the Bill of Rights specifies, such as trial by jury and freedom of speech and religion.[19]

Bakal discussed some of the relevant cases. He looked at the 1905 case *Salina v. Blaksley*, in which the Kansas Supreme Court held that the state constitutional provision protecting the right to bear arms applied only to the militia, not the individual. Bakal failed to note that *Salina* was something of an exception in terms of state law on the subject.[20] Still, he accurately reported the Kansas Supreme Court opinion. The same cannot be said of the inferences he drew from US Supreme Court cases. Bakal enlisted four Supreme Court decisions, *United States v. Cruikshank, Presser v. Illinois, Robertson et. al. v. Baldwin et. al.*, and *U.S. v. Miller*, to support the claim that the Second Amendment protected a right confined to the organized militia and not the individual. Bakal, and others who would later write in the same vein, made an important conceptual error in analyzing the Court's jurisprudence in this area. The error was basic: Bakal assumed that the Court's unwillingness to recognize an unlimited right to bear arms signaled that the right was nonexistent as far as the individual was concerned.

Thus, Bakal converted the McReynolds opinion in *Miller* from a ruling that focused on whether the arm in question was constitutionally protected to an endorsement of the idea that the Second Amendment protected only arms in the hands of the organized militia. *Cruikshank* and *Presser* were enlisted for the same purpose, even though these cases were largely about the nineteenth-century Supreme Court's views on federalism and its determination to restrict the reach of the Bill of Rights to the federal government.

Bakal's employment of another nineteenth-century Supreme Court case, *Robertson v. Baldwin*, an 1897 case involving a habeas corpus petition, was perhaps even more problematic. Justice Henry Billings Brown's opinion rejecting the petition alluded to the rights protected in the First, Second, and Fifth Amendments to argue that those rights had limitations:

> Thus, the freedom of speech and of the press (article 1) does not permit the
> publication of libels, blasphemous or indecent articles, or other publications
> injurious to public morals or private reputation; *the right of the people to keep and*
> *bear arms (article 2) is not infringed by laws prohibiting the carrying of concealed*
> *weapons*; the provision that no person shall be twice put in jeopardy (article 5)
> does not prevent a second trial, if upon the first trial the jury failed to agree, or if
> the verdict was set aside upon the defendant's motion . . . nor does the provision
> of the same article that no one shall be a witness against himself impair his
> obligation to testify, if a prosecution against him be barred by the lapse of time, a
> pardon or by statutory enactment.[21]

Far from treating the Second Amendment as some kind of peculiar provision of the Bill of Rights not applicable to the individual, or only applicable in some highly limited sense, that is, when acting as a member of the organized state militia, *Robertson* treated the right to keep and bear arms as similar to the other rights guaranteed by the first eight amendments—rights of individuals, albeit subject to the broad police power restrictions, that were common in nineteenth-century constitutional jurisprudence.

We are doing this critical examination of Bakal's work not to pick a quarrel with Bakal as such. Bakal was a popular writer and political activist, not a student of the Constitution. In 1966 when *The Right to Bear Arms* was published, there had been little in the way of academic investigation of the topic. There had also been little in the way of contested litigation on the subject. The briefs, the research for briefs, and the oral arguments that are a part of the litigation process often produce useful, if slanted, evidence. But even that was lacking to a great extent when Bakal wrote. Much of the twentieth-century commentary on the right to bear arms consisted of abbreviated discussion of the topic attached to larger examinations of the Constitution. There were few federal cases on point. All of that having been said, Bakal's arguments and mistakes would later be echoed in the argument that the Second Amendment did not protect the right of individuals and thus had nothing to say to the gun control debate.[22]

These arguments included a linguistic point that should have been dismissed on its face: the claim that the term "the people" in and of itself indicated a collective right, not a right of individuals. Neither Bakal nor those who would follow in his footsteps indicated what this understanding of the term "the people" would have done to the right of peaceable assembly and petition in the First Amendment, or the right to be secure in persons, houses, and papers in the Fourth. This tendency, in the early stages of the debate, to make overly broad claims concerning the Supreme Court's limited engagement with the Second Amendment and the language of the constitutional provision would prove to be a crucial weakness for those who argued that the amendment only protected a limited collective right as the debate matured.

Bakal challenged the enduring relevance of a notion that played a critical part in the thinking of the founding generation and subsequent generations of jurists and commentators that examined the Second Amendment. He criticized the idea that the Second Amendment could play a critical role in keeping an armed population that might play a part resisting governmental oppression. Bakal argued that the weaponry available to a modern army made the idea of any meaningful resistance to a dictatorship on the part of armed civilians problematic if not outright fanciful.[23] And yet even as Bakal wrote, events were occurring that would cast the question of arms and resistance to governmental oppression in a new light. Bakal cast his critique as a response to some of the more exuberant claims of some gun enthusiasts who argued for an armed population to combat a potential future tyrannical government. It was a point of view that often got a public airing in the 1950s and 1960s by right-wing paramilitary groups like the Minutemen. But it was by no means confined to those precincts. Liberal Democratic senators John Kennedy and Hubert Humphrey also endorsed the view that an armed population was a hedge against a potentially tyrannical government. That point of view was also championed by Illinois attorney Robert Sprecher, who would later serve on the Seventh Circuit Court of Appeals.[24] It was an idea with a long pedigree in American political philosophy and jurisprudence, having been in part the vision that had been put forward by Alexander Hamilton in *Federalist*, no. 29 and by James Madison in *Federalist*, no. 46.[25] That vision would be subsequently reiterated by Justice Joseph Story in his constitutional commentaries and by Michigan Supreme Court justice Thomas Cooley, among others. It was a view that held that if a majority of the population believed that the state had gone too far—that the government had become tyrannical—arms would give the population a means of resisting governmental oppression.[26] Even Roscoe

Pound, who called for judicial nullification of the Second Amendment, conceded that the amendment was originally adopted with the idea in mind that it would enable popular resistance to tyrannical government.[27] This traditional view was often buttressed in the popular mind by the nation's clash with totalitarian forces during the course of the twentieth century and would even play a part in the case law in the twenty-first century immediately preceding *Heller*.[28]

## RACE AND RESISTANCE

Although the traditional notion that an armed population might play a role in resisting governmental tyranny seemed problematic to Bakal and others in light of the advanced weaponry available to modern armies, there was another, less heralded intellectual tradition in America that also discussed the importance of arms as a hedge against governmental and private oppression. If the nation as a whole had escaped the problem of a macro-tyranny imposed by a dictator's usurpation or a military coup, it had not escaped the problem of micro-tyranny, ruthless suppression of disfavored minorities brought about by the systematic failure of federal and state governments to protect citizens against racial violence. The prime example of this comes, of course, from the history of Afro-Americans. There was a long history, particularly but by no means exclusively in the Southern states, of law enforcement officials refusing to protect Black people from racially motivated attacks. *Cruikshank*, incorrectly cited by Bakal and others for the proposition that the Second Amendment only applied to the militia, was really about the federal government's ability to enact and enforce protective legislation that would shield the South's newly freed Negro population and others from attacks by the Ku Klux Klan and other private parties. The Supreme Court's ruling in that case sharply curtailed the ability of the federal government to protect vulnerable minorities from private violence—violence designed to make sure Negroes and their political allies were not too vigorous in asserting their rights, particularly the right to vote in the Southern states. Violence on the part of White supremacists played a key role in establishing and maintaining the American system of petty-apartheid, Jim Crow.[29]

If the specter of a possible future tyranny had made the notion of the right to bear arms part of the nation's political philosophy and constitutional jurisprudence, the ever-present threat of lynching, race riots, and simple day-to-day racial violence had long caused champions of racial equality to embrace the idea of the right to arms as a means of a minority's survival in the face of racist hostility. It was, as we discussed in the Chapter 1, one of the ways of thinking that informed the passage of the Fourteenth Amendment and the civil rights legislation of the Reconstruction era. That way of thinking antedated the Civil War. As early as the 1820s and 1830s, free Black men were actively defending their communities against anti-Negro mobs that plagued Afro-American communities in many Northern cities.[30] Frederick Douglass advocated meeting fugitive slave catchers with armed resistance. Later in the nineteenth century, Ida Wells, who often put her own life at risk with her vigorous crusade against lynch mobs, gave the public her own prescription to curb racial violence: "The Winchester should have a place of honor in every black home." One of Afro-American labor leader A. Philip Randolph's earliest memories was of his father and other armed Black men successfully preventing the lynching of a Negro prisoner at a jail in Jacksonville, Florida. Future NAACP leader Walter White helped defend his home and family with a shotgun during the vicious Atlanta race riot of 1919.[31] African Americans had learned from painful experience that total trust and total reliance on police forces for protection was foolish at best and almost suicidal at worst. During the massive Tulsa, Oklahoma, race riot of 1921, local authorities, who had had a history of not only not stopping but indeed actively supporting lynching, deputized and handed out guns to members of White mobs, who went on to burn the city's "Little Africa" section, killing many of its residents.[32] The idea that one of the reasons to be armed was to combat potential racial violence enjoyed widespread support in Southern Black communities.

Support for armed self-defense and community defense would increase in the postwar era. There was a new spirit of racial militancy on the part of Negro veterans who had served in World War II and the Korean conflict. Having risked their lives in the service of the nation, they were increasingly unwilling to accept the American version of apartheid, Jim Crow. The 1940s–1960s was a time of often fierce struggle against the racial barriers that prevailed throughout the country but were particularly grating and obvious in the Southern states. The movement pressed its case through nonviolent means: boycotts of bus lines and stores, voter registration efforts, sit-ins at segregated restaurants, and the like. Though the efforts to break down racial barriers were nonviolent, the reaction of those who wanted to keep the Jim Crow order was not. Firebombing, kidnaping, and shootings were often the responses to efforts to register voters or to lead boycotts against stores that wouldn't serve Black customers. There had been a tradition of armed resistance to racial violence in many African American communities in the South. It was frequently under-reported in part because the Klan and other violent racists were reluctant to acknowledge that their efforts had been thwarted by armed Negroes. Successful resistance was a bad example that might spread. Members of Afro-American communities who had successfully fought or scared off racist mobs also had an interest in not heralding such incidents. Too much notice given to successful Black resistance would run the risk of retaliation by state authorities. A Black family or community might successfully resist a mob and get away with it, particularly if they had simply scared off their White attackers without killing or seriously wounding them. If state authorities, with the police and National Guard, were brought in, all would be lost.[33] In the postwar era, the Klan and other groups who sought violent encounters with the civil rights movement often found themselves facing well-trained, well-armed Black veterans. The low-cost, high-quality military surplus firearms that proved to be such a benefit to hunters, target shooters, and collectors also often served another purpose: protection of civil rights workers and Black communities.[34]

The struggle against Jim Crow would cause several Black civil rights leaders to recognize that armed self-defense would have to be a part of their civil rights advocacy. Probably the most famous of these in the 1950s was Robert Williams, a leader of the local NAACP branch in Monroe, North Carolina. Monroe had been a hotbed of Klan activity, and Williams's efforts to organize a local NAACP chapter in 1957 was both courageous and physically risky. To protect the NAACP and its civil rights efforts and the Black community more generally, Williams decided he needed better armament. As the NRA at the time was the vehicle through which civilians could buy surplus US Army weapons at significantly reduced rates, Williams turned Monroe's branch of the NAACP into an NRA-affiliated rifle club. The club had an armed confrontation with the Klan that caused the Klan to run away and the city of Monroe to ban Klan motorcades.[35]

The most organized of the Black self-defense groups working in conjunction with the civil rights movement in the 1960s was the group known as the Deacons for Defense and Justice. The Deacons, which originated in Louisiana but later spread to nearby Mississippi and Alabama, were organized to resist Klan violence. Composed largely of veterans of World War II and the Korean War, the group provided armed escorts for civil rights workers who were registering Black voters. They also protected African American communities from Klan retaliation. In Jonesboro, Louisiana, members of a chapter of the Deacons were actually deputized as auxiliary police officers, both to watch the Klan and probably to keep them under the control of the local chief of police as well.[36]

Individuals like Robert Williams and members of groups like the Deacons for Defense and Justice helped transform the South and the nation. Student Nonviolent Coordinating Committee veteran Charles Cobb was probably not exaggerating when he said that the willingness of groups like the Deacons to provide armed defense against racial violence made the civil rights movement possible.[37] Many veterans of the movement experienced occasions when local police officers were often sympathetic to the Klan, and federal officials provided little protection for the lives of Southern Negroes and the civil rights workers who worked with them. For those who lived through that history, the right to be armed proved critical. And the idea that governmental tyranny could take the form of indifference and inaction as well as active oppression became a strongly held belief. For at least some of the veterans of the civil rights movement, that experience, and that belief, would remain with them for the rest of their lives. The memory of a childhood friend who was one of the four young girls killed in the bombing of Birmingham's Sixteenth Street Baptist Church, and her recollection that her father and other Black men in the Alabama city had to guard their families and neighborhoods with rifles and shotguns, would cause future US secretary of state Condoleezza Rice, decades after the struggle against Jim Crow in the 1960s, to declare herself a "Second Amendment absolutist."[38] In 1968 Roy Innis and Floyd McKissick, leaders of the civil rights group the Congress of Racial Equality (CORE), would express opposition to one aspect of President Lyndon Johnson's proposed gun-control plan, his call for licensing of gun owners. They objected on the grounds that such a measure would give police too much discretion, allowing them to simply arbitrarily deny licenses to Black applicants. Innis would remain CORE's director and would later become a member of the board of directors of the NRA.[39]

Another person for whom the civil rights movement and the importance of the right to be armed would remain forever linked was a young White civil rights worker named Don B. Kates Jr. In the 1960s, Kates was engaged in the often-hazardous business of registering Black voters in the South. In 1979 he wrote of his experiences of a time in the recent past when individual skill with a gun, and not the law's protection, could mean the difference between life and death:

> As a civil rights worker, I saw how the possession of a firearm could shrink the threat of ultimate violence into just another more or less innocuous incident: When Klansmen catch you in some deserted area and open fire, you take cover and shoot back—if you have a gun. Then both sides depart with great speed. . . . If you don't have a gun, however, the Klansmen keep on shooting and moving closer.[40]

Kates would survive these encounters and later play a key role in the academic rediscovery of the Second Amendment. The movement to register Black voters and fight Jim Crow in the Southern states was often able to successfully defend its activities with arms because it largely followed the conservative, traditional approach that had been used in Southern Negro communities throughout the Jim Crow era and before. The public face of the movement was the unarmed, nonviolent citizen seeking service at a restaurant, or to use the public library or to register to vote. That these citizens were often guarded by armed groups like the Deacons as they traveled the dangerous back roads of the rural South or as they slept in their homes in fear of attack by night riders was not emphasized. Nor was it heralded that outside civil rights workers sometimes had to get armed escorts to the airport or train station when it was found that they were on a Klan hit list. Indeed, the NAACP, the Southern Christian Leadership Conference, and the other major civil rights groups often took pains to publicly disavow any connection with groups advocating or practicing armed self-defense, often while working with them to ensure the safety of Black communities and outside civil rights workers.[41]

If the Southern civil rights movement was able, to an extent, to allay national anxiety over the specter of Blacks arming for potential battle with the Klan, a set of developments that would occur in Northern and Western states would help to fuel national cries for stricter controls on guns. Racial inequality and indeed racist oppression were not limited to the South. They prevailed nationwide. The cities of the North and West lacked the formal Jim Crow barriers of the South, but opportunities for good jobs, decent housing, and schools that might adequately prepare a child for the workforce or college were often glaringly absent. Black people could vote in these cities, but somehow the electoral game was always rigged so that the cities had relatively few

Black elected officials and little in the way of appointed officials overseeing the school boards and the fire, sanitation, and police departments. And then there were the police departments themselves. Cases of police brutality were common. Even more common was the failure to protect the citizens in the Northern ghettoes. Southern Negroes had moved North in great numbers over the course of the twentieth century. Seeking better lives, they often found only bitter disappointment.

By the 1960s that disappointment would spill over into massive urban unrest. Riots and full-scale rebellions would occur in a large number of American cities. One student of the subject has counted a hundred major riots, in which 130 civilians and thirteen government officials were killed, between 1964 and 1967.[42] The life history of the riots or rebellions usually followed a predictable pattern: a history of poverty and high unemployment combined with a long-standing record of tensions between police and residents of particular ghetto neighborhoods. The spark added to this explosive mixture would usually be an incident with the police, an arrest where the suspect was roughed up by the police, or the shooting of a Black citizen with the police claiming that the suspect was armed and at least some witnesses arguing that the victim was unarmed. Additional incidents would pile on top of the initial confrontation, and in due course a full-fledged conflagration would ensue. Confrontations between Black communities and municipal authorities would occur throughout the nation, including in major cities like New York, Los Angeles, Newark, and Washington, DC.[43]

The urban unrest of the 1960s created additional fear because some of the rioters were armed and shot at the police and National Guardsmen sent to quell the rebellions. There is evidence that some of the ghetto residents who were firing at the police and guardsmen did so not intending to hit them, but to harass or scare them.[44] There is also considerable evidence of panic and overreaction on the part of unprepared police and National Guard forces, which only added to the number of bullets fired and casualties occurring in these situations.[45]

To this combustible mixture was added outspoken new Black voices who were making the case for self-defense and the right to bear arms in new and quite strident ways. The leaders of the Southern civil rights movement had emphasized nonviolence and lawful protest as a means of redressing long-standing Black grievances. They usually kept silent about their arms and their armed auxiliaries, preparing to use them only in self-defense and only as a last resort.

The new spokesmen rediscovered the Second Amendment and its revolutionary potential and loudly proclaimed that they were about armed struggle,
indeed revolution. Malcolm X embraced the doctrine of a muscular armed
self-defense in 1964, incorporating the Second Amendment as a tool against
racial violence. The Black Panthers, a Marxist group, would take matters a bit
further. Formed in reaction to incidents of police brutality in the Bay Area
in California, the Panthers would proclaim their Second Amendment right
to be armed and to patrol the police, following them with loaded weapons.
On May 2, 1967, in full view of California governor Ronald Reagan, the Panthers paraded into the State House with loaded rifles, pistols, and shotguns.
Two months later, the California legislature passed a bill prohibiting the unlicensed carrying of weapons. Governor Reagan, who had previously expressed
his skepticism concerning gun-control legislation, signed the measures.[46]

## ZEROING IN

The California legislature wasn't the only governmental body that was persuaded that Black militancy and firearms were a combination that required
legislative intervention. The President's Commission on Law Enforcement
and Administration of Justice, commonly called the Kerner Commission, expressed its support for measures in a report released in 1967. These measures
included state registration of all firearms and the licensing of firearms owners.
The commission also recommended the passage of federal firearms registration to be applied in those states that did not have a state registration system,
and it recommended prohibitions on out-of-state sales of handguns. It also
urged Congress to provide additional restrictions on the sale of machine guns,
mortars, and antitank weapons.[47]

The Kerner Commission's recommendations represented the revival of
efforts that had begun during Roosevelt's New Deal, only to be tabled during
the Second World War and its aftermath. There had been previous attempts
to revive Roosevelt's gun-control efforts. In 1947, President Harry Truman's
attorney general, Tom Clark, had testified before Congress in favor of a bill
that would have mandated the registration of handguns.[48]

These and similar efforts had gained little traction with postwar Congresses, but the assassination of President Kennedy and the turmoil in the
nation's inner cities caused many political leaders, journalists, and ordinary

citizens to reexamine the issue. Connecticut Senator Tom Dodd's gun-control proposals, which had first been introduced in 1962, were to be the vehicle for new gun-control legislation. Both of the slain president's surviving brothers, Robert F. Kennedy and Edward M. Kennedy, were in the Senate and provided strong voices for further restrictions on firearms ownership.[49] The Johnson administration was in full-scale support of new restrictions on the purchase of guns, particularly restrictions on and the elimination of mail-order sales that allowed purchasers to circumvent state laws. The administration also wanted a ban on the importation of surplus military weapons of the kind that Oswald had used to kill Kennedy. As might have been expected, Johnson's two attorneys general, former attorney general Nicholas Katzenbach and then current attorney general Ramsey Clark, testified on the need for stricter controls.[50] But other members of Johnson's cabinet also supported the effort. Robert McNamara, who had been appointed secretary of defense by Kennedy and continued in that position under Johnson, expressed his shock that Congress had not moved further on gun control in a published letter written in 1967 to Senator Edward Kennedy of Massachusetts.[51]

The Great Society's supporters of the mid-1960s gun-control effort differed from their New Deal predecessors in that they were more explicit in their desire to deny that the Second Amendment protected a right of individuals. The Roosevelt administration had hedged its bets on the constitutional question. The New Dealers did not directly attack the notion of a constitutional right to arms in Congress. Solicitor General Robert Jackson wrote a brief in *Miller* that argued, as one of three alternative constitutional theories, that the restrictions of the 1934 National Firearms Act were consistent with an individual right to have arms. But the gun-control advocates of the Great Society wanted more. The Johnson administration and its allies largely made the case for additional restrictions on criminological grounds, noting an average of nearly six thousand homicides per year committed with firearms in the mid-1960s.[52] But the proponents of additional firearms restrictions went further, asserting that the Second Amendment had nothing to do with individuals and served only to protect state militias from federal encroachment. That had been the position put forth by writer Carl Bakal. It would later be echoed by, among others, Maryland Appeals Court judge Reuben Oppenheimer in an article he authored in the *Baltimore Sun.* In the article the Maryland jurist argued, in essence, that because Congress had made provision for the arming and training of the National Guard, the Second Amendment's "well-regulated militia" had been provided for, and there was no need to protect the individual citizen's right to bear arms from congressional infringement.[53]

Bakal and Oppenheimer were not alone in their claim that the individual rights view of the Second Amendment could be safely ignored. The administration's report *The Challenge of Crime in a Free Society*, chaired by former attorney general Nicholas Katzenbach, summarily dismissed possible constitutional objections to increased gun controls by claiming that the Supreme Court and lower federal courts had consistently held that the Second Amendment did not protect a right of individuals. In 1967, when *The Challenge of Crime in a Free* Society was published, that claim was not supported by the Supreme Court's jurisprudence, and it was only somewhat tenuously buttressed by *Tot* and *Cases* in the circuit courts. Internal Revenue Commissioner Sheldon Cohen in testimony before the Senate Judiciary Committee in 1967 echoed the report, stating that both Katzenbach and Clark regarded the argument that the Second Amendment restricted Congress's ability to enact gun-control legislation as "preposterous."[54]

The administration's summary dismissal of the idea that the Second Amendment might limit the government's gun-control options reflected an ambitious agenda in the area of firearms regulation on the part of the Johnson's administration. The place of guns in American society was to be reined in. Gun owners were to be licensed, and guns registered.[55] Guns were to be owned only for sporting purposes. Hunting by respectable middle-class Americans who could afford a high-quality deer rifle or sporting shotgun was fine. Ownership of ten- or twenty-dollar surplus rifles by poor people was suspect. Ownership of cheap pistols was even worse. Indeed, such ownership must be curtailed. In a way, the Great Society's gun-control architects were following a lead put forward by Carl Bakal and others. The American gun culture, if it were to be allowed to continue at all, should come to more closely resemble the shooting communities of Western Europe. Hunters and target shooters, Bakal assured his readers, safely enjoyed their hobbies in Britain and on the European Continent under strict controls without their populations arming for self-defense, much less potential military activity.[56]

If the administration as a whole wanted an American gun-control regime that resembled the more restrictive policies found in much of Western Europe, it's probably fair to say that Attorney General Clark wanted American policies to change even further. In his book published in 1970, *Crime in America*, Clark decried the prominence and ubiquity of firearms in American society: "Guns were once thought to be provider, protector and defender of liberty. Today they murder."[57] As attorney general, Clark guided the Johnson administration's gun-control policy from 1967 to 1968. He was highly skeptical of private gun ownership for any but the most restricted sporting purposes, if that. Like Bakal, he dismissed the idea that widespread firearms ownership might be a hedge against a potential future tyranny. But Clark also dismissed the idea of private self-defense against criminals: "Nor can firearms in the possession of firearms protect them from crime. A state in which a citizen needs a gun to defend himself from a crime has failed to perform its first purpose. . . . The wrong people survive, because the calculating killer or the uninhibited psychotic wields the faster gun."[58] For Clark, widespread gun ownership was something that should be relegated to the nation's past and not be considered part of the future of a modern urban society.[59]

Clark and the administration were not the only ones to weigh in on the Second Amendment issue. Indeed, the question of the meaning of the constitutional right to keep and bear arms played a somewhat greater role in congressional deliberations on the 1968 Gun Control Act than had been the case with either the 1934 National Firearms Act or the 1938 Federal Firearms Act. In addition to the expected testimonies and written insertions from interest groups supporting or opposing additional firearms legislation, the Library of Congress provided research for those members of Congress interested in reviewing the Second Amendment question. In a publication titled *The Second Amendment Selected Materials*, the Congressional Research Service put together a packet of materials including a message, "The People's Right to Protection," from President Lyndon Johnson outlining the case for stricter gun controls, including licensing and registration. The packet also included a Justice Department memorandum titled "Federal Firearms Control and the Second Amendment," as well as law review literature on the topic from the mid-1960s—including a student note from the *Harvard Law Review* titled "Firearms: Problems of Control," an article by Illinois attorney Robert Sprecher in the *American Bar Association Journal*, titled "The Lost Amendment"; "The Second Amendment: A Second Look, " an article in the *Northwestern University Law Review* by Peter Buck Feller and Karl L. Gotting; and a commentary in the *Albany Law Review* by one Richard F. Riseley Jr. titled "The Right to Keep and Bear Arms: A Necessary Constitutional Guarantee or an Outmoded Provision of the Bill of Rights?" The Justice Department memorandum, the *Harvard Law Review* note, and the Feller-Gotting article argued that the Second Amendment only protected the right of the organized militia to have arms. The commentary in the *Albany Law Review* and the Sprecher article, which had been submitted into evidence as congressional testimony by Franklin L. Orth, executive vice president of the National Rifle Association, supported the view that the amendment protected an individual right. We will discuss Sprecher's article at somewhat greater length later in this volume.[60]

The Library of Congress itself produced a report to help inform Congress on the constitutional issues that the Second Amendment posed for gun-control legislation. Its report "The Second Amendment as a Limitation on Federal Firearms Legislation" did what a Library of Congress report was supposed to do, provide representatives and senators with a neutral examination of the state of the law. Vincent Doyle, the author of the report, admitted that the jurisprudence and the constitutional limits posed by the Second Amendment were, in 1968 as he was writing, unclear. Doyle indicated that the amendment posed limits on gun-control legislation, but he also indicated that the extent of the limitations was not clear. His report accepted the basic view that the Second Amendment protected an individual's right to arms and that the right was protected for the public as a whole in the public's capacity as members of the unorganized or inchoate militia. The report nonetheless indicated that Congress had broad latitude to legislate in this area and that the gun-control proposals under consideration in the summer of 1968—prohibition on mail-order sales, licensing, and registration—would not on their face be violations of the Second Amendment as long as they were not administered in a discriminatory manner.[61]

Ultimately the debates over the Second Amendment and its interpretations and limitations would play a distinctly secondary role in the passage of the Gun Control Act of 1968. It was instead the turmoil and tragedy of that tumultuous year that prompted Congress's action. The assassination of civil rights leader Martin Luther King Jr. in Memphis on April 4 and the assassination of Senator Robert F. Kennedy on June 5 caused a stunned nation to look for an answer. One answer came in the form of the gun-control legislation that had originated with Senator Dodd's proposal, now fortified by the full backing of the Johnson administration. Some of the proposals were uncontroversial. The NRA supported the proposed provision that limited the sale of mortars and antitank weapons. Other provisions, particularly the ones calling for licensing of gun owners and registration of firearms, met with stiff opposition. The debates in Congress, in the nation's editorial pages, on TV broadcasts, and in the nation's gun press continued throughout the summer and into the fall of 1968. On October 22, the bill was passed and signed into law by Lyndon Johnson. The new law was far more modest than what the administration had advocated. Licensing of gun owners and registration of firearms did not survive the legislative process. During the debates over the act, the NRA had expressed its opposition to registration, citing New York's Sullivan Law. Registration, argued NRA executive vice president Franklin Orth, had led to discretionary licensing in New York, which in turn led to a virtual handgun prohibition for most of the city's residents.[62] The NRA was successful in modifying the legislation. The NRA also played a part in changing what might be termed the tone of the gun-control measure. The administration wanted to move toward a restriction of firearms ownership to sporting purposes. That limitation was rejected in the Congressional Statement of Purpose explaining the new bill. While that statement did not mention the Second Amendment, it did indicate that the legislation was not intended to interfere with firearms ownership for any lawful purpose, including self-defense. The statement also indicated that the legislation was not intended to interfere with or eliminate private firearms ownership.[63]

The legislation did bring new restrictions. Imported firearms had to be suitable for sporting purposes. New licensing and record-keeping requirements were imposed on firearms dealers. And most important for our purposes, there were new federal requirements for the purchase and possession of firearms. An individual purchasing a firearm from a licensed dealer had to fill out a form swearing that the purchaser was not under indictment nor had been convicted of a crime punishable by more than one year in prison. A purchaser also had to swear not to be a fugitive from justice, an unlawful user of narcotics, or to have been adjudicated as having been mentally defective or committed to a mental institution. Knowingly making a false statement on the form was subject to criminal penalties. The new legislation would also make it a felony for a person previously convicted of a felony to possess a firearm.[64] It was far-reaching legislation but was nonetheless sharply criticized by gun-control supporters, including Lyndon Johnson, for not going far enough.[65]

One group who agreed that the 1968 legislation was inadequate was the United States Conference of Mayors. The mayors' organization, like many others in the early 1970s, was searching for a solution to the nation's seemingly intractable crime problem. Richard Nixon had won the US presidency in 1968 in part on his campaign promise to bring "law and order" to the nation, particularly the nation's inner cities. The Republican brand of law and order promised tougher policing, harsher penalties, fewer criminal suspects released on the constitutional "technicalities" mandated by the Warren Court's decisions on right to counsel, requirements for search warrants, and scrutiny of police interrogation methods. Urban residents certainly wanted safer streets and protection from criminals who put their lives and often meager possessions at grave risk. They suffered from crime more than the rest of the nation. Big city mayors were faced with rising crime rates that hit Black communities particularly hard. Between 1960 and 1970 the homicide rate among Black men had nearly doubled, from a rate of 42.3 per 100,000 to 78.2 per 100,000. In 1970 the homicide rate among Black men was ten times the rate among White men.[66] Increased safety was wanted, but should it come at the cost of increased incarceration and giving police departments who had always had a strained relationship with African American communities more of a free hand?

Gun control taking the nation beyond the mandates of the 1968 legislation seemed like a promising alternative. The cause was a popular theme with the nation's editorial writers. Local tragedies involving criminal actions with guns or accidental shootings of innocent persons were sure to get widespread play in the newspapers and on television. Arthur Bremer's wounding of George Wallace with a handgun while the Alabama governor was campaigning for the Democratic nomination for president in May 1972 and two attempts to assassinate President Gerald Ford in 1975 brought about at least temporary increases in the number of voices calling for stricter regulation. The Conference of Mayors added weight to the cause of handgun control. In June 1972 the conference endorsed a policy calling for the virtual elimination of private handgun ownership. The group launched a handgun-control project to develop national legislation to further that aim. The conference's 1972 statement put the issue bluntly: There was no Second Amendment right for private citizens to have arms. Handguns were not used for sporting purposes. Those who possessed handguns could not be divided into criminals and qualified or legitimate gun owners. Therefore, the private possession of handguns should be prohibited except for those in law enforcement, the armed forces, and perhaps a restricted number of private shooting clubs.[67]

The Conference of Mayors pushed its program for handgun prohibition throughout the 1970s. In 1976 it published a pamphlet titled *How Well Does the Handgun Protect You and Your Family?* that expressed a view that was becoming the conventional wisdom in the gun control community: ordinary citizens attempting to defend themselves with guns were more likely to produce catastrophe than safety.

> Private handgun ownership provides no significant deterrent to burglary and violent crime. It may in fact escalate the severity of the violence if offenders believe they must be more heavily armed than the citizenry. The use of a weapon in response to a criminal attack usually results in a greater probability of bodily injury or death to the victim. . . . Flight or verbal resistance are usually more effective in aborting the crime.[68]

But the concern of some gun-control advocates went beyond the prudential calculus that the average citizen might be incapable of safe and effective self-defense. For some in the gun-control community, arming for self-defense was not only hazardous but also a sign of civic failure on society's part and moral deficiency on the part of the individual. Ramsey Clark's 1971 statement that "a society in which a citizen needs a gun to defend himself has failed to perform its first purpose" echoed the sentiments of German-born statistician Frederick Hoffman at the hearings over the 1934 National Firearms Act—that a civilized society does not let its citizens arm for self-defense; instead it requires them to rely on the state. In later years, historian and writer Garry Wills would describe those who armed themselves for self-defense as "anti-citizens," "people arming against their own neighbors." The views that would be offered by Clark, Wills, and others were, in essence, an inversion of the notions of civic virtue that informed the late eighteenth-century generation that crafted the Second Amendment. That generation hoped for a virtuous citizenry capable of defending themselves, their communities, and their liberties. Some two centuries later Clark, Wills, and other influential voices argued that the citizen was incapable of even basic self-defense and, worse, was a menace to the social fabric if he prepared to do so. Skepticism concerning the morality of armed self-defense would play an ongoing role in the gun-control movement.[69]

The Conference of Mayors was notable in that it highlighted growing support on the part of Black political leaders for the gun-control cause. Hostile police and the threat of White mobs had caused many Negroes to arm themselves during the Jim Crow era and the civil rights movement. Urban crime and the realization that many of the fomenters and victims of this crime were their own Black neighbors had caused many Afro-Americans to support greater restrictions on gun ownership. Atlanta mayor Maynard Jackson, a graduate of historically Black Morehouse College and the predominately Afro-American North Carolina Central Law School, was among the new crop of African American politicians in the 1970s who called for stricter gun controls. In a 1975 forum sponsored by the mayors' conference, Jackson expressed support for a ban on inexpensive handguns, the so-called Saturday-night specials, as an interim step on the road to a total ban on handguns. In 1977 he authored a short law review article, "Handgun Control: Constitutional and Critically Needed," to argue the case for prohibition.[70]

## BACKFIRE

Prospects for handgun prohibition seemed promising in the 1970s. Polls indicated that the public supported stricter controls on guns. The press certainly editorialized in favor of greater restrictions. An NBC television news documentary, "A Shooting Gallery Called America?," starkly presented the problem of guns in the wrong hands in modern America. The presentation, narrated by NBC correspondent Carl Stern, interviewed both criminals and solid citizens who owned handguns. The solid citizens who owned handguns said that they did so for protection. Stern acknowledged that many of them were in circumstances where they had little other choice. But Stern's interviews with the criminals were chilling. One robber said, "I stick up many stores." When asked what happens if the store owner resisted or did not hand over the money fast enough, he replied, "Just one more store owner dead." It's likely that both those who were convinced that there was a strong need for increased restrictions on guns and those who believed that guns were essential for self-defense were confirmed in their views after seeing the documentary.[71]

Popular entertainment also weighed in on the gun controversy. Hollywood's response to guns and the use of guns in self-defense was partly tied to a new and largely unfavorable view of the military and the soldiers returning from the Vietnam War. If movies in the 1940s and 1950s celebrated the returning veteran and had made his courage on the battlefield a metaphor for the courage that everyday Americans should show when confronting evil, movies and TV had quite a different message in the 1970s. The returning veteran as ticking time bomb, poised to grab a gun and wreak havoc on his family or community, was a frequent cliché of many a hack screenwriter during the decade. And it was not just the recent combat veteran suffering from what we now call post-traumatic stress syndrome who illustrated the wisdom of keeping guns out of the public's hands. Your next-door neighbor also proved that the average citizen could not be trusted with guns. In an episode of his hit series *All in the Family*, TV producer Norman Lear enlisted his most famous creation—befuddled, buffoonish bigot Archie Bunker—to show that those who spoke in favor of gun ownership had no arguments worthy of serious consideration.[72]

Serious journalists as well as writers of popular comedies and dramas all publicly supported stricter restrictions on guns. The American Bar Association and the American Civil Liberties Union both published statements indicating their support for the view that the Second Amendment only protected the organized militia from disarmament. While the Nixon administration, despite reports that Nixon privately disliked the widespread ownership of guns in the nation, took little action in favor of additional restrictions on firearms ownership, his successors indicated an openness to further controls. The Ford administration expressed support for a ban on Saturday-night specials. Ford's attorney general, former University of Chicago law professor Edward Levi, expressed an interest in a handgun ban in high-crime urban areas. Jimmy Carter during the 1976 presidential campaign indicated his support for handgun registration. None of these measures became law, but they did indicate White House support for further controls.[73]

The Conference of Mayors had only a limited ability to further the cause of gun control as it had other items on its agenda, including increased federal funding for education, police, and other public services. Yet there was strong, or seemingly strong, sentiment for increased gun control. Two national organizations, the National Coalition to Ban Handguns and the National Coalition to Control Handguns, were formed in 1974. Although the name of the latter group suggested a limited aim, gun control—that is, licensing or registration—as opposed to gun prohibition, both groups initially agreed on the goal of banning handguns. The National Coalition to Control Handguns would gain the support and leadership of Nelson T. "Pete" Shields III. Shields had been an executive with Dupont in Delaware when his life was horribly transformed by the murder of his son Nick in 1974. Nick Shields was shot in San Francisco by one of the "Zebra" killers, a group of Black men who let loose a reign of terror in the city by randomly killing White people. Their motive was sheer racial animus. His son's murder turned Shields into a gun-control activist. In 1976 he became executive director of the National Council to Control Handguns.[74]

Shields recounted his experience as a gun-control activist and outlined the case, as he saw it, for stricter firearms regulation in his 1981 book, *Guns Don't Die—People Do*, a take-off on the slogan popular among gun-control opponents "Guns Don't Kill People, People Kill People." His book reiterated many of the themes that had become familiar to the gun-control movement in the 1960s and 1970s: handguns, especially Saturday-night specials, were the problem, not rifles or shotguns. A person was more likely to harm himself or a member of his family if he attempted to use a pistol or revolver in self-defense. The only legitimate use for handguns was target shooting. The Supreme Court had repeatedly ruled that the Second Amendment only protected the right of people in the organized militia.[75]

Shields's official position and that of the National Council was that they were not advocating a ban on handguns, but stricter regulation that could be achieved through licensing and registration. But a 1976 interview with writer Richard Harris in the *New Yorker* revealed that Shields had a more ambitious agenda. The interview told the story of Nick Shields's murder, Pete Shields's efforts at organizing the National Council to Control Handguns, and the establishment of the organization's Washington office. Shields also gave Harris statistics on the extent of handgun crime in the nation and the large number of pistols and revolvers in private hands and his plans for gun-control lobbying in the future. Shields expressed support for a handgun control bill then under consideration in the House of Representatives. The bill was criticized by many gun-control advocates, including the leadership of the National Coalition to Ban Handguns, as being too weak, but Shields argued otherwise:

> There is now a chance for some kind of a handgun control law in this country.
> . . . I'm convinced that we have to have federal legislation to build on. We're
> going to have to take one step at a time. . . . So then we'll have to start working
> again to strengthen that law, and then again to strengthen the next law, and
> maybe again and again. Right now, though, we'd be satisfied not with half a loaf
> but with a slice. . . . My estimate is from seven to ten years. The first problem is
> to slow down the increasing number of handguns. . . . The second problem is to
> get handguns registered. And the final problem is to make the possession of all
> handguns . . . totally illegal.[76]

The Shields interview indicated a fair degree of confidence on the former Dupont executive's part. After all, gun prohibition was common sense. Many of the nation's leading opinion makers endorsed the idea. In 1975 the influential *New York Times* went so far as to state that "one way to discourage the gun culture is to remove the guns from the hands and shoulders of people who are not in the law enforcement business."[77] This nonsense of an armed population resisting a tyrannical government was a bit of anachronistic folklore that could be safely put aside. As for the armed population protecting the nation from invasion? Protection from invasion was the business of the armed forces, Shields, a World War II Navy fighter pilot, told his interviewer. And, of course, armed self-protection was more likely to lead to disaster than safety. Surely in seven to eight years, less than a decade, the nation would come to see the wisdom of his position.

Shield's confidence and that of other supporters of handgun prohibition was doubtless bolstered by the prominent backers that enlisted in the cause. *Guns Don't Die—People Do* reveals that the National Coalition to Control Handguns, which would later be renamed Handgun Control Inc., received support from some of the nation's leading blue-chip law firms: Covington and Burling, Wilmer, Cutler and Pickering, and Fried, Frank, Harris, Shriver, and Kampelman. The cause of further handgun restrictions was backed by a number of quite renowned people. Shields listed television personality Steve Allen, tennis star Arthur Ashe, former California governor Edmund Brown, educator Milton Eisenhower, former attorney general Edward Levi, and advice columnist Ann Landers among his supporters.[78]

Shields's champions included more than a group of celebrities willing to put their names on an organizational letterhead. He noted that the nation's editorial writers heavily favored the cause of handgun restrictions: "As a group, American editorial writers have done a great deal to keep the cause of handgun control before the American public."[79] Shields outlined a strategy to bring about tighter restrictions: Use the sympathetic press to keep hammering home the need for further controls. Rely on the support of prominent individuals to add credibility to the cause. Bring victims of gun violence to public attention, relying on the fact that the pro–gun-control press would cover the stories in such a way as to increase support for further restrictions. And this was something that Shields and the developing gun-control movement also relied on: polls that overwhelmingly showed that the public favored further restrictions.

Massachusetts looked like a very promising place to test whether prominent supporters, a sympathetic press, favorable polling, and a strategy that highlighted tragedies suffered by individual victims could bring about the desired result—a total ban on handguns. Massachusetts was a liberal state, probably in the 1970s the most liberal in the nation. It had been the only state carried by Democratic presidential candidate George McGovern in 1972. Liberals weren't unanimous in their support for gun control; conservatives weren't unanimous in their opposition. Still, it seemed a pretty safe bet that a liberal jurisdiction would tend to favor gun control. Massachusetts already had fairly strict gun control, a requirement that an individual had to have a Firearms Identification Card in order to purchase or possess a firearm. In 1974 the Bay State had also enacted the Bartley-Fox Law, which mandated one year of imprisonment for anyone convicted of carrying a firearm without a license. Under that statute, no parole or suspended sentence was possible. It was the only crime in Massachusetts that carried a mandatory minimum sentence. Gun laws were strict in Massachusetts, but the legislature balked at gun prohibition. In 1972 and 1973 it rejected measures that would have outlawed civilian possession of handguns.

But the polls indicated that a majority of state residents favored a ban on handguns. A nonbinding test referendum in five Massachusetts communities showed 79 percent support for a ban. The attempt to ban guns in the state legislature had been thwarted because legislatures feared the single-issue voters of the state NRA affiliate, the Gun Owners' Action League. Legislators feared league members' votes and their ability to pack the legislature with raucous demonstrators when the gun issue was being debated. Perhaps the legislature could be bypassed: Massachusetts had a provision that allowed law-making by referendum. Surely that would reflect the will of the people and bring about a ban on privately owned handguns. Success in Massachusetts could be a model for handgun prohibition activists in other states.

To that end the citizens organization People v. Handguns was formed, its purpose, to push for a referendum banning handguns statewide. The wind was at the organization's back. Governor Michael Dukakis supported the effort, as did Boston police commissioner Robert DiGrazia and Middlesex County sheriff John Buckley. The League of Women Voters, the Massachusetts Council of Churches, and the Paulist Center of Boston were among the organizations expressing their support for the effort. The press was also supportive. The book *People vs. Handguns: The Campaign to Ban Handguns in Massachusetts*, in which the United States Conference of Mayors described the campaign—which it heavily supported—noted that it received strong backing from the three television network affiliates in Boston. The book also praised the *Boston Globe*, "which campaigned ceaselessly for a sensible handgun control policy. The paper's courageous and long-term commitment was reflected in many editorials, articles, cartoons, and columns, which helped expand the public awareness and understanding of the issue."[80]

Enough signatures were gathered in December 1975 to place the referendum on the ballot for the following November. Spring and summer of 1976 saw an intense campaign on both sides calling for acceptance or rejection of what became "Question 5" on the Massachusetts ballot. Election day came on Tuesday, November 2, 1976. The results shocked the gun-control movement. The referendum failed by a 2–1 margin. It failed with Democrats, Republicans, and Independents. Individuals who regarded themselves as liberals voted against it by a 64–29 margin, conservatives by 66–21. The referendum carried Cambridge by a surprisingly slim 23,559 to 16,821, revealing perhaps more support for private handgun ownership in the homes surrounding Harvard University than may have been previously thought. The referendum failed with every ethnic group in Massachusetts, with two exceptions: African Americans and Jewish Americans. But even among these two groups, support for private handgun ownership proved to be strong. Blacks, who made up 5 percent of the Bay State voters, voted 50 percent to 33 percent in favor of the ban, with 17 percent not voting on the question. Jews voted 53 percent to 47 percent in favor of the ban.[81]

The effort to ban handguns failed in Massachusetts, but it met with success in Washington, DC. The Constitution grants power to Congress to govern the District of Columbia. In 1975 Congress granted the district home rule, the ability to pass legislation, subject to congressional override. In June 1976 the District of Columbia City Council by a vote of 12–1 passed strict gun-control legislation. The legislation specified that all firearms in Washington, DC, had to be registered by November 22, 1976. Owners of pistols and revolvers who registered their weapons on or before that date would be allowed to keep them. After that date, no new handguns could be registered, with the exception of guns owned by security guards. New residents or new purchasers of rifles and shotguns could register their firearms, but they were required to keep them disassembled in their dwellings. Store owners were allowed to keep their long guns assembled in stores for defensive use. At the time the law went into effect there were an estimated 63,000 firearms in private hands in the District of Columbia. The NRA was unsuccessful in an attempt to get Congress to override the DC City Council.[82]

The failed referendum in Massachusetts and the successful ban on handgun ownership in the District of Columbia provided lessons for both sides of the gun-control debate. Massachusetts taught advocates of gun control that the seeming support for stricter controls masked a distaste for the idea of gun prohibition and the idea that the individual should be defenseless against crime. The referendum showed that this distaste was shared across the political spectrum and existed to a surprising extent even in locales that were friendly to stricter controls. The stated aims of the movement would have to be modified. Following the Massachusetts failure, the National Coalition to Control Handguns changed its name to Handgun Control Inc. It would disavow any long-term plan to ban handguns and instead press more modest claims, licensing or registration or background checks, or bans on Saturday-night specials. It would maintain its suspicion of guns for self-defense and its insistence that the Second Amendment provided no protection for ordinary citizens. But the self-confidence found in Pete Shields's *New Yorker* interview that a total ban was only a decade or so away would be gone.

For the NRA and other opponents of stricter firearms regulation, the results in Massachusetts and the District of Columbia confirmed the direction that the NRA and other groups were taking. The National Rifle Association had become more explicitly political in the 1970s. Those who felt that the shooters' organization had to move beyond its traditional strengths in hunter safety and marksmanship training had won the day over those who wanted the association to stick with its more traditional activities. But Massachusetts and the District of Columbia did more than indicate that the NRA should become more political; they also pointed to how the organization might act politically. Massachusetts and the District of Columbia confirmed something Second Amendment activists already knew. Strong support for radical gun control might be found in the cities, but such sentiment was a minority view in most states, even liberal states. The solution? Preemption! Make firearms regulation a matter of state and not municipal law. The NRA and its various state affiliates would support preemption legislation in state legislatures, and by doing so it would severely blunt the drive toward handgun prohibition that had been urged by the United States Conference of Mayors, the National Council to Control Handguns, and other groups. It wouldn't be universally successful: Morton Grove, Illinois, passed an ordinance banning handguns in 1981, and the city of Chicago enacted a ban in 1982. But despite the Conference of Mayors, the gun-control community, and the vociferous efforts of

the nation's leading editorial writers and news departments of the major networks, the movement to ban handguns had few successes. That failure would
have important consequences later on.[83]

## COURTING DISASTER

And what of the Second Amendment? Despite the best efforts of the nation's
editorial writers, the American Bar Association, and the American Civil Liberties Union, the public continued to believe that the amendment protected the
right of ordinary citizens to have arms. Polls taken in the 1970s, at the height
of the movement to ban handguns, indicated that better than 80 percent of
the public believed that the amendment granted individuals the right to have
arms. The massive effort to persuade the public otherwise had failed.[84]

But it had succeeded, or appeared to have succeeded, with the nation's
elites, public officials with national stature, editorial writers with the *New York
Times, Washington Post, Boston Globe, Los Angeles Times, New Republic, Time*
magazine, and other publications of renown. The new orthodoxy that the
Second Amendment provided no protection for the individual's right to own
a gun also met with the approval of partners in leading law firms and with
commentators on network television. A new hostility toward the view that
the Constitution protected the individual's right to have arms had developed
during the fight for the Gun Control Act of 1968 and the subsequent campaign
to ban handguns. That new hostility had already begun to be reflected in the
court cases that would appear soon after the passage of the Gun Control Act
of 1968.

Shortly after the passage of the federal legislation, and before it went into
effect, a case in the New Jersey Supreme Court set the tone for the new jurisprudence. The case, *Burton v. Sills*, involved a challenge to a state statute enacted in 1966. It mandated the licensing of manufacturers, wholesalers, and
retailers of firearms. It also required identification cards and permits for gun
purchasers. A group of plaintiffs, including three individuals associated with
shooting clubs, two firearms dealers, and a corporation to promote marksmanship, brought suit asking for injunctive relief, that is, asking the court to
stop enforcement of the law. The plaintiffs argued the statute gave authorities
too much discretion in issuing permits. While they agreed with the provisions that denied permits to minors, convicted criminals, narcotics abusers,

and other identified categories of undesirables, the complainants contested a section of the statute that allowed authorities to withhold permits from individuals who might otherwise be a threat to the public welfare even though they were not in a specified category. This, the complainants argued, gave authorities too much discretion, which could lead to abuse. The plaintiffs were denied relief at the trial court and intermediate appellate court levels.[85]

They fared no better before the New Jersey Supreme Court. The court's opinion, authored by Justice Nathan Jacobs, recognized that the statute gave officials discretion in the issuing of permits but also stated that the statute provided easy avenues for appeal, thus checking potential abuses. The complainants raised a number of constitutional claims, including the argument that the statute violated the Second Amendment. From the beginning, the case was problematic. The individuals who brought the case had not been denied permits, raising the very real question of whether they actually suffered a concrete injury for the courts to remedy. Plaintiffs conceded that the then existing case law held that the Second Amendment did not apply to the states.[86]

The problematic posture of the case did not prevent the New Jersey high court from making broad pronouncements concerning the Second Amendment. The court could have quickly disposed of the issue by citing *Presser* and indicating that only the US Supreme Court could overturn the precedent that held that the amendment did not apply to the states. Justice Jacobs felt the need to go farther. His opinion discussed the provision in the seventeenth-century English Bill of Rights protecting the right of Protestants to have arms, saying the fact that the English statute singled out Protestants meant that the right protected was a class right, not an individual right. His opinion did not elaborate whether it was a right of individual Protestants, or if Protestants had to gather in some sort of mass formation to exercise the right. Jacobs went on to note that despite the seventeenth-century provision, modern England had strict gun control—overlooking the fact the English Bill of Rights was a statute that could be easily modified or replaced with new legislation. Finally, the Jacobs opinion went beyond a discussion of the New Jersey statute, arguing that *Miller* allowed Congress broad powers to regulate in the firearms-control area as long as it didn't interfere with the organized militia of the states. *Jacobs's* views on the Second Amendment and congressional power in light of the amendment certainly went further than anything said in the McReynolds opinion in *Miller* or even the holdings in the two circuit court follow-on cases *Tot* and *Cases.* It could probably best be viewed as dicta, not central to the issues in front of the New Jersey Supreme Court. But it was powerful dicta indicating the direction that the judiciary would take in this area for the better part of the next three decades.[87]

If *Burton v. Sills* was not an appropriate occasion in which to consider the Second Amendment and how it might limit congressional power, the Gun Control Act of 1968 provided a number of cases directly on point. As intended, the provision in the federal statute prohibiting gun possession by individuals with felony records brought about the arrest and conviction of criminal offenders. Frequently the mere possession of firearms was only one and frequently the least of the offenses committed by these individuals. A number of these cases got to the federal circuit courts of appeal. The pattern was usually simple: An individual was arrested, frequently in the process of committing a crime. The individual was charged with possession of a firearm, in addition to other crimes. Sometimes the firearms charge might be leveraged to induce a plea bargain, that is, the defendant was told that the gun possession charge could be dropped if he pleaded guilty to the other offenses, or some portion of the other offenses. If the defendant was actually tried and convicted of the firearms possession charge, the matter usually ended there. But some of those who were convicted had the legal resources to pursue appeals. Counsel on appeal would usually raise a number of issues, for example, that the defendant's Fourth Amendment search and seizure rights were violated (i.e., there was no probable cause for a search), or that the interrogation violated the defendant's Fifth Amendment right against self-incrimination or his Sixth Amendment right to counsel. Along with these and various additional statutory and procedural claims, attorneys representing defendants in criminal cases or petitioners on appeal would also raise Second Amendment claims. The statutory prohibition on felons possessing firearms was a violation of the right of the people to keep and bear arms.

The courts weren't buying it. Invariably the courts upon hearing these claims would declare that the defendant's activities were not protected by the Second Amendment. Some of the cases, like the 1971 Sixth Circuit Court of Appeals case *Stevens v. the United States*, flatly denied that the Second Amendment had anything to do with the right of individuals. It was, according to the opinion written by Judge W. Harry Phillips, designed to protect the right of states to maintain their organized militias, nothing more. Interestingly enough, the Phillips opinion did include an appendix citing hearings before the Senate Judiciary Committee that led to the 1968 legislation in which a number of senators who supported the new law indicated that they did not want to infringe on the Second Amendment rights of the American public. Several other federal circuit courts, including the Fourth Circuit in *US v. Johnson* and the Seventh Circuit in *US v. McCutcheon,* also took a fairly absolutist position; that the Second Amendment did not protect the right of individuals, only the right of states to maintain militias or the right of the organized militia to be armed.[88]

Other courts were less sure. The Eighth Circuit in upholding Minnesota resident Dale Einar Synnes's conviction for carrying a revolver after a felony conviction in violation of the 1968 act, noted that a prohibition on felons possessing weapons did not obstruct the maintenance of a well-regulated militia. Judge Gerald William Heaney, who wrote the court's opinion, did not speculate on whether such a ban might be unconstitutional if applied to the population at large. Later the same year, 1971, Judge Heaney in writing an opinion upholding the conviction of firearms dealer Audry Keith Decker for failure to maintain proper records of his transactions, as required by the 1968 Gun Control Act, cited *Miller,* and noted: "The record keeping requirements . . . bear an even more tenuous relationship to the Second Amendment than did the statute involving Miller. Thus, in light of defendant's failure to present any evidence indicating a conflict between [the record keeping requirements] and the maintenance of a well-regulated militia, we decline to hold that the statute violated the Second Amendment."[89]

Again, the Heaney opinion gave no clear indication of his view of the scope of the Second Amendment and how it might or might not apply to the population at large. In one sense Heaney was doing precisely what a judge is supposed to do; resolve the case before the court. Neither *Synne* nor *Decker* involved general prohibitions that limited the public's access to firearms. Both defendants had thrown in their Second Amendment claims amid a myriad of other constitutional and statutory defenses. Judge Heaney, unlike New Jersey Supreme Court Justice Jacobs or Sixth Circuit Judge Philipps, did not feel the need to issue expansive opinions that went beyond the cases before him and the existing Supreme Court jurisprudence.[90]

Both the jurists that used firearms cases as an occasion to expand beyond *Miller* and issue opinions that would read an individual right out of the Second Amendment, and jurists like Heaney who took a more conservative approach did very little in the way of analyzing *Miller* and what the 1939 Supreme Court case might have to say to questions concerning the scope of the Second

Amendment. The circuit courts in *Tot* and *Cases* in the immediate wake of *Miller* felt the need to wrestle with the McReynolds opinion (Could the decision really mean that all military weapons were protected? When might an individual be able to claim that private use of a firearm was practice or preparation for military service?). The courts examining Second Amendment claims in the decade or so after the passage of the Gun Control Act of 1968 did no analysis of *Miller* beyond mechanically borrowing McReynolds's language saying that a firearms restriction had to be considered in light of whether it interfered with "the efficiency of a well-regulated militia." As the cases generally involved people with felony records engaged in continuing criminal activity, and who were contesting their convictions on multiple statutory and constitutional theories, little effort was made to examine the only Supreme Court precedent directly on point.

If the Second Amendment claims of criminals caught with firearms could be readily dismissed, the case of Francis J. Warin posed a bit of a problem. Warin was not a criminal. He was an engineer who designed a submachine gun somewhat similar to the one that had been used by some Special Forces units in Vietnam. He designed and had a working model of his weapon, which he possessed without paying the requisite federal tax. His actions were a violation of the 1934 National Firearms Act, now incorporated into the 1968 Gun Control Act. Warin intended to make a test case of the statutory requirement requiring that automatic weapons be registered and that their owners pay a $200 tax. The safe way to bring such a challenge would have been to have brought a civil suit challenging the constitutionality of the gun-control statutes. Warin had chosen a somewhat quixotic path: get arrested for possession of the unregistered submachinegun and argue as a defense that the federal requirements were unconstitutional.[91]

Warin was convicted in a bench trial in the US Court for the Northern District of Ohio. He appealed to the Sixth Circuit Court of Appeals. The court's opinion, authored by Judge Frederick Pierce Lively, discounted Warin's claim that the Second Amendment protected his right to have arms as a member of Ohio's sedentary militia. The Lively opinion contended that the Second Amendment protected a collective right and that the militia whose right to bear arms was protected was the organized, not the unorganized, militia. But the circuit court judge felt the need to write an opinion that would uphold the federal statute even under an individualist interpretation of the constitutional provision. Lively noted that even where the Second Amendment was applicable, it was not an "absolute barrier to Congressional regulation of firearms." The opinion quoted *Tot*, noting that "weapon bearing was never treated as anything like an absolute right at common law. It was regulated by statute as to time and place." The opinion went on to note that even the First Amendment, which occupied a more preferred place in American jurisprudence than the Second, was subject to reasonable regulation. Lively's opinion also noted that federal statutes did not tax the keeping and bearing of arms, but instead taxed the transfer of firearms. Warin's conviction was upheld. His petition for certiorari to the Supreme Court was denied.[92]

Warin's case, like the cases involving defendants who offered Second Amendment defenses to their violations of the 1968 Gun Control Act, was unlikely to cause any judge to do any heavy lifting to resuscitate the Second Amendment. Judges for the most part are cautious, pragmatic people. A party that came into court with a wild claim that the Second Amendment required society to allow convicted criminals to possess guns or that automatic weapons be essentially unregulated was not likely to produce new case law expanding the Second Amendment rights of the American people. Such a claim was more likely to produce exactly what it did produce: a jurisprudence claiming that the right to keep and bear arms essentially did not exist, or that, even grudgingly granting the right, governmental authorities had considerable leeway in regulating the right. But what about other restrictions, those that limited the right of ordinary people to own ordinary guns in their homes? A 1981 ordinance in Morton Grove, Illinois, would test how the courts might react.

Morton Grove had passed an ordinance banning handguns within municipal limits. Victor Quilici brought a suit challenging the statute's constitutionality on grounds that it violated the Illinois Constitution's provision protecting the right to keep and bear arms, and that it also violated the Second and Ninth Amendments to the US Constitution. The suit was originally filed in state court, but because the Second and Ninth Amendments involved federal questions, attorneys for Morton Grove were able to remove the case to the US District Court for the Northern District of Illinois. The district court upheld the ordinance. Victor Quilici, who was acting as both complainant and attorney, along with others, appealed to the Seventh Circuit Court of Appeals. Among the attorneys supporting Quilici's appeal was the former civil rights worker who had exchanged shots with the Ku Klux Klan, Don B. Kates Jr.[93]

The 2–1 majority opinion authored by Seventh Circuit Court judge William Bauer rejected Quilici's claims. His opinion contended that the Illinois constitutional provision protecting the right to bear arms had language indicating that that right was subject to the police power and was not absolute. In examining the Second Amendment claims, Bauer noted that *Presser* was still the law and that the Second Amendment did not apply to the states. His opinion also made a somewhat undeveloped claim that handguns were not militia weapons and would not be protected under the *Miller* doctrine. Considering that handguns were common in both military and police inventories and that *Cases* had recognized their military potential, that section of the opinion was puzzling. It can be considered a reflection of the tendency of the federal courts in the era not to give credence to Second Amendment claims even when there was a reluctant concession that an individual right might be at issue. The dissenting opinion by Judge John Coffey was mainly grounded in Illinois statutory and constitutional law. It made only a fleeting reference to the federal Constitution, placing the right to have a handgun in the home for protection more in the unenumerated right to privacy than in the Second Amendment.[94]

Victor Quilici and his associates applied to the Supreme Court for certiorari, discretionary review. His application was supported by a brief filed by the NRA's general counsel. Certiorari was denied. The battle for certiorari was more than a little ironic. The Quilici camp, having lost in the Seventh Circuit Court of Appeals, hoped that the Supreme Court would take the case, reverse Judge Bauer's decision, and declare that the Second Amendment applied to the states and that it protected a right to own handguns. Morton Grove and its supporters, which included a brief filed by Handgun Control Inc., did not want the Supreme Court to take up the Illinois town's handgun ban and possibly reverse the decision of the Seventh Circuit. The irony in this struggle over certiorari is that both sides, undoubtedly unknown to them, were courting a result in the high court directly inimical to their interests. From public statements that were made later in the 1990s we now know that Chief Justice Warren Burger and Associate Justice Lewis Powell were hostile to the individual rights view of the Second Amendment, and unless their views were radically different in 1983 when the Morton Grove case would have been heard and decided, they would almost certainly have voted to sustain the municipal pistol prohibition.[95]

Other justices who would have decided the Morton Grove case also opposed the individual rights view of the Second Amendment. In the 1972 case of *Adams v. Williams*, a case involving the conviction of a defendant by a Connecticut state court for illegal possession of a handgun, Associate Justice

Thurgood Marshall joined Associate Justice William O. Douglas in dissenting from the majority ruling stating that the defendant's pistol was found pursuant to a valid search and seizure. Douglas and Marshall argued that the majority opinion "watered down" the American public's Fourth Amendment protections, and that if any "watering down" was to be done if should be done to the Second, not the Fourth Amendment. The Douglas-Marshall opinion went on to cite *Miller* and state, "There is no reason why all pistols should not be barred to everyone except police."[96] While Douglas had left the Court in 1975 and had died in 1980, Marshall, who was very much alive and still on the Court, would have been a likely vote to sustain the Morton Grove ordinance. Attorney and independent scholar David Hardy in his exploration of Associate Justice Harry Blackmun's papers found that in considering the certiorari petition in *Quilici* and in the first draft of his majority opinion in the 1980 case of *Lewis v. United States*, which involved a convicted felon in possession of a firearm, the Minnesota jurist was inclined toward a collective reading of the Second Amendment. Blackmun didn't have a chance to express his views on the amendment because of drafting disagreements in *Lewis* and the Court's decision not to grant certiorari in *Quilici*. Had certiorari been granted, there would have been at least four votes and probably more to sustain the Bauer ruling.[97]

So why did the notion that the Constitution protected a right to bear arms, a notion that seemed to be endorsed implicitly if perhaps somewhat obliquely by postwar justices as diverse as Hugo Black, Frank Murphy, Wiley Rutledge, and William Douglas in their support for total incorporation in *Adamson,* and by John Marshall Harlan II in his enumeration of the rights of the American people in *Poe,* fare so badly in the courts after the passage of the 1968 Gun Control Act? Why did it only narrowly escape being read out of the Constitution altogether by the Supreme Court in *Quilici?* It would be easy enough to chalk the summary dismissals and cursory treatment of Second Amendment claims in the federal courts to judicial bias. Courts tend to reflect elite opinion. This includes notions of good policy as reflected in articles in the leading journals in the social sciences and well-reasoned legal arguments found in the better law reviews. It also includes the articles, commentaries, and reviews in the national press and magazines that seemingly reflect the best thinking on the nation's politics and culture, and by which judges often gauge the boundaries of respectable opinion. Jurists are also influenced by the constituencies that support or appear to support particular legal or constitutional positions.

Few of these seemed to support judicial intervention to protect the right to bear arms. The nation's jurists reflected that seeming consensus.

But something more was at work. Forces supporting the right to bear arms had not put together the ingredients necessary for a successful case. Landmark constitutional litigation, the kind that results in a case where the Supreme Court recognizes a right for the first time—that is, actually declares that a law or governmental practice is unconstitutional—requires the coming together of different elements. Such a case usually requires a cadre of lawyers skilled in constitutional advocacy. Constitutional advocacy, like appellate advocacy more generally, is a skill developed from experience. It is one that most lawyers do not have. A potential landmark constitutional case should also have a theory of the constitutional issue or right in question that has gained acceptance from a respectable contingent of the practicing bar and the academic world. Finally, landmark constitutional litigation usually requires a good argument that the proposed legal remedy, overturning a statute or governmental practice, is good policy, or at the very least that it would not be a policy disaster. The conventional wisdom of the elites of the bar and governmental policymakers at the beginning of the 1980s was that the Constitution was never meant to impede gun control or indeed gun prohibition and that such policies could significantly reduce crime, particularly criminal homicides, with no downside. These views did not rest on particularly firm foundations, but nonetheless they were the conventional wisdom at the time. They would have to be effectively challenged if successful Second Amendment litigation were to occur.

# 5. Shifting Tides

*Quilici* demonstrated that supporters of the individual rights reading of the Second Amendment had not put together the ingredients necessary for successful constitutional litigation. Litigation that would vindicate the notion that the Second Amendment protected a right of individuals, that it actually set some judicially enforceable limits on the government's ability to regulate firearms, seemed remote in 1982 when the Supreme Court denied certiorari in Victor Quilici's case. The conventional wisdom seemed to be firmly against the courts opening up what to many appeared to be a legal can of worms, the constitutional provision guaranteeing the people the right to keep and bear arms. The better voices on the bench and in the bar were arguing that the provision should be read as not applying to individuals at all. Respected policymakers were arguing that the path to reducing the nation's high rate of homicide and other violent crimes lay in strict, even prohibitory gun control, not in some late twentieth-century revival of a doctrine best left in the eighteenth. The national press and major opinion journals largely championed these views, often vigorously and repeatedly.

For these views to be challenged, there would have to be some changes in thinking. Respected voices in law and public policy would have to go against what had become the conventional wisdom concerning the Second Amendment and the linkage between large-scale private gun ownership and criminal violence. There would have to be major reconsiderations in three areas. First, there would have to be a greater public recognition on the parts of historians and other scholars who studied law and the Constitution of the essential accuracy of the individualist view of the Second Amendment. Second, a greater willingness on the part of particularly conservative scholars and jurists to acknowledge the historical legitimacy of the claim that the Fourteenth Amendment was meant to apply the Bill of Rights to the states would have to develop. And finally, there needed to be evidence from the empirical sciences that the American practice of allowing robust public gun ownership was not responsible for the nation's high rates of crime and violence. Such evidence would allow jurists to consider the evidence supporting a private right to bear arms.

They could do so free from the fear that a ruling that the Constitution placed limits on potential gun-control legislation would produce an unmitigated criminological disaster, an increase in homicide and other violence caused by people with guns. In 1982, none of these new ways of thinking seemed particularly likely to gain a large number of adherents on the part of respected commentators on law and public policy, much less to become the conventional wisdom. Without these new ways of thinking, any effort at Second Amendment litigation was quixotic, ill-advised, and likely doomed to fail.

And yet, unlikely as it may have seemed in the early 1980s, the seeds of an intellectual counterrevolution were being sown, often by scholars who were working, at least initially, unknown to each other. Some historians and legal scholars were beginning to reexamine what had been a neglected area: the history and thinking behind the Second Amendment adopted at the end of the eighteenth century. Other scholars were examining the right to bear arms and its connection to the Fourteenth Amendment. This latter exploration was in part a continuation of the incorporation debate and, in part, the result of a renewed interest in and reinterpretation of the Reconstruction era informed by the civil rights movement of the 1960s. We are going to explore some of this scholarship that was starting to emerge in the 1980s, though we won't have the chance to explore this scholarship in the depth that we would like. We also won't have a chance to do justice to the scholars and advocates, some of whom were quite able, who argued contrary points of view. Our purpose here is not to advocate for this new scholarship but instead to show how the ideas that were being put forth started out as minority voices in different scholarly communities and ultimately became conventional wisdom—or at least gained enough intellectual respectability to make academic and judicial reexamination conceivable. These academic and judicial reconsiderations ultimately made *Heller* and *McDonald* possible.

But that kind of reexamination seemed unlikely at the beginning of the decade. Still, if supporters of a constitutional right of private citizens to keep and bear arms did not have the kind of intellectual support likely to persuade appellate courts, they nonetheless had considerable ability to influence the nation's laws and public policies. They could block gun-control legislation and indeed pass positive measures providing statutory protections for gun owners and would-be gun owners. Their efforts were helped along by the absolutism of the gun-control movement in the 1970s and 1980s. The movement's public advocates often rejected the very idea of gun ownership for self-defense. This had been demonstrated in the Massachusetts referendum to ban handguns in 1976. Gun owners' groups had the ability to pressure state legislatures, resulting in the blocking of many gun-control measures. It would also take positive forms, such as the enactment or strengthening of state constitutional provisions protecting the citizen's right to have arms. And, perhaps most significantly, the gun owners' groups were instrumental in having state legislatures pass preemption measures limiting the ability of municipalities to pass local firearms restrictions. Activists in these groups also had the ability to persuade their fellow citizens on the importance of private gun ownership, particularly for personal protection. These strengths would be shown again in California in 1982 and would play a role in shaping the gun-control debate in the coming decade.

The gun-control issue would heat up in San Francisco in June 1982, when that city's board of supervisors voted by a 6–4 margin to ban handguns in the city. The measure passed with the support of then mayor Dianne Feinstein, who had become a supporter of a prohibition on handguns in part because of the assassinations of San Francisco mayor George Moscone and Harvey Milk, a member of the city's board of supervisors, some four years earlier. The municipal measure required, with a few exceptions, the surrender of privately owned pistols. One of the surrendered handguns was a .38-caliber revolver owned by Feinstein herself for protection. The ban was successfully challenged on the grounds that it conflicted with a 1969 statute that declared that firearms regulation was the province of the state government, not localities and municipalities. Then state attorney general George Deukmejian, who was planning to run for governor in the fall, had his office issue an opinion that the San Francisco ordinance was invalid under the state statute.[1]

For supporters of strict restrictions on pistol ownership, the decision by a California appellate court overturning the San Francisco ban doubtless brought a new urgency to their support for a statewide initiative to freeze handgun ownership in the West Coast state. Also introduced in 1982, the initiative Proposition 15 would have required the registration of all handguns then owned and a prohibition on the sale of new pistols or revolvers. An individual who wanted to purchase a handgun after the adoption of the initiative would have to buy one from the already registered stock of handguns, not a new one. Initial polling showed majority support for the measure. State and national newspapers ran articles supporting Proposition 15, heralding the initiative as the gateway to more far-reaching gun control measures nationwide.

It failed. When the ballot was held on November 2, 1982, it was rejected by a margin of nearly 63 to 37 percent. Some supporters of the proposition acknowledged that the NRA and its allies had simply done a better job of mobilizing grassroots constituencies to fight the measure. Pete Shields, president of Handgun Control Inc., acknowledged his disappointment but denied that the proposition's failure was a defeat. He was quoted in the *Los Angeles Times* the day after the referendum as saying, "We came as close today as we have ever come to effective handgun control."[2]

Shield's efforts to put the best face possible on the failed initiative notwithstanding, the failure of Proposition 15 and the California appellate court's earlier rejection of San Francisco's handgun ban reiterated some hard truths to gun-control advocates. Handgun bans, as opposed to various kinds of regulation, would not meet with statewide approval, even if they might be supported in some communities. Gun owners' groups had the ability to sway large segments of the public, even among those who were generally sympathetic to gun control, when the question was framed as a question of prohibition and not control. Polls on the gun issue often understated the support for gun ownership, or at least understated how many people would vote to support private handgun ownership when confronted with an actual referendum calling for a total ban.

These hard truths contributed to the minimal success of the gun-control movement's initial aim—severe restrictions on and the ultimate elimination of private handgun ownership. If Pete Shields in 1976 could envision a national campaign that would begin with registration and in less than a decade produce a ban on pistol and revolver ownership, the hard realities of the politics and sociology of gun control proved otherwise. Gun owners' organizations had become more sophisticated and explicitly political in the 1970s. In that decade the NRA had added two new branches, the Institute for Legislative Action and the Political Victory Fund, to lobby legislatures and to reward sympathetic politicians. State preemption legislation became a major goal. Its success probably prevented a number of cities from successfully passing handgun bans or near bans throughout the nation, as indeed California's preemption statute had prevented such in San Francisco. The NRA would vigorously pursue such legislation in the 1980s. By the end of that decade some forty-one of the fifty states had passed preemption statutes. And it was not just legislators who were open to persuasion. The ability of the NRA, its state affiliates, and allied organizations to mobilize voters not only in small-town and rural areas but also urban residents who wanted handguns for self-defense made referendums problematic vehicles for bringing about pistol bans.[3]

The goal of handgun prohibition would remain elusive. It would ultimately meet with success only in the District of Columbia, three Chicago suburbs—Evanston, Morton Grove, and Oak Park—and, through a municipal ordinance enacted in 1982, in the Windy City itself. The policy prescription vigorously championed by the United States Conference of Mayors, the TV networks, the nation's major newspapers, and much of the legal establishment in the 1970s and 1980s would remain an outlier in American life. The supporters of an individualist reading of the Second Amendment might not have had the tools for success in constitutional litigation, but they nonetheless were able to exert a powerful influence on the nation's laws and customs.

The success the NRA and allied organizations had in thwarting large-scale handgun prohibition would cause the gun-control movement to shift focus. Handgun Control Inc., which would become the most successful of the gun-control groups of the era, changed its stated goals. While groups like the National Coalition to Ban Handguns would continue to prescribe pistol prohibition as the solution to the nation's problems of crime and violence, Handgun Control Inc. would in the 1980s shift its emphasis, urging measures like waiting periods, background checks, and bans on handguns that it insisted were particularly dangerous, especially the so-called Saturday-night specials. Handgun Control Inc. never turned its back on the basic philosophy of the gun-control movement: that guns in civilian hands for self-defense were dangerous, somewhat illegitimate, and should largely be discouraged. But the organization did move away from Pete Shield's earlier frank admission that its ultimate goal was handgun prohibition. The organization would gain an important new recruit in 1981: Sarah Brady. Sarah Brady was the wife of presidential spokesman James Brady, who had been severely wounded and paralyzed in an assassination attempt on President Ronald Reagan. The assassination attempt, the resulting paralysis of her husband, and an incident where her five-year-old son had found a loaded pistol carelessly left in a family friend's truck, turned Sarah Brady into a gun-control activist and the public face of Handgun Control Inc. from 1981 until her death in 2015.[4]

The tragic wounding of James Brady and the subsequent enlistment of Sarah Brady into the gun-control movement further enhanced the tendency of the national press to support gun-control efforts. James Brady, as press secretary, had been a popular spokesman for the Reagan administration, and his wounding at the hands of John Hinckley Jr. naturally increased sympathy for the Brady family. Sarah Brady proved to be a sympathetic spokeswoman for the gun-control movement and one who could make her case to a press that was already largely in agreement with the cause of gun control. The sympathies of the press were reflected in newspaper editorials. They were also on display on television news broadcasts, which often showed pictures of handguns during reports on crimes, sometimes even when the crime under discussion did not involve a shooting at all. These sympathies could also be seen in the drawings of political cartoonist Herbert Lawrence Block, whose drawings in the *Washington Post* and other newspapers under the name "Herblock" frequently portrayed the NRA in gangster costumes complete with guns hidden in violin cases.[5]

The support the press had for further gun control was part of a broader support that the effort to increase firearms restrictions had gained among the nation's elites since the 1960s. The nation's bar and medical associations, national police groups, and most civil rights and civil liberties associations had all gone on record as supporting increased controls. And yet, as political scientist Kristin Goss has noted, gun-control advocates had somehow failed to transform their elite support into the kind of grassroots social movement that might bring about major political change.[6] That was by and large not the case with the NRA and its allies. The movement toward statewide preemption of firearms controls, the defeat of the Massachusetts and California referenda, and the ability to hold gun-control measures at bay in Congress and in state legislatures demonstrated an ability on the part of gun owners and their supporters to go a long way toward protecting the right to keep and bear arms, even in the face of strong hostility by the nation's elites.

But a right to bear arms that might be protected by the courts? That seemed to be too much to be hoped for even by many champions of the right. The right enjoyed popular support; it was true. Polls consistently showed that the public believed in the individual rights interpretation of the amendment even in the 1970s and early 1980s, when opinion leaders solemnly assured the nation that the Second Amendment only pertained to militias, not individual citizens.[7] Popular support remained strong, even in the face of authoritative disapproval and judicial reticence. The idea that the population had a right to bear arms had had a long-standing resonance in the American mind. It had been readily acknowledged a generation earlier, even if only in an offhand or indirect manner, by leading legal scholars like Roscoe Pound and by Supreme

Court justices Hugo Black and William O. Douglas, among others. It was part of the popular culture. The idea that the Second Amendment protected an individual's right to have arms was often taught in social studies classes in public schools.

If the popular acceptance of the view that the right to bear arms was indeed a real right that applied to individual citizens failed to excite much interest on the part of the nation's jurists in the early 1980s, it was nonetheless a view that legislators would ignore at their peril. Gun ownership was common, the right to bear arms was widely agreed upon, and many legislators from both parties shared their constituents' view that the American people, broadly speaking, had a right to have arms. The legislative victories of the NRA and its allies on the state and federal levels represented a strong, although by no means unanimous, consensus that gun ownership was a normal and proper part of the national culture. To that end, Congress and state legislatures had long acted with the idea that the rights of gun owners had to be protected even when addressing the concerns that had motivated particular gun-control statutes. Congress had demonstrated these concerns with the National Firearms Act of 1934 and subsequent gun-control legislation in 1938 and 1968. It showed an inclination to protect firearms ownership and a concern with the right to bear arms in 1941 legislation authorizing wartime requisition of property. If the Second Amendment was not the subject of judicial enforcement, it nonetheless seemed to act as something of a moral and political check on Congress and many state legislatures as well.

## SECOND THOUGHTS

But was the common assumption that the Second Amendment was meant to protect the right of the American people as individuals based on a sound reading of the text, history, or judicial precedent surrounding the amendment? It had in many ways been a largely unchallenged assumption on the part of jurists and legal commentators from men like William Rawle and St. George Tucker, who wrote almost immediately after the Bill of Rights had been adopted, to John Marshall Harlan II, who casually mentioned the right to bear arms in his concurrence in the 1961 case involving contraception, *Poe v. Ullman*. But the traditional assumption that the Constitution protected the citizen's right to have weapons for self-defense and defense of the community had received relatively little in the way of serious examination by modern constitutional scholars or practicing members of the bench or bar. The law review literature on the topic had been brief, indeed cursory. Early twentieth-century Princeton University political scientist Edward Corwin always included a paragraph on the Second Amendment in his regularly updated treatise *The Constitution and What It Means Today.* He discussed the amendment as protecting a right of individuals, subject to reasonable regulation.[8] Historians would at times make passing references to the amendment in their discussions of constitutional history. In their general treatises on constitutional law, scholars John Nowak and Laurence Tribe mentioned the Second Amendment in brief footnotes as a constitutional provision that was meant to protect state militias from federal interference. The first editions of both treatises, which would become standard references in law schools, were published in 1978. But these and other brief mentions aside, the Second Amendment by and large was a topic largely typically bypassed by the nation's constitutional scholars.[9]

The reason for this neglect was simple. Constitutional commentary tends to follow, or at times immediately precede, constitutional controversies that are likely to end up as court cases. The First Amendment would come alive as a subject for academic exploration and debate after World War I, when the Supreme Court began to embark on a course of First Amendment jurisprudence in response to speech and press restrictions imposed first by the federal and later state governments. Scholars renewed their interest in the Fourteenth Amendment and its potential implications for the actions of state governments after World War II, when the questions of racial discrimination and applications of the Bill of Rights to the states got closer scrutiny by the Supreme Court and the lower federal courts. The implications of the Fourth, Fifth, and Sixth Amendments for treatment of defendants in criminal cases provided an impetus for new academic exploration on protections for the accused in eighteenth-century America and at English common law.

This process started late with the Second Amendment. The doctrine put forth in *Presser* in 1886 that the Second Amendment only limited the federal government, combined with relatively little in the way of federal firearms legislation, created a virtual absence of serious federal case law on the right to bear arms. Like its constitutional next-door neighbor, the Third Amendment, which protects citizens from forced quartering of troops in private homes, the topic of the Second Amendment's meaning failed to excite much interest on the part of legal scholars, historians, or political scientists, the academic communities from which most constitutional commentators are drawn. There was, to be sure, a state jurisprudence interpreting state constitutional provisions guaranteeing the right to bear arms. But it is probably fair to say that that area of exploration was doubtless seen as something of an intellectual backwater unlikely to attract talented constitutional scholars who were looking to have an impact on high-profile controversies.

The growth of the gun-control movement in the wake of the turmoil of the 1960s and the insistence by many of that movement's leading lights that large-scale prohibition was the answer, and that the Constitution provided no obstacle to that objective, would change this intellectual neglect, but only slowly. Robert Sprecher's 1965 essay "The Lost Amendment" in the *American Bar Journal* provided a pioneering examination of the roots of the right to bear arms that went beyond traditional discussions of the adoption of the American Bill of Rights in the eighteenth century and the English Bill of Rights in the seventeenth. Sprecher helped introduce a discussion of classical republican theory and its influence on the right to bear arms, tracing the concept of the citizen soldier and the armed population from the writings of Plato and Aristotle in ancient Athens to the writings of early modern continental philosophers including Machiavelli and Rousseau. Sprecher noted that the linkage between a republic of free citizens and a broadly armed population serving as a militia had long been a part of continental as well as English political thought. While recognizing that the militia and the right to arms were intertwined in the Second Amendment, Sprecher also saw the right as belonging to the individual citizen. He cautioned: "But history does not warrant concluding that it necessarily follows from the pairing of the concepts that a person has a right to bear arms solely in his function as a member of the militia."[10]

Sprecher's writings and the writings of others notwithstanding, the debate on the Second Amendment would remain very much in the minor leagues in the world of constitutional commentary during the gun-control debates of the 1970s and at the beginning of the 1980s. Constitutional commentary, at least the kind of constitutional commentary that courts pay attention to, tends, for better and worse, to be the province of our legal and academic elites. Courts and students of law and related subjects pay attention to articles in the major reviews published by the leading law schools or in the more prominent journals in history and political science. Discussions of the Second Amendment in the legal literature was scattered at best, often brief articles in not particularly prominent law journals by advocates, on one side or the other of the controversy. Frequently the advocates, while lawyers, had relatively little background in constitutional history or related fields. The Second Amendment would largely remain in obscurity, the subject of occasional commentary and polemical broadsides in the popular press, but only rarely serious, systematic analysis by constitutional scholars.

That would begin to change with publication of the report "The Right to Keep and Bear Arms" by the Senate Judiciary Subcommittee in February 1982. Co-chaired by senators Orrin Hatch (R-UT) Dennis De Concini (D-AZ), the subcommittee took a distinctly individualistic view of the Constitution's guarantee of a right to keep and bear arms:

> The conclusion is thus inescapable that the history, concept and wording of the second amendment to the Constitution of the United States, as well as its interpretation by every major commentator and court in the first half-century after its ratification, indicates that what is projected is an individual right of a private citizen to own and carry firearms in a peaceful manner.[11]

The report's statement was powerful: a subcommittee of the US Senate was officially reading the Second Amendment's history in a way that said that the NRA and its supporters were essentially correct. And the subcommittee's report went further, stating that the history of the Fourteenth Amendment showed that its proponents intended to protect the right to bear arms from state infringement. No dissenting statements were issued on the findings concerning the Second Amendment by subcommittee members even though the subcommittee included strong gun-control supporters, senators Charles Mathias (R-MD), Edward M. Kennedy (D-MA), and Howard Metzenbaum (D-OH). It should be noted as well that staunch conservative senator John P. East (R-NC), who also served on the subcommittee, did not dissent from the subcommittee's finding that the Fourteenth Amendment was meant to protect the right to bear arms from state infringement. That view was at odds with then prevailing views among many conservatives, including the expressed position of then attorney general Edward Meese III, who as head of the Justice Department under President Reagan would criticize the Supreme Court's process of applying the Bill of Rights to the states through the Fourteenth Amendment.[12]

The report's appendix included essays on both sides of the constitutional controversy, including contributions by Michael Beard and Samuel Fields of the National Coalition to Ban Handguns; Roy G. Weatherup, a practicing attorney; James Featherstone, Richard Gardiner, and Robert Dowlut of the NRA General Counsel's Office; John Levin of the Chicago Kent Law School; and David Hardy, a practicing attorney who would as an independent scholar become a major contributor to the Second Amendment debate.[13]

Without slighting the other contributions, it is fair to say that Stephen P. Halbrook's essay would provide a somewhat new dimension for and prove most important to the development of the Second Amendment as a field of academic inquiry. Halbrook, who had earned a PhD in philosophy from Florida State University and was also a graduate of the Georgetown University Law Center, was a practicing attorney who had previously taught political and social philosophy at Tuskegee and Howard Universities. His experience in those historically Black universities had helped spur his interest in the linkage between the efforts to eradicate racial caste and the legacy of slavery during Reconstruction and the right to bear arms. His essay, excerpted from a larger article that appeared the previous year in the *George Mason University Law Review*, discussed the Black codes passed by Southern states in the wake of the Civil War. He did so with particular emphasis on the efforts of Southern governments to disarm freedmen. While the Black codes and the efforts to disarm the newly freed Afro-American population had previously been examined by historians, Halbrook's discussion went further in connecting that history to the Fourteenth Amendment through both an examination of the debates on the amendment itself and debates on contemporaneous and near-contemporaneous civil rights legislation. Halbrook made a strong case for incorporation and, indeed, the case that some of the best evidence in support of incorporation could be seen in the remarks of members of the Thirty-Ninth Congress concerning what they saw as the unconstitutional disarmament of the newly free Black population. After Halbrook's essay and subsequent writings on this theme, it would be difficult to seriously discuss the Constitution and the right to keep and bear arms without discussing the Fourteenth Amendment as well as the Second.[14]

Halbrook's contribution to the Senate subcommittee would be followed two years later, in 1984, by his study *That Everyman Be Armed: The Evolution of a Constitutional Right*, the first book-length treatment of the history of the Second Amendment. Like Sprecher, Halbrook discussed the right to bear arms not only as a product of Anglo-American constitutional history but also as a phenomenon that was heir to classical and early modern republican political theory concerning the armed citizen and the proper balance of power between the citizen and the state. But probably Halbrook's greatest contribution to the Second Amendment debate lay less in his linking of the American notion of the right to bear arms to the classical and modern republican traditions and more in his highlighting the comments of late eighteenth- and early nineteenth-century American statesmen and jurists on the right to bear arms. Halbrook's evidence that an individual's right to have arms enjoyed the support of both Federalists and anti-Federalists during the debates on the adoption of the Constitution and the amendments now known as the Bill of Rights, and that authoritative post-enactment commentators like William Rawle and St. George Tucker saw the Second Amendment in individualistic terms, posed real problems for those who adhered to what was at the time the dominant narrative that the Second Amendment simply applied to the organized militia. The inquiries that Halbrook made in the Senate subcommittee report would continue in *That Everyman Be Armed* and in subsequent scholarship.[15]

The Senate subcommittee report proved to be something of a milestone. It moved the Second Amendment debate from sporadic appearances in largely minor journals and purely polemical precincts to explicit consideration within the halls of Congress. The report also suggested the possibility of congressional enforcement of the Second Amendment, something that Halbrook's essay informed the reader had occurred in the Reconstruction era.

Four years later Congress would in fact take efforts to do exactly that with the passage of the Firearms Owners Protection Act. The 1986 legislation, sponsored in the Senate by James McClure (R-ID) and in the House by Harold Volkmer (D-MO), made modifications to the 1968 Gun Control Act. These modifications of a previous federal act were well within Congress's traditional role in firearms legislation. But the act did something more that went beyond Congress's traditional scope in this area: it provided a limited protection from state firearms laws for travelers passing through a state where the traveler's firearm might be banned or require a license. It was a small measure but a further indication of the possibility of congressional enforcement suggested by the 1982 Senate Judiciary Subcommittee report.[16]

That report also served as an indication that the debate over the meaning of the right to keep and bear arms would become increasingly sophisticated, attracting a new generation of advocates and scholars who would bring fresh perspectives to the debate. The year following the report, Second Amendment scholarship entered the law review big leagues with the publication of Don

B. Kates Jr.'s "Handgun Prohibition and the Original Meaning of the Second Amendment" in the *Michigan Law Review*. If the business of publishing in major law reviews is an elitist endeavor, then Kates's publication was an indication that the Second Amendment was a field now ripe for exploration by "serious thinkers." The *Michigan Law Review* is one of the nation's premier legal journals. Kates, the formal civil rights worker mentioned in earlier chapters, was a graduate of Yale Law School. In the 1970s he had been on the faculty at the St. Louis University School of Law. Very much a man of the left at the time, Kates had worked for radical attorney William Kunstler and saw part of his mission in life as convincing liberals, particularly those in the legal academy, of the essential soundness of the individual rights view of the Second Amendment. He had earlier published a book on that theme titled *Restricting Handguns: The Liberal Skeptics Speak Out.*[17]

Kates dealt with a range of issues on why the Second Amendment should be viewed as protecting a right of individuals and specifically why personal self-defense was an integral part of the protection provided. His discussion went through historical analyses of the Second and Fourteenth Amendments and into contemporary political and criminological issues. Kates noted, among other things, the irony that in contemporary American society liberals who ordinarily took a very broad view of civil liberties were often quite repressive when considering the rights of gun owners, while conservatives who frequently took a narrow view of constitutional rights and civil liberties were ironically willing to take a more generous view of civil rights connected to the right to own a gun. Kates also weighed in on the then current issue of banning handguns, arguing that a ban on handguns would have unintended consequences, including greater likelihood of unintended injuries or deaths if handguns were banned and urban residents sought to defend themselves with more powerful rifles and shotguns. Their projectiles, Kates argued, were more likely to go through walls or travel greater distances and kill or injure innocent people. Kates's arguments were persuasive, and even those who disagreed realized that Kates was a source who could not be easily dismissed. The questions of gun control and constitutional rights were proving more complex than many first thought.[18]

Later, in the 1990s and first decade of the twenty-first century, Kates would lead seminars at academic conferences trying to persuade often skeptical scholars from law and the social sciences of the essential accuracy of his views. In his seminars and scholarly writings, he also argued that prohibitory gun-control measures were often counterproductive as a criminological matter. They inhibited self-defense and denied communities the deterrent value that armed citizens posed to potential criminals. Kates was a tireless writer and speaker, and over time his efforts would persuade a number of influential students of the Constitution in American law schools.

David Hardy, another practicing attorney and independent scholar, would also begin to make his mark on the Second Amendment debate in the 1980s. Hardy's article "Armed Citizens, Citizen Armies: Toward a Jurisprudence of the Second Amendment" traced the right and duty to be armed at English law and then continued with an analysis of the development of the concepts in eighteenth-century America. Hardy's article was especially interesting because of his presentation and analysis of James Madison's speech introducing the Bill of Rights in the First Congress. Madison's speech contained a series of notes indicating why the proposed provisions were needed. These notes indicated that Madison saw the rights as rights of individuals. Hardy also noted that Madison contrasted the rights that were to be included in the new Constitution with what he saw as their somewhat cramped English ancestors. Madison noted that the English Bill of Rights was limited because it was merely an act of Parliament, not a constitutional provision or series of provisions. The notes criticized the English protection for the right to have arms, because the right only protected Protestants. Like Halbrook, Hardy's research on what members of the framing generation actually said raised uncomfortable questions for those who maintained that the Second Amendment only pertained to the organized militia.[19]

The contributions by Kates and Halbrook were especially important because they provided accurate discussions of what the Supreme Court had actually said in what were then the Court's three principal Second Amendment cases, *Cruikshank*, *Presser*, and *Miller*. We have noted that a number of supporters of the collective right or militia-only view of the Second Amendment had frequently misstated the holdings in the three cases, claiming that they supported the view that the Court had held that the amendment did not protect the right of individuals to have arms outside of the context of the organized militia. These assertions helped popularize the notion that it was well-settled law that the Second Amendment did not protect the rights of individuals. The claims were often accepted because, before the 1980s, research on Supreme Court and other court cases was often, particularly for people who were not lawyers, a somewhat tedious process. If today we are accustomed to rather easy online research, we should remember that before the 1980s, legal research, and indeed research in other areas as well, was usually a much more arduous task. To research Supreme Court cases, one had to have access to the *US Reports* or some other set of bound volumes that contain the corpus of cases decided by the US Supreme Court. These were found in law libraries at law schools, the major law firms, and bar associations. They were usually not found in local public libraries and were frequently missing from the libraries of small colleges and universities that were not connected to law schools. Many readers who read essays that claimed that *Cruikshank, Presser,* and *Miller* stood for the proposition that the Second Amendment only protected the militia's right to arms or the right to arms of persons serving in the organized militia were not inclined to make a trip to the local law school or bar association library to verify such claims. It should be added that even hardy souls who might have been so inclined were likely to be turned away by the library in question because they were not law school students or faculty members, or members of the local bar association. The inaccurate representations gained a certain amount of traction because of the relative difficulty of doing verifying research.

For those who were interested in the debate, Kates and Halbrook provided synopses of the major cases that went a long way toward putting the cases in context and indeed clarifying what they actually said. Kates provided an extensive discussion of *Miller,* noting that the 1939 case steered a middle course between the individual rights position and the collective rights position as these positions had developed in 1983 at the time of his writing. Kates noted that while the McReynolds opinion recognized an individual right, it was limited to weapons useful for militia purposes. Kates went on to argue that *Miller* implied a common-use test, that is, that weapons in common use would be the militia weapons that would be protected by the Second Amendment. It was a point that would later play a key part in Second Amendment jurisprudence.

Halbrook's *That Everyman Be Armed* went even further in dispelling some of the inaccuracies that had been disseminated concerning the Supreme Court and the Second Amendment. Halbrook did a detailed examination of *Cruikshank,* making it clear that the Court's ruling in that case was addressing the issue of private infringement of rights and that federal power under the Fourteenth Amendment could only shield against state action. *That Everyman Be Armed* went on to an equally detailed discussion of *Presser* and its conclusion that the Second Amendment did not constrain the actions of state governments. Halbrook accurately noted that the decision made no claim that the Court's holding limited the protection of the Second Amendment to members of the organized militia. He also discussed *Miller* and, like Hardy, Kates, and others, noted that the Court focused on the question of the utility of Jack Miller's shotgun for militia purposes, not on whether Miller's activities were connected to militia activity. By putting the discussion of these cases in an easily accessible book form instead of in the pages of a law journal or forcing readers to go to the case reporters, Halbrook brought members of the general public into the discussion of Supreme Court case law on the Second Amendment.[20]

The writings of Halbrook, Kates, and Hardy, and a number of others who did some of the early scholarship on the Second Amendment, were often subject to ad hominem criticism and indeed outright dismissal by their opponents. They were practicing attorneys. They frequently represented the NRA and other gun owners' advocacy group before courts and legislatures. They had an obvious agenda, to make the case for the individual rights view of the Second Amendment, and to an extent to argue against specific gun-control measures. Their arguments were addressed to the practicing bar and bench, to scholars in law and other disciplines who might be persuaded to their point of view, and to the public at large. And yet many readers found that these largely accurate criticisms were not particularly persuasive reasons to ignore their research and the writings that they published on the right to bear arms. The debate over the Second Amendment was like other questions where history, law, and public policy intertwine. Few writers, no matter how strong their professional pedigrees, or whether they are employed in presumably neutral universities or by advocacy groups, come to such discussions free of biases or preconceptions. It is probably fair to say that most readers recognized that these independent scholars were advocates for a particular point of view and realizing that, nonetheless looked at their work, weighed the arguments and the evidence offered, and came to their own conclusions as to the essential accuracy of their claims. It is also probably fair to say that the writings of these lawyer-scholars had a small audience and small impact initially, but that their influence would grow over time.

In the 1980s, practicing attorneys like Halbrook, Hardy, and Kates were starting to look anew at the Second Amendment and the issues that that constitutional provision might pose for gun control. In that same decade historians were also discovering a new-found interest in the right to bear arms. Like their colleagues in the legal academy and much of the practicing bar, historians had traditionally done fairly little in the way of exploration of the Second Amendment. This had been a somewhat curious neglect given the importance of firearms and the often-strong strains of private violence in American history. Historian Charles Debenedetti in an essay examining twentieth-century textbooks on American history would note the curious fact that while those texts frequently mentioned the significant role of firearms in the nation's history and that many historians had linked widespread ownership and use of firearms to American democracy, they rarely discussed the Second Amendment and its possible interpretations.[21]

The relative lack of discussion about the Second Amendment was part of a somewhat broader reluctance on the part of professional historians to engage with constitutional history more generally, particularly in the twentieth century. Constitutional historian Paul Murphy in a 1963 article in the *American Historical Review*, "Time to Reclaim: The Current Challenge of American Constitutional History," bemoaned the fact that the Supreme Court was often deciding constitutional issues that had important historical dimensions—the degree to which the Fifteenth Amendment was meant to protect the voting rights of racial minorities, the extent to which the Fourteenth Amendment was meant to apply the Bill of Rights to the states, how extensive the First Amendment's protection for freedom of the press or the free exercise of religion was meant to be—in the absence of much in the way of scholarship on point from professional historians. Murphy noted that historians had been more attracted to political, social, and intellectual history in the post–World War II period, leaving constitutional history an often-neglected field.[22] We would add to Murphy's observation that the neglect of constitutional history would somewhat deepen in the 1970s and 1980s and beyond as history departments and their PhD programs increased their explorations of social history often to the neglect of other areas including legal and constitutional history. This tendency was only somewhat mitigated by the fact that from the 1980s onward, a fair number of individuals with PhDs in history also earned law degrees and joined the faculties of law schools. In any event, constitutional history had traditionally been a somewhat neglected field, and that could certainly be said to be true in the early 1980s as the Second Amendment debate was gaining force. With constitutional history a somewhat neglected field, the Second Amendment, constitutional history's orphan child, received even less in the way of in-depth examination by professional historians.

That neglect started to change in the early 1980s with the heating up of the gun-control controversy. Historian Robert Shalhope, whose research had focused on civic republicanism in the early national period, in 1982 published the article "The Ideological Origins of the Second Amendment" in the *Journal of American History*, the leading journal in the field. Shalhope's examination of the concept of civic republicanism, which includes ideas of citizenship, participation, and civic virtue, led him to the conclusion that the Second Amendment was meant to support both a broad-based citizen's militia and a population armed with their own private weapons. His 1982 essay expressed an ambivalence on what modern gun-control policy should be, but Shalhope nonetheless cautioned: "But advocates of the control of firearms should not argue that the Second Amendment did not intend for Americans of the late eighteenth century to possess arms for their own personal defense, for the defense of their states and their nation, and for the purpose of keeping their rulers sensitive to the rights of the people."[23]

Shalhope's essay in the *Journal of American History* would spark a debate in the pages of the same journal with Lawrence Delbert Cress, a historian of the American militia. His article, "An Armed Community: The Origins and Meaning of the Right to Bear Arms," argued that the Second Amendment was designed to protect a well-regulated militia and that the people's right to keep and bear arms was designed to be exercised solely within the context of the militia. Cress ended his article: "The Second Amendment, concerning the right of the people to keep and bear arms, was framed in contemplation not of individual rights but of the maintenance of the states' active organized militias."[24] Cress's essay appeared in the June 1984 edition of the *Journal of American History*. The journal published a short exchange between Shalhope and Cress in December of that same year.

If a debate over the meanings of or intentions behind the Second Amendment was somewhat slow to get started among historians of the United States, there was even less engagement among historians of Stuart England with the provision in the 1689 English Bill of Rights protecting the right of Protestants to have arms. As we have noted, the provision was in a statute, one that had long since been modified, indeed in effect repealed. It posed no impediment to any modern project concerning firearms control or any other issue. Still, American jurists and commentators had long noted that the 1689 provision was in fact the predecessor of the American constitutional amendment. Among twentieth-century commentators that was largely a fact mentioned, if at all, only in very brief passing. What scholar or jurist was going to spend much time on the English ancestor of an all-but-forgotten American constitutional provision?

And yet as the controversy over gun control and the Second Amendment began to heat up, it began attracting the attention of historian Joyce Malcolm, who specialized in Stuart England, particularly the English Civil War of 1642 to 1651. In the late 1970s she was beginning research that would ultimately result in a book-length treatment of the provision in the English Bill of Rights that protected Protestants from disarmament. Her earliest work discussed the efforts of Charles II and James II to disarm large portions of the English public, particularly Protestants. In an article published in 1983 in the *Hastings Constitutional Law Quarterly*, "The Right of the People to Keep and Bear Arms: The Common Law Tradition," Malcolm argued: "The right of Englishmen to have arms was a very real and individual right. . . . The Second Amendment should properly be read to extend to every citizen the right to have arms for personal defense. The right was a legacy of the English, whose rights to have arms was, at base, as much a personal right as a collective duty."[25]

Like the writings of Halbrook, Kates, and Hardy, the scholarship produced by Shalhope, Cress, and Malcolm did not immediately bestow a new-found academic respectability on the Second Amendment. Constitutional law case books and treatises used in law schools continued to discuss the constitutional provision in brief passage, if at all. University textbooks and monographs on American history did the same. Even so, the authors who were beginning to put the Second Amendment under the microscope in the early and mid-1980s were beginning to uncover a world of thought concerning arms, rights, and the common defense connected to the Second Amendment that was more complex than the portrait that had been crafted by the gun-control movement and reflected in the largely sympathetic press. They were also uncovering a world that was more complex than the one that was being conveyed in the court decisions of the time, which tended to readily dismiss claims based on the right to keep and bear arms. The needle would move only slightly at first. But to those who were paying attention, these and other writings were beginning to sow seeds of doubt regarding what had become the conventional wisdom concerning the Second Amendment.

## THE EMPIRICAL THICKET

But the conventional wisdom regarding gun control involved more than a set of legal and historical assumptions that the right to keep and bear arms applied only to the militia. There were a host of criminological assumptions concerning guns and violence that could cause any policymaker, including a jurist who might be called upon to decide on the constitutionality of a firearms restriction, to hesitate before rendering a decision that might make public access to guns even easier. The gun-control movement and its supporters, which had included powerful voices from the Johnson, Ford, and Carter administrations as well as mayors and police chiefs from big cities, had constructed a series of powerful arguments contending that crime and violence could be traced to large-scale gun ownership and that stronger restrictions were the best way—indeed the only way—to reduce what in some communities was out and out carnage. If many Americans instinctively agreed with the bumper sticker saying, "When guns are outlawed, only outlaws will have guns," the gun-control movement nonetheless made authoritative arguments that the problem of gun violence was not simply a problem of outlaws having guns. Ordinary citizens also posed a risk. First, average citizens could not defend themselves with a gun. Self-defense with guns by untrained civilians was a myth. The gun in the hands of a crime victim or potential crime victim was likely to provoke the attacker, be taken away from the victim, turned on the would-be defender, and used to facilitate the robbery and other crimes. Better that the victim not attempt self-defense, but instead submit and leave the matter to the authorities once the danger had passed. Such arguments were often buttressed by statistics indicating that the number of murders committed with handguns significantly exceeded the number of justifiable homicides committed in self-defense. Champions of more stringent regulation also argued that many killings occurred among acquaintances, an indication that the mere presence of firearms turned what would have been relatively harmless quarrels between friends and family members into lethal confrontations. These arguments gained broad acceptance among opinion leaders in the press and on the bench and bar, if not the general public.[26]

It is probably fair to say that much of what was put forward as the conventional wisdom concerning gun ownership and availability and crime and violence rested on a not particularly firm foundation from a social science point of view. The crude statistics were present, to be sure. Researchers supporting gun control were able to show higher homicide including gun homicide rates in the United States than in Western Europe. Statistics indicated that the homicide rate was higher in the South, which had a relatively high percentage of gun owners, than it was in New England, which had a relatively low percentage. The number of potential victims who killed their would-be attackers was lower than the number of people who were killed in illegal homicides. All of this was basically true.

True, but in many ways misleading. Modern social science research that attempts to examine national issues usually relies on research that has examined the influence of a number of different variables on a particular phenomenon. This kind of research usually involves broad samples of the population over a variety of geographic regions and with attempts to ensure that the samples examined are representative of the population at large with respect to demographic, educational, and other salient characteristics of the larger population. All of this is done with a recognition that one cannot do a comparison by simply isolating one variable, in this case gun availability, and contrast locations where guns are relatively freely available with locations where they are restricted. Other variables can greatly influence rates of crime and violence—demographic variables such as age, race, and ethnicity as well as economic considerations including rates of unemployment, education levels, and so forth. We are not quantitative social scientists and will not attempt to become such in the next few pages. Nonetheless, we will say that the research done in the 1960s and 1970s—both the research that tended to support stricter controls on firearms and the research that tended to oppose it—had not by and large been subject to rigorous examination by social scientists armed with the kind of statistical tools that allowed for control for the confounding effects of different variables.

The lack of this kind of rigorous examination led the National Institute of Justice, an arm of the Justice Department, to commission in 1978 a study that reviewed the existing social-science literature on gun control with the object of critiquing the then existing research and pointing the direction that new research should take. Three sociologists, James D. Wright, Peter H. Rossi (who would serve as president of the American Sociological Association from 1979 to 1980), and Kathleen Daly performed the study, which was published in 1983 as a book, *Under the Gun: Weapons, Crime and Violence in America.* The three sociologists began by noting that as of the date of their research, "There is very little in the weapons, violence and crime literature that would qualify as hard, empirical fact." They further noted that the literature did not examine the phenomena of guns and violence through an exploration of representative national evidence; instead, such studies as had been performed were small-scale state and local studies that produced disarray and often contradictory results. Wright, Rossi, and Daly went on to note that there were no reliable estimates of the number of firearms in private hands and that the best estimates were rough approximations, easily off by tens of millions of firearms. In short, advocates on both sides of the gun-control debate in the 1970s and early 1980s were operating with little in the way of hard evidence concerning guns, crime, violence, and the likely feasibility and impact of proposed control measures.[27]

The three sociologists examined many aspects of firearms ownership and its impact on modern America, including their estimates of the size of the private firearms stock in the United States in the late 1970s: they estimated 120 million in 1978, plus or minus 20 million guns. They also explored the sociology of gun ownership, examining the influence of class, race, religion, and sex on gun ownership. And they looked at the greater incidence of gun ownership in the South compared to other regions.

Two aspects of the research reported in *Under the Gun* would point toward conclusions that would later have considerable importance for those who would argue against firearms prohibition measures and for constitutional protection for individuals who wanted to own firearms. First, the three sociologists indicated that the literature up to that point was inconclusive as to whether there was a connection between homicide and gun ownership. If a number of writers had claimed a connection, they did so in the face of incomplete evidence and flawed methodologies. Far from indicating that the increased presence of guns contributed to an increase of crime, the evidence might just as plausibly be read that increases in crime brought about increases in gun ownership. As to gun ownership being a cause of lethal accidents with guns, Wright, Rossi, and Daly examined a study that looked at lethal accidents with guns in Detroit, Michigan, and noted that 99.9 percent of gun owners did not have fatal accidents with their firearms.[28]

Wright and his colleagues also explored the questions of self-defense and crime deterrence through private firearms ownership. The conventional wisdom had been that because there were relatively few occasions in which private citizens actually killed burglars or those committing assaults, incidents of self-defense with guns were rare. *Under the Gun* rejected the view that private gun ownership was useless for self-defense and crime deterrence, indicating that, among other things, burglars had a greater risk of being shot by home or apartment dwellers than they had of being apprehended by the police. The three sociologists also noted that the evidence indicated that potential victims of aggravated assault who were armed were less likely to be victimized than those who were not. Wright and his colleagues also noted that victims who resisted were on the whole more likely to be injured than those who did not resist. Their report also noted that the question of gun ownership and general deterrence, that is, the possibility that criminals were less like to commit burglaries, robberies, rapes, and assaults because they feared potential encounters with armed civilians, was an issue that had not been adequately addressed by the criminological community. *Under the Gun* also indicated that survey data showed that a significant number of Americans actually used firearms in self-defense. Wright and his colleagues argued that the sense of reassurance that they could defend themselves that firearms ownership brought to many Americans was a quality-of-life benefit that should not be easily dismissed.[29]

In a later study, *Armed and Considered Dangerous: A Survey of Felons and Their Firearms*, published in 1986, Wright and Rossi surveyed convicted felons. Their research indicated that the prevalence of arms in civilian hands in fact acted as a substantial deterrent to certain types of crimes. Convicted felons who answered the Wright-Rossi surveys responded that encountering armed civilians was a major concern among criminals, indeed a greater concern than the fear of arrest and conviction. Most of the respondents indicated that they took pains to avoid potential victims who they suspected were armed. One answer was particularly telling: 64 percent of the felons surveyed stated that one reason burglars avoided entering houses when people were home was fear of being shot.[30]

The earlier study undertaken by Wright, Rossi, and Daly would be the first major social-science study that introduced a serious note of caution concerning what had been the conventional wisdom concerning the issues of gun ownership, crime, violence, and self-defense. *Under the Gun* would later be followed in the 1980s, 1990s, and beyond by empirical studies by criminologist Gary Kleck and economist John Lott, among others, suggesting that Wright, Rossi, and Daly were right about their skepticism concerning what had been the conventional wisdom concerning guns, crimes, and violence. In fact, these latter researchers found even more robust evidence that privately owned guns were frequently used in self-defense and that such weapons had strong overall general deterrent effects.[31]

These studies had, and still have, their critics. There is a robust empirical literature debating firearm availability, crime, suicide, deterrence, and related issues that are beyond the scope of our discussion. But we would like to point out the importance of the Wright, Rossi, and Daly study and others that would follow. In the 1970s a number of jurists were eagerly following the advice that former Harvard dean Roscoe Pound had given the bench and bar in 1957: Reinterpret the Second Amendment! Erase the idea that it protected a citizen's right to have arms! That was done by New Jersey Supreme Court justice Nathan Jacobs when he went far beyond existing precedent and the demands of the case before him to use a challenge to his state's firearms licensing scheme to write an opinion that read an individual right out of the Second Amendment. US Supreme Court justices William O. Douglas and Thurgood Marshall urged the Supreme Court to follow in that vein when they argued for a "watering down" of the Second Amendment. Hostility to the constitutional provision almost certainly influenced the thinking behind the Supreme Court's refusal to hear Victor Quilici's challenge to the Morton Grove handgun ban.

Simply put, a number of jurists had become convinced that a recognition of the Second Amendment as a right of individuals would be a policy disaster, whatever the merits of such a recognition might be from a historical and constitutional point of view. *Under the Gun* began the process of undermining the certitude that prevailed among many educated people, including many jurists, that large-scale gun ownership was an unmitigated policy disaster. It did not erase the belief among many jurists and commentators that gun control and a corollary interpretation of the Second Amendment that would not interfere with restrictive measures was the better course. But a major study by three respected sociologists did make the once-firm certainty that radical gun control was the solution to American problems of crime and violence, a little less certain.

## NO STATE SHALL ABRIDGE

But a judicial willingness to reexamine the Constitution and the limits that it might pose for firearms restrictions would require more than an acknowledgment that the Second Amendment was originally conceived of as a constitutional provision that would protect a right of individuals. That willingness would also require something more than empirical examinations by social scientists indicating that the link between gun availability and crime and violence was less firm than gun-control advocates had claimed. In the 1980s, gun restrictions were still largely the product of state laws. Despite the fervent wishes of its proponents, the Gun Control Act of 1968 posed few obstacles to gun ownership by the general public. And the NRA and its allies had been quite successful in beating back attempts to have Congress pass new legislation— bans on cheap handguns, derisively labeled Saturday-night specials, or registration of handguns. The serious restrictions that did exist had been passed by state and municipal governments. To get at these, as had been shown in the Morton Grove litigation, the courts would have to be willing to reexamine the incorporation question.

Incorporation was still a quite controversial doctrine in the 1980s when the new scholarship making the case for the individual rights view of the Second Amendment was beginning to appear. The Supreme Court under the leadership of Chief Justice Earl Warren had gone a long way toward achieving Justice Hugo Black's vision of applying the Bill of Rights to the states, doing so with the First Amendment's speech, press, and religion clauses and with the guarantees for the rights of the accused found in the Fourth, Fifth, and Sixth Amendments. But the Warren Court had done so within the framework of the process of selective incorporation, whereby the Court would determine which rights were fundamental, not the text of the Bill of Rights. That process had bypassed the Third Amendment's prohibition on forced quartering of soldiers in private homes, the Fifth Amendment's guarantee of a grand jury hearing in criminal cases, the Seventh Amendment's guarantee of a right to jury trials in civil cases, and the excessive fines provision of the Eighth Amendment. Constitutional scholars generally agreed that the courts had implicitly incorporated the Eighth Amendment's mandate requiring reasonable bail in criminal cases, though there was no specific Supreme Court case stating such. And, of course, for our purposes, the Second Amendment's guarantee of the right of the people to keep and bear arms had not been incorporated. The process of directly considering whether specific provisions of the Bill of Rights applied to the states had slowed with the retirement of Earl Warren, the appointment of Warren Burger as chief justice, and the dawning of a more conservative Court. In two cases decided in 1972, *Apodaca v. Oregon* and *Johnson v. Louisiana*, the Court sustained state felony convictions on the basis of less-than-unanimous verdicts. Even though the Court agreed that the Sixth Amendment required unanimous verdicts for convictions in federal courts, the plurality opinions in both cases held that the Fourteenth Amendment did not require unanimous verdicts by state juries in noncapital cases. The doctrine of selective incorporation gave states a fair amount of latitude in their approach to what had long been considered one of the fundamental rights of the individual in Anglo-American jurisprudence, trial by jury.[32]

The doctrine was also open to considerable criticism. Edwin Meese III, who served as attorney general under Ronald Reagan, in a 1985 speech before the American Bar Association criticized the Court's incorporation doctrine as a threat to federalism, the ability of the states to craft laws and policies that would meet their needs, particularly in the criminal justice arena. All this, according to Meese, was the result of a judge who made legal doctrine with little sound historical foundation.[33]

Meese's arguments on this score were buttressed by legal historian Raoul Berger. A vigorous and polemical writer, Berger picked up where Charles Fairman had left off in the 1950s, arguing that the Fourteenth Amendment had not been adopted with the aim of making the Bill of Rights binding on the states. Berger, who was constantly challenged and vigorously defended his views in law journals, was popular in the 1980s among conservative commentators. His writings were favorably reviewed in the *National Review* and other conservative journals and were frequently cited as evidence that the idea of applying the Bill of Rights to the states was without decent historical foundation. It should be added that the very methodology the Supreme Court used to incorporate the Bill of Rights bolstered the criticisms made by opponents of the doctrine. Instead of the straightforward total incorporation urged by Justice Black in *Adamson*, the Court incorporated the Bill of Rights on a case-by-case basis. In place of incorporating the Bill of Rights through the Fourteenth Amendment's "privileges or immunities" clause, a phrase that suggests substantive rights of citizens and one that had been employed by the drafters of the Fourteenth Amendment when they indicated their intention to make the states respect the Bill of Rights, the Court had incorporated portions of the first eight amendments through the Fourteenth Amendment's due process clause, a clause that suggested to most laypeople and many lawyers as well a right to fair procedures, not substantive rights. The Court's methodology left it and the incorporation doctrine vulnerable to the charge that incorporation owed more to the policy preferences of individual justices than the demands of the Constitution.[34]

The debate over incorporation would engage the interest of Michael Curtis, then a practicing attorney in North Carolina (he would later join the faculty of Wake Forest Law School). Curtis would challenge Berger and the other critics of incorporation, often in back-and-forth battles in the nation's law reviews. But Curtis would do something more. He would in 1986 produce a major book examining the history of incorporation. The book, *No State Shall Abridge: The Fourteenth Amendment and the Bill of Rights*, provided a detailed look at the development of the antislavery Republican Party's political theory before the enactment of the Fourteenth Amendment. His examination looked at the debate over the amendment in the Thirty-Ninth Congress and the debate over the Fourteenth Amendment in the states. Curtis spent considerable time challenging the arguments of Charles Fairman and Raoul Berger, the two principal academic critics of incorporation. Curtis's research also bolstered many of the points Stephen Halbrook had previously made concerning the link between the Second and Fourteenth Amendments. Like Halbrook, Curtis noted that the 1867 Freedman's Bureau Bill, passed a year after Congress had sent the Fourteenth Amendment to the states, included language indicating a desire to protect the right to keep and bear arms. Curtis, like Halbrook, also noted that several congressmen expressed the view that the Civil Rights Act of 1866 would protect the right to bear arms of the newly emancipated Black population.[35]

## ENTERING THE MAINSTREAM

Slowly this new literature started to be read and have an impact. By 1988 Laurence Tribe, who had summarily assured his readers a decade earlier that the debates over the Second Amendment clearly indicated that the framers were only concerned with protecting state militias from federal interference, had revised his discussion in the second edition of his treatise on constitutional law. The Harvard Law School professor noted that the debates on the amendment indicated that the framers also had a desire to protect the individual's right to self-defense. Tribe cited Kates's article in the *Michigan Law Review*.[36]

By the late 1980s the view that the Second Amendment protected a right of individuals was gaining increased currency, helped by the views of the conservative Republican presidential administrations of Ronald Reagan and George H. W. Bush. If the Johnson administration in the liberal 1960s had supported a view of the Second Amendment that was congenial to gun-control advocates and one that essentially read the right to bear arms out of the Bill of Rights, the conservative Reagan and Bush administrations, elected with the support of the NRA, supported a view of the Second Amendment that saw the constitutional provision as protecting the rights of individuals.

Political party and ideological leanings were not perfect predictors of where an individual stood on the issue of gun control and the Second Amendment. Staunch liberal Representative John Dingell (D-MI) was a strong supporter of the NRA, sat on the organization's board of directors, and helped set up the association's political arm, the Institute for Legislative Action. Conservative chief justice Warren Burger authored an essay in *Parade Magazine* denouncing the individual rights view of the Second Amendment as a "fraud."[37] Nonetheless, it is fair to say that the Democratic Party as a whole was more sympathetic to gun control than the Republican Party as a whole and that Republican administrations were more likely to show sympathy for the individual rights view of the Second Amendment than Democratic ones. An early example of this is found in an article authored by political scientist and legal scholar Nelson Lund. The article, titled "The Second Amendment: Political Liberty and the Right to Self-Preservation" and published in the *Alabama Law Review*, made an argument based on the amendment's language that the constitutional provision protecting the right to keep and bear arms was meant to protect individuals. In 1987 when the article appeared, Lund had already served as an attorney-advisor to the Justice Department's Office of Legal Counsel. He would later serve as law clerk to Justice Sandra Day O'Connor.[38]

Lund's article was not the only indication that there was considerable sympathy for the individual rights interpretation of the Second Amendment in the Reagan and Bush administrations. Oral argument presented by the Bush administration in two cases gave indication of the administration's support for an individual rights interpretation of the Second Amendment. In oral argument in the case of *United States v. Verdugo-Urquidez*, a case involving whether the Fourth Amendment's protection against warrantless searches extended to foreign nationals in foreign countries, Lawrence S. Robbins, the assistant to the solicitor general, argued that the people protected by the Fourth Amendment were the citizens of the United States and not people in the world at large. He went on to argue that the term "the people" in the Bill of Rights was a term of art meant only to include those who were part of the political compact that made up the American polity:

It's worth comparing the other provisions in the Bill of Rights that also use the phrase "the people" because they cannot be understood unless you recognize that "the people" was a limiting concept.

The other provisions that use that phrase are the Ninth and Tenth Amendment which make utterly no sense except in terms of this compact that I am describing; the Second Amendment which refers to the right to bear arms, which can't plausibly be assumed to be a right of persons overseas to have arms.[39]

The majority opinion, authored by Chief Justice William Rehnquist, picked up on Robbins's argument stating that the term "the people" seemed to have been a term of art employed in select parts of the Constitution. Rehnquist went on to note "while this textual exegesis is by no means exclusive, it suggests that 'the people' protected by the Fourth Amendment, and by the First and Second Amendments . . . refers to a class of persons who are part of a national community."[40]

For those who wanted recognition of the Second Amendment as a right of individuals, Robbins's argument and the Rehnquist opinion were encouraging. This was not some restatement of the idea that the amendment only applied to the militia or that it was somehow a right of the states despite its language referring to the people. No, the oral argument and the chief justice's opinion stated that the Second Amendment protected a right of the people in much the same way the First and Fourth Amendments did. It was, of course, dicta, and like the dicta in Harlan's opinion in *Poe* it was unlikely to affect how federal or state courts would decide actual cases where firearms restrictions were at issue. But for supporters of the right to bear arms it was a bit of an oasis of relief in what had been a hostile judicial landscape.

Further indication that the right to bear arms had highly placed friends in the Bush Justice Department would come the following year, 1990, in the case of *Perpich v. Department of Defense*. The case involved whether the Defense Department could send a state's National Guard out of the country for training in peacetime without the governor's consent. This time the government was represented by Kenneth Starr, the solicitor general. Starr was anxious to differentiate the National Guard that had been organized under federal law as a reserve component of the US Army and, later, US Air Force and that figured into Department of Defense planning for worldwide mobilization and deployment, from the militia discussed in different parts of the Constitution, including the Second Amendment. He noted that Congress had organized the

National Guard under its power to raise armies, not under its power to organize and discipline the militia. He also noted that for the first one hundred
years of the militia's existence, militia members supplied their own arms instead of receiving arms from the state or federal governments. Starr went on
to note that the purpose of the right of the people to keep and bear arms was
so that they could have arms for militia service.[41]

The arguments of the government and the opinions in the two cases represented something of a retreat from the absolutist position that the Second
Amendment was not designed to protect the rights of individuals. Both cases
could be read as providing some recognition of a personal right to firearms, although again it should be stressed that this indirect and off-hand recognition
was a far cry from the possibility that the courts would look at firearms restrictions and possibly pronounce them unconstitutional. The fact that there had
been some minor throat clearing concerning the Second Amendment in two
Supreme Court cases unrelated to the gun control controversy, or that there
had been a few articles and books discussing the right to bear arms, seemed
not to alter the conventional wisdom that deemed the Second Amendment a
constitutional dead end and dead letter. It's probably fair to say that most supporters of gun control in the late 1980s regarded the constitutional issue as settled. Gun-control measures would not be disturbed by the courts. Passing gun
control would be a matter of convincing legislatures on the wisdom of specific
measures, not convincing courts as to their constitutionality. This view was
frequently echoed in the largely sympathetic press. As late as December 1989,
National Public Radio correspondent Nina Totenberg could confidently claim
that the Second Amendment had not engaged the attention of constitutional
scholars and that even the NRA could not furnish her with the names of constitutional scholars in law schools who believed that the Second Amendment
protected the rights of individuals.[42]

Her certitude proved to be premature. The world of Second Amendment
commentary and analysis would change forever with the December 1989 publication of Sanford Levinson's article "The Embarrassing Second Amendment" in the *Yale Law Journal*. Levinson, a legal scholar and political scientist
at the University of Texas, warned the national community of constitutional
commentators that they dismissed too quickly, and at their peril, the arguments made by those who asserted that the Second Amendment protected the
rights of individuals. Levinson quickly reviewed *Cruikshank* and *Presser*, noting that both cases occurred before the Supreme Court had begun to seriously

examine the incorporation issue. His discussion of *Miller* indicated that the organized-militia-only view of the case was wrong and that the McReynolds opinion should be viewed as protecting the right of individuals to own weapons useful for the common defense: "It is difficult to read *Miller* as rendering the Second Amendment meaningless as a control on Congress. . . . Arguments about the constitutional legitimacy of a prohibition by Congress of private ownership of handguns or, what is much more likely, assault rifles, might turn on the usefulness of such guns in military settings."[43]

The effect was magnetic. Levinson was a major constitutional scholar at a major law school publishing in one of the nation's premier law journals that the individual rights view of the Second Amendment had to be taken seriously, and, what's more, that it was probably right. Independent scholars like Kates, Halbrook, and Hardy could be dismissed, unfairly, because of their connections to the gun owners' rights movement. Historians like Malcolm or Shalhope might be ignored because they were exploring a past that many people found difficult to disentangle and understand. But Levinson was in the mainstream of modern constitutional commentary, a premier scholar of the nation's fundamental charter and a bona fide political liberal. His essay would prove hard to ignore.

And it wasn't ignored. Levinson's essay insured that the era when the Second Amendment was an ignored and little commented on provision of the Constitution had come to an end. Other scholars began looking at the issue. Levinson had written his article in part as a thought experiment—to get others to examine a constitutional problem that had been generally overlooked in the legal academy. He did so in part because he had been intrigued by one aspect of the Second Amendment debate; the idea that an armed population might make popular resistance to tyrannical government possible. Other scholars would follow. The Second Amendment was one great area of the Constitution and the rights of the American people that remained largely unexplored. For scholars who felt that they had written their umpteenth article on the First Amendment and freedom of the press or the Fourteenth Amendment and equal protection, here was new territory, an exciting prospect.

So, they came. Levinson's 1989 essay would be followed in subsequent years by writings by other major legal scholars whose research supported the view that the Constitution protected an individual's right to have arms. In 1991 Raymond T. Diamond, then at the Tulane Law School, coauthored an article discussing the importance of an individual right to bear arms in light

of the history of racial violence in American history. In 1994 William Van Alstyne, a leading liberal constitutional law scholar and at the time a professor at
Duke Law School, wrote an article supporting the individual rights view of the
Second Amendment. That same year, Joyce Malcolm extended her research
on the English right to bear arms, producing the first book-length treatment
of the subject in *To Keep and Bear Arms: The Origins of an Anglo-American
Right*.[44]

One of the more important scholars to accept the individual rights view of
the Second Amendment was Akhil Amar of the Yale Law School. The individual rights view of the amendment dovetailed with Amar's thinking in the late
1980s and early 1990s that constitutional scholars needed a new approach to
the study of the Bill of Rights. Amar's approach emphasized two perspectives:
first, that the provisions of the Bill of Rights should be studied as interrelated
parts of an integrated whole, not simply as a listing of isolated rights. In this
regard Amar urged constitutional scholars to consider that in the right to keep
and bear arms and the right to trial by jury specified in the Bill of Rights in
tandem, both through the militia and the jury, the Constitution was calling
for community participation in providing for society's physical security and
in judging cases. Similarly, he urged constitutional scholars to reconsider the
Fourteenth Amendment as having done more than simply incorporate the Bill
of Rights against the states. Instead, he believed that the Fourteenth Amendment served to transform the rights specified in the first eight amendments.
The Second Amendment of 1791, which for Amar was a right of White men to
have their individual weapons primarily for the purpose of participating in the
militia, was transformed by the Fourteenth Amendment of 1868 into a right
of all citizens, particularly the newly emancipated Black population, to have
weapons for self-defense.[45]

By the 1990s, writings supporting the idea that the Second Amendment
protected an individual right became so numerous and gained such widespread support among law professors that one scholar called that view "the
standard model." What was once on the margins of the constitutional conversation had gained a strong measure of intellectual acceptance, even among
those who favored stricter gun controls. And this new conventional wisdom
was beginning to spread beyond the law reviews and history journals. Essay-
ists in newspapers and magazines were beginning to pay attention to the once
obscure amendment in ways that they never had before. Predictably enough,
many advocates of stricter gun control asserted that the amendment did not

protect a right of individuals while opponents of gun control argued that it did. But there were some interesting voices who, convinced by the emerging scholarship in the early 1990s, argued that the Second Amendment posed a real constitutional barrier to a result they hoped for—stricter gun control. *New Republic* columnist Michael Kinsley, a member of Handgun Control Inc., reluctantly conceded in an article in the *Washington Post* in 1990 that the Second Amendment presented real barriers to gun control. Conservative columnist George Will, also an advocate of stricter gun control, made a similar concession in the *Post* the next year. Robert Sprecher's "Lost Amendment" was lost no longer.[46]

# 6. One Case, Many Controversies

By the late 1980s it was becoming increasingly clear to many gun-control advocates that the earlier hopes of Pete Shields and others that national measures to control handguns would be adopted and later ripen into prohibitions or near prohibitions were unlikely to be realized. The failure of Proposition 15, the handgun freeze in California, and the failure of the Massachusetts referendum to ban handguns indicated that even in jurisdictions with substantial numbers of liberal voters there was great skepticism concerning measures that would take away what ordinary people regarded as a means of self-defense. The new scholarship on the Second Amendment and the skepticism expressed by some social scientists concerning the criminological benefits of proposed gun-control measures only added to the woes of gun-control activists. These new developments would probably not, at the time, have been enough to persuade courts to give the individual rights view of the Second Amendment a sympathetic hearing. But taken together, these developments undoubtedly increased the reluctance of Congress and the state legislatures to adopt far-reaching gun-control measures.

Josh Sugarman of the Violence Policy Center was one gun-control activist who was concerned that the movement to ban handguns had effectively stalled and that with that stalling the whole movement for stricter gun control was in peril. Throughout the 1980s there had been some discussion within the gun-control movement of moving away from the traditional focus on handguns to a new focus on what was being termed "assault weapons." A few points are worth mentioning here. There had been a long tradition of civilian ownership of military small arms in the United States, and to a great extent that tradition had been supported by the Army with its sale of surplus weapons to the public and the service's support for various civilian marksmanship programs. During the 1960s the armed forces of the United States and most other nations switched from the bolt-action and semiautomatic rifles used in World War II to select-fire rifles capable of firing in either the semiautomatic or the fully automatic mode. As fully automatic weapons were strictly regulated by the 1934 National Firearms Act, there was a demand for semiautomatic versions of the same rifles, frequently on the part of veterans who had learned to use select-fire rifles during their service during and after the Vietnam era. The US Army participated in civilian marksmanship contests with the M1A and AR-15 rifles—semiautomatic versions of the service's select-fire M14 and the M16 rifles. In many ways it was a continuation of the Army policy that had placed millions of semiautomatic M1 rifles and M1 carbines into the public's hands after the Second World War.

But the 1980s were not the 1950s. The hot and cold wars of the mid–twentieth century that had brought a broad range of men—sharecroppers and movie stars, truck drivers and philosophy professors—into the armed forces and onto the rifle ranges of the different services were becoming a distant memory. Large segments of the population knew little about firearms. Fewer people knew the difference between automatic and semiautomatic weapons. Sugarman believed that this public ignorance could help revive the gun-control movement. In a 1988 paper written for the Violence Policy Center, "Assault Weapons and Accessories in America," Sugarman outlined what would become the new direction for the movement:

> Although handguns claim more than 20,000 lives a year the issue of handgun restriction consistently remains a non-issue with the vast majority of legislators, the press and public. . . . Assault weapons . . . are a new topic. The weapons' menacing looks, coupled with the public's confusion over fully automatic machine guns versus semi-automatic assault weapons—anything that looks like a machine gun is assumed to be a machine gun—can only increase the chance of public support for restrictions on these weapons. In addition, few people can envision a practical use for these weapons.[1]

Sugarman's words proved prophetic. The 1989 massacre of five children in a California schoolyard by Patrick Purdy would set the national gun-control debate on a new course. Purdy, a drifter with a criminal record and a history of anti-Asian animus, used a semiautomatic version of the AK-47 rifle to kill five pupils, all of Vietnamese or Cambodian descent. In reaction the California legislature passed a statute outlawing selected rifles deemed assault weapons. Other states followed suit. In 1994 Congress, under pressure from the Bill Clinton administration, passed a ban on the purchase of new rifles deemed assault weapons. The legislation had a sunset provision and expired in 2004.[2]

We do not have the time or space to get too far into the assault weapons controversy. But let us suggest that the ongoing debate over assault rifles may have produced an unintended result. The appearance of the assault weapons issue probably helped drain whatever energy might have remained in the movement to ban or enact very strict controls on the purchase and possession of handguns. Since the emergence of gun control as a national issue in the 1960s, supporters of stricter gun controls had tended to emphasize that the movement was not a broad-based effort at gun prohibition, but instead an effort to limit access to firearms deemed particularly dangerous. The claim as to which firearms were particularly dangerous frequently changed. At various times bolt-action military surplus rifles, handguns in general, or cheap handguns were all claimed to have especially dangerous characteristics that made them suitable for rigorous controls. Presumably other firearms would not be the object of particularly prohibitive measures. The gun-control movement had to take this posture partly for tactical reasons. In a country with large-scale firearms possession, a political effort to attack all gun ownership would be doomed to failure. And indeed, many supporters of firearms controls were themselves gun owners and would reject the idea of universal prohibition.

The emergence of the assault weapons issue would echo previous controversies. Assault weapons were the new bad guns. They were the public menace, the focus of editorial comment and legislative debate. Handguns, the previous focus of control efforts, became a matter of secondary concern. The criminological facts would have suggested the opposite. The number of homicides committed with rifles of all kinds were a fraction of those committed with pistols and revolvers.[3] But the assault weapons issue put the handgun debate in the shadow. Indeed, even as the gun-control movement was gaining some traction with the assault weapons issue, more and more states were passing legislation liberalizing the right to carry handguns outside the home. By the beginning of the twenty-first century, statutes in a majority of states recognized a right to carry handguns for protection outside the home. The assault weapons issue coincided with and may have played a part in legitimating handguns. That legitimation may very well have played a role in *Heller.*[4]

These developments represented something of a cultural shift. But the legal issue remained. Scholarship in the 1980s and 1990s had gone a long way toward supporting the view that the Constitution protected, or was meant to protect, gun ownership. Supporters of stricter firearms regulation saw the need to answer the recent scholarship that had done much to revive the intellectual respectability of the individual rights view. Lawyers associated with the gun-control movement, most particularly Dennis Henigan of Handgun Control Inc., had written extensively criticizing the individual rights view of the Second Amendment. But, as the gun owners' rights movement had realized earlier, supporters of stricter controls and the collective rights view of the amendment recognized that their case would be bolstered—indeed, needed to be bolstered—by work done by sympathetic scholars in universities. Gun-control supporters made an effort to recruit professors in law schools and history departments who could provide systematic and high-profile rebuttals to the scholarship supporting the individual rights view.

One result of the effort to recruit scholars to present a view of the Second Amendment that should not be a hindrance to gun-control efforts was a symposium on the amendment that appeared in the *Chicago Kent Law Review* in the year 2000. The volume was edited by Carl Bogus, a professor at the Roger Williams School of Law and a former member of the board of directors of Handgun Control Inc. The edition contained articles by well-known historians and legal scholars including legal historian Paul Finkelman, historian of Tudor Stuart England Lois Schwoerer, historian of the early national era Jack Rakove, and constitutional law scholar Michael Dorf, among others.[5]

That same year, one participant in the symposium, Michael Bellesiles, published the book *Arming America: The Origins of a National Gun Culture*, which promised to upend all previous assumptions concerning gun ownership and the constitutional right to bear arms. Bellesiles, a specialist in early American history, argued that gun ownership was rare in Colonial America and through the Revolutionary War period and the early decades of the nineteenth century. The rarity of firearms ownership, coupled with what Bellesiles claimed were often stringent regulation of firearms on the local level, argued for a Second Amendment that was not meant to be protective of an individual right to have arms. The thesis initially created great excitement among American historians and those who followed the Second Amendment and gun-control issues. Supporters of stricter gun control were particularly heartened by Bellesiles's study, believing that it would prove fatal to the individual rights view of the right to bear arms. The hopes that *Arming America* would be a stake in the heart of the individual rights view were dashed as more and more scholars started to take a closer look at Bellesiles's sources only to find that his claims were simply not supported by his supposed sources. *Arming America* would end up casting, fairly or unfairly, a pall on the work of scholars who supported the collective rights view of the Second Amendment. The debate would nonetheless continue.[6]

It would continue, and get a higher and higher profile, at the start of the twenty-first century, when it was becoming increasingly likely that the Supreme Court would take a case involving the Second Amendment. The amendment had become a hot topic for law reviews. It had become a reliable staple in the nation's op-ed pages. A number of states had adopted assault weapons bans. Many observers and gun owners thought these bans could or should be the object of a Supreme Court case that might settle the matter once and for all. In 2002 a short-lived television series, *First Monday*, presenting a fictional Supreme Court presided over by a chief justice played by actor James Garner, featured an episode where a Second Amendment case was brought before the Court. In the dramatization, the Court by a narrow 5 to 4 margin ruled in favor of the individual right to own arms.[7]

And it was not only academic writings, op-ed pieces, and TV dramas that caused many observers to believe that the time was ripe for the Court to weigh in on the debate. The political winds had shifted. The Clinton administration had been strongly in favor of stricter gun controls. The new administration of George W. Bush had won an excruciatingly narrow electoral victory over Clinton's vice president Al Gore with strong support from the NRA. The new administration quickly made known its support for the view that the Second Amendment protected a right of individuals. In April 2001, Bush's attorney general, John Ashcroft, wrote a letter to the NRA's Institute for Legislative Action expressing support for the individual rights view. Ashcroft's letter concluded, "It is clear that the Constitution protects the private ownership of firearms for lawful purposes." The views expressed in that letter would later become official administration policy, expressed in an "Attorney General's Opinion" in 2004.[8]

With a healthy body of scholarship in law reviews supporting the claim that the Second Amendment was meant to support the individual's right to have arms and with a new administration that was friendly toward that point of view, many people argued that a decision to bring a case should be made and without further delay. The NRA had had internal meetings and meetings with sympathetic scholars to discuss bringing a case. The gun laws of the District of Columbia were the obvious choice. The district had a total ban on handguns in the home for self-defense. Coupled with that, rifles and shotguns had to be rendered inoperable so that they too could not be used to defend home and family. And DC was federal territory. A litigant could bring a pure Second Amendment case unencumbered by the pesky incorporation issue. It was promising.

It was also risky. A case that would actually get to the Supreme Court and produce a definitive pronouncement on the Second Amendment could bring fantastic results—for example, if the Court stated that the Second Amendment protected a right of the individual and overturned a restrictive gun law. But the NRA's leadership also feared another equally or perhaps more likely possibility: a decision that stated that at the end of the day, the constitutional provision that seemingly protected the right of the people to keep and bear arms actually did something far less, perhaps only protecting state militias, or only protecting people in organized state militias, or some variation on those two themes. The courts had not been friendly to the individual rights view of the amendment; why assume that the Supreme Court would now reverse what had been some seven decades of judicial hostility? Why gamble everything on a long shot? Could anybody be sure there were five justices willing to go out on a limb and vote to declare the DC law unconstitutional?

While that internal debate was raging at the NRA, the worst fears of the shooter's organization and other gun owners' rights activists were almost realized: a Second Amendment case with enough legs to get to the Supreme Court was being brought by a litigant involved in criminal activity. There were very real fears in the Second Amendment community that the first time the Court heard a fully litigated case on the meaning of the Second Amendment, it would do so with a claimant who was not at all sympathetic.

The case involved a charge of a violation of the prohibition against possessing firearms by those under a restraining order due to accusations of domestic violence. The 1994 Crime Bill, which had included the assault weapons ban, also contained a provision popularly known as the Violence Against Women Act. The provision included a restriction making it unlawful for a person under a restraining order due to the threat of domestic violence to possess a firearm. That restriction seemed designed for Texas physician Timothy Joe Emerson. Emerson had purchased a gun in 1997. During the course of the following year his marriage had deteriorated. His wife filed for a divorce, claiming that her estranged husband had threatened to kill a friend of hers. Emerson believed that his wife and the friend were having an affair. After the restraining order was issued, Emerson was accused of brandishing the weapon at his wife. Emerson was indicted for violating the Violence Against Women Act. He filed a motion to dismiss the indictment, arguing, among other infirmities, that the statute violated his rights under the Second Amendment.[9]

The motion was heard in the Western District of Texas by US District

Court judge Sam Cummings. In April 1999, Judge Cummings sided with Emerson, issuing an opinion stating that the Second Amendment guaranteed an individual right to private gun possession and that the statute Emerson was charged with violating infringed his right to keep and bear arms. Cummings wrote that the statute

> is unconstitutional because it allows a state court divorce proceeding, without particularized findings of the threat of future violence, to automatically deprive a citizen of his Second Amendment rights. The statute . . . does not require . . . that the person under the order represents a credible threat to the physical safety of the intimate partner or child. . . . If the statute only criminalized gun possession based upon court orders with particularized findings of the likelihood of violence, then the statute would not be so offensive.
>
> It is absurd that a boilerplate state court divorce order can collaterally and automatically extinguish a law-abiding citizen's Second Amendment rights.[10]

This was historic. For the first time since 1938, when Judge Ragon had quashed the indictments of Jack Miller and Frank Layton, a federal court held that the Second Amendment protected an individual right to private gun ownership and that a federal statute restricting gun ownership was unconstitutional. For supporters of the right to keep and bear arms it was historic and troubling. The ruling would be appealed. What would happen in the appellate courts? Would the fate of the Second Amendment be decided by the case of an unsympathetic litigant? Would it ultimately be killed by the wrong case at the wrong time?

The Justice Department appealed the ruling to the Fifth Circuit Court of Appeals. Emerson and the government were joined by a broad array of amici—gun-control groups, gun owners' advocates, advocates against domestic violence, university professors on both sides of the issue, and think tanks of various political and policy persuasions, among others. All recognized that this could be the case that got to the Supreme Court and defined the Second Amendment, perhaps for all time. The parties and amici filed their briefs and waited and waited. The Fifth Circuit was in no hurry. Almost two and a half years passed between Judge Cumming's dismissal of Emerson's indictment and the Fifth Circuit's decision. In a lengthy opinion written by Judge William Garwood, the Fifth Circuit discussed the text and history of the Second Amendment and the meager Supreme Court case law associated with it. The

panel agreed with Judge Cummings that the Second Amendment protected
an individual's right to keep and bear arms, but it rejected his conclusion that
the Violence Against Women Act violated Emerson's rights. The court held:

> We agree with the district court that the Second Amendment protects the right
> of individuals to privately keep and bear their own firearms that are suitable as
> individual, personal weapons . . . regardless of whether the particular individual
> is then actually a member of a militia. However . . . we also conclude that the
> [protective order] here is sufficient, albeit likely minimally so, to support the
> deprivation, while it remains in effect, of the defendant's Second Amendment
> rights. Accordingly, we reverse the district court's dismissal of the indictment on
> Second Amendment grounds.[11]

The ruling did Emerson little good. On remand, he was convicted of violating the statute and sentenced to thirty months in prison followed by three
years of supervised release. Emerson petitioned the Supreme Court for certiorari. Frequently a split in the circuits, particularly on a constitutional question, can prompt the Court to take a case. But even with the circuit split the
Supreme Court was unlikely to take this case. The Court receives an average of
7,000–8,000 cert petitions each year. It decides to hear or grants cert for some
eighty cases annually. Although the Fifth Circuit was, at that point, the only
circuit court to recognize the Second Amendment as protecting the right of
an individual, and although most other circuits had disagreed, Emerson's case
was still unlikely to get a hearing from the high court. The Fifth Circuit had
declared that the relevant provisions of the Violence Against Women Act were
constitutional. Emerson's conviction would be valid under either the Fifth
Circuit's individual rights interpretation of the Second Amendment or the
militia-only interpretations of other circuits. There was little reason for the
Supreme Court to take the rare step of granting a cert petition. On June 10,
2002, the Supreme Court denied Emerson's petition. For supporters of the
individual rights view, that denial was undoubtedly fortuitous. Emerson was
a problematic plaintiff bringing a case with less than compelling facts. Such
considerations can be critical when the Court is deciding to examine an issue
in essence for the first time.[12]

The Fifth Circuit's decision may have done little for Emerson, but it went
a long way to help increase the respectability of the individual rights position.
For the first time a circuit court had, in unambiguous terms, endorsed the

view that the Second Amendment protected the rights of individuals. What's more, the Fifth Circuit opinion had done so after a fairly detailed discussion of the text and history of the amendment. For opponents of the individual rights view, the opinion demanded a response.[13]

That response would come from the Ninth Circuit the following year in the case of *Silvera v. Lockyer*. The case involved a Second Amendment challenge to California's assault weapons ban. Ninth Circuit judge Stephen Reinhardt used the case to rebut the Garwood opinion in *Emerson*. Reinhardt's opinion examined the text and history of the Second Amendment to make the case that the constitutional provision was meant to protect the arms of the organized militia and not the population at large. The Reinhardt opinion might be seen as a direct rebuttal meant to buttress the collective rights view. It was, interestingly enough, unnecessary for the purposes of sustaining the California legislation. The assault weapons ban was state law, and as the reigning Supreme Court doctrine was that the Second Amendment was not incorporated, the Ninth Circuit was presumably bound to declare that the ban was not a violation of the Second Amendment because the amendment did not apply to the states. By writing an opinion that was a rebuttal to the Fifth Circuit opinion in *Emerson*, Judge Reinhardt only helped to highlight the fact that the circuits were now split on the question.[14]

The high-profile circuit split, and the fact that one circuit court had embraced the individual rights reading of the Second Amendment, caused many observers to believe that the time had come to bring a case that could go all the way to the Supreme Court. Among those wondering whether such a case might be possible and prudent were two attorneys who worked at the Institute for Justice, Clark Neily and Steve Simpson. The institute is a libertarian public-interest law firm known primarily for constitutional litigation against various forms of economic regulation. Experienced litigators, Neily and Simpson both knew that for the Court to be persuaded to adopt an individual rights reading, the suit would have to be brought by an extremely sympathetic plaintiff in a very restrictive jurisdiction. Ideally, the plaintiff should be a law-abiding citizen who lived in a high-crime area whose laws made it nearly impossible to own a gun for self-defense.[15]

BRINGING THE CASE

Like the NRA, Neily and Clark recognized that the District of Columbia was the logical choice. But could such a case get to the Supreme Court? Despite the odds, Neily and Simpson wanted to press forward. They spoke to their boss, institute director Chip Mellor, outlining the proposal. In Mellor they faced a skeptic who believed that the Second Amendment was outside of the institute's core mission, economic regulation. Nonetheless, Mellor gave Neily permission to explore litigation possibilities.[16]

Litigation would be expensive and time-consuming. Neily realized he would need to find a benefactor willing to underwrite the litigation and a first-rate firearms lawyer to prosecute the case. For financing, Neily, a graduate of the University of Texas School of Law, sought out Bob Levy, a wealthy entrepreneur and investor known to support libertarian causes. Levy, who had earned a PhD in business administration from American University in 1966, had returned to law school as an older student. He received his JD from the George Mason University School of Law in 1994. Levy, like Neily, had clerked for Judge Royce Lamberth of the US District Court for the District of Columbia. Levy was now at the Cato Institute, a DC-based libertarian think tank. Libertarians tend to be skeptical of government regulation frequently in ways that fall outside of the conventional left-right spectrum in American politics and often in ways that both liberals and conservatives tend to find vexing. Libertarians are almost invariably critics of what they see as governmental overregulation of economic activity and are also disinclined to support state regulation of private sexual activity. Libertarians have also tended to be skeptical of many gun-control measures. Levy fell into this category. He agreed to fund the litigation. Now Levy and Clark needed a lawyer.[17]

They first approached Stephen Halbrook. The Second Amendment scholar was a seasoned litigator and firearms law expert. At the time Halbrook was already a Supreme Court veteran, having prevailed in the high tribunal in three cases. Halbrook was intrigued, but Levy hesitated when Halbrook quoted him his usual hourly rate. Given the time it would take to build a good case, Halbrook's fee would likely be a substantial one—with no guarantee either that the Court would agree to hear the case or, if it did, that Neily and Levy would prevail. They kept looking.[18]

Neily and Levy moved on to Alan Gura, a young lawyer who Levy knew from libertarian circles. Gura was thirty-one years old and worked in a small law firm in Alexandria, Virginia. Gura had once interned for the Institute for Justice. He was self-confident, believed he could win, and was willing to work for a relative pittance. Gura realized that the reputation he would gain by winning such a landmark case would more than make up for the fees he was agreeing to forgo. Gura knew the value of what he was offering. He extracted a promise from Levy that if the case made it to the high court, Gura would argue the case and would not be dropped in favor of a marquee appellate advocate from a big law firm's Supreme Court litigation shop. Neily and Levy had their lawyer.[19]

The plan, a lawsuit challenging the District of Columbia handgun ban, encountered early resistance from the National Rifle Association. Gura and Levy met with NRA general counsel Robert Dowlut and other representatives from the organization, who tried to discourage pursuing the case. The NRA feared a definitive unfavorable ruling from the Supreme Court. The organization's lawyers and outside counsel were doubtful that there were five justices willing to uphold the individual rights view of the right to bear arms. A modern adverse ruling, particularly in the case of a near total prohibition like the District of Columbia's, would not be remote and ambiguous like *Miller*. Nor could it be readily explained away like much of the case law in the lower federal courts. It would instead be devastating. Such a ruling might set the rights of gun owners back by decades and could destroy the individual rights view of the Second Amendment for all time. The stakes could not have been higher. Gura and Levy thought the shooter's organization was being unduly risk averse. They decided to press ahead without the NRA's help. The NRA saw a situation that could spin out of control with disastrous results. The organization looked for measures that might prevent the worst outcome—a case getting to the Supreme Court, with the Court deciding definitively in favor of a collective reading of the Second Amendment. The three libertarian lawyers and the NRA supported the same cause but were now adversaries, not allies.[20]

That adversarial relationship led to the filing of two separate cases. Gura, who had been preparing all along to bring suit against the District of Columbia, went first. On February 10, 2003, he brought a complaint challenging DC's handgun ban. Filing on behalf of six plaintiffs, Shelly Parker, Dick Anthony Heller, Tom G. Palmer, Gillian St. Lawrence, Tracey Ambeau, and George Lyon, Gura did what is often done in public-interest litigation: he selected plaintiffs whose personal stories illustrated why the case was not only an academic legal argument but also compelling from a human point. The lead plaintiff, Shelly Parker, an African American woman, had been threatened by drug dealers who objected to her efforts to combat crime in her neighborhood. She seemed perfect: a law-abiding woman who was attempting to improve living conditions for herself and her neighbors and was targeted by criminals as a result. She wanted a handgun for self-defense, but the district's laws prevented her from legally possessing one. The second plaintiff, Dick Anthony Heller, was a security guard and was designated as a special police officer under district law. He could carry a gun in the course of his duties guarding the Thurgood Marshall Judicial Center but was legally prohibited from using a firearm to guard himself at home, even though he lived in a high-crime neighborhood. Tom Palmer was a gay man who had been the victim of assault because of his sexual orientation. He wanted to be able to have firearms at home for self-defense. The other plaintiffs all asserted a need to have firearms in their homes for self-defense. Gura only sued the district and rested his complaint on Second Amendment grounds alone.[21]

Gura's suit alarmed the NRA. A suit against the District of Columbia's firearms bans seemingly could not be avoided. Years of internal debate on the subject had been overtaken by events. With the mutual distrust between Gura and Levy on the one hand and the NRA on the other, the NRA decided to act in a way that might, from its point of view, mitigate the damage and perhaps hedge a bet. The organization hired Stephen Halbrook and his co-counsel Richard Gardiner to bring its own action against the district, which they did on April 4, 2003. Like Gura, Halbrook gathered a mixture of sympathetic plaintiffs, all of whom had compelling claims that they had been or were likely to be victims of the high rate of violent crime in the nation's capital and needed to have a functional firearm at home for defense. The lead plaintiff was Sandra Seegars, who lived in a high-crime neighborhood and had been a crime victim. Like Gura, Halbrook drafted a complaint that argued that the district's statute violated the Second Amendment. But Halbrook did more. First, his complaint was filed not only against the District of Columbia but also against Attorney General John Ashcroft. The reasoning was simple. The Justice Department under Ashcroft had taken the position that the Second Amendment protected the rights of individuals. The Justice Department could not defend the district's statute on a Second Amendment challenge and remain consistent with the department's new position.[22]

Halbrook did something else: he included three additional counts that went beyond the Second Amendment claim. According to Halbrook's complaint, the District of Columbia's legislation was legally problematic because it exceeded the district's authority under Congress's Home Rule Act, which authorized the DC city council to enact usual and reasonable regulations controlling firearms. Halbrook also took the position that the DC firearms ban violated the Civil Rights Act of 1866 and the due process clause of the Fifth Amendment. Lawyers who engage in public-interest litigation often have a dilemma deciding whether their main obligation is to the named client that they are representing or to the broader legal principle that they are trying to vindicate. The answer to that question can often determine whether a lawyer offers the court a single legal theory on which to base its decision or multiple theories, any one of which might provide the client with the sought-after relief. It also might determine whether an attorney uses a strategy that employs an untested or disfavored legal theory in the hopes of establishing a new legal precedent or uses a more established legal claim. Halbrook recognized that at that point the Second Amendment claim was a disfavored one. By making the additional claims, he hoped to avoid the worst result, a court focusing solely on the Second Amendment and declaring that the amendment did not protect the rights of individuals.[23]

Both suits went forward in the federal district court for the District of Columbia. They would go forward against a background of unsuccessful NRA efforts to have the district's statute repealed through congressional legislation. Had Congress, which has ultimate power over the district's laws, done so, the cases would have been moot. That did not happen. Instead, the district court heard the cases.[24]

The court got to the claims of the plaintiffs represented by Halbrook first. On January 14, 2004, the district court issued its decision. The judgment went against the plaintiffs, although there was at least a partial victory for Halbrook's decision to bring suit against Ashcroft as well as the District of Columbia. The Justice Department in its reply to Halbrook's complaint conceded the basic point that the Second Amendment protected a right of individuals and that the plaintiffs indeed did have a right to have firearms in their homes for self-defense. Instead of contesting that point, the Justice Department argued that the plaintiffs lacked standing to bring suit because they had not been prosecuted or threatened with prosecution under the DC statute. The government's reply noted the plaintiffs had not even attempted to register their firearms. They therefore lacked standing, and the issues were not ripe for the district court to review.[25]

The Justice Department had gotten around its dilemma—how to defend the DC statute without repudiating the attorney general's position that the Second Amendment protected an individual right—by invoking technical rules that can make litigation difficult, even when a party appears to have a constitutional or other legal claim that calls for resolution by the courts. The requirement that a plaintiff has standing is rooted in the constitutional requirement that the courts decide actual cases in controversy and not issue advisory opinions or give opinions on hypothetical cases. Before a plaintiff can have her day in court, she must show that a particular law or governmental practice is causing concrete injury. The federal government's position was that Sandra Seegars and her co-plaintiffs had not suffered injury and hence their claims should be dismissed.[26]

If the Justice Department did not contest Seegars's Second Amendment claims, the government of the District of Columbia did. The district's response was to argue that the Second Amendment did not protect a right of individuals and that therefore the plaintiffs had no legal claim against the district. The district court separated the claims of the plaintiffs. Lead plaintiff Sandra Seegars and three of the other plaintiffs had not previously attempted to register pistols in the District of Columbia. The district court dismissed their claims on the grounds argued by the Justice Department—that the plaintiffs lacked standing. A fifth plaintiff, Gardine Hailes, owned a legally registered shotgun in the District of Columbia. The court ruled that she had standing to contest the district's requirement that the weapon be rendered inoperable for home defense. The substantive complaints would have to be addressed. The court dismissed the claims made by Halbrook and Gardiner rooted in the Civil Rights Act of 1866, the congressional statute authorizing DC firearms legislation, and the due process clause of the Fifth Amendment. The district court then turned to Hailes's Second Amendment claim. Judge Reggie B. Walton did a fairly detailed review of the history of the Second Amendment and the then existing case law and issued an opinion stating that the amendment did not apply to residents of the District of Columbia and only applied to members of the organized militia.[27]

Gura's case would meet a similar fate in the district court. On March 31, 2004, Judge Emmet G. Sullivan dismissed the claims of Parker and the others on the grounds that the Second Amendment was meant to apply to the militia and not individuals. Judge Sullivan included some brief praise for Gura's argument but concluded that the weight of both Supreme Court and lower federal court precedent was firmly in favor of the militia-only view of the amendment.[28]

Gura had expected to lose, but the delay cost him the race to appellate court. Because Halbrook's suit had been dismissed earlier; he, not Gura, would be the first to file an appeal with the US Court of Appeals for the DC Circuit. The DC Circuit delayed Gura's appeal until it could rule on Halbrook's. Halbrook was, at least temporarily, in control of the litigation over the DC gun laws. On February 8, 2005, a three-judge panel of the DC Circuit issued an opinion upholding the trial court ruling. The appellate court opinion authored by Judge Stephen F. Williams agreed that the four plaintiffs seeking to be allowed to have pistols in their homes lacked standing. Curiously enough, the court also determined that Gardine Hailes lacked standing as well because she was not under threat of imminent prosecution. The appellate court side-stepped the constitutional issue, neither endorsing nor contesting the district court's Second Amendment reasoning. The circuit court instead mentioned in brief passing that there were differing views on the subject, noting the Fifth and Ninth Circuit disagreements in *Emerson* and *Silveira*. Judge David B. Sentelle, a member of the panel, issued a dissenting opinion arguing that the plaintiffs likely had a valid Second Amendment claim that should be considered and not be thwarted by the rules of standing. Sentelle further observed that the courts had developed far more liberal rules in determining if an individual had standing in cases involving free speech claims and First Amendment protections, and that the court should adopt that posture with respect to the Second Amendment claims in this case. The DC Circuit Court denied the petition for rehearing en banc in June 2005, and the Supreme Court denied certiorari in January 2006.[29]

While Halbrook and Gardiner's efforts on behalf of Sandra Seegar and the others were being defeated by the rules of standing, Alan Gura was proceeding with his representation of Shelly Parker and her co-plaintiffs. On December 7, 2006, Gura argued his case before the DC Circuit. Gura's draw at the appellate court might have given him some confidence. The three-judge was made up of two Reagan appointees, Karen Henderson and Laurence Silberman, and one George W. Bush appointee, Thomas Griffith. All were seen as reliable conservatives who would likely be sympathetic to the individual rights reading of the Second Amendment. Oral argument was set for December 2006; it would be Gura's first argument before a federal appeals court. Silberman clashed with the district's lawyer during oral argument. He forced him to concede that at least some plaintiffs could challenge DC's laws without having applied for a permit. The signs looked promising for a favorable decision.[30]

In fact, Silberman wrote the majority opinion. He first examined the standing issue that had thwarted Seegars and her co-plaintiffs. His opinion noted the standing requirements had been decided in *Seegars*, and that those requirements disqualified Shelly Parker and four of her co-plaintiffs. But the standing requirements did not disqualify Dick Heller. The DC special police officer had previously taken the necessary but seemingly futile step of attempting to register a handgun in the district. Heller had actually been planning for some time, along with his friend Dane Von Breichenrud, a libertarian activist, to find a way to challenge DC's firearms statute. Breichenrud advised Heller to attempt to register a handgun in the district. Heller did so. It was a small matter, but it was enough to allow the court of appeals to find standing and consider the core constitutional issue.[31]

Judge Silberman's opinion was decisive: the Second Amendment unequivocally protected the right of individuals. The right was individual, not collective, and was not conditioned on any formal service in or affiliation with a militia:

> We conclude that the Second Amendment protects an individual right to keep and bear arms. That right existed prior to the formation of the new government under the Constitution and was premised on the private use of arms for activities such as hunting and self-defense, the latter being understood as resistance to either private lawlessness or the depredations of a tyrannical government (or a threat from abroad). In addition, the right to keep and bear arms had the important and salutary civic purpose of helping to preserve the citizen militia. The civic purpose was also a political expedient for the Federalists in the First Congress as it served, in part, to placate their Antifederalist opponents. The individual right facilitated militia service by ensuring that citizens would not be barred from keeping the arms they would need when called forth for militia duty. Despite the importance of the Second Amendment's civic purpose, however, the activities it protects are not limited to militia service, nor is an individual's enjoyment of the right contingent upon his or her continued or intermittent enrollment in the militia.[32]

Judge Silberman then defined the "arms" included within the scope of the right to include weapons in common use at the time of the ratification of the Bill of Rights "and their lineal descendants." The latter obviously included handguns. While conceding that the District of Columbia might reasonably restrict the exercise of this right, he concluded that "once it is determined . . . that handguns are 'Arms' referred to in the Second Amendment, it is not open to the District to ban them." Among other things, the ban on "carrying" of pistols without a license would apply to moving from room to room in one's house or apartment.[33]

In the opinion, Silberman also addressed DC's defense of the requirement that long guns had to be kept disabled. The district sought to defend that provision by arguing that a judge would likely give that requirement a narrow reading if deciding a case involving legitimate self-defense in the home. Silberman replied, "That might be so, but judicial lenity cannot make up for the unreasonable restriction of a constitutional right." He concluded that the safe storage provision, "like the bar on carrying a pistol within the home, amounted to a complete prohibition on the lawful use of firearms for self-defense" and was unconstitutional.[34]

To Gura and Levy's surprise, Judge Karen Henderson dissented. In her dissent, she read *Miller* to endorse the collective rights position, and felt bound to follow that case. In addition, she endorsed the district's argument that the Second Amendment did not even apply to the district. The argument went like this: The Second Amendment refers to the necessity of a militia for the security of a free *state*. The District of Columbia is not a state, but rather a federal enclave; ergo, the Second Amendment does not apply to it. If nothing else, her dissent was a reminder that Gura and Levy could not count on the votes of every conservative jurist. That had been the NRA's concern when it had initially discouraged the suit.[35]

## THE ROAD TO ONE FIRST ST., NE

Gura's victory in the DC Circuit Court put the shoe on the other foot. Having lost in the DC Circuit, the district began to feel pressure from gun-control advocates to cut its losses for fear that Gura and Levy might actually prevail at the Supreme Court. The Court, after all, had changed. Following the death of Chief Justice William Rehnquist, John Roberts was sworn in in September 2005 to replace him. Justice Sandra Day O'Connor retired at the end of the 2004–2005 term and was replaced in January 2006 by Third Circuit judge Sam Alito.

As is usual in Supreme Court litigation, both sides tried to handicap the Court and guess which justices were likely to support or oppose their positions. For Gura, and other supporters of the individual rights position, two justices appeared to have signaled a favorable position in earlier writings. Justice Antonin Scalia in his scholarly writings about the Court and the Constitution had shown sympathy for the individual rights position.[36] Justice Clarence Thomas in a concurring opinion in *Printz v. United States*, a case involving the power of the federal government to compel state law enforcement officials to enforce federal gun-control statutes, indicated that he believed that the gun-control legislation might be suspect on Second Amendment grounds.[37] While Justice O'Connor had been a moderate—at times siding with the Court's conservative wing, at other times siding with the liberal justices—her replacement Alito was seen as more conservative and likely to support the individual rights view. Newly minted chief justice Roberts in his confirmation hearing had rejected the idea that the militia-only view of the amendment was settled law. For both sides, the great unknown was Justice Anthony Kennedy. Like Justice O'Connor, the justice from California was not a lock for either camp. What the Court would do was unclear, a worry for both sides.[38]

Despite the misgivings of many gun-control advocates, the district decided to continue the case and petition for certiorari. To handle the case, the district's attorney general, Linda Singer, first turned to Alan Morrison, an experienced appellate advocate who had taught at the Harvard, New York University, and Stanford schools of law. Singer had hired Morrison as special counsel. With the *Heller* case on track for Supreme Court review, Singer had to make a decision on DC's representative. Todd Kim, the district's solicitor general, might have been the logical choice. But Morrison pointed out to Kim and Singer that Kim had never argued a case before the high court, while he, Morrison, was a veteran Supreme Court litigator with a strong track record. Kim and Singer agreed that Morrison should handle the case. Morrison started working on the district's brief before cert was granted. In a later interview Morrison would state that he had confidence in the district's position, but that the case was not a "slam-dunk." Morrison believed that the district was right to appeal. This was welcome news to DC mayor Adrian Fenty, who was determined to see the fight through. Singer, Morrison, and their legal team filed a petition for certiorari in September 2007. Their petition was granted on November 20.[39]

Gura and Levy's joy at winning in the DC Circuit Court was tempered by the fact that the court upheld the denial of standing to all of their plaintiffs but Heller. The loss of Parker, a Black woman threatened by neighborhood drug dealers, was especially unfortunate. She would no longer be the lead and named plaintiff. *Parker v. District of Columbia* would become *District of Columbia v. Heller.* In place of the sympathetic Parker, who had a compelling personal story, they were going to the nation's highest tribunal with Dick Heller. Heller's political opinions could at times sound like a gun-control supporter's worst stereotype of a paranoid, antigovernment "gun nut." He compared the district's government with that of the Soviet Union. He expressed the view that the people needed to be armed not just to fight off everyday criminals but potentially to revolt against the US government. Although the idea that the population should be armed to be able to resist a potentially tyrannical government had been part of the political philosophy behind the right to bear arms from Madison's *Federalist*, no. 46 in 1788 to Ninth Circuit judge Alex Kosinski's dissent in *Silveira* in 2003, it was not the prime argument that Gura and his team wanted to place before the Supreme Court. Gura impressed upon Heller the need for emphasizing self-defense at home, not hypothetical revolutions. Dick Heller might not have been Gura's ideal client, but he was Gura's client nonetheless.[40]

Shortly after Morrison began to work on the briefs and prepare for oral argument, he became collateral damage resulting from infighting among Fenty's staff and DC attorney general Singer. Fenty had hired Peter Nickles as his general counsel and special advisor. Nickles and Singer clashed repeatedly; Singer felt that Nickles was usurping her authority, especially after he ordered her to drop a lawsuit against the Bank of America over money stolen from the district by a bank employee. The *Washington Post* then ran a story about the lawsuit, noting that Nickles's old law firm represented the bank. Singer resigned, and the *Post* ran a follow-up story about the feud between her and Nickels. Nickels then succeeded Singer as attorney general and began a purge of all those in the office seen as Singer loyalists. Thinking Morrison was among those still loyal to Singer, Nickels fired Morrison as well. Morrison's last day was January 4, 2008, the day that the district's brief was due. Oral argument was just over two months away. A new lawyer would have to step into Morrison's shoes, starting from square one, framing the arguments and preparing for oral argument.[41]

That burden fell on Walter Dellinger, a North Carolina native and Yale Law School graduate who had clerked for Justice Hugo Black and had a distinguished career as a professor at Duke Law School. During the Clinton administration, Dellinger served as the head of the Office of Legal Counsel (which advises the president on constitutional law matters), as well as acting solicitor general. Dellinger was an experienced Supreme Court advocate, and since becoming professor emeritus at Duke, he conducted appellate litigation for the law firm O'Melveny and Myers in DC. Preparing for oral argument before the US Supreme Court is an arduous task in the best of circumstances; preparing in two months when someone else was supposed to argue the case meant Dellinger's labor was now Herculean. Compounding his difficulties further, Dellinger had already been scheduled to appear before the Supreme Court that term representing Exxon in a bet-the-company case challenging the constitutionality of a $2.5 billion punitive damage award to plaintiffs who were harmed by the wreck of the Exxon *Valdez* in 1989 and the resulting oil spill.[42]

For Gura, preparation was even more daunting. He had won in the district and the DC Circuit Court, but he was still a rookie at big-ticket federal appellate litigation. And on March 18, 2008, he was scheduled for the biggest ticket of them all—the United States Supreme Court. Dellinger needed to juggle his schedule and learn a lot quickly about what at the time was an arcane, rarely considered area of the law: the Second Amendment. But Gura needed more. He had to further polish his skills as an appellate advocate. All appellate litigators work to improve their advocacy through the use of moot courts. Moot courts give lawyers the chance to sharpen their arguments through their responses to questions—especially questions that may be hostile or seemingly totally out of left field. Moot courts also give attorneys a chance to experience traps, traps in which a jurist may try to force a seemingly modest concession out of an advocate. That modest concession might lead to giving away the whole argument. Gura went through a number of moot courts in early 2008. One of them was at the Supreme Court Institute's Supreme Court Moot Court Program at Gura's alma mater, Georgetown. The institute offers any litigant scheduled to argue before the Supreme Court the opportunity to practice in a setting made to look very much like the high court.

Gura had another mooting that might have been more significant. Held on March 6 at the George Mason University Law School and organized by 2004 George Mason graduate Alice Beard, this moot court occurred twelve days before Gura's scheduled Supreme Court appearance. It included several individuals quite familiar with the Second Amendment: Eugene Volokh, a leading constitutional law scholar at UCLA; and independent scholars David Hardy and David Kopel. The moot panel also included Gura's rival in the DC litigation, Stephen Halbrook. The judges probed the range of difficult issues that would likely confront Gura during oral argument. If Judge Silberman in the DC Circuit Court was correct, which arms were protected? If modern arms, why not machine guns? One judge pointed out that unless Gura found a way to distinguish machine guns from other modern firearms, the Court would likely reject the whole concept of an individual right to arms. The mooting at George Mason had two sessions. After each session the judges and Gura did postmortems discussing on which points to hold firm, and which points to concede. They debated how Gura should respond if asked by a justice whether the Second Amendment included a right to carry firearms or simply a right to have arms in the home? Judge Silberman in the DC Circuit opinion had stated that the arms protected were arms that were in common use among the public; wasn't that circular reasoning? If the 1934 National Firearms Act hadn't put automatic weapons under tight restrictions, wouldn't machine guns now be in common use? The moot court anticipated every question that the justices conceivably could ask. They hoped.[43]

Dellinger and Gura awaited March 18, their date before the Supreme Court.

## THE BRIEFS

Oral argument is only a small part of the case that a party puts before the Supreme Court. Much of the parties' legal and factual case comes in the form of written briefs. Brief writing is partly a strategic exercise; how narrow or how broad an issue does a party want the court to consider? Gura would later explain his briefing strategy in *Heller*: "Strategic civil rights litigation depends on crafting a narrow case, one which forces the courts to answer the fewest number of questions. Our objective was to have the Second Amendment defined as securing a meaningful individual right—not resolve the constitutionality of every possible gun regulation."[44]

In *Heller*, the briefs on both sides largely reflected the arguments made in the DC Circuit Court. The district argued that (1) the right contained in the Second Amendment was inextricably linked to militia membership; (2) the amendment did not apply to the district itself; and (3) that even if the amendment guaranteed an individual right unconnected with militia service, the district's laws were reasonable regulations of that right.[45] Gura's brief was written with the aid of Levy and Neily. It argued that the Second Amendment protected an individual right without regard to participation in a militia. They argued accordingly that the handgun ban and the ban on the possession of operable firearms in the home were both unconstitutional. Their brief scoffed at the notion that the District of Columbia was a "Constitution-free zone." "Washington," they wrote, "was not planned as a 'Forbidden City' in which federal officials would be shielded from the hazards of interaction with the otherwise free people of the United States."[46]

Their brief also argued that "strict scrutiny" should be the standard of review for cases involving the Second Amendment, as opposed to a "reasonableness" standard (as proposed by the district) or "heightened" scrutiny (as argued by the United States). Standards of review are a judicially created criterion for measuring the constitutionality of governmental action. They are necessary because the simple statement of a constitutional principle would give the courts little guidance on how to resolve concrete cases. For example, it is one thing to say that the state must guarantee equal protection to all persons within its jurisdiction; it is quite another to ask whether that authorizes (or prohibits) the use of race in higher-education admissions decisions. Strict scrutiny is regarded as the most demanding standard of review. Generally applied when the government infringes upon certain "fundamental" rights, it requires the government to demonstrate that the regulation is necessary (or narrowly tailored) to a "compelling" governmental interest. The US government was worried that this might render certain federal restrictions on firearms ownership—the ban on possession by felons or the ban on private possession of most fully automatic weapons, for example—vulnerable to constitutional challenge, and it sought to convince the Court to adopt a less rigorous standard of review. The government's position is discussed in more detail below.[47]

In addition to the principal briefs of the parties, and their reply briefs, scores of amicus curiae—"friend of the court"—briefs were filed in *Heller*. An amicus brief is one that is filed by a nonparty to the case, ostensibly to provide the court with information not contained in the parties' briefs that might be useful or helpful in resolving the dispute. High-profile cases like *Heller* produce a slew of briefs from state attorneys general, members of Congress, university professors, and myriad interest groups. Often amicus briefs are simply variants on the parties' arguments or stress the potential that the court's ruling may have on particular interests. Constitutional scholar Ilya Shapiro's research indicates that more amicus briefs were filed in *Heller* than in any other Supreme Court case up to that time.[48]

Dueling briefs filed by differing groups of scholars are common in high-profile cases, and they could be found in abundance in *Heller*. One group of criminal justice scholars argued that DC's handgun ban was effective and therefore reasonable. Another group of criminologists disagreed, concluding that there was no evidence the handgun ban had done much to make the district safer. The range of groups that weighed in on one side or another encompassed the broad range of American civil society, including law professors, historians, civil rights groups, law enforcement personnel, members of Congress, state attorneys general, organizations concerned with military preparedness, physicians, firearms organizations, and public-interest groups of all stripes. There was even a brief filed by a group of linguists who argued that the rules of grammar mandated reversal of the court of appeals' decision.[49]

## ORAL ARGUMENT

Ordinarily each side receives only thirty minutes to argue its case before the Supreme Court. Time is monitored by lights that alert lawyers when their time is running out and when it has expired. The time limit is rigorously enforced. *Heller* was unusual because in addition to Alan Gura and Walter Dellinger, Paul Clement—the solicitor general of the United States—was allowed time to give the federal government's views as well. Ordinarily two cases are scheduled beginning at 10 A.M. *Heller* was scheduled to be heard alone on Tuesday morning, March 18, 2008. Those hoping to get one of the few seats available to watch the oral argument began lining up days before. At 10:06, Chief Justice Roberts announced that the Court "will hear argument today in Case 07–290, District of Columbia versus Heller."[50]

Dellinger's argument tracked the district's brief. First, he would strenuously argue that the right to keep and bear arms guaranteed by the Second Amendment was inseparable from some form of militia service. Later he argued that even if the scope of the right included some right of private gun ownership for self-defense, the District of Columbia was permitted to prohibit certain categories of weapons if, in its opinion, those weapons posed some particular danger to the public, as long as some other alternatives were available (like the rifles and shotguns the district permitted people to possess).

Finally, he argued that the district would concede that while the law required the permitted rifles and shotguns to be unloaded and inoperable, if those laws were broken while an individual was engaged in self-defense, that individual should not be prosecuted.[51]

Chief Justice Roberts challenged Dellinger, asking why, if the framers wished to protect only state militias, the Second Amendment referred to "the right of the people." When Dellinger responded that "the people" and the "militia" were considered one and the same, Roberts suggested that his answer harmed his case. The right, Dellinger responded, was "a right to participate in the common defense and you have a right invocable (*sic*) in court if a federal regulation interferes with your right to train" for the militia. Given the state of the scholarly debate between the "collective" and "individual" interpretations of the Second Amendment prior to *Heller*, Dellinger's concession at the outset that, whatever its scope, the Second Amendment guaranteed a right that individuals could invoke in court was an interesting one. This point would later be conceded even by *Heller*'s dissenters.[52]

Dellinger was then challenged by Justice Kennedy about his argument that the entire amendment had to be read with that military purpose in mind. Dellinger maintained that "keep and bear arms" would have been understood to have a military connotation. Kennedy asked, "It had nothing to do with the concerns of the remote settler to defend himself and his family against hostile Indian tribes and outlaws, wolves and bears and grizzlies and things like that?" Dellinger maintained that it did not.[53]

Justice Scalia then weighed in, arguing that the first clause (referring to the militia) and the second clause (referring to the right to keep and bear arms) were not only *not* in tension, but rather were perfectly complementary. "Why isn't it perfectly plausible . . . to assume that since the framers knew that the way militias were destroyed by tyrants in the past was not by passing a law against militias, but by taking away the people's weapons," they would have written the amendment the way they did? "The two clauses go together beautifully," he argued, "since we need a militia, the right of the people to keep and bear arms shall not be infringed." Dellinger replied that it made no sense "to require the arm to be militia-related if the right is not, and the key phrase is 'bear arms.'"[54]

In response to a question from Justice Ruth Bader Ginsburg, Dellinger argued that the only restraint imposed by a militia-centered Second Amendment would be on a federal law that interfered in some way with a state's requirements for its militia. Dellinger agreed with Justice Ginsburg's comment that no such law existed, essentially conceding that, under his reading, the amendment did no contemporary work. But, he added, "You don't make up a new use for an amendment whose prohibitions aren't being violated."[55]

Justices Alito and Scalia then challenged Dellinger on his reading of the interplay between the militia clauses of Article I and the Second Amendment.[56] If the purpose of the Second Amendment was to prevent the disarmament of the militia, how did Dellinger square that purpose with the near-plenary power Congress possessed over the militia? Dellinger replied that the Second Amendment gave some security to the institution but didn't completely return it to the state control, as many desired. "Those who wanted to retake State authority over the militia didn't get everything they wanted." "They got nothing at all," protested Justice Scalia. "So long as it was up to the Federal Government to regulate the militia and to ensure they were armed, the Federal Government could . . . disband the State militias." Dellinger demurred, saying that it was "by no means clear" that the federal government had the power to abolish the militia.[57]

Dellinger then suggested that the best argument for Heller's side was that "the amendment's purpose is militia protective, but . . . over-inclusive," and that "preserving the individual right, presumably to have guns for personal use, was the best way to ensure that the militia could serve when called." He went on, though, to reject the "libertarian ideal" where the right is "an unregulated right to whatever arm, wherever kept, however you want to store it, and for the purposes an individual decides." And in response to a question by Justice John Paul Stevens, he reiterated his point by noting that many late eighteenth-century state constitutional provisions stressed the common defense aspects of the right to keep and bear arms.[58]

After a brief discussion about the relevance of the right to keep and bear arms in the 1689 English Bill of Rights, Dellinger pivoted, arguing that if the Court were to recognize a right to keep and bear arms unrelated to military service, it ought to follow the lead of state courts that interpreted similar rights to keep and bear arms enshrined in state constitutions and adopt "a reasonableness standard that has allowed [those state courts] to sustain sensible regulation of dangerous weapons." To which Roberts responded, "What is reasonable about a total ban on possession?" Handguns, he replied, are considered by the district to be especially dangerous, thus—because "there is no showing that rifles and shotguns are not fully satisfactory to carry out" self-defense, for example—it is not unreasonable for the district to enact a categorical ban on that class of weapons. If the Court adopted strict scrutiny, or something close to it, Dellinger warned, "It's hard to see . . . why machine guns or armor-piercing bullets or other dangerous weapons wouldn't be categorically protected."[59]

Justice Scalia was skeptical: "I didn't read it that way. I thought the opinion below said it had to be the kind of weapon that was common for the people" to possess. Dellinger replied that the DC Circuit's opinion "protects weapons suitable for military use that are lineal descendants" and that machine guns and "improved bullets" are covered, unless the Court adopts "the kind of reasonableness standard that we suggest." He then returned to his argument that it was reasonable for DC to categorically ban handguns, which are "concealable and moveable" and "can be taken into schools, into buses, into government office buildings, and that is [a] particular danger . . . in a densely populated urban area." In response to a comment by Chief Justice Roberts, Dellinger again disputed the characterization of DC's law as a total ban. "The District has made clear," he noted, "that there is no doubt it interprets its laws to allow a functioning gun."[60]

But wasn't it true, asked Justice Alito, that "even if you have a rifle or a shotgun in your home . . . the code prevent[s] you from loading it and unlocking it except when it's being used for lawful, recreational purposes within the District of Columbia," meaning it couldn't be used for self-defense? Dellinger demurred, "That is not the city's position, and we have no dispute with the other side on the point of what the right answer should be." He went on to concede that "we have no argument whatsoever with the notion that you may load and have a weapon ready when you need to use it for self-defense," citing the "near universal rule of criminal law that there is a self-defense exception" available.[61]

Seeing that his time was running low—and having requested to reserve some of his time for rebuttal—Dellinger attempted to sit down. Ordinarily, the thirty-minute allotment for each side's oral argument is strictly enforced. The late chief justice William Rehnquist was a ruthless timekeeper, famous for silencing advocates in midsentence, even in mid-word! Chief Justice Roberts, however, asked Dellinger to remain at the podium for a few minutes, and assured him the additional time would not be charged against his rebuttal. It was only fair, Justice Kennedy volunteered, "because I did interrupt Justice Breyer."[62]

Justice Stephen Breyer then asked a "question" that was less of a question and more of an invitation to Dellinger to succinctly restate his position. The

Second Amendment would be interpreted one of two ways, he began. "One possibility is that the amendment gives nothing more than a right to the State to raise a militia. A second possibility is that it gives an individual right to a person, but for the purpose of allowing people to have guns to form a militia." He continued: "Assume the second. If you assume the second, I wanted you to respond if . . . to . . . the Chief Justice's question of why, on the second assumption, this [total] ban on handguns . . . is . . . a reasonable regulation viewed in terms of the purposes as I described them?[63]

First, Dellinger replied, the amendment refers to a "well-regulated militia"—which drew an interjection from Justice Scalia, who demanded, "Doesn't 'well regulated' mean 'well trained'" as opposed to "'massively regulated'"? Whatever it meant, Dellinger parried, it "is different than the libertarian right" for which Dick Heller was arguing. Then he offered five reasons why the categorical handgun ban was "reasonable," assuming that was the appropriate standard of review. First, other weapons (rifles and shotguns) were permitted. Second, the ban of these "particularly dangerous weapons" served "significant [and] important regulatory interest[s]." Third, ensuring a viable militia was, if not the exclusive aim of the Second Amendment, "the most salient objective." Thus, the ban, fourth, touched on "the penumbra or the periphery, not the core" of the amendment. Finally, as opposed to preventing "national legislation [displacing] the laws in all of the States, rural as well as urban," the legislation here was "responsive to local needs." It would be "extraordinary," he concluded, if the District of Columbia, the seat of national government, could not "control dangerous weapons."[64]

Next up was US solicitor general Paul Clement, who was appearing as amicus curiae in support of the District of Columbia. Sort of.

Paul Clement was born in Cedarburg, Wisconsin, a picturesque town just north of Milwaukee. He graduated from Georgetown University, received a master's degree in economics from Darwin College, Cambridge, and earned his law degree from Harvard. He was an editor on the *Harvard Law Review* when Barack Obama was editor in chief. In his early career, he clerked for Justice Scalia, was an associate at the law firm of Kirkland and Ellis, and served as chief counsel to a subcommittee of the Senate Judiciary Committee, before becoming a partner in King and Spalding's DC office. Clement then joined the George W. Bush administration in the solicitor general's office, serving as principal deputy solicitor general before succeeding Ted Olson as solicitor general in 2004.[65]

Both as a private practitioner and while in government, Clement had argued scores of cases before the US Supreme Court—more, reportedly, than any other active lawyer. A 2012 *New York Times* profile described him as bringing "exhaustive preparation and acute insight" to cases he argued. He is "admired by colleagues and adversaries," the profile continued, "for the straightforward clarity of his preparation"; he is known for arguing without notes and "maintain[ing] a breezy but respectful rapport with the justices."⁶⁶

The Bush administration's involvement in *Heller* was controversial. Gun-rights supporters were surprised and angered when the government filed a brief in support of the District of Columbia, arguing that the court of appeals had applied an inappropriately stringent standard of review. As if to signal his disagreement with the administration, Vice President Dick Cheney even took the step of signing on to a congressional brief endorsing a strict standard of review not in his capacity as vice president but as president of the Senate. The administration assumed a posture that was less than fully supportive of the challenge to the DC legislation because federal law enforcement officials feared that if some version of strict scrutiny was adopted by the Court, a number of federal restrictions on gun ownership—a lifetime ban on gun possession by convicted felons and the near total ban on fully automatic weapons, for example—might be vulnerable to Second Amendment challenge.⁶⁷

Clement, therefore, wanted to make two points at oral argument: First, that the government's position was that the Second Amendment guaranteed "an individual right that does not depend on eligibility for or service in the militia." Second, that the proper standard of review would permit that right to "coexist with reasonable regulations of firearms."⁶⁸

Clement's clarity of presentation and easy rapport with the justices was on display during his argument. He generally spoke in complete paragraphs, courteously responding to questioning from the justices, but then always resuming the thread of his argument. As he began his opening, he faced questions from Justices Stevens and Ginsburg about the nature of the right. Had the preamble been omitted, Justice Stevens asked, would the amendment have the same meaning? No, Clement replied, "We don't take the position that the preamble plays no role in interpreting the amendment." Justice Stevens followed up by asking whether the amendment guaranteed one right or two. Two, Clement said, but "two rights that are closely related."⁶⁹

But even if there was a right to "keep" arms, as well as a right to "bear" them, pressed Justice Ginsburg, that doesn't mean the right to keep all arms or any arm, did it? Clement conceded that it did not, specifically offering the example of plastic guns or guns designed to evade metal detectors as those that would not be "'arms' within the meaning of the Second Amendment and are not protected at all." But, he observed, it would be much more difficult to categorically exclude, say, machine guns from a definition of arms, "given that they are the standard-issue weapons for today's armed forces and the State-organized militia." His observation was a way to introduce his second point: that whatever standard of review the Court adopted, it ought *not* be one that endangered laws like the federal machine gun ban.[70]

Justice Kennedy then jumped in, asking whether it was the government's position that "this amendment has nothing to do with the right of people living in the wilderness to protect themselves, despite maybe an attempt by the Federal Government . . . to take away their weapons?" Clement responded that the thing likely "foremost in the framers' mind was a concern that the militia not be disarmed such that it would be maintained as a viable option to the standing army" and that the way to do this would be to ensure that individuals' rights to private arms possession be protected.[71]

As he had of Walter Dellinger, Justice Stevens then asked whether it was significant that only a couple of state analogues to the Second Amendment specifically protected an individual right, and that the others seemed "quite clearly" to guarantee a collective right. Clement parried this with the observation that the proposal to add "in the common defense" to the language of the Second Amendment was rejected. Likewise, Justice Kennedy asked about the relevance of the 1689 English Bill of Rights to the Second Amendment. Clement agreed, noting that the right to petition, too, had its roots in the 1689 statute.[72]

The English Bill of Rights, Justice Ginsburg interjected, "was always understood to be subject to the control and limitation and restriction of Parliament," and she noted, "that's what we're talking about here . . . legislative restrictions." True, conceded Clement, but that was true for all those provisions. And, he might have added, the US Bill of Rights was adopted against the backdrop of an emerging understanding that constitutions were higher law, could not be superseded by ordinary legislation, and could be enforced against contrary legislative enactments by courts exercising judicial review. Justices David Souter and Stevens then piled on. Souter noted that the right to keep and bear arms provision in the English Bill of Rights "had an express reference to permission by law," that is, by parliamentary authority. Stevens further noted that the provision had "the additional limitation to 'suitable to their conditions,'" and that a "large number of people were not permitted to have arms."[73]

Clement agreed, but then, in a kind of verbal ju-jitsu, he used both questions to restate his main points. The qualifying language, he said, is why "we think something less than strict scrutiny is appropriate." But the English Bill of Rights is also "highly relevant in considering the threshold question of whether there's an individual right here at all" because "the parallel provisions in the English Bill of Rights that were borrowed over included the right to petition and the right to keep and bear arms." Both, he noted, "are rights given to the people."[74]

Justice Souter then pressed Clement on his earlier assertion that the amendment protects two rights. "If the people can keep them and they have them for use in the militia as well as to hunt deer," he mused, "why do we have to have a further reference . . . to a right to bear" arms? Clement responded that the right to keep went to private possession in the home; but one would need the corresponding right to "bear" them when one went out to hunt, for example. He denied, in response to a further query from Souter, that "bear arms" had, as the district was arguing, an exclusively military connotation. Justice Scalia came to his aid, asking whether when Scots and Catholics were barred from bearing arms in England, "it didn't mean that [they] could not join militias; it meant they couldn't carry arms."[75]

With his time running short, Clement finally got to the second part of his argument—what standard of review was appropriate when entertaining a Second Amendment challenge to a firearm regulation? As its appearance in the English Bill of Rights suggested, the right to keep and bear arms mentioned in the Second Amendment was a preexisting one, and it had "always coexisted with reasonable regulation of firearms." But, Justice Scalia interrupted, the freedom of speech in the First Amendment was also preexisting and there were some types of speech (libel, for example) that was excluded from its protection; however, "We've never held that simply because it was pre-existing and that there were some regulations upon it, that we would not use strict scrutiny." Clement didn't answer Scalia directly, other than to agree that some regulations—here Clement specifically referred to the federal ban on firearm possession by felons—were "so well established that you don't even view them as Second Amendment . . . infringement[s]." This led Justice Kennedy to ask, "what about possessing arms for purposes of "protecting yourself against in-truders in the home?"[76]

Clement took his opportunity to make clear that "notwithstanding the fact that the preamble makes it clear that the preeminent motive was related to ensuring that the militia remained a viable option vis-à-vis the standing army," the right guaranteed by the amendment is more broad than that. But if that's true, asked Justice Alito, "then how could the District code survive under any standard of review where they totally ban the possession of the type of weapons . . . most commonly used for self-defense" or where it requires that shotguns and rifles be unloaded and disassembled or locked? Clement replied that the district should have an opportunity, after the Court articulated the correct standard of review, to defend its law, allowing "for a relatively robust self-defense exception to the trigger lock provision."[77]

"I don't understand that," an incredulous Justice Scalia interjected, "if you have time, when you hear somebody crawling in your . . . bedroom window, you can run to your gun, unlock it, load it, and fire? Is that going to be the exception?" Clement backtracked, saying that if that were the exception, "it could clearly be inadequate," then suggesting alternatively that if someone were charged with having a loaded, unlocked gun on their nightstand, with no children present, "that would be a good test case to decide whether or not their construction would provide for an exception . . . in that case."[78]

Justice Ginsburg then asked whether it made "a practical difference whether we take your standard or strict scrutiny that was in the D.C. Circuit's opinion? There is a whole panoply of Federal laws restricting gun possession. Would any of them be jeopardized under your standard?" Not under the stan-dard he was urging, Clement replied, adding that "if you apply strict scrutiny, I think the result would be quite different, unfortunately." That exchange led Chief Justice Roberts to muse:

Well, these various phrases under the different standards that are proposed, "compelling interest," "significant interest," "narrowly tailored," none of them appear in the Constitution; and I wonder why in this case we have to articulate an all-encompassing standard. Isn't it enough to determine the scope of the existing right that the amendment refers to, look at the various regulations that were available at the time, including you can't take the gun to the marketplace and all that, and determine how . . . this restriction and the scope of this right looks in relation to those?

I'm not sure why we have to articulate some very intricate standard. I mean, these standards that apply in the First Amendment just kind of developed over the years as sort of baggage that the First Amendment picked up. But I don't know why when we are starting afresh, we would try to articulate a whole standard that would apply in every case?[79]

Clement replied that the government would welcome a decision that "was focused very narrowly on this case." Addressing concerns that adopting strict scrutiny or something like it would put federal gun laws at risk, Justice Scalia pointed out that the DC Circuit Court's opinion said the amendment protected only those weapons "that would be useful in militia and that are commonly . . . held today? I don't know what you're worried about. Machine guns . . . armored bullets, what else?" Clement said that it was "more than a little difficult to say that the one arm that's not protected by the Second Amendment is that which is the standard issue armament for the National Guard, and that's what the machine gun is."[80]

"But this law didn't involve a restriction on machine guns," Chief Justice Roberts interjected, "it involved an absolute ban. . . . Why would you think an opinion striking down an absolute ban would also apply to a . . . narrower one directed solely to machine guns?" Clement pointed out that pre-1976 handguns were exempt from DC's prohibition, as pre-1986 machine guns, of which there were about 160,000, were grandfathered in under federal law. In any event, Clement noted, the opinion talked not only about arms used in the militia at the time but also mentioned "lineal descendants. Just as this Court would apply the Fourth Amendment to something like heat imagery . . . then I do think that reasonably machine guns come within the term of 'arms.'"[81]

Now it was Alan Gura's turn, and he was not slow out of the gate. In fact, he spoke his opening sentence so quickly that Justice Scalia asked him to talk more slowly. The first point he made is that the self-defense exception that the District of Columbia was claiming it recognized had been litigated in a prior court of appeals case in the 1970s, where the court held that the *lack* of a self-defense exception was "a legitimate policy choice of the City Council," and again when the district agreed to a stipulation that DC law was a "functional firearms ban." In addition, people had been prosecuted "for the possession or for the carrying of a prohibited firearm when the police ruled the shooting [had] been lawful self-defense."[82]

Justice Breyer—who was known to pose lengthy, convoluted hypotheticals to counsel—was the first with a question. Suppose, he began, "that there is an individual right, but the purpose of that right is to maintain a citizen army" and that basic purpose "informs what's reasonable and what isn't reasonable." Further assume, he continued, "that we are going to decide whether something is proportionate or apply an intermediate standard in light of the purpose." Given that 200–300 people were killed annually and 1,500–2,000 people wounded each year in the district, "Why isn't a ban on handguns . . . a reasonable or a proportionate response on behalf of the District?"[83]

Citing briefs submitted by retired military officers, Gura responded that the handgun ban "weakens military preparedness" because civilian gun ownership and use means that "they are better prepared and able to use them" if they join the military. If the goal is firearms proficiency, Justice Breyer asked, can't people do it with rifles? Or go to gun ranges in neighboring states? If you want people to be good with guns so they might make decent soldiers, if *that* is what the Second Amendment is about, then is it "unreasonable for a city with a very high crime rate . . . to say no handguns here?"[84]

Here Justice Scalia jumped in, telling Gura, "You want to say yes. . . . That's your answer." Gura took the hint: "The answer is yes . . . it's unreasonable, and it fails any standard of review that might be offered under . . . a construction of individual rights." Justice Stevens then interrupted to ask whether Gura attached "any significance to the reference to the militia in the Second Amendment?" Gura began to answer "yes," but before he could explain, Chief Justice Roberts said, "So a conscientious objector who likes to hunt deer for food . . . has no rights under the Second Amendment" because he would not be part of the militia?[85]

"No," Gura explained, "the militia clause informs . . . a purpose" and gives some "guidepost," but "it's not the exclusive purpose of the Second Amendment." But is the militia clause a limitation on the legislature, Justice Ginsburg wanted to know. Gura replied that it informs the class of arms the Second Amendment protects, as the Court suggested in *Miller*.[86]

If that is true, if the militia clause defines the class of arms protected, Justice Stevens asked, then why doesn't it likewise "limit the kind of people who may have arms?" Because, argued Gura, that would mean that Congress could "redefine people out of that right. Congress could . . . declare that nobody is in a militia, and then nobody [could enforce the right to keep and bear arms] against the government."[87]

Justice Ginsburg pointed out that "the people" required to serve in the militia were males ages 17–45, to which Gura replied, that, yes, there were people not eligible or subject to militia service who nevertheless had guns. "Which shows," suggested Justice Scalia, "that maybe you're being unrealistic in thinking that the second clause is not broader than the first. . . . The second clause goes beyond the militia and says the right of the people to keep and bear arms."[88]

When Gura agreed, Justice Souter asked, "Then why have the first clause? What is it doing?" Gura explained that it was a way to pay tribute to the militia ideal. "Could it also be simply to reaffirm that the provisions in the main text of the Constitution remain intact?" suggested Justice Kennedy. It became clear that Kennedy wished to steer the conversation in a different direction. Before Gura could finish his answer, Kennedy pressed him on the other purposes served by the Second Amendment. "I want to know whether or not, in your view . . . the amendment protects, or was designed to protect . . . the settler in the wilderness and his right to have a gun against some conceivable Federal enactment which would prohibit him from having any guns?" Gura readily agreed, citing Sir William Blackstone's mention of the right, which Gura argued that the framers had sought to expand.[89]

Returning to his favorite theme, Justice Breyer pointed out that Blackstone qualified the right by describing "it as a right to keep and bear arms 'under law.' He clearly foresees reasonable regulation of that right." Isn't the real issue, pressed Breyer, whether it is reasonable to ban handguns when other weapons are available to individuals? He added that early militia statutes said only officers had to bring pistols, which to Breyer suggested they weren't "as crucial."[90]

Gura responded with a concession that weapons not appropriate for civilian use, such as machine guns, could be banned. Many gun-rights advocates would later harshly criticize Gura for his concession, but as he noted in post-argument interviews, he felt the concession was a prudent one he had to make. Gura's concession led to a colloquy among the justices about the meaning of *Miller*.[91]

Why would machine guns be excluded, asked Justice Ginsburg, given that they were the standard armament in the military? "But," Gura replied, "it's not an arm of the type that people might be expected to possess commonly in ordinary use. . . . *Miller* spoke about [militia members] bring[ing] with them arms of the kind in common use supplied by themselves." He added that the proper time frame for assessing what is in "common use" is always the present. Even if you were to consider "lineal descendants" of weapons in use in 1791, Gura maintained, "it's hard to imagine how a machine gun" would qualify as in common use.[92]

Justice Kennedy then suggested maybe the problem was with the *Miller* decision itself. "I would have to agree with Justice Ginsburg," he ventured, "that a machine gun is probably more related to the militia now than a pistol is. But . . . that seems to me to be allowing the militia clause to make no sense out of the operative clause in present-day circumstances." Kennedy reiterated his question: "Why is that of any real relevance to the situation that faces the homeowner today?" Seeming to catch the drift of Kennedy's comments, Gura agreed that *Miller* was "ultimately not very useful guidance for courts" and proposed instead a "commonsense rule" that courts consider whether any particular type of arm was one that "you could really reasonably expect civilians to have."[93]

Gura's reference to "commonsense rules" piqued Justice Breyer's interest. He proposed an analogy between an eighteenth-century Massachusetts law prohibiting the keeping of loaded firearms in the house and mandated storage of powder and bullets in the upper floors of buildings to prevent fires because fire departments didn't exist. "We now have police departments, and the crime wave might be said similar to what were fires then," therefore "you can say no handguns in the city because of the risk of crime."[94]

Gura pointed out that, at the time, the term "firearms" didn't include pistols, and that the purpose of the statute was not to prevent people from engaging in self-defense because the latter was deemed harmful. Justice Breyer seemed then to reconsider his own analogy but added that what he was getting at was that instead of focusing on the *type* of weapon at issue, courts should perhaps look to "the purpose of the regulation" and whether "it makes sense in terms of having the possibility of people trained in firearms," referring to the military briefs Gura mentioned at the start of his argument.[95]

Justice Stevens then returned to his favored line of questioning: whether it was significant that of the state Second Amendment analogues, only two specifically mentioned self-defense. Gura pointed out that even some of those provisions were given that gloss by later judicial decisions. Stevens then asked about the English Bill of Rights: "Do you think the term 'suitable to their conditions' limited the number of people who had access to arms for self-defense?" Gura replied that the Second Amendment was "quite clearly an expansion on" the English right. He added that he thought the English antecedent was useful for certain things, but seemed to have trouble coming up with an example. Justice Scalia helpfully supplied one: "It's useful for such purposes as what 'keep and bear arms' means." He further observed that the Americans wanted a militia "separate from the state, separate from the government," instead of the English version.[96]

After a brief exchange with Justice Souter, Chief Justice Roberts asked Gura whether the trigger-lock provision was akin to safe storage regulations mentioned earlier by Justice Breyer. Gura replied that "the modern trigger-lock provisions are aimed squarely at self-defense in the home" and that modern powder doesn't present the same type of fire risk. What about children gaining access, Roberts pressed. When Gura noted that a child could access a disassembled gun, Roberts was skeptical: "You don't necessarily expect a young child to be able to reassemble the pistol." Gura ended up conceding that safe storage laws would satisfy even strict scrutiny but argued this was not a safe storage provision; this provision was intended to keep people from people able to use a gun in self-defense in their homes.[97]

Justice Breyer asked whether it made sense to have courts second-guessing city councils and legislatures on their decision to enact laws like the trigger-lock provision. "When a fundamental right is at stake," Gura replied, "there is a role for judicial review." He noted that DC's law was an outlier as well. This led Justice Ginsburg to inquire about licensing. Could you license handguns even if you couldn't ban them? In another concession that would later anger some gun-rights supporters, Gura gave a qualified "yes." And age limits, asked Chief Justice Roberts? Gura said these were valid, though he thought "it would be very difficult to have an age limit that goes beyond 21, because that's the majority age for most things in the United States."[98]

Was Gura essentially arguing that the amendment enshrines a right to keep and bear arms that "shall not be unreasonably infringed instead of shall not be infringed," queried Justice Stevens? Gura was cautious: "Well, yes . . . to some extent, except the word 'unreasonable' is the one that troubles us because we don't know what this unreasonable standard looks like." Once again, Justice Scalia offered Gura help: "You wouldn't put it that way. You would just say it is not being infringed if reasonable limitations are placed on it."[99]

Chief Justice Roberts asked whether reasonable restrictions would be defined in light of those existing at the time of ratification, like a ban on public carrying, and their "lineal descendants." As part of our common law tradition, Gura replied, "we look to framing our practices in traditional understandings of that right to see both the reasonableness of the restrictions that are available as well as the contours [of the right]."[100]

Justice Souter then asked whether legislators could consider crime statistics and allow those statistics to inform restrictions placed on gun ownership. Yes, Gura replied, but "there are constitutional limitations enforced by courts that are going to limit those policies." After a couple of brief questions about the reasonableness of bans on shipping sawed-off shotguns and machine guns in interstate commerce (Gura agreed it was reasonable) and a question about banning guns on college campus (it depends, Gura answered), time expired and Gura sat down.[101]

When Walter Dellinger rose for his rebuttal, Chief Justice Roberts asked him how long it took to remove a trigger lock and load a weapon. Dellinger said it took him three seconds. Justice Scalia quipped, "You turn on . . . the lamp next to your bed so you can turn the knob at 3–22–95." Dellinger said, yes, some locks had numerical codes. Roberts joined in, "So then you turn on the lamp, you pick up your reading glasses," eliciting laughter from the gallery.[102]

Roberts then asked, "Does it really make sense to say that the best self-defense arm is a rifle, as opposed to a pistol?" Dellinger replied that there had been "no showing" that a rifle or shotgun was not adequate for self-defense.[103] After arguing that the trigger-lock requirement and the handgun ban were not necessarily connected—that the Court could say that whatever weapon is permitted must be available for self-defense—Dellinger made one last bid for Justice Kennedy's vote:

> I know, Justice Kennedy, that you would be concerned about a national
> government which sets a single standard for rural and urban areas, for East and
> West, North and South. Here you have legislation that is adopted by a group of
> citizens in the District, operating under the authority of Congress, but it is local
> legislation. And if it's still good law, that States and local governments across the
> country can strike these balances. . . . It would be deeply ironic to preclude the
> District of Columbia as being the only place that could enact legislation free of
> the strictures of the Second Amendment.
>
>   What is critical here is not to apply the kind of categorical standard the court
> below did or a kind of strict scrutiny that would strike this law down. This is an
> area, unlike areas where government regulation is presumptively illegitimate,
> [where the] text contemplates regulation of inherently dangerous weapons. It's

a kind of right where even if you recognize it, deference needs to be given to the legislative resolution rather than have courts try to decide how best to resolve the statistical and methodological debates.[104]

Dellinger then thanked Chief Justice Roberts and sat down. The case was submitted at 11:43 A.M.

# 7. A Silence Broken

The briefs had been filed, the arguments made—and then came the waiting. Gura, Levy, Neily, their sometimes allies, sometimes adversaries in the NRA, and tens of millions of everyday citizens who supported the view that the Constitution protected the right of ordinary people to have arms had cause for optimism. From his questions during oral argument, it seemed clear that they had Justice Scalia's vote. Justice Thomas seemed likely too, based on his mention of the Second Amendment in his concurring opinion in the 1997 case *United States v. Printz.* Chief Justice Roberts and Justice Alito also seemed sympathetic, based on their questions, and their expressed skepticism concerning the District of Columbia's position that a near-total ban on the possession of weapons for self-defense was reasonable. Most heartening of all, though, must have been Justice Kennedy's apparent position. Kennedy's questions indicated that he supported the notion that the Second Amendment guaranteed an individual the right to keep and bear arms for self-defense, whatever other militia-related purposes it was intended to serve.

But questions remained. Even if the Court embraced the individual rights reading, would its characterization of the right be a broad one? Or would it write a narrower opinion, as the government seemed to want it to do? Would its articulation of the right's scope make it a useful springboard to challenge other federal gun laws? And, of course, to be useful to litigants challenging restrictive state and local laws, moreover, a victory in *Heller* would be incomplete until the Supreme Court addressed the issue of incorporation of the right to keep and bear arms through the Fourteenth Amendment. That would require additional litigation, with at least some of the uncertainty that had accompanied *Heller* itself.

Once a case is submitted, the justices must vote on the case, then assign someone to write the opinion. The justices deliberate in secret on cases during one of their two weekly Justices' Conferences, held on Wednesdays and Fridays when the Court is in session. No clerks or secretaries are permitted in the conference room while the justices discuss the cases. (By custom, the junior justice must act as doorkeeper when messages are sent to the conference while it meets.) During discussion of the cases, the chief justice speaks first; then the associate justices speak in descending order of seniority. Votes are cast in the same order. If the chief justice is in the majority, he assigns the drafting of an opinion to himself or another justice; if he is not, then the senior-most justice in the majority makes the assignment. Drafts are circulated. Sometimes justices will join unconditionally; other times, they will request modifications to the draft opinions. This can be tricky for the opinion's author. Acceding to one justice's request might alienate another justice and cause the author to lose her majority. Justices may agree with the outcome but pen concurring opinions to explain why they disagreed with some or all of the majority's reasoning. A justice who disagrees with the outcome will often write or join dissenting opinions.[1]

After opinions are drafted, circulated, argued over, and ultimately finalized, majority, dissenting, and concurring opinions are written. In May and June, as the term draws to a close, opinions are announced on Mondays; additional days are often designated as "opinion days" as the Court works to clear its docket before the end of its term. High-profile cases, like *Heller*, which are usually among the Court's most controversial, are typically among the last to be announced in a term. This is especially true if the case was argued after the new year, as *Heller* was.

Because conference deliberations are held in secret, we often know very little about what goes into the Court's decision-making processes. Only when a justice's papers are released, often years after his or her death, do we get a clearer picture of what occurred behind the scenes. Until then, the process is something of a black box. We will discuss later in this chapter Justice Stevens's autobiography, which provides something of a glimpse into the Court's deliberations on *Heller*. But we do not have the papers of the other justices who participated in the decision. In the period between oral argument and the Court's rendering of a decision, guesses as to how the Court might decide are frequent, but these are nothing more than guesses, based on pure speculation. Court-watchers often speculate on how individual justices might vote. These speculations are frequently based on the questions individual justices posed at oral argument, the general judicial philosophy that different justices have espoused, and any remarks or writings they may have published on particular issues.[2]

*Heller* was announced on June 26, 2008. The Court, by a 5–4 vote, found for Heller. Chief Justice Roberts had assigned the majority opinion to Justice Scalia. His opinion was joined by Justices Kennedy, Thomas, Alito, and the chief justice. Justices Stevens, Souter, Ginsburg, and Breyer dissented. Justices Stevens and Breyer each wrote a dissenting opinion that all of the other dissenting justices joined. Even by the prolix standards of contemporary Supreme Court opinions, *Heller* was a behemoth. Justice Scalia's majority opinion takes up sixty-three pages in the *U.S. Reports*; the combined length of the two dissents is eighty-six pages—an eye-watering 152 pages of opinion, dissents, and introductory material.

Chief Justice Roberts's choice of Justice Scalia to write the majority opinion was significant. Scalia was a proponent of one strain of originalist jurisprudence—understanding or deciding cases based on the meaning of the words of a constitutional provision as they were generally understood at the time of the writing of the provision. This might be distinguished from an earlier form of originalist jurisprudence that was interested in finding the original intent that motivated those who passed a particular constitutional provision by looking at the debates that occurred during the provision's framing. We had a brief glance at that strain of originalism in chapter 3 in our discussion of Justice Hugo Black's support for total incorporation of the Bill of Rights through the Fourteenth Amendment.[3]

As a proponent of adhering to the original understanding or original public meaning of constitutional provisions, Justice Scalia's view was that when the Supreme Court exercised judicial review, it should impute to a provision of the Bill of Rights the contemporary meaning that the framers and ratifiers of the provision would have ascribed to the document when Congress debated and voted on it in 1789, or the meaning as it would have been recognized and understood by state ratifiers between 1789 and 1791. Scalia once wrote an article where he described originalism as the "lesser evil" as compared with other, nonoriginal methodologies. Originalism curbed judicial discretion, in his view, and minimized the opportunities for judges exercising judicial review merely to replace the policy preferences of elected and accountable branches of government with their own. He wrote that

> The Constitution, though it has an effect superior to other laws, is in its nature the sort of "law" that is the business of the courts—an enactment that has a fixed meaning ascertainable through the usual devices familiar to those learned in the law. If the Constitution were not that sort of a "law," but a novel invitation to apply current societal values, what reason would there be to believe that the invitation was addressed to the courts rather than to the legislature?[4]

Unlike his colleague Clarence Thomas, Justice Scalia would temper originalism with adherence to precedent. Thus, his originalism was, he admitted, somewhat "faint-hearted." Some originalist critics of his majority opinion would later argue that his faint-heartedness prevailed in *Heller*.[5]

*Heller* opened with a brief recitation of the facts and summarized the holdings of the lower courts. Then it proceeded to consider the meaning of the Second Amendment, with Justice Scalia noting the main point of contention between the District of Columbia and Gura and Levy. Does the amendment guarantee the right to possess a firearm only in connection with militia service? Or is the right broader, protecting a right to possession unconnected with militia service? Does the right include the right to use arms for traditionally lawful purposes, including "self-defense within the home"?[6]

The Second Amendment, he noted, had a "prefatory clause" and an "operative clause." The prefatory clause was the portion that read, "a well-regulated militia being necessary for the security of a free state," while the operative clause read, "the right of the people to keep and bear arms shall not be infringed." The key question was whether the prefatory clause limited the right recognized in the operative clause. Justice Scalia, however, began his opinion by examining the meaning of the *operative* clause, promising to "return to the prefatory clause to ensure that our reading of the operative clause is consistent with the announced purpose."[7]

His discussion of the operative clause then carefully parsed the phrases "the right of the people" and "to keep and bear Arms." A "salient feature" of the amendment "is that it codifies a 'right of the people.'" The Second Amendment, along with other amendments that use the phrase, "unambiguously refer to individual rights, not 'collective' rights, or rights that may be exercised only through participation in some corporate body."[8]

> "The people" seems to have been a term of art employed in select parts of the Constitution. . . . [Its uses] sugges[t] that "the people" protected by the Fourth Amendment, and by the First and Second Amendments, and to whom rights, and powers are reserved in the Ninth and Tenth Amendments, refers to a class of persons who are part of a national community or who have otherwise developed sufficient connection with this country to be considered part of that community.[9]

So, what was the "right to keep and bear Arms" that individuals possessed? Justice Scalia began by defining "Arms." Quoting contemporary dictionaries, he concluded that the term was not limited to a military context and "was applied, then as now, to weapons that were not specifically designed for military use and were not employed in a military capacity."[10] Nor did it only apply to those arms that existed in the eighteenth century, any more than the First Amendment protects only eighteenth-century forms of communications.[11]

He then turned to the terms "keep" and "bear." Because "no party has apprised us of an idiomatic meaning of 'keep Arms,'" Justice Scalia wrote, "the most natural reading . . . in the Second Amendment is to 'have weapons.'" Further, he observed that "keep Arms" had no special militia-related connotation. It was, rather, "simply a common way of referring to possessing arms, for militiamen *and everyone else.*" As for the meaning of "to bear," he argued that it "refers to carrying [arms] for a particular purpose—confrontation," and "did not refer only to carrying a weapon in an organized military unit." He pointed to James Wilson's interpretation of the Pennsylvania constitutional right as recognizing the right of self-preservation and noted that "was also the interpretation of those state constitutional provisions adopted by pre–Civil War state courts." While he conceded that there was a use of "bear Arms" that meant to serve as a soldier, he stated that use "*unequivocally* bore that idiomatic meaning only when followed by the preposition 'against.'"[12]

Justice Scalia then addressed Justice Stevens's focus, at oral argument and in his dissent, on James Madison's original draft of the Second Amendment, which included a conscientious-objector clause exempting from compulsory military service any "person religiously scrupulous of bearing arms." For Stevens, that was proof that "bear arms" had an exclusively military connotation. First, Scalia observed, that provision was ultimately deleted from the final version. That aside, though, the deleted provision "was not meant to exempt from military service those who objected to going to war but had no scruples about personal gunfights." Rather, the most natural reading would be that "those opposed to carrying weapons for potential violent confrontation would not be 'compelled to render military service,' in which such carrying would be required."[13]

For Justice Scalia, the combination of these textual elements meant "that they guarantee the individual right to possess and carry weapons in case of confrontation." This reading was bolstered, he continued, by the fact the framers considered the provisions of the Bill of Rights to codify preexisting rights imported—in expanded form—from England, where reaction to Stuart policies produced the 1689 English Bill of Rights, which included certain protections for arms bearing. However, over the next century, "the right to have arms had become fundamental for English subjects," he wrote, citing Blackstone and others. "Thus, the right secured in 1689 as a result of the Stuarts' abuses was, by the time of the founding, understood to be an individual right protecting against both public and private violence."[14]

The opinion then pivoted to the prefatory clause. A "well-regulated militia" referred to the body of able-bodied men available for military service, with "well-regulated" implying "nothing more than the imposition of proper discipline and training." As for the declaration that the militia is "necessary to the security of a free State," Justice Scalia said that "state" meant "polity," not the security of individual states. At the founding, moreover, militia were thought to be necessary because they were "useful in repelling invasions and suppressing insurrections," made large standing armies unnecessary, and enabled resistance to tyranny.[15]

So, did the prefatory clause qualify or narrow the right guaranteed in the operative clause? Not at all, concluded Justice Scalia. The framers' reading of history "showed that the way tyrants had eliminated a militia consisting of all the able-bodied men was not by banning the militia but simply by taking away the people's arms, enabling a select militia or standing army to suppress political opponents." Thus, he pronounced it "entirely sensible" that the prefatory clause "announces the purpose for which the right was codified: to prevent elimination of the militia." But it wasn't "the only reason Americans valued the ancient right;" in fact, "most undoubtedly thought it even more important for self-defense and hunting. But the threat that the new Federal Government would destroy the citizens' militia by taking away their arms was the reason that right . . . was codified in a written Constitution."[16]

Justice Scalia bolstered the majority's reading of the Second Amendment with analogous provisions in state constitutions. He particularly noted that some provisions arguably couching the right in collective self-defense terms were later interpreted by courts to have a much broader scope.[17]

Scalia then looked to post-ratification and post–Civil War commentary, case law, and legislation concerning the Second Amendment. Early nineteenth-century legal commentators like St. George Tucker, William Rawle, and Joseph Story all described the right in individual terms unrelated to military service. Likewise, "many early-19th century state cases indicated that the Second Amendment right to bear arms was an individual right unconnected to military service, though subject to certain restrictions." While he conceded that the1840 Tennessee case *State v. Aymette* did adopt what he termed an "odd" middle position—that membership in a formal military organization was not a necessary condition for firearms ownership, but their use was limited to collective self-defense against tyranny—he noted that no one was urging that reading in the courts. He also noted that the Tennessee Supreme Court adopted a more traditional individual rights position two decades later.[18]

Equally telling, for Justice Scalia, was how the right to keep and bear arms was treated in the years following the Civil War. He cited discussions of the Freedman's Bureau Act and the Civil Rights Act of 1871, wherein members of Congress expressed concern with the systematic disarmament of freed slaves in the South, as proof that Congress understood "that the Second Amendment protected an individual right to use arms for self-defense."[19] Post–Civil War commentators, such as Thomas Cooley, too, "understood the right not as connected to militia service, but as securing the militia by ensuring a populace familiar with arms."[20]

Justice Scalia's opinion then addressed the Court's relatively meager case law, concluding that none of the cases "foreclose[d] the conclusions we have reached about the meaning of the Second Amendment." The pre-incorporation *Cruikshank* and *Presser* decisions merely confirmed that the Second Amendment bound the federal government, but not states. To the extent *Presser* held that states could ban private military organizations from drill or parade except where authorized by law, Scalia noted, "no one supporting [an individual rights] interpretation has contended that States may not ban such groups."[21]

That left the enigmatic *Miller* decision. As we shall see, Justice Stevens read *Miller* to restrict the exercise of the right to military purposes. Justice Scalia, in contrast, thought it equally clear "that the Court's basis for saying that the Second Amendment did not apply was . . . that the *type of weapon at issue* was not eligible for Second Amendment protection." Had the Court not thought the Second Amendment guaranteed an individual right, "it would have been odd to examine the character of the weapon rather than simply note that the two crooks were not militiamen."[22]

Moreover, the *Miller* Court didn't even purport to undertake an extensive examination of the Second Amendment's history. Justice Scalia alluded to the fact that only the government filed briefs and appeared at oral argument: "The Government's *Miller* brief . . . provided scant discussion of the history of the Second Amendment—and the Court was presented with no counter-discussion." All *Miller* stood for, in his reading, was that "the Second Amendment does not protect those weapons not typically possessed by law-abiding citizens for lawful purposes, such as short-barreled shotguns."[23]

Finding that precedent did not stand in the way of adopting the individual rights reading the Court articulated in its opinion, Scalia then traced the scope of the right and hinted its limits. He began with the observation that, like all rights, the scope of the right to keep and bear arms was not unlimited.[24] Then came the paragraph that, for many critics, confirmed that Justice Scalia's originalism was faint-hearted indeed:

> Although we do not undertake an exhaustive historical analysis today of the full scope of the Second Amendment, nothing in our opinion should be taken to cast doubt on longstanding prohibitions on the possession of firearms by felons and the mentally ill, or laws forbidding the carrying of firearms in sensitive places such as schools and government buildings, or laws imposing conditions and qualifications on the commercial sale of arms.[25]

In a footnote, he added that "these presumptively lawful regulatory measures" were "examples; our list does not purport to be exhaustive."[26] Then—in a passage that was likely music to Solicitor General Clement's ears—he continued:

> It may be objected that if weapons that are most useful in military service— M1-6 rifles and the like—may be banned, then the Second Amendment right is completely detached from the prefatory clause. But as we have said, the conception of the militia at the time of the Second Amendment's ratification was the body of all citizens capable of military service, who would bring the sorts of lawful weapons that they possessed at home to militia duty. It may well be true today that a militia, to be as effective as militias in the 18th century, would require sophisticated arms that are highly unusual in society at large. Indeed, it may be true that no amount of small arms could be useful against modern-day bombers and tanks. But the fact that modern developments have limited the degree of fit between the prefatory clause and the protected right cannot change our interpretation of the right.[27]

From that passage, one could surmise that the federal ban on machine guns was safe, whatever the precise scope of the right guaranteed by the Second Amendment.

Finally, Justice Scalia examined the DC laws in light of the right to keep and bear arms as he had articulated it. "The inherent right of self-defense has been central to the Second Amendment right," he observed. The District of Columbia had banned an entire class of arms (handguns) and extended that ban into the home. "Under any of the standards of scrutiny that we have applied to enumerated constitutional rights, banning from the home 'the most preferred firearm in the nation'" for self-defense "would fail constitutional muster." While the opinion refused to commit to any particular standard of review, in a footnote, Scalia seemed to exclude at least one. In response to a point Justice Breyer made in his dissent that the law would likely survive "rational basis" scrutiny, Scalia conceded that it would. But, he continued, "if all that was required to overcome the right to keep and bear arms was a rational basis, the Second Amendment would be redundant with the separate constitutional prohibitions on irrational laws and would have no effect."[28]

Justice Scalia then critiqued Justice Breyer's application of the interest-balancing approach he proposed in his dissenting opinion, which Scalia characterized thus: "Because handgun violence is a problem, because the law is limited to an urban area, and because there were somewhat similar restrictions in the founding period," the handgun ban was constitutional. "We know of no other enumerated constitutional right," Scalia observed, "whose core protection has been subjected to a freestanding 'interest-balancing' approach." The very enumeration of the right, he argued, means that balance has already been performed. "A constitutional guarantee subject to future judges' assessments of its usefulness is no constitutional guarantee at all."[29]

He then attempted to preempt the criticism that the Court left much unsaid about the scope and application of the Second Amendment. Because "this case represents this Court's first in-depth examination of the Second Amendment, one should not expect it to clarify the entire field."[30]

Justice Scalia concluded with an acknowledgment that handgun violence was a serious problem. Nothing in the opinion meant the district could not *regulate* handguns, but, he noted, "the enshrinement of constitutional rights necessarily takes certain policy choices off the table. These include the absolute prohibition of handguns held and used for self-defense in the home." While some may think the Second Amendment obsolete, he concluded, "it is not the role of this Court to pronounce the Second Amendment extinct."[31]

Justice Stevens's opinion was the first dissent because he was the senior justice in opposition to the majority opinion—and it sought to refute Justice Scalia's opinion point-by-point. In light of the debate between collective and

individual rights theorists that characterized the Second Amendment scholarship from the 1980s, through the 1990s, and into the 2000s, however, the
dissent began with an interesting concession: "The question presented by this
case is not whether the Second Amendment protects a 'collective right' or an
'individual right.' Surely it protects a right that can be enforced by individuals.
But a conclusion that the Second Amendment protects an individual right
does not tell us anything about the scope of that right."[32]

Summarizing his reading of the available historical evidence, Stevens wrote
that "neither the text of the Amendment nor the arguments advanced by its
proponents evidence the slightest interest in limiting any legislature's authority to regulate private civilian uses of firearms." He claimed that this was the
view of the amendment advanced in *Miller*, a view that "hundreds of judges
have relied on" in the years since that decision.[33]

Justice Stevens began his exegesis of the amendment—unlike Justice Scalia's opinion—with the prefatory clause. The prefatory clause, which he argued reflected the concerns of similar state constitutional analogues, omits
"any statement of purpose related to the right to use firearms for hunting or
personal self-defense," despite the fact that provisions so encompassing those
purposes were known to the framers. This omission, for Justice Stevens, "confirms that the Framers' single-minded focus in crafting the constitutional
guarantee 'to keep and bear arms' was on military uses of firearms, which they
viewed in the context of service in state militias."[34]

As for "the right of the people," Stevens argued that if it is true that some
classes of persons (i.e., felons) were excluded from exercising the right, then
that makes the Second Amendment *unlike* other amendments that reference
"the people" in their text. "The Court," he avers, "offers no way to harmonize
its conflicting pronouncements." In his view, the use of the words "the people" does not "enlarge the right . . . to encompass use or ownership of weapons
outside the context of service in a well-regulated militia."[35]

And "to keep and bear arms"? Unlike the majority, whose opinion "treats
them as two 'phrases'—as if they read 'to keep' and 'to bear,'" Justice Stevens
argued that "they describe a unitary right: to possess arms if needed for military purposes and to use them in conjunction with military activities." Again
he noted the availability of language in contemporary state constitutions that
referred to civilian uses of weapons and concluded that the absence of such
language in the Second Amendment implied that the framers limited the right
to a military context.[36]

Reviewing the same drafting and ratification history canvassed by the majority, Justice Stevens arrived at a completely different conclusion:

> The history of the adoption of the Amendment . . . describes an overriding concern about the potential threat to state sovereignty that a federal standing army would pose, and a desire to protect the States' militias as the means by which to guard against that danger. But state militias could not effectively check the prospect of a federal standing army so long as Congress retained the power to disarm them, and so a guarantee against such disarmament was needed. . . . The evidence plainly refutes the claim that the Amendment was motivated by the Framers' fears that Congress might act to regulate any civilian uses of weapons.[37]

Justice Stevens likewise drew different lessons from the English Bill of Rights, Blackstone, and the nineteenth-century sources relied on by the majority. The 1689 right enshrined by the English, Stevens argued, was irrelevant to the concerns that animated the framers. Moreover, its restriction to Protestants and its "as allowed by law" qualification rendered it very limited. Because Blackstone cited the Bill of Rights as the source for the natural right to have arms to exercise the natural right of self-defense, Stevens concluded that such rights remained subject to the qualifications of the original right to keep and bear arms.[38]

As for the nineteenth-century sources, Justice Stevens dismissed them as being too remote from the drafting of the amendment to be accorded much weight. The post-enactment commentators "tended to collapse the Second Amendment with . . . the English Bill of Rights, and they appear to have been unfamiliar with the drafting history of the Second Amendment." The nineteenth-century legislators, moreover, made their statements "long after the framing of the Amendment and cannot possibly supply any insight into the intent of the Framers; and all were made during pitched political debates, so that they are better characterized as advocacy than good-faith attempts at constitutional interpretation."[39]

Justice Stevens also disputed the majority's reading of *Miller*. "If the Second Amendment were not limited in its coverage to military uses of weapons," he asked, "why should the Court . . . have suggested that some weapons but not others were eligible for Second Amendment protection?"[40]

His dissent closed with a sense of slightly ominous foreboding at the prospect of the litigation to come. Until *Heller*, he wrote, it had been understood that regulation of firearms was permissible as long as the regulations did not "interfere with the preservation of a well-regulated militia." Now, however, "the Court's announcement of a new constitutional right to own and use firearms for private purposes upsets that settled understanding but leaves for future cases the formidable task of defining the scope of permissible regulations."[41]

In his dissent, Justice Breyer was primarily concerned with articulating how he would decide whether a particular firearms regulation infringed the Second Amendment. Like Justice Stevens, Justice Breyer emphatically declared that the right guaranteed by the amendment was an individual one. He also assumed that one purpose of the amendment was to "further[] an interest in possessing guns for purposes of self-defense." But like all rights, it was subject to regulation.[42] Any standard of review, he argued, would result in a de facto interest-balancing test—even strict scrutiny. This is so, he argued, because preventing crime has been found to be a "compelling governmental interest," and the question would then be the extent that government could prove that something like DC's handgun ban is "necessary" or "narrowly tailored." "Thus, any attempt *in theory* to apply strict scrutiny to gun regulations will *in practice* turn into an interest-balancing inquiry . . . the only question being whether the regulation at issue impermissibly burdens [Second Amendment rights] in the course of advancing" public-safety concerns.[43] He continued:

> I would simply adopt such an interest-balancing inquiry explicitly. The fact that important interests lie on both sides of the constitutional equation suggests that review of gun-control regulation is not a context in which a court should effectively presume either constitutionality (as in rational-basis review) or unconstitutionality (as in strict scrutiny). Rather, "where a law significantly implicates competing constitutionally protected interests in complex ways," the Court generally asks whether the statute burdens a protected interest in a way or to an extent that is out of proportion to the statute's salutary effects upon other important governmental interests. Any answer would take account both of the statute's effects upon the competing interests and the existence of any clearly superior less restrictive alternative.[44]

Applying his approach, which included deference to the district's conclusions about the necessity of banning handguns in an effort to curb violent crime, he concluded that "the District's measure is a proportionate, not a disproportionate, response to the compelling concerns that led the District to adopt it."[45]

## ON HOLDING, DICTA, AND PERSUASION

We are going to spend a little time providing a brief analysis of Justice Scalia's opinion in the next few pages. We concentrate on the majority opinion because it provided the law as it was decided in *Heller*. Our focus is on the Scalia opinion also because in many ways it was the most challenging of the three, both, we suspect, for the justice to write and for the reader to understand the various contours that the opinion took. Scalia used an originalist methodology to craft his opinion, and while we agree with the essential accuracy of his view of the original understandings and meanings of the Second Amendment, we would nonetheless agree with critics like political scientist and legal scholar Nelson Lund that the conservative jurist's opinion is not wholly satisfactory either from an originalist point of view or even from the perspective of judicial reasoning. Our discussion here is less an effort to criticize the decision and more an attempt to use Scalia's opinion as a tool to discuss some of the difficulties that can occur in the effort to adhere to a strictly originalist jurisprudence.[46]

What is problematic in the Court's opinion lies less in the holding and more in what lawyers would call dicta. Lawyers are frequently concerned with parsing judicial opinions and trying to separate holding, the ruling in the case, the law that must be followed, from dicta, parts of an opinion that go beyond answering the questions presented by a case. These discussions can frequently be quite important. They often give direction to lower courts as to which path should be followed in given areas, but they are arguably not the law. Of course, supporters of a particular principle discussed in a case strive to get that principle recognized as part of the holding while opponents of the principle seek to have it minimized as mere dicta, extraneous to the ruling and hence not binding precedent in future cases.

The holding in *Heller* can be reduced to three propositions: (1) The Second Amendment protects an individual's right to keep and bear arms without a requirement that the individual is using the arms in a militia capacity; (2) Statutes banning handguns in the home violate the Second Amendment; and (3) Statutes that prohibit having operable firearms in the home for purposes of immediate self-defense also violate the Second Amendment. In making these propositions the holdings in the case, the Court was answering the questions posed by Dick Heller. The answers flowed quite logically from Justice Scalia's reading of the history and text of the Second Amendment. Some disagree with that reading, but if one accepts that reading, the three propositions seem reasonably consistent with an originalist reading of the amendment.

If the holding in the Court's decision flows reasonably enough from the text and history as Scalia presented them, the parts of the decision that might be labeled dicta are not especially easy to reconcile with the originalist discussion that Scalia presented. The majority recognized limitations to the right to bear arms that would resonate with early twenty-first-century American sentiments on firearms regulation whether or not those sentiments were consistent with the eighteenth-century thinking that put the Second Amendment into the Constitution. Thus, the opinion presumed the constitutionality of bans on firearms possession by people with felony convictions and histories of mental illness. The majority opinion also indicated that guns could be banned from sensitive places. Whether one might argue that these concessions in the Scalia opinion were similar to restrictions that existed in the eighteenth century, it seems likely that they were included in the opinion to sway twenty-first-century opinion, particularly that of the four other justices.[47]

We want to focus on one area where Justice Scalia was forced to move away from an originalist analysis: what weapons does the Second Amendment protect? Scalia, like James McReynolds before him in *Miller*, accepted that the Second Amendment was meant to protect the arms of the population as a whole in part to enable the population to serve as a militia of the whole when needed. McReynolds's opinion indicated that weapons that were useful for the common defense might receive constitutional protection but set no limiting principle as to whether some weapons, though useful for the common defense, might be too deemed too dangerous to receive constitutional protection. Nor did he discuss how such a determination might be made.

Scalia in *Heller* offered a way to make that determination. His opinion indicates that small arms in common use among law-abiding citizens are constitutionally protected. The conservative jurist reasoned that as citizens at the time of the adoption of the Second Amendment were expected to perform their duties as members of the militia with weapons that were commonly found among law-abiding citizens at the time, then those firearms generally owned by law-abiding members of the public in modern America are constitutionally protected in twenty-first century America. Scalia rejected the idea that the right was confined to eighteenth-century firearms: "The Second Amendment extends, prima facie to all instruments that constitute bearable arms, even those that were not in existence at the time of the founding."[48]

Despite this recognition that the right to bear arms extends to modern, bearable firearms, the Scalia opinion stressed that fully automatic weapons like the military's M16, even though they might be the most useful small arms for a citizen militia, did not enjoy constitutional protection because they were not in common use among members of the law-abiding public. The reasoning, of course, is circular. Automatic weapons are not in common use among members of the law-abiding public in modern America in part because they were placed under very tight restrictions with the passage of the National Firearms Act in 1934. It is not hard to envision an alternative history in which the 1934 act had not been passed and in which large quantities of automatic weapons would have been sold to the American public via the surplus market after the World War II. One can also conceive of an alternative history in which the 1934 act and other legislation had put strong restrictions on handgun ownership, creating, over time, a situation where handgun ownership would have been relatively uncommon by 2008 when *Heller* was decided. Scalia's common-use test leaves the question of what type of arms are protected up to historical accident—what arms happened to be legally available and in general use when the Court had its first serious examination of the Second Amendment? Even putting that difficulty aside, one might also consign the discussion on automatic weapons to the dicta bin for an even simpler reason. Automatic weapons were not the issue before the Court. So why was it in the opinion?

Justice Scalia could not have just simply written an opinion stating that the Second Amendment protected the right of Dick Heller and others to have a gun in the home for self-protection and let the matter rest. Judicial opinions are exercises in persuasion. A jurist must first persuade enough of his colleagues to join an opinion to gain a majority. He must then persuade the broader legal community, including the lower courts, and the greater public at large, of the soundness of his reasoning. This was especially true in *Heller*, which, previous cases—including *Miller*—notwithstanding, was essentially the Second Amendment's debut before the high court.

Scalia's first task was to persuade four other justices to sign onto an opinion vindicating the claims of Dick Heller. The questions posed during oral argument seemed to indicate that a bare majority of five supported the view of the Second Amendment that would have granted Dick Heller the relief he sought. But that consensus was perhaps less sure than it seemed. The wild card in the case was Justice Anthony Kennedy. Was Kennedy as sure a bet as his questions concerning intrepid settlers defending their log cabins against hostile Indians and marauding grizzlies might have indicated? Probably more than the other justices on the Court at the time, Kennedy's jurisprudence did not fit into conventional categories of liberal or conservative. In the spring 2008 when *Heller* was being argued and decided, Kennedy was the swing justice, often the pivotal player on a Court closely divided between four justices generally regarded as liberals and four usually characterized as conservatives. Kennedy's pivotal and shifting role on the Court would be on dramatic display in the early summer of 2008. On June 25 he was the author of the majority opinion in the case of *Kennedy v. Louisiana,* agreeing with the Court's four liberal justices that the execution of a man who had raped but not killed a child was a violation of the Eighth Amendment's prohibition on cruel and unusual punishment. The next day he would vote with the Court's four conservatives to strike down the DC handgun ban.[49]

So, Kennedy was persuadable. Indeed, most justices are. Almost every student of the Supreme Court, or of particular cases, has looked at the papers of individual justices and seen evidence of how justices came to change their views and votes based on the persuasive efforts of other justices and at times even the persuasive efforts and maneuverings of law clerks.[50] We don't yet have the papers of the justices involved in *Heller,* but we do have the autobiography of Justice Stevens—and it is quite revealing concerning the discussions among the justices about the case. After the initial vote, Stevens, a supporter of stricter gun control and a supporter of the view that the Second Amendment's protection does not extend beyond the militia context, made an effort to persuade Justices Thomas and Kennedy to change their votes. In his autobiography, Stevens indicated he had occasional discussions with Justice Thomas and frequent conversations with Justice Kennedy in an effort to pull one of them away from the slim majority inclined to declare the District of Columbia's statute unconstitutional. The different amount of time allocated by Stevens to Thomas and Kennedy was probably a reflection of which justice he believed was more likely to be persuaded. Ultimately Stevens's efforts were to no avail; both Thomas and Kennedy would remain with the *Heller* majority. But Stevens does indicate in his autobiography that he believed that his efforts may have caused Justice Scalia to modify his opinion. Whatever Scalia's initial inclinations might have been to write an opinion that recognized limitations on the right to keep and bear arms, they could only have been enhanced by the realization that he was in a competition with Stevens for Kennedy's vote. Scalia's willingness to include dicta supporting restrictions on firearms ownership by individuals with felony convictions, permitting localities to bar the carrying of weapons in sensitive places, or the issue we discussed, treating automatic weapons differently from other modern firearms, may have meant the difference in Scalia's writing the Court's opinion or a dissent.[51]

Justice Scalia's efforts at persuasion required a nonoriginalist concession on the kinds of weapons that were constitutionally protected. The distinction between the military small arms issued to the British and Continental armies and the musket, rifles, and pistols found in eighteenth-century American homes were slight. A fully originalist logic would have dictated that the automatic small arms like the M16 would have enjoyed constitutional protection, especially if the Second Amendment's primary purpose was to make possible a large-scale popular militia. But could the opinion recognize that large-scale participation in the militia was the amendment's first purpose? Accepting that would force the opinion into dangerous territory. It would require emphasizing the idea that a major motivation behind the Second Amendment was to enable the citizenry to fight a government gone bad, a potential tyranny. That would lead to the conclusion that the weapons of the US Army, or at least its small arms like the M16, were constitutionally protected for the public at large. Whatever the historical accuracy of such a claim, it was not an argument that would be persuasive.

We argue that it was this effort to write a persuasive opinion that caused Justice Scalia in *Heller* to produce a Second Amendment with a shift in emphasis as to the amendment's primary purpose. What might be termed the legislative history, the history of the amendment's drafting that we discussed in the first chapter, reveals a primary purpose in providing constitutional protection for the right to bear arms in order to facilitate the militia. The majority opinion in *Heller* relegates the militia to a secondary role in Second Amendment analysis. Instead, private purposes—defense of self and home—become the heart of what is constitutionally protected. This shift in emphasis was not necessary to produce an originalist opinion that vindicated the rights of Dick Heller and other DC residents to have firearms at home for self-defense. A sound originalist case could certainly have been made that the right to bear arms had long been recognized as including the private right to self-defense as well as the right to bear arms for participation in the common defense. That case is buttressed by the English history that preceded the drafting of the Second Amendment, including Sir Edward Coke's recognition in the seventeenth century of a right to use weapons in defense of the home and the recognition in late seventeenth-century England that even the despised Catholics had the right to have arms in their homes for self-defense. Certainly, comments by early national-era jurists James Wilson and St. George Tucker linking the Second Amendment to the personal right of self-defense would have only strengthened the case for reading an individual self-defense component into the Second Amendment without disturbing the traditional view that broad-based participation in the common defense was the primary purpose of the amendment.[52]

But by shifting the Second Amendment's emphasis from broad-based participation in the common defense to a constitutionally protected right to self and home defense, the majority produced a Second Amendment in line with early twenty-first-century sensibilities. The militia and broad-based citizen participation in such were acknowledged but placed in the background. Instead of the question in *Miller*—was a particular weapon part of ordinary military equipment and thus a candidate for constitutional protection?—the focus became whether a particular weapon or type of weapon was generally owned by the public at large. The 1934 restriction on automatic weapons was a fait accompli that would not be disturbed. The new debate on semiautomatic military style rifles was not engaged even though these firearms were owned by large numbers of members of the public and police departments and might arguably be useful for one type of militia service, civilian aid to law enforcement. The militia and anything that smacked of citizen participation in such was in a curious place. It was acknowledged in the law, was part of the Second Amendment debate, but it smacked of an extremism best avoided. The right to self-defense in the home was widely supported. Only a handful of jurisdictions had banned the ownership of handguns in the home. Bans on firearms for self-defense in the home had been overwhelmingly rejected by the American public. The District of Columbia was an outlier. An opinion rejecting the DC law and placing self-defense in the home at the heart of what was protected by the Second Amendment would be safe ground. It would resonate with the American public and at least four other justices. That was the opinion Justice Scalia wrote.

REACTION

As the first Supreme Court case to examine the Second Amendment and the controversial issue of gun control in seven decades, *Heller* naturally brought swift reaction from all points of the political compass. Some of that reaction was predictable. The *New York Times*, which had been a staunch supporter of firearms restrictions since its championing of New York's Sullivan Law before World War I, was harshly critical. In an editorial, "the Gray Lady" pronounced *Heller* "an audaciously harmful decision" and a "a radical break from seventy years of Supreme Court precedent."[53] In Justice Scalia's opinion, the editorial saw dire consequences:

> This is a decision that will cost innocent lives, cause immeasurable pain and
> suffering and turn America into a more dangerous country. It will also diminish
> our standing in the world, sending yet another message that the United States
> values gun rights over human life.
>
>      The gun lobby will now trumpet this ruling as an end to virtually all gun
> restrictions, anywhere, at all times. That must not happen.[54]

Liberal constitutional scholar Erwin Chemerinsky accused the majority of abandoning judicial restraint and embracing the sort of activism conservatives usually criticize. "In striking down the law," he wrote, "Justice Antonin Scalia's majority opinion, joined by the court's four other most conservative justices, is quite activist in pursuing the conservative political agenda of protecting gun owners." Historian Saul Cornell, whose writings did much to influence Justice Stevens's dissent in *Heller*, argued that Scalia's opinion sounded "like Bach played on a kazoo."[55]

But criticism and praise for the decision did not neatly fall along liberal and conservative lines. Senator Patrick Leahy, chairman of the Senate Judiciary Committee and a liberal Democrat from Vermont, a state with large intersecting liberal and gun-owning populations, noted:

> The Supreme Court has recognized the personal right to bear arms guaranteed
> in the *Second Amendment* and expressly held for the first time that our Bill of
> Rights includes this right among its guarantees of individual liberty and freedom.
> This is a good thing. This opinion should usher in a new era in which the

constitutionality of government regulations of firearms is reviewed against the
backdrop of this important right. . . .

Since before the nation's founding, Americans have used firearms for
protection and sporting purposes. I have enjoyed target shooting since my days
at St. Michael's. I know Vermonters will be relieved and encouraged to see their
rights recognized just as they were when the Supreme Court preserved the Great
Writ of habeas corpus in its decision earlier this month.[56]

Leahy would not be the only liberal to express agreement with the decision. Harvard constitutional scholar Laurence Tribe stated: "It's only the two
extremes who have any reason to be disappointed. One extreme is those who
say there is no individual right, which may be good policy but is not consistent
with the Constitution, and the other extreme is that the right to bear arms is
absolute and not subject to regulation, which is also not consistent with the
Constitution."[57]

Whereas liberals like Patrick Leahy and Laurence Tribe were willing to express general approval of the decision in *Heller*, some conservatives criticized
Scalia's opinion as either faulty in its originalist analysis or on the grounds that
the ruling in *Heller* would lead to a bad policy result, limiting the ability of the
democratically elected branches to choose gun-control measures in an effort
to attack criminal violence. Two federal court judges appointed by Ronald
Reagan, J. Harvey Wilkinson III, a judge on the Fourth Circuit Court of Appeals, and Richard Posner, a judge on the Seventh Circuit Court, attacked the
reasoning and result in the Scalia opinion.[58]

If conservative jurists Wilkinson and Posner were alarmed at *Heller*, they
were concerned in part because they realized that the decision overturning
the DC prohibition would be followed quickly by attacks on state restrictions,
accompanied by claims that the Second Amendment should be incorporated
and applied to the states. This possibility may have alarmed Wilkinson and
Posner, but it excited progressive legal activists David Gans and Doug Kendall. Writing in December 2008, Gans and Kendall, lawyers at the liberal Center for Constitutional Accountability, realized that incorporation was likely.
Alan Gura had already filed suit to overturn Chicago's handgun ban—an
issue we will explore in the next chapter. But what kind of incorporation?
Gans and Kendall, like many others, recognized that the traditional vehicle
for applying the Bill of Rights to the states, the Fourteenth Amendment's due
process clause, was historically and logically problematic. Might the Second

Amendment issue finally provide an opportunity to revive the Civil War amendment's privileges or immunities clause and rectify the mistake that was made in *Slaughter-House*? The authors indicated their belief that a revival of the privileges or immunities clause would put the constitutional right to privacy on a somewhat surer footing than it had with a reliance on substantive due process. Gans and Kendall foresaw what would be a major subtheme in the battle over incorporation: whether it would be argued and achieved through what had become the established route of incorporation through the due process clause, or through a revival of privileges or immunities. It may seem like an obscure and pedantic difference, but it was one that would increase the division between Gura and his allies and the NRA.[59]

# 8. *McDonald*

Suits against the city of Chicago and surrounding suburbs were filed as soon as *Heller* was decided. The NRA filed one such suit against the city of Chicago and another against the city of Oak Park, Illinois, a Chicago suburb. Alan Gura and David Sigale, an Illinois attorney, likewise filed suit against Chicago. Their lead plaintiff this time was Otis McDonald, an elderly African American veteran of the Korean War. McDonald wanted a handgun for self-defense. He was prohibited from doing so by the Windy City's ban on handguns. McDonald lived on the South Side of Chicago, a neighborhood plagued with crime and violence. In addition to McDonald, Gura represented former Evanston, Illinois, police officer Adam Orlov and David Lawson, a resident of Chicago who had been a victim of burglary.[1]

Gura had decided on an unconventional strategy in order to secure incorporation of the Second Amendment. Instead of employing what had become the traditional vehicle for incorporation—the due process clause of the Fourteenth Amendment—Gura decided to argue that the amendment's privileges or immunities clause should be the vehicle for applying the Bill of Rights to the states. This strategy had two difficulties. First, a long string of precedents going back to the nineteenth century indicated that if the federal judiciary was going to apply a provision of the Bill of Rights to the states, it would do so through the Fourteenth Amendment's due process clause. Second, the Supreme Court had declared in the *Slaughter-House Cases* in 1873 that the privileges or immunities clause placed few restrictions on state governments—certainly not the restrictions that the Bill of Rights placed on the federal government. Gura's strategy was risky.

But if Gura's strategy seemed like one that might risk the Court's disapproval, it was consistent with a new scholarly consensus that agreed that incorporation indeed total incorporation was correct after all. That new consensus also recognized that the privileges or immunities clause was originally intended to be the vehicle for applying the Bill of Rights to the states. The due process clause as the vehicle for incorporation had been heavily criticized. Most scholars and commentators were aware that it was based on a somewhat shaky historical foundation. Even the *New York Times*, which had long been a vociferous supporter of gun control, recognized that *McDonald* would likely produce a decision in favor of incorporation and argued in an editorial that the Court should take the occasion to restore the Fourteenth Amendment's privileges or immunities clause and rectify the error that it had made in *Slaughter-House*.[2]

But the due process clause was the vehicle that the Supreme Court and the lower federal courts had used to apply the Bill of Rights to the states. The precedent was firm and unlikely to change. This pointed to the second problem with Gura's strategy. The *Slaughter-House Cases* were widely believed to have rendered the privileges or immunities clause a virtual constitutional dead letter. In addition to convincing the Supreme Court to incorporate the Second Amendment against state and local governments, Gura had given himself the daunting task of convincing a majority of the Court to overrule a venerable, if often criticized, precedent. Gura's strategy would increase the friction between himself and the NRA's legal team.

The cases were first heard by Milton Shadur, a judge appointed to the US District Court for the Northern District of Illinois by President Jimmy Carter. As expected, Judge Shadur dismissed the cases, finding that *Quilici v. Village of Morton Grove* controlled. "*Quilici*," he wrote in an unreported opinion, "is an on-all-fours decision by our Court of Appeals that takes the opposite position from that now pressed by plaintiffs in all three cases before this Court."[3]

The parties dutifully appealed their cases to the Seventh Circuit, where a panel that included Judges Richard Posner and Frank Easterbrook likewise ruled in the cities' favor. In his opinion, Judge Easterbrook observed that because overruling its own cases was the Supreme Court's prerogative, the circuit court was unable to avoid the fact that the *Slaughter-House Cases* held that the privileges or immunities clause did not incorporate the Bill of Rights. As for the plaintiffs' selective incorporation argument, Easterbrook observed that "'selective incorporation' cannot be reduced to a formula" and expressed doubts that the right to keep and bear arms was "'deeply rooted in this nation's history and tradition."[4] He continued:

> Plaintiffs' reliance on William Blackstone . . . for the proposition that the right
> to keep and bear arms is "deeply rooted" not only slights the fact that Blackstone
> was discussing the law of another nation but also overlooks the reality that
> Blackstone discussed arms-bearing as a political rather than a constitutional right.

The United Kingdom does not have a constitution that prevents Parliament and the Queen from matching laws to current social and economic circumstances, as the people and their representatives understand them. It is dangerous to rely on Blackstone (or for that matter modern European laws banning handguns) to show the meaning of a constitutional amendment that this nation adopted in 1868. . . . Blackstone also thought determinate criminal sentences (e.g., 25 years, neither more nor less, for robbing a post office) a vital guarantee of liberty. . . . That's not a plausible description of American constitutional law.[5]

Judge Easterbrook concluded by observing that among its features, the Constitution creates a federal republic "where local differences are to be cherished as elements of liberty rather than extirpated in order to produce a single, nationally applicable rule." Federalism, too, is a "deeply rooted tradition"— more so, he claimed, "than is a right to carry any particular type of weapon. How arguments of this kind will affect proposals to 'incorporate' the second amendment," he wrote, "are for the Justices rather than a court of appeals."[6]

Following their loss at the Seventh Circuit, both the NRA and Gura filed petitions for certiorari. Again, the NRA won the race to the courthouse, filing its petition the day after the court of appeals decision; Gura followed suit a week later. The usual collection of sports shooting enthusiasts, university professors, think tanks, and civil rights organizations joined in urging the Supreme Court to take up the case. In addition, the attorneys general of over thirty states filed a brief likewise urging the Court to take the case and incorporate the Second Amendment. Chicago and Oak Park filed briefs in opposition urging the Court not to take up the privileges or immunities issue.[7]

No doubt to Gura's delight, although the NRA was first to file, on September 30, 2009, the Supreme Court denied the NRA's petition and granted Gura's. Under the Supreme Court's rules, however, because the NRA was a party in the consolidated appeal heard by the Seventh Circuit, it was entitled to file briefs as a "respondent in support of the petitioner."[8]

Gura's brief, which was filed in mid-November 2009, contained something of a surprise. Fully 90 percent of its seventy-three pages was devoted to urging the Court to strike down the *Slaughter-House Cases*, along with *Cruikshank* and *Presser*, and incorporate the Second Amendment through the privileges or immunities clause. The first part of their brief argued that the right to keep and bear arms was a "privilege or immunity" as understood both in the early republic and in the nineteenth century. It argued further that the framers of the Fourteenth Amendment intended to apply those rights against the states and that those ratifying the amendment, as well as contemporary legal commentators, likewise understood that to be a consequence of ratification.[9]

The second part of the brief argued that the Court must overrule the *Slaughter-House Cases*, *Cruikshank*, and *Presser* as profoundly erroneous and anachronistic, and that stare decisis should not preserve those cases. Only in the last five pages of the brief did Gura address incorporation through the due process clause. *Heller*, he concluded, "has defined the contours of the Second Amendment right: it identified the right's origins, traced its history, and described its core purposes. Applying these variables to this Court's established selective incorporation doctrine yields a judgment of reversal."[10]

By contrast, the NRA's brief was a little less than two-thirds the length of Gura's, and its emphasis leaned heavily on the standard selective incorporation arguments. The first part argued that, as a matter of original understanding, the framers of the Fourteenth Amendment intended to secure the right to keep and bear arms against state infringement. "There can be," it argued, "no real debate that the right to keep and bear arms is guaranteed against infringement by the States somewhere in the Fourteenth Amendment." The only question was "where [in the Amendment] that right is found."[11]

The second part of the brief answered that question: the due process clause of the Fourteenth Amendment as viewed through the lens of the Court's selective incorporation jurisprudence. The NRA's brief noted that other than the Second Amendment, only the Fifth Amendment's grand jury requirement and the Seventh Amendment's jury trial provision have not been incorporated. And those, the brief pointed out, "both involv[e] legal procedure rather than fundamental rights."[12] It went on to observe that

> while the Court has phrased the incorporation test in various ways over the
> years, the lynchpin has been the importance of the right in question to what has
> variously been described as "liberty," "a free society," "free government," the
> "liberty at the base of all our civil and political institutions," or "ordered liberty."
> As well, the central, abiding, and indispensable element of every formulation is
> that rights be deemed fundamental in our system of government.[13]

Did the Second Amendment meet these criteria? The NRA said the answer "should be a foregone conclusion in light of everything that has come before. Given the extensive history" discussed in the first part of the brief, "the case for incorporation of the Second Amendment is stronger than for any other right in the Bill of Rights." The NRA noted as well that incorporation via the due process clause did not require the Court to overrule existing precedent.[14]

For good measure, however, the NRA's brief made two alternative privileges or immunities clause arguments as well. The first argued that the Court should simply declare the right to keep and bear arms to be a right of national citizenship of the sort mentioned in the *Slaughter-House Cases*; it further argued that support for this position could be found in subsequent cases like *Cruikshank* and *Presser*, albeit in dicta. In its second alternative argument, the NRA argued that if precedent could *not* be read to support the proposition that the right to keep and bear arms was a privilege or immunity of national citizenship, then it ought to overrule those precedents and revisit the scope of the privileges or immunities clause. Were it to do so, "the historical record culminating in the passage of the Fourteenth Amendment provides compelling support for the propositions that the [privileges or immunities clause] was intended to incorporate much of the Bill of Rights, and certainly the Second Amendment, against the States."[15]

Chicago and Oak Park's brief spent considerable space attempting to rebut both the due process and privileges or immunities clause arguments made by Gura and the NRA. To incorporate under the due process clause, a right must be "implicit in the concept of ordered liberty," the cities argued. In some cases, a handgun ban might enhance, not inhibit, ordered liberty. Incorporating the Second Amendment would "place at risk, in addition to handgun bans, many other firearms regulations that may equally be viewed as necessary to reduce fear, violence, and injury, and therefore to foster, not threaten a system of ordered liberty." Federalism principles should counsel respect for choices like those made by the cities—a point made forcefully by Judge Easterbrook in his opinion. Further, the brief noted that countries sharing an Anglo-American legal heritage that have more strictly regulated privately owned firearms was a further argument that "ordered liberty" was not jeopardized by strict firearms regulations. Indeed, the brief also argued that state and local treatment of firearms has varied over the years and that those regulations have generally been subjected to a "reasonableness" test by state courts.[16]

Finally, the cities' brief seemed to reargue the *Heller* decision itself, arguing that the framing-era history of the Second Amendment did not support incorporation. It also rejected the argument that even "assuming that there is an unenumerated right to self-defense that extends beyond its recognition as a defense to criminal charges, such a right would . . . support incorporation of the Second Amendment." Nor was the fact that most other provisions of the Bill of Rights had been incorporated relevant. "To establish that a particular provision of the Bill of Rights applies to the States, that particular provision—not some other one—must be so fundamental that it warrants displacing the ability of state and local governments to make their own sovereign choices and legislate for their own conditions."[17]

As for the privileges or immunities clause, the cities leaned heavily on an appeal to stare decisis as a compelling reason not to revisit the *Slaughter-House Cases* and use that clause as the means of incorporation. Moreover, the cities argued, the historical record surrounding the passage and ratification of the privileges or immunities clause did not support the "total incorporation" position. To the extent that the framers expressed concerns about discriminatory disarmament of the Freedmen, the brief argued, that would not necessitate incorporation of the Second Amendment. It would merely require application of the Fourteenth Amendment's antidiscrimination principle to ensure any firearms regulations were race-neutral. "Overruling *Slaughter-House* and its progeny, and overturning the settled law governing the application of the first eight amendments to the States," the brief concluded, "should require an overwhelming justification"; the cities argued that the petitioners had not furnished one.[18]

As in *Heller*, the Court was inundated with amicus briefs. Fifty-one briefs were filed, most in support of the petitioners. Many of the amicus briefs began life as briefs supporting or opposing the petition for certiorari. Amici ran the usual gamut of historians, law professors, law enforcement groups of various stripes, members of Congress, firearms interest groups, think tanks, and civil rights groups, Among the more interesting ones were a brief filed on behalf of nearly forty states in support of petitioners, and a separate brief filed on behalf of several liberal and libertarian law professors who were urging the Court to adopt Gura's privileges or immunities argument. A somewhat unexpected brief was filed by California's liberal attorney general Edmund "Jerry" Brown in support of the petitioners. Brown, a Democrat, who had previously served as California's governor and who would return to that office in 2011, signed a brief supporting incorporation of the Second Amendment. The brief argued that incorporation was needed to protect the rights of the state's citizens to have arms because the state constitution lacked a right-to-bear-arms provision.[19]

There were two interesting briefs filed in support of neither party. One, filed on behalf of the Brady Center to Prevent Gun Violence (previously Handgun Control Inc.), the International Association of Chiefs of Police, the International Brotherhood of Police Officers, and the National Black Police Association, urged the Court explicitly to adopt intermediate scrutiny as the standard of review for state and local firearms regulations. The other, written by the NAACP Legal Defense Fund, urged the Court to incorporate the Second Amendment using its traditional selective incorporation jurisprudence. The organization expressed fear that incorporation through the privileges or immunities clause alone might jeopardize previous civil rights and civil liberties decisions grounded in the due process clause. The NAACP Legal Defense Fund urged that if the Court chose to revive the privileges or immunities clause, it should do so in a way that would not jeopardize previous due process precedents.[20]

Civil rights attorney Dale Ho, a coauthor of the Legal Defense Fund's brief, has written that many advocates on the right and left who hoped to revive the privileges or immunities clause did so with concerns that went far beyond the Second Amendment claims at stake in *McDonald*. Scholars and practicing lawyers on the left hoped that the privileges or immunities clause might provide a firmer grounding for what had become the Court's modern substantive due process jurisprudence, a jurisprudence that had embedded an unenumerated right to sexual privacy into the nation's constitutional law. A number of advocates on the right hoped that a revived privileges or immunities clause might bring with it the return of early twentieth-century notions of freedom of contract, casting constitutional doubt on various forms of economic regulation including minimum wage and maximum hours laws.[21]

## GURA V. THE NRA: ROUND TWO

There was to be one more skirmish between Alan Gura and the lawyers for the NRA. Concerned that Gura's insistence on emphasizing the privileges or immunities clause argument might shortchange the due process clause argument, the NRA filed an unusual motion to divide oral argument between itself and Gura in early January 2010. Paul Clement, who filed the brief motion on behalf of the NRA, sought ten of Gura's thirty allotted minutes. Clement argued that the division "would materially assist the Court and ensure a full exploration of both the alternative grounds for reversing the decision below which are included in the question presented." Using the due process clause to incorporate the Second Amendment, the motion contended, was "the most direct way to apply the Second Amendment to States and localities," but the petitioners "have concentrated their argument on a Privileges or Immunities Clause theory that would require overruling at least three of this Court's precedents." Dividing time would ensure "that both issues encompassed within the question presented are fully explored at oral argument."[22]

Gura vigorously opposed the NRA's motion in his own filing objecting to a division of time. The NRA, he argued, "lacks any unique interest justifying its insertion into the argument." And the "speculation" that Gura would not adequately argue the due process clause question was "unjustified." For the NRA to argue the latter "would at best be redundant." Gura argued that under the Court's own rules, the NRA was ineligible to argue because it was not a petitioner and entitled only to "file documents."[23] Further, Gura defended his giving relatively little space to the due process argument:

> Petitioners worked closely with the amici in seeking to avoid duplication of effort, hosting a coordination conference attended by several NRA attorneys and attorneys for NRA-funded amici. . . . Petitioners correctly anticipated that the familiar due process issues would be overwhelmingly covered in other briefs, and therefore perceived no value in belaboring the same points in briefing beyond their own merely comprehensive treatment of the issue.[24]

Granting the NRA's motion would discourage coordination, "as efforts to reduce duplication could produce motions to divide argument time based on claims that the parties did not devote 'enough' pages to an issue."[25]

The Supreme Court granted the NRA's motion on January 25, 2010. In a blog post about the Court's decision, veteran Court reporter Tony Mauro quoted Paul Clement as saying the Court's grant was a "signal that the Court is interested in ensuring that all the avenues to incorporation . . . are fully explored at oral argument," adding that he "look[ed] forward to working with" Gura.[26]

Gura shot back, "The suggestion that I wouldn't present all the arguments to the Court was uncalled for." He added, "I hope this time Paul understands that handgun bans are unconstitutional"—a reference to Clement's position as solicitor general in *Heller* that the DC handgun ban should be subjected to heightened, but not strict, scrutiny and that the case should have been remanded to the lower courts for analysis under that standard.[27]

## ORAL ARGUMENT

On March 2, 2010, Gura began his oral argument at 10:13 A.M. He opened with his discussion of the privileges or immunities clause and why it was the proper vehicle for incorporating the provisions of the Bill of Rights. He immediately ran into rough sailing. Why overrule a 140-year-old precedent, Chief Justice Roberts demanded. Gura's reply: stare decisis should not be observed when the original precedent was erroneous from the start. Justice Sonia Sotomayor asked about reliance interests. Wouldn't overruling the *Slaughter-House Cases* suggest that states could not have nonunanimous juries or require juries in all civil cases? Gura answered that "states may have grown accustomed to violating the rights of American citizens, but that does not bootstrap those violations into something that is constitutional."[28]

Justice Ginsburg then asked about the scope of his argument. What else, in addition to the first eight amendments, would be included among the "privileges or immunities"? Specifically, "What unenumerated rights would we be declaring privileges and immunities under your conception of it?" Gura demurred, saying that while it was "impossible to give a full list of all the unenumerated rights that might be protected by the Privileges and Immunities Clause, just as it is impossible to do so under the Due Process Clause, at least with respect to the Privileges and Immunities Clause we have wonderful historical guideposts" to inform judges' decisions.[29] It was at this point that Justice Scalia pounced, essentially putting paid to Gura's bid to revive the privileges or immunities clause and inter the *Slaughter-House Cases* once and for all. Their exchange is worth quoting at length:

> JUSTICE SCALIA: Mr. Gura, do you think it is at all easier to bring the Second Amendment under the Privileges and Immunities Clause than it is to bring it under our established law of substantive due process?
>
> MR. GURA: It's—
>
> JUSTICE SCALIA: Is it easier to do it under privileges and immunities than it is under substantive due process?

MR. GURA: It is easier in terms, perhaps, of—of the text and history of the original public understanding of—

JUSTICE SCALIA: No, no. I'm not talking about whether . . . the *Slaughter-House Cases* were right or wrong. I'm saying, assuming we give, you know, the Privileges and Immunities Clause your definition, does that make it any easier to get the Second Amendment adopted with respect to the States?

MR. GURA: Justice Scalia, I suppose the answer to that would be no, because—

JUSTICE SCALIA: Then if the answer is no, why are you asking us to overrule 150, 140 years of prior law . . . when you can reach your result under substantive due—I mean, you know, unless you are bucking for . . . a place on some law school faculty—

(Laughter.)

MR. GURA: No. No. I have left law school some time ago and this is not an attempt to—to return.

JUSTICE SCALIA: What you argue is the darling of the professoriate, for sure, but it's also contrary to 140 years of our jurisprudence. Why do you want to undertake that burden instead of just arguing substantive due process, which as much as I think it's wrong . . . even I have acquiesced in it?

(Laughter.)

MR. GURA: Justice Scalia, we would be extremely happy if the Court reverses the lower court based on the substantive due process theory that we argued in the Seventh Circuit.[30]

Pressed again by Justice Ginsburg about what might be covered, in addition to the first eight amendments, Gura suggested some of the rights mentioned in the 1866 Civil Rights Act, such as the right to acquire, hold, and transfer property. But, Ginsburg responded, these were rights that weren't necessary enjoyed by all citizens everywhere, like women, for instance. Gura replied that women were citizens of the United States at the time but agreed that rights weren't fully enforced 140 years ago and that we now have a better understanding of rights than we did then. This led Justice Ginsburg to ask whether that process was a one-way ratchet. "I mean, if the notion is that these are principles that any free society would adopt, well, a lot of free societies have rejected the right to keep and bear arms," she observed.[31]

Gura responded that, on his reading, the Court's most recent selective incorporation decisions emphasized that it was our history and tradition that served as a reference point for determining if a right was fundamental. He further explained, "as understood by the people who ratified the Fourteenth Amendment . . . It's not a free-flowing license . . . for judges to announce un-enumerated rights. However, to the extent that we have unenumerated rights which the framers and ratifiers didn't literally understand, they nonetheless left us guideposts." Justice Scalia interrupted, "Well, what about rights rooted in the traditions and conscience of our people? Would . . . that do the job?" Gura said that it would, to which Scalia replied, "That happens to be the test we have used under substantive due process."[32]

Justice Stevens next began a colloquy with Gura over the scope of the incorporated Second Amendment right. Would a right to keep and bear arms incorporated through the due process clause, he asked, be the same as that right guaranteed by the Second Amendment, even if that amendment did not exist? He said that it would and, in response to a clarification by Chief Justice Roberts and Justice Kennedy, would incorporate not only the right but also any gloss put on the right by the Supreme Court's own decisions. This would be true, Gura agreed, whether incorporation took place via the due process clause or the privileges or immunities clause.[33]

Justice Breyer then asked whether Gura had considered that perhaps the right guaranteed by the Second Amendment was "different," warranting different treatment than other rights when it came to incorporation. The application of other rights, he observed, do not usually involve balancing liberty interests on the one hand with the potential loss of life on the other. "To be specific," Breyer continued, "suppose Chicago says . . . by banning handguns . . . in the city, we save several hundred human lives every year. And the other side says, we don't think it is several hundred and, moreover, that doesn't matter. How do you decide the case?"[34]

Gura replied that the answer was to be found not in "which side has the better statistics, but rather to what the framers said in the Constitution, because that policy choice was made for us in the Constitution." So, the city can't ban guns, even if the ban saves lives?, asked Breyer. "The city cannot ban guns that are within the common use as protected by the right to arms," Gura clarified. Justice Scalia added that there is debate over the cost in lives of the *Miranda* rule informing those in custody that they have a right to remain silent, but that the Court had never engaged in balancing social costs against individual liberty in those cases. Gura concluded his argument by noting that the Court has long concluded—as it had in *Heller*—that laws limiting enumerated constitutional rights are subjected to heightened judicial scrutiny.[35]

Paul Clement then rose to make the substantive due process argument on behalf of the NRA. The case for incorporation, he announced confidently, was a "remarkably straightforward" one. Justice Stevens interrupted to ask Clement whether an incorporated Second Amendment would have the identical scope to the right as it applied to the federal government. He reminded Clement that the Court had permitted states to employ nonunanimous juries in some cases. Clement said that he regarded the Sixth Amendment as something of an outlier and that so-called jot-for-jot incorporation was the norm.[36]

Well, Justice Stevens demanded, when was the last time the Court incorporated a substantive provision of the Bill of Rights? Clement said that he guessed it was in *Mapp v. Ohio*,[37] which held that the Fourth Amendment required that evidence gathered pursuant to an illegal search be excluded from trial. Stevens and Clement then disagreed whether *Mapp* involved a procedural or a substantive right, and Justice Scalia intervened, observing that

> I guess we have applied substantive due process with regard to the necessity of permitting homosexual conduct [in *Lawrence v. Texas*] and with respect to the necessity of permitting abortion on demand [in *Planned Parenthood v. Casey*]. We have not adopted a more rigid rule for the Federal Government than we have adopted for the States in either of those instances, have we?[38]

Clement replied that was indeed correct, adding, "Though I guess I would stress that . . . whatever the debates about substantive due process when it comes to unenumerated rights . . . the gist of this Court's incorporation doctrine is that the textual provisions of the Bill of Rights stand in a favored position with respect to incorporation."[39]

But, protested Justice Stevens, "We've never said it had to be literally all the way down the line, or we couldn't have done the . . . non-unanimous criminal jury case."[40] True, Clement responded, but he noted that seems to be the exception that proved the rule. It was, he ventured,

> interesting that the one place that I see where the Court has not effectively translated all the case law is one of the procedural rights, the Sixth Amendment criminal jury right. And I think with respect to the substantive rights—and I think the . . . similarity between the First and the Second Amendments are very stark in this respect—this Court has incorporated essentially not just the amendment and not just the right, but all of the jurisprudence as well.[41]

Clement then argued that a good working definition of what a fundamental right is would be one that was a "preexisting right[ ] that didn't depend on the Constitution for their existence." Arguing that was true of the Second Amendment, a consequence of that "would be to carry over the jurisprudence under the Second Amendment," which was not "carrying over a lot [just] carrying over the *Heller* case." He added that "it's going to be difficult enough to develop the Second Amendment jurisprudence that you wouldn't want to make it more difficult by having to develop a Federal Second Amendment jurisprudence and then some sort of shadow version of that jurisprudence for the States," especially when the Court's modern incorporation cases explicitly rejected such a federal-state dichotomy. And, he continued, if you treat the Second Amendment like other incorporated rights, "the case is really straightforward." Comparing the First and Fourth Amendments to the Second, he noted that "they have the same textual guarantee to the people, they trace their origins to preexisting rights back to the English Bill of Rights, back to even earlier constitutional history."[42]

As time wound down, Justice Breyer referred to a law professors' brief arguing that Blackstone saw the right to keep and bear arms primarily as a right to raise an army through Parliament and asked Clement whether that made a difference as to incorporation. Turning the question to his advantage, Clement responded first that the *Heller* majority had concluded Blackstone was talking mainly about self-defense; then he added that "the one thing that I think we can come to a conclusion about Blackstone is the very fact that Blackstone dwelled on the right is good evidence that it's a fundamental right that should apply to the States."[43]

Chicago was represented by James A. Feldman, who maintained a solo appellate practice in Washington, DC, and taught as an adjunct professor at the University of Pennsylvania Carey Law School. A graduate of Harvard Law School, Feldman clerked for Judge Skelly Wright on the Court of Appeals for the District of Columbia and for Justice William Brennan. After a stint in private practice, he joined the solicitor general's office, where he stayed for almost twenty years. He had argued nearly fifty cases before the Supreme Court when he agreed to argue on Chicago's behalf.

Feldman began his argument by stating the Second Amendment should not be incorporated because it was not "implicit in the concept of ordered liberty," and he immediately ran into a flurry of questions by Justices Scalia and Kennedy and Chief Justice Roberts.

Scalia jumped in first, asking whether the implicit-in-the-concept-of-ordered-liberty formula was the test employed in the most recent incorporation cases.[44] When Feldman responded that the phrase had been used as recently as the Court's assisted suicide cases, Justice Kennedy noted that it was the test employed by Justice John Marshall Harlan II, who dissented from many of the Court's incorporation decisions—especially those incorporating the Bill of Rights' criminal procedure provisions.[45]

Feldman gave no quarter. The Supreme Court held in *Barron v. Baltimore* that the Bill of Rights did not apply to the states; and there was no clear evidence that the framers of the Fourteenth Amendment intended to apply the first eight amendments in toto to the states. Therefore, "the Court has always understood that when it's applying the Due Process Clause, what it asks is not just is something in the Constitution but is this something that is so fundamental it's a necessary condition." Justice Scalia interrupted with a question about jury trials. Were they implicit in the concept of ordered liberty? Even England did not guarantee them in all criminal cases, he observed. Feldman replied that with a procedural right in a particular procedural system, context mattered.[46]

"I think that's . . . exactly right," replied Chief Justice Roberts, "and that is what the Court elaborated on in [*Duncan v. Louisiana*[47]]. I do think the focus is our system of ordered liberty, not any abstract system of ordered liberty. You can say Japan is a free country, but it doesn't have the right to trial . . . by jury." The concept "only makes sense, I think, if you limit it to our system. Under our system . . . the right to a jury is essential." And if you believe that, Roberts continued, then "why wouldn't you think, for all the reasons given in *Heller*, that the Second Amendment right is essential to our system, whatever it may be with respect to France or England or anywhere else?"[48]

Feldman protested that the fundamental nature of the Second Amendment was not at issue in *Heller*. Justice Kennedy joined in: Wasn't *Heller*'s rationale that the right to keep and bear arms had to be considered independently of the militia case precisely because of its fundamental character? That because "the public meaning of the Second Amendment was that there was an individual right to bear arms," it was considered fundamental? "If it's not fundamental," Kennedy observed, "then *Heller* is wrong, it seems to me." Chief Justice Roberts piled on, arguing that "I don't see how you can read *Heller* and not take away from it the notion that the Second Amendment, whether you want to label it fundamental or not, was extremely important to the framers in their view of what liberty meant." Feldman conceded it was considered important, but it was codified in the Bill of Rights out of concern that the federal government would disarm the militia, not out of concern for individual self-defense.[49]

Chief Justice Roberts noted that the question of the Second Amendment's incorporation and its application to specific state and local regulations were two separate questions and suggested that Feldman was conflating them. "All the arguments you make against incorporation . . . are arguments you should make in favor of regulation under the Second Amendment." Take laws against concealed carry, he offered; maybe "you should not be able to have concealed carry—well, maybe that's right. But that doesn't mean you don't incorporate the Second Amendment to allow you to enforce that type of regulation."[50]

Feldman disagreed with the chief justice's characterization of his argument. "The argument I am making," he clarified, is that "the framers would have been satisfied to leave [the regulation of self-defense] to the States" and that self-defense is "something that has always been effectively regulated through the political process and especially at the State and local level. And through our history, as technology has changed, State and local regulation has altered to draw the balance that has to be drawn."[51]

Kennedy then asked whether self-defense is part of the liberty guaranteed by the due process clause. Feldman agreed for the sake of argument. If so, then how can you write an opinion holding that the right to keep and bear arms is not fundamental, but *Heller* was correctly decided?, Justice Kennedy asked. Feldman demurred, saying only that the Second Amendment "took a preexisting right that had not been . . . codified in the Constitution, and it said, this self-defense right [was needed] in the Constitution . . . in order to protect the militia against being disarmed by the Federal Government." That, quipped Roberts, "sounds an awful lot to me like the argument we heard in *Heller* on the losing side."[52]

Now it was Justice Alito's turn to joust with Feldman:

JUSTICE ALITO: Let me see if I understand your argument. I thought you said
    a minute ago that if a State or local government were to ban firearms
    completely, this Court might hold that that violates substantive due process
    because the right to use a firearm for self-defense . . . might be held to be
    implicit in the concept of ordered liberty; is that right?
MR. FELDMAN: That is correct.

JUSTICE ALITO: But I thought you began by saying that the right to keep and bear arms is not implicit in the concept of ordered liberty.

MR. FELDMAN: . . . I don't actually think the right to keep and bear arms itself is. Perhaps the right to self-defense is, and then like other rights . . . if the Court were to hold that that is constitutionally protected, the question would be is the State now giving you sufficient means to exercise that right? Not whatever means you want but sufficient means so that you reasonably can exercise for that right. I would think that would be the only way that that kind of analysis could go if you start off from self-defense.[53]

"But," asked Justice Scalia, "isn't that militia purpose just as much defeated by allowing the States to take away the militia's arms as it would be by allowing the Federal Government to take away the militia's arms?"[54] This spurred Justice Breyer to imagine James Madison rank-ordering the rights protected by the Second Amendment. According to Breyer, Madison

would say insofar as that right to bear arms is important for the purpose of maintaining the militia, it's high on the ordered liberty chart. Insofar as the right to bear arms is there to shoot burglars, it's low on the ordered liberty chart. And if that's what they would say, it's conceivable that part of this amendment . . . which would prevent a law that would disarm people to the extent they couldn't form militias [would be incorporated]. But that part which would disarm people to the extent that they couldn't shoot burglars . . . would not be incorporated.[55]

Feldman, however, was unwilling to draw such fine lines. When Chief Justice Roberts asked whether he was arguing that the Court should distinguish between various purposes of the amendment, incorporating some but not all of them, Feldman said no. "So your argument is all in or all out?" asked Roberts. Feldman replied yes. Justice Alito also pointed out that to be consistent, adopting Justice Breyer's approach would mean revisiting all of the Court's previous incorporation decisions and deciding which among them would warrant incorporation in part or in total.[56]

Feldman eventually returned to the point that states traditionally had regulated firearms with a view to the peculiarities of state and local conditions, that these regulations—if reasonable—were upheld by courts, and that state and local governments should be allowed to do so. An incorporated Second Amendment might inhibit their ability to do that, and the political safeguards were sufficiently robust to protect the right to self-defense.[57] By contrast, with other incorporated amendments there has been concern

> that there is a . . . discrete minority or a highly unpopular view that is not going to get a fair shake in the political process. I don't think that has ever been the case here. And as far as I know, the framers didn't think that was the case with respect to the right to keep and bear arms. It's a right that gets controlled in accordance with local conditions, with local cultures, and with local views about the necessarily difficult questions about how best to protect public safety.[58]

Justice Kennedy then questioned whether Feldman wasn't again conflating the incorporation issue with that of the scope of the incorporated amendment. Can't you both incorporate *and* permit reasonable regulation of the right? Feldman responded with something of a non-sequitur: *Heller*, he said, foreclosed interest balancing and said Chicago could not ban handguns.[59]

What if, asked Justice Sotomayor, we incorporated and said "reasonable regulation" was part of the incorporation? Her question prompted Justice Ginsburg to ask whether reasonable regulation wasn't part of *Heller* already.[60] The disconnect seemed to be that Chicago was arguing that under certain circumstances bans on classes of weapons—like handguns—would be reasonable in light of local conditions, but that was precisely what *Heller* said DC could *not* do. Given jot-for-jot incorporation, that would mean that a handgun ban would not be among the reasonable regulations Chicago might impose. As Feldman explained in conclusion:

> Our view would be that what Chicago has done here, which is permit you to . . . have long guns but ban handguns, is the kind of regulation that throughout our history jurisdictions . . . that are most familiar with their own particular needs and their own particular problems, and in a position to balance . . . the need for self-defense with the risk to the use of firearms—for violence, for accidental death and or suicide—that the City of Chicago has come up with something that is well within our tradition.[61]

Gura had reserved time for rebuttal but spent it all answering skeptical questions about his argument for reviving the privileges or immunities clause. Given that most of the Bill of Rights had been incorporated, asked Justice Kennedy, what, other than jury trials and requiring the use of grand jury indictments, was left? What unenumerated rights? Gura again refused to be pinned down: "We can't give a full description of all unenumerated rights that are going to be protected by the Fourteenth Amendment." This equivocation prompted Justice Scalia to ask whether Gura wasn't bothered by the lack of determinacy. Chief Justice Roberts observed that would give judges lots of flexibility, perhaps even more than in substantive due process cases.[62] Gura disagreed. The privileges or immunities clause "had a specific understanding and that there are guideposts left behind in texts and history that tell us how to apply it, unlike the due process. But at least we know one thing, which is that in 1868 the right to keep and bear arms was understood to be a privilege or immunity of citizenship."[63] And with that, the case was submitted at 11:13 A.M.

THE OPINION

June 28, 2010, the day the Supreme Court announced its decision in *McDonald*, was, of course, a day marked by great anticipation by the litigants and their supporters. It was also a special and somewhat bittersweet day for the members of the Court. Justice Stevens was retiring. The ninety-year-old Republican who had become a mainstay of the Court's liberal wing was stepping down after thirty-five years on the high court. By all appearances he would be missed by his colleagues liberal and conservative alike. On this, the last day of the Court's term and Justice Stevens's tenure, Chief Justice Roberts read a letter from active and retired justices praising Stevens's service on the Court. Roberts added a note of levity by saying that he would give Stevens time for rebuttal. In tribute to the Chicago-born justice who had made bow ties his signature, the Court's gallery was filled with lawyers and spectators who had donned bow ties in the justice's honor. Reporter Jess Bravin of the *Wall Street Journal*, noting the attire of most of the men at Court that day, observed that Stevens "may have finally found his majority."[64]

But if the justice had achieved a consensus that day on a sartorial issue, the majority that Stevens sought rejecting the incorporation of the Second Amendment would elude the retiring justice. Despite the skepticism that most justices seemed to have for Gura's efforts to revive the privileges or immunities clause, it seemed likely from the beginning that a majority of the justices would vote for incorporation. The majority that had decided *Heller* was still on the Court. It seemed unlikely that they had agreed to hear and decide *Heller* just to address the prohibition in the District of Columbia—if so, they could have simply let the decision of the DC Circuit Court stand. No, it was more likely that the Court had granted certiorari in *Heller* because a majority believed that the time had come to address the Second Amendment issue and to give the amendment nationwide application. That would require incorporation. The *Heller* majority were not alone. Even before *Heller* was decided, Harvard professor Mark Tushnet, a constitutional law scholar very much on the left side of the American legal academy, wrote that "surely the right to keep and bear arms is at least as important as other rights that have been selectively incorporated. . . . Intellectual honesty requires that the courts take the next step and decide that the Fourteenth Amendment guarantees the right to keep and bear arms against state regulations."[65] Few were surprised, then, when the Court's decision was announced on June 28, 2010. This time, however, it was Justice Alito, not Justice Scalia, who was tasked with writing what ended up being a four-vote plurality opinion applying selective incorporation to the Second Amendment. A fifth vote for incorporation was furnished by Justice Thomas.[66]

After reciting the basic facts and mentioning the two theories the petitioners advanced for incorporating the right to keep and bear arms, Justice Alito briefly recounted the history of incorporation and mentioned the *Cruikshank* and *Presser* cases, which held that the right applied only to the federal government. The petitioners, he wrote, "argue . . . that we should . . . hold that the right to keep and bear arms is one of the 'privileges or immunities of citizens of the United States.'" However, he continued, "petitioners are unable to identify the [privileges or immunities] Clause's full scope." Further, he remarked that "there [is no] consensus on that question among the scholars who agree that the *Slaughter-House Cases'* interpretation is flawed."[67]

In any event, he concluded, there was no need to reconsider those cases because "for many decades, the question of the rights protected by the Fourteenth Amendment against state infringement has been analyzed under the Due Process Clause of that Amendment." He then shut the door firmly on Alan Gura's primary argument, stating flatly that "we . . . decline to disturb the *Slaughter-House* holding."[68]

Justice Alito then proceed to discuss the evolution of the Court's incorporation jurisprudence; specifically, the varying criteria the Court has used over the years to decide whether a specific provision of the Bill of Rights would be applicable to states. To determine whether the Second Amendment would likewise be incorporated, Alito said, "We must decide whether the right to keep and bear arms is fundamental to *our* scheme of ordered liberty" or "whether [the] right is 'deeply rooted in this Nation's history and tradition.'" *Heller* "points unmistakably to the answer," he wrote.[69]

He went on to note that self-defense was a basic right recognized from time immemorial. Further, *Heller* placed self-defense at the core of the Second Amendment and noted that the right was an integral part of the nation's history and traditions. In an interesting twist, though Justice Alito briefly discussed founding-era history from Blackstone to the early commentaries on the Constitution by Story and Rawle, he spent the bulk of his historical survey focusing on pre–Civil War and Reconstruction sources.[70]

Alito rightly noted that as "the fear that the National Government would disarm the universal militia" faded in the nineteenth century, the "right to keep and bear arms was highly valued for purposes of self-defense," especially among abolitionists facing violence at the hands of proslavery forces. During Reconstruction, both newly freed slaves and African Americans who served in the Union Army "returned to the States of the old Confederacy, where systematic efforts were made to disarm them and other blacks." Thus disarmed, they were then subjected to a reign of terror carried out by private groups, often with at least tacit support of public officials.[71]

After legislative attempts to secure the right to keep and bear arms were deemed insufficient, Congress proposed the Fourteenth Amendment. As Alito noted, "Today, it is generally accepted that the Fourteenth Amendment was understood to provide a constitutional basis for protecting the rights set out in the Civil Rights Act of 1866," which included the right to keep and bear arms. Moreover, "Evidence from the period immediately following the ratification of the Fourteenth Amendment only confirms that the right to keep and bear arms was considered fundamental."[72]

Justice Alito rejected Chicago's reading of history, which would have reduced the Fourteenth Amendment to constitutionalizing only an antidiscrimination rule. First, he noted, that would mean that nondiscriminatory abridgement of First or Fourth Amendment rights would be permissible. "We assume that this is not [Chicago's] view," leading him to conclude that "what they must mean is that the Second Amendment should be singled out for special—and specially unfavorable—treatment," which he declined to do. Chicago's reading of history also ignored the 1867 Freedman's Bureau Act, which explicitly acknowledged the right to keep and bear arms. "Third, if the

39th Congress had outlawed only those laws that discriminate on the basis of race or previous condition of servitude, African-Americans in the South would likely have remained vulnerable to attack by many of their worst abusers: the state militia and state peace officers." Moreover, the antidiscrimination reading "disregards the plight of whites in the South who opposed the Black Codes" and would have been left at the mercy of their opponents "as had abolitionists in Kansas in the 1850s." Finally, Alito noted that when the Thirty-Ninth Congress debated the disbanding of Southern state militias, it decided against disarming their members. Thus, he concluded, "It cannot be doubted that the right to bear arms was regarded as a substantive guarantee, not a prohibition that could be ignored so long as the States legislated in an evenhanded manner."[73]

What Chicago really opposed, wrote Alito, was the *Heller* decision itself; specifically, its recognition of an individual's right to keep and bear arms in the home for self-defense. And it would have the Court "treat the right recognized in *Heller* as a second-class right, subject to an entirely different body of rules than the other Bill of Rights guarantees" that the Court has incorporated over the years.[74]

Chicago argued that the only substantive rights incorporated should be those that *no* civilized legal system would fail to recognize. Because many Western democracies severely restricted gun ownership, the right to keep and bear arms should not be incorporated, it reasoned.[75]

That incorporation test, Justice Alito replied, "is . . . inconsistent with the long-established standard we apply in incorporation cases." To adopt it at this late date would have dramatic implications, especially in the area of criminal procedure, because "many of the rights that our Bill of Rights provides [for criminal defendants] are virtually unique to this country," he pointed out. As for the attempt to distinguish between substantive and procedural rights, Alito further noted that the Court's incorporation of the establishment clause in 1947 put paid to that argument.[76]

Justice Alito also rejected what amounted to a Second Amendment exceptionalism argument that the right to keep and bear arms was different because it has public safety implications. First, Alito noted that the argument assumed a point in question: whether increased private possession of firearms increased or decreased gun deaths. Assuming there is some increase, though, the Second Amendment is not the only provision of the Bill of Rights that implicates public safety. As he noted, many dissenters from the Warren Court's campaign to incorporate most of the criminal procedure protections made equivalent public safety-based arguments. Those critics—as did Chicago—also opposed incorporation of those protections on federalism grounds.[77] But, he replied:

> Time and again . . . those pleas failed. Unless we turn back the clock or adopt a special incorporation test applicable only to the Second Amendment, municipal respondents' argument must be rejected. Under our precedents, if a Bill of Rights guarantee is fundamental from an American perspective, then, unless stare decisis counsels otherwise, that guarantee is fully binding on the States and thus limits (but by no means eliminates) their ability to devise solutions to social problems that suit local needs and values. As noted by the 38 States that have appeared in this case as amici supporting petitioners, "state and local experimentation with reasonable firearms regulations will continue under the Second Amendment."[78]

Justice Alito went on to reject Chicago's arguments that incorporation would lead to increased and expensive litigation (like the exclusionary rule?, he responded); that Chicago's ban should be upheld because other state and local firearms have been upheld (yes, but none were as draconian as Chicago's); and attempts to reargue *Heller*'s central holding that the right guaranteed by the Second Amendment was an individual one, unconnected to military service. Justice Alito's opinion also repeated the safe harbor language from *Heller* to illustrate the point that "despite municipal respondents' doomsday proclamations, incorporation does not imperil every law regulating firearms."[79]

The opinion closed with a restatement of *Heller*'s central holding: "The Second Amendment protects the right to possess a handgun in the home for the purpose of self-defense." He added, "Unless considerations of *stare decisis* counsel otherwise, a provision of the Bill of Rights that protects a right that is fundamental from an American perspective applies equally to the Federal Government and the states."[80]

Alan Gura's efforts to resuscitate the privileges or immunities clause were not entirely in vain. Justice Alito's opinion only garnered four votes. Justice Thomas, however, who concurred in the result, wrote a separate concurring opinion that argued at length that the privileges or immunities clause—not the due process clause—was the proper vehicle for incorporating provisions of the Bill of Rights. The Thomas concurrence criticized the Court's due process jurisprudence, stating that:

I cannot accept a theory of constitutional interpretation that rests on such a tenuous footing. This Court's substantive due process framework fails to account for both the text of the Fourteenth Amendment and the history that led to its adoption, filling the gap with a jurisprudence devoid of a guiding principle. I believe that the original meaning of the Fourteenth Amendment offers a superior alternative and that a return to that meaning would allow the Court to enforce the rights the Fourteenth Amendment is designed to protect with greater clarity and predictability than the substantive due process framework has so far managed.[81]

Thomas's concurrence continued with a detailed historical analysis. It partially included an analysis of the uses of the terms "privileges" and "immunities" in Anglo-American history. The concurrence also offered a detailed discussion of the role that racial violence in the South had in prompting the Reconstruction-era Congresses to enact civil rights legislation and to adopt the Fourteenth Amendment and send it to the states for ratification.[82]

Justice Breyer's dissent, which was joined by Justices Ginsburg and Sotomayor, largely repeated his arguments from *Heller* that the Second Amendment was not primarily concerned with guaranteeing the right of armed individuals to engage in self-defense.[83] In his view,

The police power, the superiority of legislative decision-making, the need for local decision-making, the comparative desirability of democratic decision-making, the lack of a manageable judicial standard, and the life-threatening harm that may flow from striking down regulations all argue against incorporation. Where the incorporation of other rights has been at issue, some of these problems have arisen. But in this instance, all these problems are present, all at the same time, and all are likely to be present in most, perhaps nearly all, of the cases in which the constitutionality of a gun regulation is at issue. At the same time, the important factors that favor incorporation in other instances—e.g., the protection of broader constitutional objectives—are not present here. The upshot is that all factors militate against incorporation—with the possible exception of historical factors.[84]

Turning back to history, Justice Breyer surveyed much of the same evidence canvassed in the plurality opinion but reached very different conclusions. Surveying eighteenth- and nineteenth-century sources, Breyer concluded that state and local governments were regulating the right to keep and bear arms—and that courts were upholding these regulations as long as they were "reasonable."[85] He closed his opinion writing that

> Nothing in 18th-, 19th-, 20th-, or 21st-century history shows a consensus that the right to private armed self-defense, as described in *Heller*, is "deeply rooted in this Nation's history [or] tradition" or is otherwise "fundamental." Indeed, incorporating the right recognized in *Heller* may change the law in many of the 50 States. Read in the majority's favor, the historical evidence is at most ambiguous. And, in the absence of any other support for its conclusion, ambiguous history cannot show that the Fourteenth Amendment incorporates a private right of self-defense against the States.[86]

The opinion also featured an odd debate between Justices Stevens and Scalia. Seeming to jettison the Court's long-standing approach to incorporation, Stevens chose to analyze the question as a "substantive due process" case.[87] He concluded:

> The fact that the right to keep and bear arms appears in the Constitution should not obscure the novelty of the Court's decision to enforce that right against the States. By its terms, the Second Amendment does not apply to the States; read properly, it does not even apply to individuals outside of the militia context. The Second Amendment was adopted to protect the States from federal encroachment. And the Fourteenth Amendment has never been understood by the Court to have "incorporated" the entire Bill of Rights. There was nothing foreordained about today's outcome.[88]

Justice Stevens's analytical framework and its application to the case provoked Justice Scalia to respond that the allegedly "cautious" approach Stevens outlined was a sham. If "Justice Stevens' account of the constraints of his approach did not demonstrate that they do not exist," he wrote, "his application of that approach to the case before us leaves no doubt."[89] None of the "several reasons for concluding that the . . . right to keep and bear arms is not fundamental enough to be applied against the State" persuaded Justice Scalia.[90] Even more, "each is either intrinsically indeterminate, would preclude incorporation of rights we have already held incorporated, or both. His approach . . . does nothing to stop a judge from arriving at any conclusion he sets out to reach."[91]

AFTERMATH

*McDonald* mattered. The case that began with an elderly man's quest to be allowed to have a pistol to defend himself in his home would change constitutional law in important ways. It provided a kind of finishing vindication of those commentators who had long argued that the Fourteenth Amendment had fundamentally altered American federalism. Justice Alito's plurality opinion combined with Justice Thomas's concurrence represented a tacit agreement by a majority of the Supreme Court that the application of the Bill of Rights to the states had been a major purpose of the Fourteenth Amendment from the beginning. Part of that agreement was an implicit recognition that the Court's traditional methodology of selective incorporation could not be sustained even if the Court claimed to be using it. In the wake of *McDonald*, the Court would move to strengthen the principle that the Bill of Rights applied to the states with the same strength that it did to the federal government. In the 2019 case of *Timbs v. Indiana* the Court unanimously agreed that the Eighth Amendment's prohibition on excessive fines applied to the states. Justice Ginsburg, the author of the Court's opinion and a dissenter in *McDonald*, cited *McDonald* for the proposition that the Civil War amendments had fundamentally altered the nation's federal system. She went on to quote *McDonald* that "incorporated Bill of Rights guarantees are [e]nforced against the states under the Fourteenth Amendment according to the same standards that protect those personal rights against federal encroachment." *Timbs* was also noteworthy in that Justice Thomas in a separate concurrence reiterated his view that the privileges or immunities clause was the proper vehicle for incorporation of the Bill of Rights and Justice Gorsuch in his own concurrence indicated that Justice Thomas was probably correct from an originalist point of view.[92]

The doctrine, reiterated in *McDonald*, that incorporated provisions of the Bill of Rights were to be applied to the states with the same rigor that they were applied to the federal government caused the Court to reexamine the question of unanimous juries. In 2020 the Court in *Ramos v. Louisiana* reversed the position that it previously held in *Apodaca v. Oregon* and *Johnson v. Louisiana* permitting convictions for felonies by less than unanimous juries. After *Ramos* the only provisions of the Bill of Rights that remained unincorporated were the Third Amendment's prohibition on the quartering of troops in private homes, the Fifth Amendment's right to a grand jury in criminal cases, and the

Seventh Amendment's right to a jury trial in civil cases. *McDonald* can only be said to have accelerated the processes of fulfilling the vision of Fourteenth Amendment author John Bingham, who intended to make the states respect the Bill of Rights.[93]

But *McDonald* was about more than the Bill of Rights in general. It was specifically about the Second Amendment. What impact would it have on the right to keep and bear arms? One scholar has noted that the Supreme Court's decision in *McDonald* would bring the constitutional provision into the ambit of "ordinary constitutional law." After *McDonald*, the old debates about the meaning of the Second Amendment and whether it applied to the states and their various subdivisions were to be put aside. The Second Amendment would become the subject of routine litigation. Given that a right was recognized, what kind of regulation is permissible?[94]

In the decade following *McDonald*, the answer from the federal judiciary was that state and local governments would retain a great deal of latitude in firearms regulation. Lower federal courts have produced differing results. The Fourth and Ninth Circuits upheld restrictive licensing schemes, making it difficult for most citizens to get licenses to carry handguns outside the home for protection.[95] In contrast, the DC Circuit and Seventh Circuit Courts held that bans on carrying firearms outside the home were unconstitutional, thus giving a constitutional right to carry handguns outside the home in the District of Columbia and Chicago, two cities that before *Heller* had banned the ownership of pistols altogether.[96] Circuit courts that addressed bans on firearms deemed to be assault weapons generally ruled that such bans did not violate the Second Amendment.[97]

In the first decade after *McDonald*, the Supreme Court demonstrated something of a reluctance to return to the Second Amendment fray. Rulings in lower federal courts giving state governments broad latitude to regulate firearms were met with petitions for certiorari. The Supreme Court, with one exception, declined to use these cases as occasions to define the scope of permissible regulation under the Second Amendment. The one exception was a case where the highest court of a state, the Supreme Judicial Court of Massachusetts, issued an opinion that seemed to challenge the very logic of the *Heller* decision. The Massachusetts high court's decision held that electric stun guns were not protected by the Second Amendment in part because they used a technology unknown to the framers. That decision was reversed in a per curium (unsigned) opinion by the Supreme Court. The Court's opinion in that case, *Caetano vs. Massachusetts*, should be seen less as a unanimous endorsement of the Second Amendment by the Court and more as evidence of total agreement by the justices that lower courts are bound to follow the Supreme Court's decisions until those decisions are reversed by the Court itself.[98]

Justices Thomas, Gorsuch, and Kavanaugh all expressed frustration at various points with the Court's failure to grant certiorari and develop further a Second Amendment jurisprudence for the lower courts to follow. The Court almost did that in its 2019 term when it granted certiorari in *New York State Rifle and Pistol Association v. New York City*. The case involved a provision of the New York City handgun licensing scheme. New York City law requires a premises permit to own a handgun in one's home or place of business. Premises permit owners were only permitted to take their handguns to ranges within New York's five boroughs. A permit owner who could lawfully possess a handgun outside of New York City was not permitted to take the weapon to a range outside the city or to use it to protect a residence in another jurisdiction, even if such was permitted by the law of the other jurisdiction. Faced with the likelihood that that provision would be declared unconstitutional, the New York state legislature passed legislation permitting premises permit holders to travel with their firearms outside of New York City. A majority of the Court declared the case moot in light of the changes over the dissents of Justices Thomas, Alito, and Gorsuch.[99]

# 9. *Bruen*, an Unanticipated Epilogue

THE CASE PRESENTED

On April 26, 2021, the Supreme Court signaled that its reluctance to return to the Second Amendment fray had come to an end. On that date, the high court, made more conservative by the death of Associate Justice Ruth Bader Ginsburg and President Donald Trump's appointment of Associate Justices Neil M. Gorsuch, Brett M. Kavanaugh, and Amy Coney Barrett, granted certiorari in the case of *New York State Rifle and Pistol Association v. Corlett*. The case, later known as *New York State Rifle and Pistol Association v. Bruen*, involved the issuance of licenses to carry handguns outside the home for self-defense. It began with two residents of New York State, Robert Nash and Brandon Koch, who had restricted licenses to carry handguns for the limited purposes of hunting and target shooting. Both men wanted to be able to get general licenses to carry their firearms for self-defense. The case would bring about a far-reaching Supreme Court decision affirming that the Second Amendment protected a right to carry firearms outside the home for protection. *Bruen* would also prescribe a new methodology for courts to use when considering Second Amendment claims. This new methodology, according to the majority opinion authored by Justice Thomas, would emphasize the history and tradition of firearms regulation and not the balancing of claimed rights and asserted governmental interests that had been the Court's prevailing methodology in constitutional litigation. With this methodology, the Court through *Bruen* would instruct lower courts to see if a method of regulation was consistent with the type of regulation that existed at the time of the adoption of the Second Amendment or perhaps the Second and Fourteenth Amendments.

For over a decade after the decisions in *Heller* and *McDonald* the question remained, would the Court recognize a right to armed self-defense outside the home? The case that began in New York State in 2018 as *New York State Rifle and Pistol Association v. Beach* became the vehicle that would ultimately answer the question. The subject of the challenge was New York's procedure for granting permits to carry concealed weapons. New York's law, which was over a century old when the suit was filed, vested broad discretion in municipal and county law enforcement agencies and judges to grant or deny licenses to carry handguns. Theoretically a state resident, twenty-one years old or older with no felony convictions, with "good moral character" and a "legally recognized reason" for wanting to carry a firearm, was eligible for a license. But in practice the ability to get a permit to carry was a bit more complicated— significantly more complicated, in fact. In some jurisdictions—New York City was the prime example—the stated policy of licensing authorities was that licenses would not be granted to persons who wished to carry a weapon for self-defense unless they could point to very specific threats made against them. In practice in New York City and some other jurisdictions in New York, almost all the private citizens who were able to get licenses to carry handguns for self-defense were security guards and individuals who regularly carried large sums of cash in the course of their employment. We say "almost all" because New York City authorities, despite the strict licensing regime, had long been notorious for providing licenses to carry to residents who were rich and famous, including such modern-day New York celebrities as talk-show host Sean Hannity, actor Robert De Niro, radio personalities Alexis Stewart and Howard Stern, and, before he became president, New York celebrity Donald J. Trump.[1]

Following the incorporation of the Second Amendment in *McDonald*, several plaintiffs unsuccessfully challenged various aspects of New York's concealed-carry licensing regime.[2] Because those earlier cases constituted binding precedent in the Second Circuit, the only hope of the third group of plaintiffs to challenge the licensing laws was that the US Supreme Court would relent and agree to hear the case. And on April 26, 2021, that is precisely what the Court did. In so doing, the Court limited the question presented to the following: "Whether the State's denial of petitioners' applications for concealed-carry licenses for self-defense violated the Second Amendment."[3]

The petitioner's brief made a straightforward argument. First, as a textual matter, the Second Amendment's reference to the right to "bear" arms as well as "keep" them meant that an individual has a right to carry arms outside the home. Second, they argued that history and tradition favored the right to carry arms outside the home. The English restriction that one not go publicly armed "to terrify the King's subjects" crossed the Atlantic and settled itself into laws in the early republic, they argued. The petitioners argued that the nineteenth-century state cases upholding bans on concealed carry "relied on the erroneous premise that the Second Amendment and analogous provisions in state constitutions did not protect the individual right to keep and bear arms for self-defense." They continued, "These decisions have, of course, been 'sapped of authority by *Heller*.'"[4] Finally, they argued that *Heller* and *Caetano* both implicitly recognized the right to carry arms outside the home. In *Heller*, "the Court went out of its way to note that 'nothing in our opinion should be taken to cast doubt on . . . laws forbidding the carrying of firearms in sensitive places such as schools and government buildings. . . . That caveat would have been nonsensical if the Second Amendment does not protect the right to carry arms outside the home at all." The vacatur of the Massachusetts Supreme Judicial Court's decision in *Caetano* and instructions to follow *Heller* "would have sent the Supreme Judicial Court on a fool's errand if the Second Amendment does not protect the right to possess arms outside the home in the first place."[5]

Having argued that the right to keep and bear arm extends beyond the home, the petitioners then argued that New York's "proper cause" requirement could not survive constitutional scrutiny. Not only did it exclude most New York citizens from exercising a fundamental right, but also "the threshold 'proper cause' determination is left to the broad discretion of a licensing officer."[6] The petitioners concluded with an argument that—assuming intermediate scrutiny was the proper standard—the Second Circuit did not properly apply it in its prior cases.

> New York has taken the extreme step of banning typical, law-abiding citizens from carrying any type of handgun anywhere unless they can distinguish themselves from their fellow law-abiding citizens, even though they have an equally valid constitutional right to keep and bear arms. That is not a serious effort to avoid "burden[ing] substantially more [protected conduct] than is necessary to further the government's legitimate interests."[7]

What the Second Circuit did, they argued, was "nothing more than the kind of 'interest-balancing' that *Heller* rejected."[8]

In most respects, New York's brief was a mirror image of the petitioners.' The state first attempted to rebut the notion that the right to carry outside the home was at least implied by *Heller*. And it cited an 1897 case in which the Court (in dicta) stated that the Second Amendment did not prohibit bans on concealed carry. The brief also disputed the petitioners' characterization of *Heller* as prefiguring a right to carry outside the home. Both English common law as well as American law, the state argued, barred public carrying of weapons except in unpopulated areas. As the state summarized, "For over seven centuries, Anglo-American jurisdictions used public-carry restrictions to maintain safety in places where people gather to worship and conduct business." Moreover, the respondents challenged the petitioners' characterization of licensing officers' discretion as "boundless" and "unreviewable." They observed that "New York courts will set aside a licensing decision that is 'arbitrary and capricious' or otherwise contrary to law." The state noted that applicants could amend their applications and the fact that New York State encompasses very rural as well as densely populated areas, so it was only natural that "what is required to show a non-speculative need for self-defense may differ depending on local conditions."[9]

New York then argued that its concealed-carry regime was consistent with history and tradition going back to colonial times. Indeed, the state argued that its current regime provides a much broader right than earlier laws "that existed from fourteenth-century England through the founding era" that "broadly prohibited carrying firearms where people typically congregated, such as at fairs and markets." It also alleged that it would be inconsistent with the "sensitive places" exception recognized in *Heller* for the Court to recognize a right to carry publicly anywhere the need for self-defense may arise.[10]

Finally, the state argued that intermediate scrutiny is the appropriate standard of review for Second Amendment claims and that New York's licensing regime easily passes muster. "As implemented, New York's concealed-carry licensing system is akin to the types of time, place, and manner regulations of expression that [the] Court has long subjected to intermediate scrutiny." The restrictions, it noted, like time, place, and manner regulations, were not aimed at the protected activity itself, but sought to address secondary effects that the activity might have on the surrounding community: "New York's 'proper cause' requirement . . . does not seek to inhibit handgun carrying for lawful self-defense—the '*central component*' of any public-carry right . . . but rather aims to limit the violence attending handgun *misuse.*"[11]

The state regarded it as almost self-evident that the promotion of public safety and the reduction of gun violence was an "important governmental interest." It further argued that there was indeed a substantial relationship between the "proper cause" requirement and the furtherance of those goals. "A wealth of empirical evidence supports New York's judgment that limiting the public carrying of handguns to those who have proper cause reduces the risk of gun violence to the public," the brief stated. It went on to cite a host of studies to support its position and pointed out that the requirement "does not burden 'substantially more' protected activity 'than is necessary to further the government's legitimate interest.'" It concluded with the observation that respect for federalism counseled the Court to show deference to New York's policy choices regarding the public carrying of firearms.[12]

As it had in *Heller*, the United States requested permission to participate in oral argument, and the Biden administration filed its own brief. While its argument largely tracked that of New York's, the beginning of the United States's brief stressed the broad legislative authority to regulate firearms generally; it then went on to argue that history and tradition authorized the regulation of concealed firearms and that New York's proper purpose requirement did not violate the Second Amendment.[13] All the attendant risks to public safety occasioned by unrestricted concealed carry, the United States argued, are mitigated by the proper-cause requirement.

> It ensures that the only people who carry handguns in public are those who need to do so. And because licensing officers may restrict the right to carry to the purpose that justified issuance of the license, the proper-cause requirement ensures that even those who carry guns do so only when they must and where they must. The proper-cause requirement thereby reduces the prevalence of unnecessary guns in public places, diminishing all the dangers discussed above— the risk that guns will be used to commit a crime, be fired in anger, be fired when they should not have been, or otherwise endanger police officers and bystanders.
>
> At a minimum, courts should defer to New York's judgment that the proper-cause requirement effectively serves those interests.[14]

In their reply, the petitioners spent much of their brief arguing that the early laws regulating public carrying of weapons did, in fact, require an intent to terrorize or be armed "offensively" as an element of the offence and were not—as the state argued—broad injunctions about appearing armed in public. It further argued that the state's version of intermediate scrutiny was improper, shifting as it did the burden from the state to individuals. Where a fundamental right was involved, the kind of deference the state was arguing for likewise undermined the heightened nature of the test. The empirical evidence the state proffered in support of its claim that the proper-purpose requirement substantially furthered its aim was similar to that rejected in *Heller*. There "the Court made clear that the District could not ban [handguns] even if doing so would have public safety benefits because the relevant tradeoffs were settled by the Second Amendment."[15]

As was true in the previous cases, numerous amici briefs—over eighty total—were also filed by many of same groups who participated in *Heller* and *McDonald*. Consistent with earlier filings, most of the briefs restated or amplified the arguments for or against New York's law that were made by the parties themselves. One amicus brief sought to remind the Court that restrictive licensing schemes often had dire consequences for residents of dangerous inner-city communities. The brief filed by a group of Black public defenders in New York City informed the Court that restrictive licensing often forced inner-city residents to make a Hobson's choice: go defenseless on streets dominated by violent criminals, or get pistols for self-protection and risk punitive sanctions from the very criminal justice system that failed to protect them:

> The consequences for our clients are brutal. New York Police have stopped, questioned and frisked our clients in the streets. They have invaded our clients' homes with guns drawn, terrifying them, their families, and their children. They have forcibly removed our clients from their homes and communities and abandoned them in dirty and violent jails and prisons for days, weeks, months and years. They have deprived our clients of their jobs, children, livelihoods and ability to live in this country. And they have branded our clients as "criminals" and "violent felons" for life. They have done this only because our clients exercised a constitutional right.[16]

Oral argument was scheduled for November 3, 2021, and the scheduling was unusual for two reasons. First, the Court allotted two hours for arguments, instead of the usual single hour. Second, changes that the Court made to its oral argument format when it was hearing cases remotely during the COVID-19 pandemic that began to plague the nation in 2020 created a different dynamic: instead of the usual verbal scrum, the lawyers were allowed to speak uninterrupted for a few minutes at the outset and then the justices asked questions in order of seniority, meaning that Justice Clarence Thomas would speak first after Paul Clement's opening remarks.

Clement began with the claim that New York had conceded that "carrying a handgun outside of the home for purposes of self-defense is a constitutionally protected activity" and in so doing, had essentially doomed its case because its licensing regime "makes it a crime for a typical law-abiding New

Yorker to exercise that constitutional right." That right, he continued, should not turn on whether a government official thinks that your desire to defend yourself is sufficiently compelling.[17]

Justice Thomas then asked for an analogous restriction that would pass muster, and Clement mentioned older laws restricting arms in "sensitive areas." He then noted that extensive bans on public carrying—open or concealed—surfaced in the post-Reconstruction era and that the cases in which those bans were invalidated were praised in *Heller*. When asked which historical analogue should prevail if there were a conflict between a Founding-era restriction and one around the time of Reconstruction, Clement said the latter, but added, "I don't know that the original founding history is going to be radically different than that at Reconstruction."[18]

"How could it stop there?" asked Justice Kagan. "In *Heller*, we made very clear that laws that restricted felons from carrying or possessing arms and laws that forbade mentally ill people from doing the same . . . basically put the stamp of approval on those laws. And those laws really came about in the 1920, didn't they?" Clement replied that disarmament of Founding-era felons was unnecessary because then all felonies were capital crimes and that skepticism of post-1871 cases upholding restrictions is warranted because it was around that time that the collective rights view of the Second Amendment was gaining purchase in some state courts.[19]

Justice Breyer asked how the Court was supposed to resolve the conflicts among historians as to what was permitted or prohibited and also how could the Court find out what New York *actually* does in issuing licenses, noting that there are conflicting claims. "There's been no trial," he said. "How are we supposed to know what we're talking about in terms of what New York does?" Clement argued that what New York did generally was irrelevant because the issue here was whether his clients had been denied their fundamental rights by being required to demonstrate an atypical need to carry for self-defense. Justice Kagan pointed out, however, that Clement's brief emphasized the fact that the New York licensing regime in general "deprives most people of the right to carry arms in self-defense."[20]

Justice Breyer then asked Clement if his position, in essence, was that as long as the statutory requirements of good moral character and the like were met, his client could "carry a concealed gun around the streets or the town or outside just for fun?" Clement conceded that one wouldn't necessarily be entitled to carry anywhere the licensee wished, but he argued that unlike someone seeking a concealed carry permit to hunt or target shoot, if you cite self-defense as a reason, you have to further demonstrate a particularized threat.[21]

Clement and Justice Sotomayor then engaged in a back-and-forth discussion about the degree of deference to which states are entitled to regulate concealed weapons. Justice Sotomayor argued that her reading of the history suggested that the right to publicly carry has been regulated extensively as compared with regulations regarding guns in the home. Clement replied that while it was true that there have been periods where concealed carry was banned, in those states open carry was permitted. *Heller*, he noted, concluded that those cases upholding the bans stood for the proposition that you could permit open carry and ban concealed carry or vice-versa, but you couldn't ban both. The only way you can carry a handgun in New York is to have an unrestricted license, which is the relief the petitioners seek, he continued, objecting to Sotomayor's claim that Clement "was asking [the Court] to make the choice [open vs. concealed carry] for the legislature." Sotomayor then asked why a proper-purpose requirement was any different than older laws that conferred discretion on officials to decide who was eligible to have guns and who wasn't. Clement replied that he couldn't think of an analogue that gave officials discretion to review the degree to which a licensee actually *needed* to carry for self-defense. Even surety laws—those laws requiring someone who was armed to post bond in case they injured anyone with their weapons—he pointed out, preserved the individual's right to have arms.[22]

Chief Justice Roberts then began pressing Clement to define "sensitive areas" in which he conceded states can regulate guns. What about places that serve alcohol? What about football stadiums? The question seemed to catch Clement off guard, but he recovered and suggested two general principles. First, he said, "Restriction of access to the place is something that I think would be consistent with the way government buildings and schools have worked" in that not just everyone has access. Second, he distinguished sensitive place restrictions from carry restrictions because "a true sensitive place restriction is not going to limit your ability to carry concealed, but it's going to . . . say, this is a place where no weapons are allowed." He then added that you could "start with the place and try to understand is this a place where, given the nature of the place, its function, its restrictions on access, that weapons are out of place? And, if so, that's probably a sensitive place."[23]

Justice Kagan stayed with the chief justice's line of questioning and pressed Clement on "how those [principles] cash out in the real world," asking

Clement about New York City subways and universities or stadiums. Clement seemed to struggle, to the point of evading Kagan's question about ballparks by noting that most are privately owned and so any restrictions would not involve governmental action implicating the Constitution at all. But Justice Kagan was not so easily put off: "Suppose," she continued, "the state says no protest or event that has more than 10,000." Clement responded by saying he didn't think that would be a sensitive place, to which Justice Barrett interjected, "But why not?" She seemed to suggest that there was no reason to think of sensitive places as a closed class. "Can't we just say Times Square on New Year's Eve is a sensitive place? Because . . . people are on top of each other [and] we've had experience with violence, so we're making a judgment, it's a sensitive place." Clement recharacterized Barrett's example as a time, place, and manner restriction, and contrasted that regulation with one involving sensitive spaces.[24]

At that point, Justice Alito stepped in with a suggestion: start with the personal right to keep and bear arms for self-defense as the baseline, then "analyze the sensitive place question by asking whether this is a place where the state has taken alternative means to safeguard those who frequent that place." While conceding that it wouldn't cover every situation, Alito suggested it would be a start. Clement, however, was wary; cities, he worried, could restrict carrying by saying it had staffed parts of a city with extra police officers.[25]

Justice Breyer then returned to his theme: that allowing people to carry concealed weapons in densely populated urban areas would inevitably result in deaths. "I think," he said, "that people of good moral character who start drinking a lot and who might be there for a football game or—some kind of soccer game can get pretty angry at each other, and if they each have a concealed weapon, who knows?" Clement noted that the forty-three states that are more or less "must issue" states, including states with very large cities, "have not had demonstrably worse problems with this than the five or six states that have the regime that New York has."[26]

After Justice Thomas established that for all the discussion of carrying in New York City, the petitioners lived in rural, upstate New York, Justice Sotomayor queried just how much of a restriction the petitioners were laboring under and how much their ability to engage in self-defense was hampered. Clement responded that the restrictions prohibited the petitioners from concealed carry in any location open to or frequented by the public. In any event, Clement continued, "I think what it means to give somebody a constitutional right is that they don't have to satisfy a government official that they have a really good need to exercise it or they face atypical risks."[27]

After a colloquy with Justice Kagan over the utility of history in assessing the validity of New York's licensing regime, Clement got a question from Justice Gorsuch regarding the lower-court application of *Heller* and *McDonald*. Clement responded that he thought "text, history, and tradition" were an appropriate way to handle Second Amendment claims and that the Court should take the opportunity to make that clear, but "if this Court prefers to the level of scrutiny route" it should either adopt strict scrutiny or, if it sticks with intermediate scrutiny, "probably the single-most important thing to remind the lower courts is that intermediate scrutiny requires narrow tailoring." He added that New York's law would fail narrow tailoring because of its requirement that one who has shown no propensity to misuse firearms was being denied the ability to defend himself without government permission.[28]

But Justice Kavanaugh expressed concern that insofar as strict and intermediate scrutiny tests are balancing tests, adopting them in the Second Amendment context would end up "making it a policy judgment basically for the courts." He also clarified that the only challenge was to the permitting regime here and that it wasn't necessary for the Court to resolve all the questions surrounding sensitive places where one is prohibited from carrying. Clement suggested that might be a reason for the Court to adopt strict scrutiny; he conceded that the lower courts have "made a muddle of it and the . . . experience of the last 13 years is probably a very good reason to prefer a text, history, and tradition approach to this area of the law."[29]

Barbara Underwood, the solicitor general of New York and former attorney general of the state, then made her argument. A graduate of Radcliffe College and Georgetown University Law Center, Underwood clerked for Judge David Bazelon on the DC Circuit Court and for Justice Thurgood Marshall. After teaching at Yale, Brooklyn, and NYU law schools, she entered government service both as a state prosecutor and in the US solicitor general's office.

Underwood began her statement by emphasizing that throughout Anglo-American legal history, the carrying of firearms had been regulated in various ways. "In total, from the founding era through the 20th Century, at least 20 states have at one time or another either prohibited all carrying of handgun in populous areas or limited it to those with good cause." She continued, "New York's law fits well within that tradition of regulating public carry."[30] Should there be questions about how the law operates in practice, the appropriate remedy, she argued, was to remand for fact-finding at trial.

Justice Thomas noted that the state focused quite a bit on population density but observed that the petitioners lived in an area that was less populous. Doesn't that imply that rules for unrestricted permits should be more permissive in those areas? Underwood agreed and argued that was what happened in this case—the licensing officer took account of the fact this was upstate New York, not Manhattan. But, asked Chief Justice Roberts, isn't it in populated urban areas where you might be *more* likely to need a gun for self-defense? How does that square with the self-defense right recognized in *Heller*? Underwood replied that bans on carrying weapons to markets or fairs demonstrates that, historically, population density was considered and that having lots of people (and police) around has its own deterrent effect on crime. Chief Justice Roberts expressed skepticism that one would have much need to carry in remote or isolated areas as compared to cities.[31]

After emphasizing that New York's law requires individuals to experience a particularized threat, one not shared with the public at large, in order to satisfy the law's requirement, Justice Alito asked how that requirement squares with "the core right to self-defense, which is protected by the Second Amendment?" Underwood disputed the premise, arguing that the Amendment "doesn't allow for all . . . to be armed for all possible confrontations in all places." Justices Alito and Kavanaugh pressed her on the fact that law-abiding people who worked at night or alone could not get an unrestricted license but substantial numbers of people in New York and elsewhere were carrying guns illegally. Kavanaugh wanted to know "why isn't it good enough to say I live in a violent area and I want to be able to defend myself?" It might be, Underwood agreed, but you'd have to convince the licensing officer. "Well, that's the real concern," he replied, "with any constitutional right? If it's the discretion of an individual officer, that seems inconsistent with an objective constitutional right." Pressed by Justice Kavanaugh, Underwood defended the New York licensing requirement, arguing, "I believe there is evidence about the success that New York has had in keeping . . . gun violence down that is attributable to the reduced number of guns that are being carried and particularly in these densely populated places."[32]

Justice Kagan asked Underwood to make the argument why there should be the flexibility built into New York's regime when ordinarily we don't adjust the scope of other constitutional rights according to geography. Underwood emphasized that New York's system, operating as it does at a local level, allows officials to take account of local conditions. "If the history warrants taking local conditions and local population density and so forth into account, it's hard to think of another way to . . . effectively do that."[33]

An exchange with Justice Breyer suggested that he favored remand for a trial so a factual record could be developed. He referenced an amicus brief that argued that states with more liberal licensing regimes did, in fact, experience higher levels of violence. He also asked for a rough estimate of the number and types of licenses issued annually. Justice Alito followed up by asking what safeguards existed to ensure officials weren't abusing their discretion, especially regarding licensing applications for self-defense. Underwood replied that the licensing officials had to provide written reasons for a denial.[34]

There followed a somewhat tense exchange between Justice Alito and Underwood. In its brief, the state quoted an 1814 North Carolina law that was summarized by the state as prescribing the arrest of all who "shall ride or go armed." The statute actually read "shall ride or go armed *offensively*," and the state had omitted that last word in its brief. "Do you think that's an irrelevant word?" Alito asked. Underwood replied that "it would have been better to put it in and make an explanation, but I do think it's an irrelevant word because we have substantial authority for the proposition that guns were deemed to be offensive weapons." Justice Alito replied that "if any possession of weapons outside the home was illegal, then there would be no need to put in the term 'offensively.'"[35]

Justice Kagan then asked Underwood to explain why a "sensitive place" regime would not be a good substitute for New York's licensing law. First, she said, it probably wouldn't satisfy the petitioners; and second, it would be very difficult to comprehensively define "sensitive places" outside some fairly obvious characteristics. Questioning ended with Justice Barrett asking Underwood whether *Heller*, which covered some of the same historical ground at issue in the current case, tied the Court's hands or whether the Court could adopt the state's reading of that same historical material. Underwood replied that the Court was free to do so "because I think the *Heller* decision made very clear that it was not deciding anything other than the right to keep arms in the home."[36]

Next to address the Court for the United States was Principal Deputy Attorney General Brian Fletcher. Fletcher, a graduate of Yale College and Harvard Law School, had clerked for then DC Circuit Court judge Merrick Garland

and later for Justice Ruth Bader Ginsburg. He served as an associate White House counsel in the Obama administration and did a stint in private practice before becoming an assistant solicitor general. In 2020 he joined Stanford Law School's faculty before returning to the solicitor general's office.

Fletcher sought to "focus on laws that either prohibited or required a showing of good cause to carry a concealable weapon, like a pistol." In his view, New York's proper cause requirement was "firmly grounded in our nation's history and tradition of gun regulation." He rattled off several states and the dates in which they enacted gun laws, noting that "those laws remain in force in seven states today, and more than 80 million Americans live under their protection." Fletcher argued that the petitioners' argument was question-begging because it assumed the right to concealed carry that was in question. History and tradition, Fletcher argued, was all in the state's favor. Justice Kavanaugh asked whether those were states that permitted open carry. No, he replied, "If I were here defending a regime that just prohibited concealed carry and allowed open carry, I would have many . . . more states." Nevertheless, he added, this is not like the restrictive laws in *Heller* and *McDonald*, which he characterized as outliers. Again and again, Fletcher cited examples from the nineteenth and twentieth centuries to make the case that laws like New York's were consistent with the history and traditions regarding firearms regulations.[37]

Justice Alito asked about the provenance of New York's law and the fact that it was allegedly enacted to disarm minority groups and recent immigrants from Southern Europe. Fletcher replied that "similar laws have been enacted and maintained not just in New York and not just at that moment in time but in a number of different states . . . throughout large swaths of our nation's history [and] . . . is good reason to believe that this is not just prejudice, that this is a legitimate regulation." Alito then suggested that the laws Fletcher cited were inconsistent with the original understanding of the Second Amendment. Fletcher parried by invoking *Heller*'s concession that the right was subject to some regulation and that fact suggested that the laws he cited that restricting carrying or required a showing of good cause are quite consistent with the amendment. But as you get later into the nineteenth and early twentieth centuries, Alito prodded, what light can laws passed then shed on the scope of the right? Fletcher had an answer: "I think it's [fair] to extend the analysis into the 20th Century [because] [*Heller*] validated as presumptively lawful felon-in-possession requirements, bans on the possession of firearms by the mentally ill that date to much later than the 19th Century."[38]

Fletcher was asked by Justice Sotomayor to describe the outer boundaries of permissible regulation and the appropriate standard of review, but Fletcher refused to be drawn in. Specifying a standard of review was unnecessary because *Heller* itself instructs courts to look to history and tradition. He did concede that the Second Amendment *does* extend beyond the home and that total bans on the carrying of any type of firearm for any purpose would likely have no "historical precedent." As for what regulations were permitted, Fletcher offered a "couple of guideposts." There was, he continued, "a tradition of laws . . . that prohibit the carrying of concealable weapons without any exception for self-defense [or] any good cause exception like the one that you have in the New York law." If a total ban on concealed carry is consistent with the Second Amendment, then so would a law, like New York's, that contains those exceptions and offers the opportunity for someone to get a concealed-carry permit if they satisfy all of the requirements, including one requiring a particularized need to carry for self-defense.[39]

Justice Gorsuch sought Fletcher's views on how the Court should instruct lower courts to approach Second Amendment cases. Again, Fletcher cited the need to decide those cases with appeals to "text, history, and tradition," but he added that if history gives out and can furnish no analogies, then courts should ask whether the regulation is a reasonable one, which he argued is embodied in intermediate scrutiny.[40]

The final colloquy was with Justice Kavanaugh, who asked Fletcher how—assuming he was correct on the history, and these were seen as consistent with the Second Amendment—to square that tradition with another tradition in US constitutional law that is skeptical of requiring official permission before individuals exercise their constitutional rights. Fletcher replied that he understood the problem of discretion and that perhaps the Court would require "some more predictable or stringent or prescriptive guidelines."[41]

In his very crisp rebuttal, Paul Clement made four points. First, he argued, to the extent that the rationale for maintaining "may issue" was that any other regime would result in more guns in circulation, that was not a permissible state interest. That, in turn, underscored "how completely non-tailored this law is. It might be well tailored to keeping the number of handguns down, but it's not well tailored to identifying people who pose a particular risk or anything else because it deprives a typical New Yorker of their right to carry for self-defense." As for population density, he emphasized that many large cities are located in "shall issue" states and have experienced no appreciable increase in gun crime; he referred the justices to an amicus brief that made that point statistically. He also stressed that the permits are different than permitting for, say, a parade, because you have to demonstrate an especially good reason to want to exercise your right in order to get that permit. Clement said that much of the cases and statutes Fletcher cited was either criticized in *Heller* or was the product of the rise of the collective rights theory of the Second Amendment, which was well-known by the early twentieth century.[42]

He argued that there's no need to remand; the issues are quite clear. First, the fact that you have to show you have a special need for self-defense is reason enough to invalidate it. Rights exercised at governmental sufferance aren't rights at all, he said, they are privileges. Second, the discretion results in making criminals of otherwise law-abiding citizens who want only to protect themselves. Moreover—referring to the state's argument that a "must carry" regime would impact policing because they have to assume everyone is armed—he concluded, "One of the ways essentially making everybody in New York City a presumptive person who is unlawfully carrying is that leads to stopping and frisking everybody."[43]

Just before noon, Chief Justice Roberts thanked counsel and submitted the case.

## THE OPINION

The Court issued its opinion a little over six months later, on June 23, 2022. Justice Thomas wrote the opinion for himself, Chief Justice Roberts, and Justices Alito, Barrett, Gorsuch, and Kavanaugh. It was notable that early in the opinion, Justice Thomas rejected the tiered scrutiny framework and intermediate scrutiny standards around which—with some variation—all the lower courts had coalesced. The correct standard, he wrote, was as follows: "When the Second Amendment's plain text covers an individual's conduct, the Constitution presumptively protects that conduct. The government must then justify its regulation by demonstrating that it is consistent with the Nation's historical tradition of firearm regulation."[44] Only if the government carries its burden will the individual conduct go unprotected by the Second Amendment. Thomas acknowledged that history could only get one so far, but that fidelity to the Second Amendment demanded that courts incorporate technological advances or regulations unknown in the eighteenth century into the case law. In such cases, analogical reasoning would be appropriate. While he declined to provide "an exhaustive survey of the features that render regulations relevantly similar under the Second Amendment," he wrote that *Heller* and *McDonald* pointed to two metrics: "how and why the regulations burden a law-abiding citizen's right to armed self-defense."[45] He concluded,

> To be clear, analogical reasoning under the Second Amendment is neither a regulatory straitjacket nor a regulatory blank check. On the one hand, courts should not "uphold every modern law that remotely resembles a historical analogue," because doing so "risk[s] endorsing outliers that our ancestors would never have accepted." On the other hand, analogical reasoning requires only that the government identify a well-established and representative historical analogue, not a historical twin. So even if a modern-day regulation is not a dead ringer for historical precursors, it still may be analogous enough to pass constitutional muster.[46]

Thomas then applied his history-and-tradition approach to New York's law. There is little question, he argued, that the Second Amendment applies in public. The amendment's use of the word "bear," he wrote, "naturally encompasses public carry." *Heller*, moreover, spoke of the right to "'carry weapons in case of confrontation.'" And while self-defense in the home was at the center of the right, "to confine the right to 'bear' arms to the home would nullify half of the Second Amendment's operative protections." The text, therefore, "presumptively" guaranteed the petitioners' right to bear arms in public for self-defense.[47]

Justice Thomas next embarked upon a lengthy examination of the historical materials New York offered in support of its contention that its proper-cause requirement was "consistent with this Nation's historical tradition of firearm regulation." He looked at regulations from "(1) medieval to early modern England; (2) the American Colonies and the early Republic; (3) antebellum America; (4) Reconstruction; and (5) the late-19th and early-20th centuries."

The main point of contention between the petitioners and New York was how to characterize the laws regulating the carrying of weapons. The petitioners claimed, and the Court agreed, that the tradition began in England and was transplanted to the colonies—later states—which barred the carrying of weapons in public in order to menace others. As Justice Thomas concluded:

The historical evidence from antebellum America does demonstrate that *the manner* of public carry was subject to reasonable regulation. Under the common law, individuals could not carry deadly weapons in a manner likely to terrorize others. Similarly, although surety statutes[48] did not directly restrict public carry, they did provide financial incentives for responsible arms carrying. Finally, States could lawfully eliminate one kind of public carry—concealed carry—so long as they left open the option to carry openly.[49]

As for the evidence from Reconstruction and the latter part of the nineteenth century, Justice Thomas conceded that, yes, Texas and West Virginia had something like New York's special-purpose requirement but dismissed them as outliers. He likewise dismissed the restrictions placed on public carry in the western territories. They were temporary and covered a very small percentage of the population. In addition, they were never subject to judicial scrutiny, so there is no guarantee that, if challenged, they would have been upheld.[50] He summarized the results of the survey:

> Apart from a few late-19th-century outlier jurisdictions, American governments simply have not broadly prohibited the public carry of commonly used firearms for personal defense. Nor, subject to a few late-in-time outliers, have American governments required law-abiding, responsible citizens to "demonstrate a special need for self-protection distinguishable from that of the general community" in order to carry arms in public.[51]

New York, he concluded, had not carried its burden of proving that special-need requirements to carry publicly is part of the historical tradition of firearms regulation in the United States. He added for good measure the observation that "The constitutional right to bear arms in public for self-defense is not a second-class right, subject to an entirely different body of rules than the other Bill of Rights guarantees. We know of no other constitutional right that an individual may exercise only after demonstrating to government officers some special need."[52]

Justice Kavanaugh concurred to emphasize that (1) states were still free to impose licensing requirements for concealed carry licenses, and (2) nothing in *Bruen* ties a state's hands in passing "a 'variety' of gun regulations." Justice Barrett's concurrence flagged "two methodological points that the Court does not resolve." First, the Court didn't specify how much weight is to be accorded post-ratification practice in ascertaining original meaning. Scholars have proposed various—sometimes conflicting—approaches. Second, she noted that the Court didn't resolve the question whether 1791 or 1868 is the proper historical baseline for establishing the scope of an individual right.[53]

Justice Breyer wrote the dissent for himself and Justices Sotomayor and Kagan. His opinion opened with an impassioned description of the scope of gun violence in the United States, from rates of deaths and injuries to mass shootings; the fact that gun violence is on the rise; and the danger posed to police officers and the urban-rural divide regarding guns. In response to Justice Alito, whose concurring opinion took specific issue with this part of the dissent, Breyer defended that section of the opinion, writing that the statistics demonstrate that problems associated with guns in the United States are "complex [and] should be solved by legislatures rather than courts."[54]

Returning to a theme he pursued at oral argument, Justice Breyer criticized the majority for not remanding to the lower courts. "The parties," he complained, "have not had an opportunity to conduct discovery, and no evidentiary hearings have been held to develop the record." For example, he continued, the majority characterized the New York law as granting too much discretion and offering "'little recourse if their local licensing officer denies a permit,'" but "without an evidentiary record, there is no reason to assume that New York courts applying [the arbitrary and capricious] standard fail to provide license applicants with meaningful review." Nor was there information on how the "proper cause" standard was actually applied.[55]

A related critique of the majority was its—in Justice Breyer's opinion—flattening of the differences among the forty-three states that the Court said had adopted "must issue" laws and how they operate in practice. "Because the Court strikes down New York's law without affording the State an opportunity to develop an evidentiary record, we do not know how much discretion licensing officers in New York have in practice or how that discretion is exercised, let alone how the licensing regimes in the other six 'may issue' jurisdictions operate."[56]

Second, Justice Breyer objected to the "history-and-tradition" methodology adopted by the Court and predicted that it would cause innumerable problems, especially in the lower courts. He argued that the rejection of some form of interest balancing marked a break with *Heller* itself. Surprisingly, Breyer wrote as if he were resigned to the Court adopting strict scrutiny in Second Amendment cases.[57] He called the Court's "near-exclusive reliance on history" "deeply impractical." Aside from the obvious objection that judges are trained as lawyers and not as historians, Breyer raised other "troubling" questions:

> Do lower courts have the research resources necessary to conduct exhaustive historical analyses in every Second Amendment case? What historical regulations and decisions qualify as representative analogues to modern laws? How will judges determine which historians have the better view of close historical questions? Will the meaning of the Second Amendment change if or when new historical evidence becomes available? And, most importantly, will the Court's approach permit judges to reach the outcomes they prefer and then cloak those outcomes in the language of history?

Not only does the Court not answer those questions, he wrote, it seemed to downplay the fact that history will likely take you only so far in assessing contemporary regulations. Breyer was deeply skeptical that resort to "analogical reasoning" will be much help because the Court is similarly opaque as to how that is supposed to work. "Even seemingly straightforward historical restrictions on firearm use may prove surprisingly difficult to apply to modern circumstances."[58] Breyer predicted that "as technological progress pushes our society ever further beyond the bounds of the Framers' imaginations, attempts at 'analogical reasoning' will become increasingly tortured." Sole reliance on history, he argued, "is unjustifiable and unworkable."[59]

Justice Breyer then conducted a similarly lengthy review of the historical materials analyzed by the majority but drew the opposite conclusion. He regarded the "historical examples of regulation similar to New York's licensing regime [as] legion." The laws, he argued, while not identical, "*resembled* New York's law, similarly restricting the right to publicly carry weapons and serving roughly similar purposes." Put another way, he concluded that they were at least analogous to New York's law. He asked, "If the examples discussed above, taken together, do not show a tradition and history of regulation that supports the validity of New York's law, what could?" Almost plaintively, he lamented, "Sadly, I do not know the answer to that question. What is worse, the Court appears to have no answer either."[60]

Justice Breyer's dissent reiterated many of the consequentialist arguments that he had made earlier in his dissent in *Heller*. His objections could not change the fact that the Thomas opinion had produced a far more muscular version of the Second Amendment and the protections that it provided than had been the case with *Heller* and *McDonald*. Instead of the tentative 5 to 4 majorities that had prevailed in the earlier cases, Thomas's opinion in *Bruen* enjoyed a more robust 6–3 majority. In place of the intramural debate found in *McDonald* over whether the Second Amendment applied to the states through the due process clause or the privileges or immunities clause of the Fourteenth Amendment, Thomas's opinion simply indicated that the Fourteenth Amendment applied the Second Amendment to the states, a view joined by five other justices without further elaboration. And *Bruen* prescribed a methodology that should be quite favorable to complainants arguing that Second Amendment claims have been violated. Thomas's opinion places the burden on governmental entities to prove that their regulatory efforts are consistent with the historical tradition of firearms regulation in the United States. Governmental interest, for the *Bruen* Court, does not outweigh the individual's right to have commonly used arms for self-defense unless there is strong evidence that the type of regulation challenged has strong historical roots in American law.

It is still too early to tell what *Bruen's* full impact will be. But there are early indications that the decision is already having a major difference. Immediately after *Bruen*, the Supreme Court remanded two cases in which the Fourth and Ninth Circuits had upheld bans on so-called assault weapons and large-capacity magazines for reconsideration consistent with *Bruen*.[61] As of the writing of this chapter in early August 2022, authorities in several states that had previously had "good reason" requirements for pistol permits similar to the invalidated New York statute indicated that they would adjust their firearms laws to conform to the new ruling. On July 7, 2022, Holly T. Shikada, attorney general of Hawaii, in an opinion prepared for that state's governor, David Igo, indicated that *Bruen* made Hawaii's previous practice of requiring an applicant to show special need in order to secure a pistol permit unconstitutional. In the same month, Governor Larry Hogan of Maryland directed that the state police department should eliminate the "good and substantial reason" requirement for permits to carry a pistol. Massachusetts also dropped its "good reason" requirement for a license to carry handguns soon after *Bruen*. New York, which had been the respondent in *Bruen*, indicated that it would accept the Court's decision, but it also passed legislation that expanded the number of places declared sensitive places, in which no one outside of law enforcement officers could carry firearms. The legislation also restricted the sale of body armor and created a presumption that businesses prohibited the carrying of weapons on their property unless the business owner specifically indicated otherwise. The initial responses to *Bruen* have been far-reaching.[62]

## EPILOGUE

We noted at the beginning of this volume, in the Introduction, that the Second Amendment had been bypassed and somehow missed the constitutional bus in the twentieth century. It finally caught that bus in the first quarter of the twenty-first. The cases brought to the Supreme Court by libertarian activist Dick Heller, Korean War veteran Otis McDonald, and later New York State residents Brandon Koch and Robert Nash are now part of the nation's legal history. Early signs indicate that the courts may be on the verge of embarking on an era of relatively robust judicial protection of the right to bear arms. We cannot say how long that era might last or if the nation's courts might sometime in the future do what some legal commentators have urged and essentially reverse the early twenty-first century decisions and declare that the Constitution provides no meaningful impediment to firearms regulation including outright gun prohibition.

There is an irony that has accompanied the effort to strip the right to bear arms from the constitutional protections that belong to the American people. That effort has made gun control, as distinct from gun prohibition, very hard to achieve politically. Gun control might be thought of as policies that might do what reasonably can be done to keep firearms out of the hands of people likely to commit crimes with guns or to keep firearms away from individuals with histories of psychological disturbance that make their misuse of firearms likely. If we accept this definition, a firm indication by the courts that they will read the Constitution as protecting firearms ownership for a broad range of legal purposes including self-defense and lawful participation in the defense of one's community, and that that reading is shared by jurists across the ideological spectrum, may very well be the best friend the cause of gun control could have. The four decades that elapsed between the enactment of the Gun Control Act of 1968 and the Supreme Court's decision in *Heller* saw the growth of the NRA and other gun owners' rights organizations into a mass movement precisely because the gun-control movement had a strong prohibitionist contingent that openly acknowledged that large-scale prohibition was the ultimate goal and that control measures, background checks, waiting periods, licensing, and registration were simply way stations on the road to the final destination. This acknowledgment produced a mass movement in reaction. Whether the NRA has five million members, as its senior officials claimed at the organization's height about five years ago, or whether it has considerably fewer members, as some of the organization's critics have argued, it is still one of the largest voluntary associations in the country. One should also take into account the fact that the NRA is not alone, but simply the largest of several groups opposing gun-control measures. Even if, as many of its critics hope, the NRA is severely diminished as a result of an ongoing lawsuit that was brought against the organization by New York attorney general Letitia James in 2019,[63] other groups with similar aims are likely to recruit the organization's millions of members and supporters. It is no exaggeration to call the anti–gun-control effort a mass movement, one that has mobilized largely in response to the threat of gun prohibition.[64]

All of this raises the question of whether or not we might have had a different national dialogue on gun control and might perhaps have accomplished more if the courts had stated from the beginning of the modern phase of the national gun-control debate in the late 1960s that while control measures were constitutionally permissible, prohibitions were not. One wonders if such a dialogue might yet be possible if the judiciary, starting with the Supreme Court, begins to send, or with *Bruen*, continues to send a clear signal or a series of clear signals that the enforcement of the rights protected by the Second Amendment would be rigorous, that there would be no perfunctory approvals of control measures that in effect turned the right to keep and bear arms into a second-class right, or a somewhat reluctantly granted privilege. We have by and large done that with the First Amendment's protections of freedom of speech and freedom of assembly. We as a nation have come to accept time, place, and manner restrictions on speech and assembly—requirements for permits for parades and rallies are examples of this—precisely because we know the courts will not permit authorities to allow such regulatory measures to morph into prohibitions on unpopular forms of political or artistic expression. There is little reason why a similar consensus could not be achieved with respect to firearms regulation if the judiciary fully stepped up to the constitutional plate and provided a clear indication that the enforcement of Second Amendment rights would be robust.

If that consensus could be achieved, we might have an informed debate on what screening measures, background checks, waiting periods, licensing, and other measures would best serve the two public goals of increasing public safety while also protecting the right to keep and bear arms.

We suspect that that debate, if it is conducted with honesty and rigor, will produce results that will not totally satisfy either side in the great American gun debate. Avid supporters of gun control would find that the Constitution sets real limits on gun control, limits that the courts are only beginning to articulate. Supporters of the right to bear arms would find that screening measures, background checks, and licenses would probably pass constitutional muster. Supporters of greater controls would find, or should find, that high fees that make it difficult for poor people to get licenses are an infringement on the right to have arms, as are the banning of certain types of firearms simply because they have fearsome cosmetic features. Both sides could very well find to their disappointment that even if agreement could be found on control measures, such measures might only have a marginal impact, if any, on the problem of violent crimes committed with firearms. The nation's long experience with illegal markets for prohibited or restricted products cautions against too much optimism about the ability of screening measures to keep deadly weapons out of the wrong hands.

But in an atmosphere where the courts acknowledge that the Second Amendment protects a real right, we can have a real debate about the efficacies and downsides of proposed gun-control measures, free from the threat of potential prohibitions. We aren't there yet, but Dick Heller, Otis McDonald, and Brandon Koch and Robert Nash have set us on that path.

# Notes

## INTRODUCTION

1. *District of Columbia v. Heller*, 554 U.S. 570 (2008); *McDonald v. City of Chicago*, 130 S.Ct. 320 (2010).

2. *United States v. Miller*, 307 U.S. 174 (1939).

3. Leonard W. Levy, *Origins of the Bill of Rights* (New Haven, CT: Yale University Press, 1999), esp. 1–43; Melvin I. Urofsky and Paul Finkelman, *A March of Liberty: A Constitutional History of the United States, Vol. II, From 1898 to the Present* (New York: Oxford University Press, 2011), 684–694, 734–735. *Near* was not formally decided on First Amendment grounds, but on the grounds that the due process clause of the Fourteenth Amendment protected freedom of the press from infringements by state government.

4. Gary Kleck, *Targeting Guns: Firearms and Their Control* (Hawthorne, NY: Aldine de Gruyter, 1997), 11–14; Adam Winkler, *Gunfight: The Battle over the Right to Bear Arms in America* (New York: W. W. Norton, 2011), 10–11, 15–20. Political scientist Kristin Goss has argued that the gun-control movement's early focus on highly restrictive gun control measures in the 1970s probably inhibited its ability to gain mass support and long-term effectiveness. See Kristin A. Goss, "Policy, Politics, and Paradox: The Institutional Origins of the Great American Gun War," *Fordham Law Review* 73, 2 (2004): 681–714.

5. For the leading example of the latter point of view, see generally Saul Cornell, *A Well Regulated Militia: The Founding Fathers and the Origins of Gun Control in America* (New York: Oxford University Press, 2006).

6. See, inter alia, Stephen P. Halbrook, *The Founders' Second Amendment: Origins of the Right to Bear Arms* (Chicago: Ivan R. Dee, 2008); Levy, *Origins*, 133–149.

7. For a discussion concerning the importance of the history of American race relations and the history of the Fourteenth Amendment to the debate on the right to have arms in American Constitutionalism, see Robert J. Cottrol and Raymond T. Diamond, "The Second Amendment: Toward an Afro-Americanist Reconsideration," *Georgetown Law Journal* 80, 2 (December 1991): 309–361.

8. B. Bruce Briggs, "The Great American Gun War," *Public Interest* 45 (Fall 1976): 37–62, esp. at 38. Communications scholar Brian Anse Patrick analyses media support for gun control and hostility toward the National Rifle Association in Brian Anse Patrick, *The National Rifle Association and the Media: The Motivating Force of Negative Coverage* (London: Arktos, 2013). See also the discussion by one of the authors (Brannon Denning) of the elite bar, and pre-*Heller* lower court judicial hostility to the individualist reading of the Second Amendment, in Brannon P. Denning, "Can the Simple Cite Be Trusted? Lower Court Interpretations of *United States v. Miller* and the Second Amendment," *Cumberland Law Review* 26 (1995–1996): 961–1004.

9. James D. Wright, Peter H. Rossi, and Kathleen Daly, *Under the Gun: Weapons, Crime and Violence in America* (New York: Aldine de Gruyter, 1983), 238–240.

10. For two early examples of lawyers affiliated with the NRA who authored articles supporting the individualist view of the Second Amendment, see David I. Caplan, "Restoring the Balance: The Second Amendment Revisited," *Fordham Urban Law Journal* 5 (1976): 31–53; and Robert Dowlut, "The Right to Arms: Does the Constitution or the Predilection of Judges Reign," *Oklahoma Law Review* 36 (1983): 65–106.

11. The academic reconsideration began in the legal academy with the publication of Sanford Levinson, "The Embarrassing Second Amendment," *Yale Law Journal* 99 (1989): 637–659. There were other important exponents of the individual rights view of the amendment before Levinson, including historians Robert Shalhope and Joyce Lee Malcom.

12. For the best discussion of the history of the Fourteenth Amendment and incorporation, see Michael Kent Curtis, *No State Shall Abridge: The 14th Amendment and the Bill of Rights* (Durham, NC: Duke University Press, 1986). The *Slaughter-House Cases* (16. Wall. [83 U.S.] 36) effectively ended the possibility that the Fourteenth Amendment's privileges or immunities clause would be a vehicle for protecting citizens from violations of provisions of the Bill of Rights by the states.

13. Carol D. Leonnig, "Gun Ban Ruling Has Fenty on the Spot; Pursuing Case Would Be Risky," *Washington Post*, May 17, 2007 (Metro section, Westlaw version).

14. See, e.g., Charles E. Cobb Jr., *This Nonviolent Stuff'll Get You Killed: How Guns Made the Civil Rights Movement Possible* (New York: Basic Books, 2014); Lance Hill, *The Deacons for Defense: Armed Resistance and the Civil Rights Movement* (Chapel Hill: University of North Carolina Press, 2004); Nicholas Johnson, *Negroes and the Gun: The Black Tradition of Arms* (Amherst, NY: Prometheus Books, 2004).

## CHAPTER 1: CONSTITUTIONAL PREDICATES

1. Abraham D. Lavender, "United States Ethnic Groups in 1790: Given Names as a Suggestion of Ethnic Identity," *Journal of American Ethnic History* 9, 1 (Fall 1989): 36–66, esp. at 40; Thomas L. Purvis, "The European Ancestry of the United States Population, 1790: A Symposium," *William and Mary Quarterly* 41, 1 (January 1984): 85–101, esp. at 98.

2. For a discussion that examines the complexities of the adoption of English law in Britain's North American colonies and the importance of civil law, Scottish law, and other legal influences in the American colonies, see David S. Clark, "Comparative Law in Colonial British America," *American Journal of Comparative Law* 59, 3 (Summer 2011): 637–674.

3. See, e.g., *Dr. Bonham's Case*, 8 Co. Rep. 114 (1610); Theodore F. T. Plucknett, "Bonham's Case and Judicial Review," *Harvard Law Review* 40 (1926): 30–70; Daniel J. Hulsebosch, "The Ancient Constitution and the Expanding Empire: Sir Edward Coke's British Jurisprudence," *Law and History Review* 21, 3 (Autumn 2003): 439–482.

4. Edward Coke, *The Third Part of the Institutes of the Laws of England* (Buffalo, NY: William S. Hein, 1986), 160–161.

5. Joyce Lee Malcolm, *To Keep and Bear Arms: The Origins of an Anglo-American Right* (Cambridge, MA: Harvard University Press, 1994), 1–15.

6. Malcolm, *To Keep and Bear Arms,* 1–15; Steven Gunn, "Archery Practice in Tudor England," *Past and Present* 209, 1 (2010): 53–81.

7. Malcolm, 1–15.

8. Malcolm, 16–62, 113–134; Lois Schwoerer, *The Declaration of Rights* (Baltimore: Johns Hopkins University Press, 1981), 267–291.

9. An Act Declaring the Rights and Liberties of the Subject and Settling the Succession of the Crown (English Bill of Rights of 1689), The Avalon Project: Documents in Law History and Diplomacy, http://Avalon.law.yale.edu/17th_century/England.asp.

10. An Act Declaring the Rights and Liberties of the Subject.

11. Howard L. Lubert, "Sovereignty and Liberty in William Blackstone's Commentaries on the Laws of England," *Review of Politics* 72, 2 (Spring 2010): 271–297, 271–272; Lawrence M. Friedman, *A History of American Law,* 3rd ed. (New York: Simon & Schuster, 2005), 238–240.

12. St. George Tucker, ed., *Blackstone's Commentaries with Notes of Reference to the Constitution and Laws of the United States and of the Commonwealth of Virginia in Five Volumes* (Orig. pub., Philadelphia: William Young Birch and Abraham Small, 1803). Edited with an Introduction by Paul Finkelman and David Cobin (Union, NJ: Lawbook Exchange, 1996), hereinafter, *Blackstone's Commentaries,* Book I, Part II, 143.

13. See Theodore F. T. Plucknett, "Bonham's Case and Judicial Review," *Harvard Law Review* 40 (1926): 30–70.

14. English Bill of Rights of 1689.

15. *Blackstone's Commentaries,* Book I, Part II, 140.

16. *Blackstone's Commentaries.*

17. *Blackstone's Commentaries,* 411–412.

18. Abbot E. Smith, *Colonists in Bondage: White Servitude and Convict Labor in America, 1607–1776* (New York: Norton, 1971), 30–34.

19. Robert J. Cottrol and Raymond T. Diamond, "The Second Amendment: Toward an Afro-Americanist Reconsideration," *Georgetown Law Journal* 80, 2 (December 1991): 309–362, esp. at 323–327.

20. Cottrol and Diamond, "The Second Amendment," 323–327.

21. Cottrol and Diamond, 323–327.

22. See, generally, Paul Finkelman, "James Madison and the Bill of Rights: A Reluctant Paternity," *Supreme Court Review* 1990 (1990): 301–347.

23. Cecelia M. Kenyon, ed., *The Anti-Federalists* (Indianapolis, IN: Bobbs-Merrill, 1966), 228.

24. Robert Middlekauff, *The Glorious Cause: The American Revolution, 1763–1789* (New York: Oxford University Press 1982, 2005), 354–355, 503–515.

25. Alexander Hamilton, James Madison, and John Jay, No. 29 in *The Federalist,* ed. J. R. Pole (Indianapolis: Hackett Publishing, 2005), 156.

26. *Federalist,* no. 46, 258–259.

27. Bureau of the Census, U.S. Department of Commerce, *Statistical History of the United States from Colonial Times to the Present* (1976), 16.

28. Robert H. Churchill, "Gun Ownership in Early America: A Survey of Manuscript Militia Returns," *William and Mary Quarterly* 60, 3 (July 2003): 615–642, esp. at 625–639; James Lindgren and Justin L. Heather, "Counting Guns in Early America," *William and Mary Law Review*, 43, 5 (2002): 1777–1842.

29. 1. Stat. 271 (1792).

30. Neil H. Cogan, ed., *The Complete Bill of Rights: The Drafts, Debates, Sources and Origins* (New York: Oxford University Press, 1997),169–205.

31. Gordon S. Wood, *Empire of Liberty: A History of the Early Republic, 1789–1815* (New York: Oxford University Press, 2009), 70; Robert E. Shalhope, "To Keep and Bear Arms in the Early Republic," *Constitutional Commentary* 16 (Summer 1999): 269–281.

32. U.S. Constitution Art. 1, Sec. 8, Subsection 15.

33. *Blackstone's Commentaries*, Book I, Part II, 343.

34. Cogan, *The Complete Bill of Rights*, 177.

35. Cogan, 169.

36. Cogan, 169.

37. Cogan, 182.

38. Cogan, 177.

39. Cogan, 177.

40. Cogan, 177.

41. Cogan, 177.

42. See, e.g., Paul Finkelman, "A Well-Regulated Militia: The Second Amendment in Historical Perspective," *Chicago Kent Law Review* 76, 1 (2000): 195–236.

43. James Wilson, *Works of James Wilson*, vol. II. Kermit Hall and Mark David Hall, eds. (Indianapolis, IN: Liberty Fund, 2007).

44. William Rawle, *A View of the Constitution of the United States of America*, 2nd ed. (Durham, NC: Carolina Academic Press, 2009), 125–126.

45. *Blackstone's Commentaries*, Book I, Part II, 143.

46. Joseph Story, *Commentaries on the Constitution of the United States* (Durham, NC: Carolina Academic Press, 1987), 708.

47. *Barron v. Baltimore*, 32 U.S. 243 (1833).

48. Robert J. Cottrol, *The Long, Lingering Shadow: Slavery, Race and the Law in the American Hemisphere* (Athens: University of Georgia Press, 2013), 93–109.

49. Martha S. Jones, *Birthright Citizens: A History of Race and Rights in Antebellum America* (New York: Cambridge University Press, 2018), 102–105; Cottrol and Diamond, "The Second Amendment," 335–338; Paul Finkelman, "Prelude to the Fourteenth Amendment: Black Legal Rights in the Antebellum North," *Rutgers Law Journal* 17 (Spring and Summer 1986): 415–482, 476.

50. *Aymette v. State*, 21 Tenn. (2 Hum.) 154 (Tenn. 1840); *State v. Buzzard*, 4 Ark. (Pike) 18 (Ark. 1842).

51. Arkansas State Constitution, ratified 1836, Article II, Section 21 (http://ahc.dig ital-ar.org/cdm/ref/collection/p16790coll1/id/8); see also Tennessee State Constitution, Article I, Section XXVI (http://tngenweb.org/law/constitution1835.html).

52. See generally *State v. Buzzard*, 4 Ark. 18 (Ark. 1842).

53. *Aymette v. State*, 21 Tenn. 154 (Tenn. 1840).

54. *Nunn v. Georgia*, 1 Georgia (Kelly) 243, 251 (Ga. 1846).

55. *Dred Scott v. Sanford*, 60 U.S. (19 How.) 393, 417 (1857).

56. Robert J. Cottrol, *The Afro-Yankees: Providence's Black Community in the Antebellum Era* (Westport, CT: Greenwood Press, 1982), 63, 94; see also Billy Higgins, "Peter Caulder: A Free Black Soldier and Pioneer in Antebellum Arkansas," *Arkansas Historical Quarterly* 57, 1 (1999): 80–99.

57. Saul Cornell, *A Well-Regulated Militia* (New York: Oxford University Press, 2006), 130–131.

58. *Friendly Persuasion*, Allied Artists, 1956.

59. Harold Hyman and William M. Wiecek, *Equal Justice under Law: Constitutional Development 1835–1875* (New York: Harper & Row, 1982), 319–324.

60. *Certain Offenses of Freedmen. Laws of Mississippi.* 1, 165 (November 29, 1865).

61. *The Congressional Globe: Containing the First Session of the Thirty-Ninth Congress.* F & J Rives, ed. (Washington, DC, 1866), 1839.

62. W. E. B. Dubois, *Black Reconstruction in America, 1860–1880* (New York: Meridian Books, 1968), 270–273, 280–284; Hyman and Wiecek, *Equal Justice under Law*, 246, 277–278, 386–438.

63. *Cong. Globe*, 39th Cong. 1st Sess. 1089–90 (1866).

64. *Cong. Globe*, 39th Cong. 1st Sess. 2764–2767 (1866). The most complete examination of the incorporation issue is Michael Kent Curtis, *No State Shall Abridge: The Fourteenth Amendment and the Bill of Rights* (Durham, NC: Duke University Press, 1986). For an important discussion of the right to keep and bear arms and its salience during the Reconstruction era see, Stephen P. Halbrook, *Freedmen, the Fourteenth Amendment and the Right to Bear Arms, 1866–1876* (Westport, CT: Praeger, 1998). We will return to a discussion of the incorporation issue in Chapters 3 and 8.

65. *Slaughter-House Cases*, 83 U.S. 36 (1873).

66. 16 Stat. 140 (1870).

67. *United States v. Cruikshank*, 92 U.S. 542 (1875). For two book-length treatments of the Colfax Massacre and the importance of the Cruikshank case, see LeeAnna Keith, *The Colfax Massacre: The Untold Story of Black Power, White Terror, and the Death of Reconstruction* (New York: Oxford University Press, 2009); and Charles Lane, *The Day Freedom Died: The Colfax Massacre, the Supreme Court, and the Betrayal of Reconstruction* (New York: Holt, 2009).

68. *Presser v. Illinois*, 116 U.S. 252, 265–266 (1886).

69. *Civil Rights Cases*, 109 U.S. 3 (1883).

70. *Andrews v. State*, 50 Tenn. 165 (Tenn. 1871).

71. Thomas M. Cooley, *The General Principles of Constitutional Law* (Boston: Little, Brown, 1898), 298.

72. Kermit Hall and Peter Karsten, *The Magic Mirror: Law in American History*, 2nd ed. (New York: Oxford University Press, 2009), 161; James W. Loewen, *Sundown Towns: A Hidden Dimension of American Racism* (New York: New Press, 2005), 47–115.

## CHAPTER 2: "NEGRO LABORERS," "LOW-BROWED FOREIGNERS," AND THE "EFFICIENCY OF A WELL-REGULATED MILITIA"

1. "Henry Repeating Rifle, c.1862," https://web.archive.org/web/201510240 33210 /http://www.ket.org/artstoolkit/statedivided/gallery/resources/henry/henry_more.pdf, "Henry Rifle," http://www.civilwar.si.edu/weapons_henry.html; Jerry Lee, "The Lever-Action Rifle: An American Classic," *American Rifleman*, May 9, 2011.

2. Lee Kennett and James La Verne Anderson, *The Gun in America: The Origins of a National Dilemma* (Westport, CT: Greenwood Press, 1975), 92–93, 97.

3. Eugene Volokh, "State Constitutional Rights to Keep and Bear Arms," *Texas Review of Law and Politics* 11 (Fall 2006): 191–217.

4. See Louis Cantor, "Elihu Root and the National Guard: Friend or Foe?," *Military Affairs* 33, 3 (December 1969): 361–373; see also Jeff Bovarnick, "*Perpich v. United States Department of Defense: Who's in Charge of the National Guard?*," *New England Law Review* 26 (Winter 1991): 453–494. The 1990 Supreme Court case *Perpich v. Dept. of Defense* outlined the twentieth-century statutory history that took the National Guard from its original status as a body organized under Congress's authority to arm and discipline the militia, to a body organized under Congress's authority to raise armies. Legislation passed in 1986 gave Congress the power to call the National Guard to active duty in peacetime without the consent of state governors. See *Perpich, et. al., v. Dept. of Defense, et. al.*, 496 U.S. 334 (1990).

5. See, generally, Eric Foner, *Reconstruction: America's Unfinished Revolution, 1863–1877*, updated ed. (New York: Harper, 2014).

6. Robert J. Cottrol and Raymond T. Diamond, "'Never Intended to Be Applied to the White Population': Firearms Regulation and Racial Disparity—the Redeemed South's Legacy to a National Jurisprudence?," *Chicago Kent Law Review* 70, 3 (1995): 1307–1335, 1327–1333; Nicholas Johnson, *Negroes and the Gun: The Black Tradition of Arms* (Amherst, NY: Prometheus Books, 2004), 107–112.

7. *Watson v. Stone*, 148 Fla. 516 (1941). Justice Buford (concurring specially), p. 523. Italics added.

8. Kennett and Anderson, *The Gun in America*, 167–169.

9. See, e.g., Humbert S. Nelli, "Italians and Crime in Chicago: The Formative Years, 1890–1920," *American Journal of Sociology* 74, 4 (January 1969): 373–391; Robert J. Goldstein, "The Anarchist Scare of 1908: A Sign of Tensions in the Progressive Era," *American Studies* 15, 2 (Fall 1974): 55–78.

10. "City Wide Raid on Concealed Weapons," *New York Times*, February 14, 1911; "Bargains in Guns at the Pawnshops" *New York Times*, August 30, 1911.

11. "The Right to Bear Arms," *New York Times*, August 31, 1911.

12. "Seven Ways to Compute the Relative Value of a U.S. Dollar Amount, 1774 to the Present," MeasuringWorth, 2015,http://www.measuringworth.com/uscompare; Catalog No. 124, Sears, Roebuck and Co., Chicago, 1912, 906–909.

13. Carolyn Moehling and Anne Morrison Piehl, "Immigration, Crime and

Incarceration in Early Twentieth Century America," *Demography* 46 (November 2009):739–763; Ramiro Martinez, Jr. and Matthew T. Lee, "On Immigration and Crime," *The Nature of Crime: Continuity and Change*, vol. 1 (2000), 485–524. Accessed via the National Criminal Justice Reference Service, https://www.ncjrs.gov/criminal_justice2000 /vol_1/02j.pdf.

14. *Congressional Record (Senate)*, March 11, 1924, 3946.

15. *City of Salina v. Blaksley*, 72 Kan. 230 (1905).

16. Lucillius A. Emery, "The Constitution Right to Keep and Bear Arms," *Harvard Law Review* 28, 5 (1915): 473–477.

17. *Muller v. Oregon*, 208 U.S. 412 (1908); Louis Brandeis, *Brief for the State of Oregon in Muller v. Oregon* (1907).

18. *Giles v. Harris*, 189 U.S. 475 (1903).

19. William Tucker, *The Science and Politics of Racial Research* (Chicago: University of Illinois Press, 1994), 61. See also Ruth Engs, *The Eugenics Movement: An Encyclopedia* (Westport, CT: Greenwood Press, 2005), 34–35.

20. *Salina*, 72 Kan. at 232.

21. *Salina*, 72 Kan. at 232.

22. The Supreme Court's view of Congress's powers under the commerce clause would change dramatically with the New Deal. The case that best illustrates that change was the 1942 case *Wickard v. Filburn*, 315 U.S. 110 (1942), in which the Court held that the power to regulate interstate commerce included the power to regulate the activities of a farmer growing wheat on his land for his own use.

23. Lawrence M. Friedman, *A History of American Law*, 3rd ed. (New York: Simon & Schuster, 2005), 305–306.

24. Charles V. Imlay, "The Uniform Firearms Act," *American Bar Association Journal* 12, 11 (November 1926): 767–769.

25. Sam B. Warner, "The Uniform Pistol Act," *Journal of Criminal Law and Criminology* 29, 4 (Nov./Dec. 1938): 529–554, 543–547, 551.

26. U.S. Census Bureau, 1920 Census, "Urban and Rural Population Metropolitan Districts and Center of Population," 5–21, http://www2.census.gov/prod2/decennial /documents/16440598v2ch02.pdf.

27. Christopher Capozzola, "The Only Badge Needed Is Your Patriotic Fervor: Vigilance, Coercion, and the Law in World War I America," *Journal of American History* 88, 4 (March 2002): 1354–1382; James A. Sandos, "The Plan of San Diego: War and Diplomacy on the Texas Border, 1915–1916," *Arizona and the West* 14, 1 (Spring 1972): 5–24; Ronnie C. Tyler, "The Little Punitive Expedition in the Big Bend," *Southwest Historical Quarterly* 78, 3 (January 1975): 271–291, 275–276.

28. Kennett and Anderson, *The Gun in America*, 138–141; Chris McNab, "Man-Stopper: Colt M1911," *MHQ: The Quarterly Journal of Military History* 26, 2 (Winter 2014): 17.

29. *War Department Basic Field Manual Browning Automatic Rifle, Caliber .30 M1918A2 with Bipod* (Washington, DC: US Government Printing Office, 1940), 1. The field manual indicated that the Brown's effective rate of fire was 120 to 150 rounds per minute.

30. Bruce Canfield, "Thompson Submachine Gun: The Tommy Gun Goes to War," *American Rifleman*, February 15, 2011, http://www.americanrifleman.org/articles/2011/2/15/thompson-submachine-gun-the-tommy-gun-goes-to-war/.

31. Auto-Ordnance Corp. Pre-World War 2 Advertisements, www.auto-ordnance corporation.com.

32. David S. Lux, "Tommy Gun," in *Guns in American Society*, ed. Gregg Lee Carter (Santa Barbara, CA: ABC-CLIO, 2012), 586–587.

33. Robert Hodges Jr., *The Browning Automatic Rifle* (Oxford: Osprey Publishing, 2012), 37.

34. *The Public Enemy*, Warner Bros., 1931; *Little Caesar*, Warner Bros., 1931, *Scarface*, Warner Bros., 1932; Movie Price Information from DaveManuel.com, http://www.dave manuel.com/whatitcost.php, accessed July 9, 2015.

35. Curt Gentry, *J. Edgar Hoover: The Man and the Secrets* (New York: W. W. Norton, 1991), 167–188.

36. *H.R. 9066: Hearing Before the Committee on Ways and Means*, 73rd Cong., 4, 6, 8, 19, 23–24 (1934) (statement of Homer Cummings, Attorney General of the United States); *H.R. 9066: Hearing Before the Committee on Ways and Means*, 73rd Cong., 100–102, 162–163 (1934) (statement of Joseph Keenan, Assistant Attorney General of the United States).

37. *H.R. 9066: Hearing Before the Committee on Ways and Means*, 73rd Cong., 147–148 (1934) (statement of Charles Imlay, representing the National Conference on Uniform Law).

38. *H.R. 9066: Hearing Before the Committee on Ways and Means*, 73rd Cong., 4–6, 15–17, 19, 24–26 (1934) (statement of Homer Cummings, Attorney General of the United States); *H.R. 9066: Hearing Before the Committee Ways and Means*, 73rd Cong., 86–87, 92–95 (1934) (statement of Joseph Keenan, Assistant Attorney General of the United States).

39. Ibid., 22; ibid., 91–92.

40. H. Rep. No. 1780 (1934); *H.R. 9066: Hearing Before the Committee on Ways and Means*, 73rd Cong., 81, 107–115, 121–122, 124, 126, 160 (1934) (statement of Milton A. Reckord, Adjutant General of the State of Maryland, Executive Vice President of the National Rifle Association); *H.R. 9066: Hearing Before the Committee on Ways and Means*, 73rd Cong., 39–42, 48, 54–56, 59 (1934) (statement of Karl T. Frederick, President, National Rifle Association of America).

41. *H.R. 9066: Hearing Before the Committee on Ways and Means*, 73rd Cong., 105 (1934) (statement of J. Weston Allen, Chairman, National Crime Commission).

42. *Hearings Before a Subcommittee of the Committee on Commerce, United States Senate, Seventy Third Congress, Second Session on S.885, S.2258 (Bills to Regulate Commerce in Firearms and S. 3680)* May 28 and 29, 1934, 32–51, quotation at 41.

43. Max Weber, *Economy and Society: An Outline of Interpretive Sociology*, ed. Guenther Roth and Claus Wittich (Berkeley: University of California Press, 1978), 56.

44. David B. Kopel, "The Great Gun Control War of the Twentieth Century—and Its Lessons for Gun Laws Today," *Fordham Urban Law Journal* 39, 5 (2012): 1529–1530.

45. Pieter Spierenburg, "Democracy Came too Early: A Tentative Explanation for

the Problem of American Homicide," *American Historical Review* 111, 1 (February 2006): 104–114, 110.

46. Edwin S. Corwin, *The Constitution and What It Means Today* (Princeton, NJ: Princeton University Press, 1924), 86–87.

47. Carol Skalnik Leff and Mark H. Leff, "The Politics of Ineffectiveness: Federal Firearms Legislation, 1919–38," *Annals of the American Academy of Political and Social Science* 455 (May 1981): 48–62, 55–62.

48. See generally, Brian L. Frye, "The Peculiar Story of *United States v. Miller*," *NYU Journal of Law and Liberty* 3, 48 (2008): 48–82, esp. at 50–52.

49. Frye, "The Peculiar Story of *United States v. Miller*," 58–60.

50. *United States v. Miller, et. al.*, 26 F. Supp. 1002 (1939).

51. Brief for the United States at 7, *United States v. Miller*, 307 U.S. 174 (No. 696) (1939).

52. *United States v. Miller*, 307 U.S. 174 at 178.

53. *United States v. Miller*, 307 U.S. 174 at 178.

54. *United States v. Miller*, 307 U.S. 174 at 183.

55. Frye, "The Peculiar Story of *United States v. Miller*," 68–69.

## CHAPTER 3: ARMS, WAR, AND LAW IN THE AMERICAN CENTURY

1. Sam B. Warner, "Uniform Pistol Act," *Journal of Criminal Law and Criminology* 29, 4 (1938): 529–554.

2. *United States v. Tot*, 131 F.2d 261 (1942).

3. *Cases v. United States*, 131 F.2d 916 (1942).

4. We should probably make a technical point here. Semi-automatic pistols are frequently referred to as "automatic pistols" even though the term is inaccurate. An automatic weapon is a weapon that will continue to fire as long as the shooter depresses the trigger and ammunition is available in the weapon's feeding device. A semi-automatic weapon requires that the shooter pull the trigger each time he or she wishes to discharge a round. There are true automatic pistols (not to be confused with machine pistols, a synonym for submachine guns), but these are rare. Had Tot had a true automatic pistol, he would likely have been charged under both the 1934 National Firearms Act for possessing an unregistered automatic weapon and the 1938 Federal Firearms Act.

5. *Tot*, 131 F.2d 261 (1942).

6. *Tot*, 131 F.2d at 266–267.

7. *Tot*, 131 F.2d at 266–267.

8. *Tot v. United States*, 319 U.S. 483 (1943); Brief for Petitioner, *Tot v. United States*, 319 U.S. 463 (1943) (No. 569).

9. *Cases v. United States*, 131 F.2d 916 (1942).

10. *Cases*, 131 F.2d 916 (1942).

11. *Cases*, 131 F.2d 916.

12. Thomas A. Bailey and Paul B. Ryan, *Hitler vs. Roosevelt: The Undeclared Naval War* (New York: Free Press, 1979); Michael Gannon, *Operation Drumbeat: The Dramatic True Story of Germany's First U-Boat Attacks along the American Coast in World War II* (New York: HarperPerennial, 1991), 90–93.

13. David Woolner, "The 'Special Relationship' between Great Britain and the United States Began with FDR," Roosevelt Institute, July 22, 2010, http://www.rooseveltinstitute.org /new-roosevelt/special-relationship-between-great-britain-and-united-states-began-fdr.

14. An Act to Authorize the President of the United States to Requisition Property Required for the Defense of the United States, Public Law 77–274, *U.S. Statutes at Large* 55 (1941): 742.

15. *U.S. Statutes at Large* 55 (1941): 742.

16. Representative Hall, speaking on S. 1579, on August 5, 1941, 77th Cong., 1st sess., *Congressional Record* 87, part 6, 6778.

17. Michelle Hall, "By the Numbers: End of World War II," CNN, September 2, 2013, https://www.cnn.com/2013/09/02/world/btn-end-of-wwii; "History at a Glance: Women in World War II," National World War II Museum, accessed November 5, 2022, https:// www.nationalww2museum.org/students-teachers/student-resources/research-starters /women-wwii.

18. "Glenn Miller," Arlington National Cemetery, accessed November 5, 2022, http:// www.arlingtoncemetery.mil/Explore/Notable-Graves/Other-Prominent-Figures/Glenn Miller.

19. United States Department of Veterans Affairs, "America's Wars," accessed November 6, 2022, https://www.va.gov/opa/publications/factsheets/fs_americas_wars.pdf. This fact sheet indicates that more than sixteen million individuals served in the US Armed Forces during World War II, nearly six million served during the Korean War, and nearly nine million served during the Vietnam War. These figures do not give an exact count of the number of people who served between 1940 and 1973. A number of individuals served multiple times, sometimes in different services. The figures also do not reflect individuals who served during this period in peacetime. Thus, an individual like entertainer Elvis Presley who was drafted in 1958 and discharged in 1960 was not counted in this fact sheet because his service occurred during peacetime.

20. Don Graham, *No Name on the Bullet: A Biography of Audie Murphy* (New York: Viking Press, 1989), 16–17; David A. Smith, *The Price of Valor: The Life of Audie Murphy, America's Most Decorated Hero of World War II* (Washington, DC: Regnery, 2015), 6.

21. Joseph P. Roberts Jr., ed., *The American Rifleman Goes to War: The Guns, Troops and Training of World War II as Reported in the NRA's Magazine.* (Washington, DC: National Rifles Association, 1992), 198–199.

22. U.S. Department of the Army, "Operator and Organizational Maintenance Manual Including Repair Parts and Special Tools List: M-1 Garand," March 17, 1969.

23. U.S. Department of War, *Basic Field Manual: U.S. Carbine, Caliber .30, M1* (Washington, DC: Government Printing Office, 1942).

24. Lee Kennett and James LaVerne Anderson, *The Gun in America: The Origins of a National Dilemma* (Westport, CT: Greenwood Press), 216–222.

25. Nicholas Harman, *Dunkirk, The Patriotic Myth* (New York: Simon & Schuster, 1980), 105–106; Walter Lord, *The Miracle of Dunkirk* (New York: Viking Press, 1982), 88–89, 226–227. For the record, we had thought of and decided to use the Dunkirk example before the release of the 2017 movie that dramatized these events. Christopher Nolan, director and writer, *Dunkirk* (Warner Bros., 2017).

26. David Fernbach, "Tom Wintringham and Socialist Defense Strategy," *History Workshop* 14, 1 (Autumn 1982): 63–91; Corinna M. Peniston-Bird, "'All in It Together' and 'Backs to the Wall': Relating Patriotism and the People's War in the 21st Century," *Oral History* 40, 2 (Autumn 2012): 69–80.

27. Roberts, *The American Rifleman Goes to War.*

28. Fernbach, "Tom Wintringham and Socialist Defense Strategy," 63–91.

29. Charles R. Fisher, "The Maryland State Guard in World War II," *Military Affairs* 47, 1 (February 1983): 1–14; P. Whitney Lackenbauer, "Guerrillas in Our Midst: The Pacific Coast Rangers, 1942–1945," *B.C. Studies* 155 (Autumn 2007): 31–67.

30. Franz-Karl Stanzel, "German Prisoners of War in Canada, 1940–1946: An Autobiography-Based Essay," *Canadian Military History* 27, 2 (2018): 1–19; J. Malcolm Garcia, "German POWs on the American Homefront," *Smithsonian Magazine*, September 15, 2009, https://www.smithsonianmag.com/history/german-pows-on-the-american-home front-141009996/.

31. Gannon, *Operation Drumbeat.*

32. *The Coast Guard at War: The Temporary Component of the Coast Guard Reserve* (Washington, DC: Coast Guard Public Information Division, 1948).

33. George Orwell, "Don't Let Colonel Blimp Ruin the Home Guard," in *The Complete Works of George Orwell*, vol. 12, ed. Peter Davison (London: Seeker & Warburg, 1998), 362–365.

34. Alan Clark, *Barbarossa: The Russian German Conflict, 1941–1945* (New York: Quill, 1965), 151–155.

35. David K. Yelton, *Hitler's Volkssturm: The Nazi Militia and the Fall of Germany, 1944–1945* (Lawrence: University Press of Kansas, 2002).

36. Ronald H. Spector, *Eagle against the Sun: The American War with Japan* (New York: Vintage Books, 1985), 544–545; Sadao Asada, "The Shock of the Atomic Bomb and Japan's Decision to Surrender: A Reconsideration," *Pacific Historical Review* 67, no. 4 (November 1998): 477–512, 511; Thomas R. H. Havens, "Women and War in Japan, 1937–1945," *American Historical Review* 80, 4 (October 1975): 913–934, 915.

37. Kennett and Anderson, *The Gun in America*, 216–221.

38. Frances Goodrich, Albert Hackett, Frank Capra, and Jo Swerling, *It's a Wonderful Life: From the 1946 Liberty Film* (New York: St. Martin's Press, 1986), 99.

39. Graham, *No Name on the Bullet*, 88–91; John Houston, director and screenwriter, *The Red Badge of Courage* (Metro-Goldwyn Mayer, 1951); Jesse Hibbs, director, *To Hell and Back* (Universal, 1955); William A. Wellman, director, *Battleground* (Metro-Goldwyn Mayer, 1949); Robert Pirosh, director and writer, *Go for Broke* (Metro-Goldwyn Mayer, 1951); Donald Dewey, *James Stewart: A Biography* (Atlanta: Turner Publishing,

1996), 239–251, 254–257, 343–352, 355–360, 388–390; Norman Macdonnell, producer, *Gunsmoke* (CBS Studios, 1955).

40. Fred Zinneman, director, *High Noon* (Stanley Kramer Productions, 1952); John W. Cunningham, "The Tin Star," *Collier's Magazine,* December 6, 1947.

41. Gary Kleck, *Point Blank: Guns and Violence in America* (New York: DeGruyter, 1991), 378.

42. Roscoe Pound, *The Development of Constitutional Guarantees of Liberty* (New Haven, CT: Yale University Press, 1957), 90–91.

43. *Adamson v. California,* 332 U.S. 46, 48–49 (1947).

44. See Chapter 1, notes 62–64.

45. *The Butcher's Benevolent Ass'n New Orleans v. The Crescent City Live-Stock Landing & Slaughter-House Co.,* 16 Wall. (83 U.S.) 36, 77–78 (1873).

46. Gregory Elinson, "Judicial Partisanship and the *Slaughterhouse Cases:* Investigating the Relationship between Courts and Parties," *Studies in American Political Development* 31, 1 (April 2017): 24–46.

47. *The Butcher's Benevolent Ass'n New Orleans v. The Crescent City Live-Stock Landing & Slaughter-House Co.,* 16 Wall. (83 U.S.) 36, 71–72 (1873).

48. *United States v. Cruikshank,* 92 U.S. 542, 547–48 (1876).

49. *Presser v. Illinois,* 116 U.S. 252, 258 (1886).

50. Thomas Tandy Lewis, "The Ironic History of Substantive Due Process; Three Constitutional Revolutions," *International Social Science Review* 76 (2001): 21–35.

51. Michael G. Collins, "October Term 1896: Embracing Due Process," *American Journal of Legal History* 45, 1 (January 2001): 71–97.

52. 211 U.S. 78 (1908).

53. *Twining v. New Jersey,* 211 U.S. 78 (1908) (emphasis added).

54. *Twining v. New Jersey,* 211 U.S. 78 (1908).

55. *Gitlow v. New York,* 268 U.S. 652 (1925).

56. *Near v. Minnesota ex rel. Olson,* 283 U.S. 697 (1931).

57. *Powell v. Alabama,* 287 U.S. 45 (1932).

58. *Brown v. State of Mississippi,* 297 U.S. 278 (1936).

59. *Palko v. Connecticut,* 302 U.S. 319 (1937).

60. *Palko,* 302 U.S. 319 (1937).

61. *Adamson v. California,* 332 U.S. 46 (1947).

62. Jeffrey D. Hockett, "Justices Frankfurter and Black: Social Theory and Constitutional Interpretation," *Political Science Quarterly* 107, 3 (Autumn 1992): 479–499.

63. *Adamson,* 332 U.S. at 59–62 (1947).

64. *Adamson,* 332 U.S. at 70–72.

65. *Adamson,* 332 U.S. at 70–72.

66. *Adamson,* 332 U.S. at 70–72; William Gillette, *The Right to Vote: Politics and the Passage of the Fifteenth Amendment* (Baltimore: Johns Hopkins University Press, 1965), 26–35, 151.

67. In the immediate wake of *Adamson,* legal scholars Charles Fairman and William W. Crosskey continued the debate between Justices Black and Frankfurter. Charles

Fairman, "Does the Fourteenth Amendment Incorporate the Bill of Rights?," *Stanford Law Review* 2, 1 (December 1949): 5–139; William W. Crosskey, "Charles Fairman, Legislative History and the Constitutional Limits on State Authority," *University of Chicago Law Review* 22, 1 (Autumn 1954): 1–143. For a good examination of the Crosskey-Fairman debates, see Pamela Brandwein, "Dueling Histories: Charles Fairman and William Crosskey Reconstruct 'Original Understanding,'" *Law and Society Review* 30, 2 (1996): 289–334. The debate over incorporation would be later taken up by other scholars. Michael Kent Curtis, *No State Shall Abridge: The Fourteenth Amendment and the Bill of Rights* (Durham, NC: Duke University Press, 1986); Raoul Berger, *The Fourteenth Amendment and the Bill of Rights* (Norman: University of Oklahoma Press, 1989); Akhil Reed Amar, *The Bill of Rights: Creation and Reconstruction* (New Haven, CT: Yale University Press, 1998).

68. Felix Frankfurter, "Memorandum on 'Incorporation' of the Bill of Rights into the Due Process Clause of the Fourteenth Amendment," *Harvard Law Review* 78, 4 (February 1965): 746–783.

69. *Johnson v. Eisentrager*, 338 U.S. 877 (1950).

70. *Johnson*, 338 U.S. 877 (1950).

71. *Brown v. Bd. of Educ.*, 347 U.S. 483 (1954).

72. *Baker v. Carr*, 369 U.S. 186 (1962); *Reynolds v. Sims*, 377 U.S. 533 (1964).

73. *Mapp v. Ohio*, 367 U.S. 643 (1961).

74. *Miranda v. Arizona*, 384 U.S. 436 (1966).

75. *Gideon v. Wainwright*, 372 U.S. 335 (1963).

76. *Moore v. Gallup Cnty. Judge*, 45 N.Y.S.2d 63, 67–68 (1943); *New York v. Raso*, 170 N.Y.S.2d 245, 249 (1958).

77. Kennett and Anderson, *The Gun in America*, 220–223.

78. David Kopel, *The Samurai, the Mountie and the Cowboy: Should America Adopt the Gun Controls of Other Democracies?* (Buffalo, NY: Prometheus Books, 1992), 343.

79. Nicholas Johnson, *Negroes and the Gun: The Black Tradition of Arms* (Amherst, NY, Prometheus Books, 2014), 49; Charles E. Cobb, *This Nonviolent Stuff'll Get You Killed: How Guns Made the Civil Rights Movement Possible* (New York: Basic Books, 2014), 7.

80. Kennett and Anderson, *The Gun in America*, 226–228.

81. *Guns*, January 1959, 34; *Guns*, January 1961, 34, 59; Lawrence H. Officer and Samuel H. Williamson, "Annual Wages in the United States, 1774–Present," MeasuringWorth, accessed December 6, 2022, https://www.measuringworth.com/datasets/uswage/result .php.

## CHAPTER 4: FROM CASUAL ACCEPTANCE TO VIRTUAL DESUETUDE

1. *Roe v. Wade*, 410 U.S. 113, 169 (1973) (Stewart, J., concurring); *Moore v. City of East Cleveland*, 431 U.S. 494, 502 (1977); *Planned Parenthood v. Casey*, 505 U.S. 833, 848 (1992).

2. *Poe v. Ullman*, 367 U.S. 497, 543 (1961) (Harlan, J., dissenting) (emphasis added).

3. *Poe,* 367 U.S. at 515–516; *Adamson v. California,* 332 U.S. 46, 89 (1947) (Black, J., dissenting).

4. Charles G. Rau, "Those Distinguished Awards," *American Rifleman Magazine* 102, 2 (February 1954): 28–30.

5. Carl Bakal, *The Right to Bear Arms* (New York: McGraw-Hill, 1966), 192.

6. Bakal, *The Right to Bear Arms,* 7.

7. Philip Schreier, "The Guns of U.S. Presidents," *American Rifleman,* February 15, 2016, https://www.americanrifleman.org/content/the-guns-of-u-s-presidents/; Phil Bourjaily, "JFK's M1 Garand Goes Up for Auction," *Field & Stream,* August 3, 2015, https://www.fieldandstream.com/blogs/field-notes/jfks-m1-garand-goes-up-for-auction/; "Know Your Lawmakers, *Guns,* April 1960, 4.

8. Frank C. Daniel to John F. Kennedy, letter, April 19, 1961, Papers of John F. Kennedy, John F. Kennedy Presidential Library, accessed November 6, 2022.

9. Vincent Bugliosi, *Four Days in November: The Assassination of President John F. Kennedy* (New York: W. W. Norton, 2007), 319.

10. Bugliosi, *Four Days in November,* 434–442.

11. *Report of the President's Commission on the Assassination of President John F. Kennedy* (Washington, DC: Government Printing Office, 1964).

12. Ramon Germania, "Buying Rifle Is Easy: Legislation Sidetracked, Guns Bought Abroad," *Washington Post,* November 25, 1963, A9.

13. "Dodd Will Tighten Bill on Gun Sales," *New York Times,* November 28, 1963, 20.

14. Philip Benjamin, "New Group Urges Laws to Curb Sale of Firearms," *New York Times,* December 4, 1963.

15. George Gallup, "The Gallup: A Majority for Permit to Buy Gun," *Washington Post,* January 16, 1964, A15.

16. "Gun Aversion Laid to Death of Kennedy," *Washington Post,* March 14, 1964, A5.

17. Jack Gouls, "The Firearms Issue: 'C.B.S. Reports' Presents a Provocative Examination of a National Problem," *New York Times,* June 11, 1964.

18. Bakal, *The Right to Bear Arms;* Wolfgang Saxon, "Carl Bakal, 86: Offered a Warning on Firearms," *New York Times,* April 3, 2004.

19. Bakal, 296–297.

20. Eugene Volokh, "State Constitutional Rights to Keep and Bear Arms," *Texas Review of Law and Policy* 11, 1 (Fall 2006): 191–217, 205–207.

21. *Robertson v. Baldwin,* 165 U.S. 275, 281–282 (1897) (emphasis added).

22. Bakal, *The Right to Bear Arms,* 296–297; Saul Cornell, "A New Paradigm for the Second Amendment," *Law and History Review* 22, 1 (2004): 161–67; Thomas M. Cooley, "Constitutional Limitations on Firearms Regulation," *Duke Law Journal* 1969, 4 (1969): 773–801.

23. Bakal, *The Right to Bear Arms,* 280–282.

24. *Guns,* February 1960, 4; *Guns,* April 1960, 4; Robert A. Sprecher, "The Lost Amendment," *American Bar Association Journal* 51, 7 (1965): 554–557, 665–669.

25. Alexander Hamilton, James Madison, and John Jay, No. 29 in *The Federalist,* ed. J. R. Pole (Indianapolis: Hackett Publishing, 2005), 152–158.

26. Thomas M. Cooley, *General Principles of Constitutional Law* (Boston: Little, Brown, 1898).

27. Roscoe Pound, *The Development of Constitutional Guarantees of Liberty* (New Haven, CT: Yale University Press, 1957), 90–91.

28. *Silveira v. Lockyer*, 328 F.3d 567, 571 (2003) (Kozinski, J., dissenting from denial of rehearing en banc).

29. Robert J. Cottrol and Raymond T. Diamond, "The Second Amendment: Toward an Afro-Americanist Reconsideration," *Georgetown Law Journal* 80, 2 (1991): 347–349.

30. Cottrol and Diamond, "The Second Amendment," 340–342.

31. Jervis Anderson, *A. Philip Randolph: A Biographical Portrait* (New York: Harcourt, 1972), 41–43.

32. Rudia Haliburton Jr., "The Tulsa Race War of 1921," *Journal of Black Studies* 2, 3 (March 1972): 333–357, 339.

33. Nicholas Johnson, *Negroes and the Gun: The Black Tradition of Arms* (Amherst, NY: Prometheus Books, 2014), 24–26.

34. Johnson, *Negroes and the Gun*, 21.

35. Charles E. Cobb, *This Nonviolent Stuff'll Get You Killed: How Guns Made the Civil Rights Movement Possible* (Durham, NC: Duke University Press, 2015), 110–111.

36. Lance Hill, *The Deacons for Defense: Armed Resistance and the Civil Rights Movement* (Chapel Hill: University of North Carolina Press, 2004), 31–39.

37. Cobb, *How Guns Made the Civil Rights Movement Possible.*

38. George F. Will, "GOP Can Transform Politics with African-American Vote," *Tampa Bay Times*, September 27, 2005.

39. "Johnson's Gun Control Plan Opposed by CORE Official," *New York Times*, July 15, 1968, 18.

40. Don B. Kates Jr., "The Necessity of Access to Firearms by Dissenters and Minorities Whom Government Is Unwilling or Unable to Protect," in *Restricting Handguns: The Liberal Skeptics Speak Out*, eds. John B. Salter Jr. and Don B. Kates Jr. (Croton-on-Hudson, NY: North River Press, 1979), 186.

41. Hill, *The Deacons for Defense*, 6–7.

42. Joseph Boskin, "The Revolt of the Urban Ghettoes, 1964–1967," *Annals of the American Academy of Political Science* 382 (March 1969): 1–14.

43. *Report of the National Advisory Commission on Civil Disorders* (Washington, DC: Government Printing Office, 1968).

44. Boskin, "The Revolt of the Urban Ghettoes," 11.

45. *Report of the National Advisory Commission on Civil Disorders*, 36–37.

46. Carolyn R. Calloway, "Group Cohesiveness in the Black Panther Party," *Journal of Black Studies* 8, 1 (September 1977): 55–74; Adam Winkler, "The Secret History of Guns," *Atlantic*, September 2011; Richard Berghole, "Reagan Will Fight for Gun Ownership: Opposes Firearms Ban, Says Issue Not Involved in Texas Shootings," *Los Angeles Times*, August 3, 1966, 3.

47. Chapter 10, "Control of Firearms," in *The Challenge of Crime in a Free Society:*

*A Report by the President's Commission on Law Enforcement and the Administration of Justice* (Washington, DC: Government Printing Office, 1967), 239–243.

48. Alexander De Conde, *Gun Violence in America: The Struggle for Control* (Boston: Northeastern University Press, 2001), 156.

49. "Bob Kennedy Blames Rifle Group for Deaths," *Los Angeles Times*, August 25, 1967, 4; "Edward Kennedy Presses for Speed on Gun Controls," *New York Times*, August 17, 1966, 34.

50. *Federal Firearms Legislation: Hearings before the Subcomm. to Investigate Juvenile Delinquency of the S. Comm. on the Judiciary*, 89th Cong., 1st sess. (May 19, 1965) (statement of Nicholas deB. Katzenbach, Attorney General, United States), 33–57; *Anti-Crime Program: Hearings before the H. Comm. on the Judiciary*, 90th Cong., 1st sess. (March 16, 1967) (statement of Ramsey Clark, Attorney General, United States), 203–237.

51. George Lardner Jr., "McNamara Deplores Lack of Firearms Control Law," *Washington Post*, July 2, 1967, A3.

52. *The Challenge of Crime in a Free Society*, 239.

53. Reuben Oppenheimer, "Gun Control and the Second Amendment," *Baltimore Sun*, September 22, 1968, K3.

54. *The Challenge of Crime in a Free Society*, 241–242; *Federal Firearms Act: Hearings before the Subcomm. to Investigate Juvenile Delinquency of the S. Comm. on the Judiciary*, 90th Cong., 1st sess. (July 10, 1967) (statement of Sheldon Cohen, Commissioner, Internal Revenue Service), 59–60.

55. Lyndon B. Johnson, "Remarks upon Signing the Gun Control Act of 1968, October 22, 1968," in *Public Papers of the Presidents of the United States*, vol. 2 (Washington, DC: Government Printing Office, 1970), 1059–1060.

56. Bakal, *The Right to Bear Arms*, 10–11.

57. Ramsey Clark, *Crime in America: Observations on Its Nature, Causes, Prevention and Control* (New York: Simon & Schuster, 1970), 102.

58. Clark, *Crime in America*, 107.

59. Clark, 101–116.

60. Congressional Research Service, *The Second Amendment: Selected Materials* (Washington, DC: Library of Congress, June 1968).

61. Vincent Doyle, *The Second Amendment as a Limitation on Federal Firearms Legislation* (Washington, DC: Library of Congress Legislative Reference Service, 1968).

62. *Crime Legislation for the District of Columbia: Hearings before the H. Comm. on the District of Columbia*, 88th Cong. (May 1, 1963) (statement of Franklin L. Orth, Executive Vice President, National Rifle Association of America), 127–129.

63. Gun Control Act of 1968, Public Law 90–618, *U.S. Statutes at Large* 82 (1968): 1213–1214.

64. *U.S. Statutes at Large* 82 (1968): 1224.

65. Robert Young, "Johnson Signs Gun Bill, Asks Tighter Curbs," *Chicago Tribune*, October 23, 1968, A4.

66. Centers for Disease Control and Prevention, National Center for Health Statistics, "Compressed Mortality File 1968–1978," CDC Wonder online database, compiled

from Compressed Mortality File CMF 1968–1988, Series 20, No. 2A, 2000, accessed November 7, 2022, http://wonder.cdc.gov/cmf-icd8.html.

67. Joseph D. Alviani and William R. Drake, "Handgun Control: Issues and Alternatives," (Washington, DC: United States Conference of Mayors, Handgun Control Project, 1975), 45.

68. Matthew G. Yeager, Joseph D. Alviani, and Nancy Loving, "How Well Does the Handgun Protect You and Your Family?: Technical Report 2," (Washington, DC: United States Conference of Mayors, January 1, 1976).

69. Don B. Kates Jr., "The Value of Civilian Arms Possession as a Deterrent to Crime or Defense against Crime," *American Journal of Criminal Law* 18, 2 (1991): 4, 7.

70. Maynard Holbrook Jackson Jr., "Handgun Control: Constitutional and Critically Needed," *North Carolina Central Law Journal* 8, 2 (Spring 1977): 189–198.

71. Lucy Jarvis, producer, *A Shooting Gallery Called America*, aired April 29, 1975, NBC.

72. *All in the Family*, season 3, episode 1, "Archie and the Editorial," directed by Norman Campbell, written by Norman Lear, George Arthur Bloom, Don Nicholl, and Johnny Speight, featuring Carroll O'Conner, Jean Stapleton, Rob Reiner, and Sally Struthers, aired September 16, 1972, in broadcast syndication, NBC.

73. John M. Crewdson, "Levi Says U.S. Is Studying Ways to Curb Pistols in Urban Areas," *New York Times*, April 7, 1975; Leslie Wheeler, *Jimmy Who?: An Examination of Presidential Candidate Jimmy Carter—The Man, His Career, His Stands on the Issues* (Woodbury, NY: Barron's Educational Series, 1976), 185.

74. "Nelson Shields 3d, 69, Gun-Control Advocate," *New York Times*, January 27, 1993.

75. Pete Shields and John Greenya, *Guns Don't Die—People Do* (New York: Arbor House, 1981), 46, 49–55.

76. Richard Harris, "A Reporter at Large: Handguns," *New Yorker*, July 26, 1976, 57–58.

77. "The Gun Culture," *New York Times*, September 24, 1975.

78. Shields and Greenya, *Guns Don't Die—People Do*, 100.

79. Shields and Greenya, 8.

80. Judith Vandell Holmberg and Michael Clancy, *People vs. Handguns: The Campaign to Ban Handguns in Massachusetts* (Washington, DC: United States Conference of Mayors, 1977).

81. Holmberg and Clancy, *People vs. Handguns*, 81–86.

82. Paul W. Valentine, "Rush of Paperwork," *Washington Post*, September 24, 1976; Karlyn Barker and Paul W. Valentine, "Effort to Kill D.C. Gun Law Hits Snag," *Washington Post*, September 18, 1976.

83. Eric Zorn, "Morton Grove Gun Ban Quietly Turns 5," *Chicago Tribune*, June 15, 1986; Associated Press, "Chicago Council Votes Ban on New Handguns," *New York Times*, March 20, 1982.

84. James D. Wright, Peter H. Rossi, and Kathleen Daly, *Under the Gun: Weapons, Crime and Violence in America* (New York: DeGruyter, 1983), 238–241.

85. *Burton v. Sills*, 240 A.2d 462, 467–468 (N.J. Super. Ct. Law. Div. 1967), *aff'd*, *Burton v. Sills*, 240 A.2d 432, 434 (N.J. Super. Ct. App. Div. 1968).

86. *Burton v. Sills*, 248 A.2d 521, 526 (1968).

87. *Burton*, 248 A.2d at 526–530 (1968).

88. *Stevens v. United States*, 440 F.2d 144 (6th Cir. 1971); *United States v. Johnson*, 497 F.2d 548 (4th Cir. 1974); *United States v. McCutcheon*, 446 F.2d 133 (7th Cir. 1971).

89. *United States v. Decker*, 446 F.2d 164, 166–167 (8th Cir. 1971).

90. *Decker*, 446 F.2d at 166–167.

91. *United States v. Warin*, 530 F.2d 103, 108 (6th Cir. 1976).

92. *Warin v. United States*, 426 U.S. 948 (1976).

93. *Quilici v. Vill. Morton Grove*, 695 F.2d 261 (7th Cir. 1982).

94. *Quilici*, 695 F.2d 261, 271–272 (7th Cir. 1982).

95. Warren Burger, interview by Charlayne Hunter-Gault, *PBS NewsHour*, Public Broadcasting Service, 1991; Josh Getlin, "No Constitutional Right to Ownership: Powell Calls for Stricter Control on Handguns," *Los Angeles Times*, August 8, 1988.

96. *Adams v. Williams*, 407 U.S. 143, 150 (1972).

97. David T. Hardy, *The Papers of Justice Harry Blackmun: Insights into the Supreme Court and the Second Amendment* (in the authors' possession).

## CHAPTER 5: SHIFTING TIDES

1. 65 Ops. Cal. Att'y. Gen. 457 (August 3, 1982), https://oag.ca.gov/opinions/search ?combine=82–305; "San Francisco to Appeal Ruling on Gun Ordinance," *New York Times*, October 15, 1982.

2. Lee Dembart and Kevin Roderick, "Voters Overwhelmingly Reject Handgun Law," *Los Angeles Times*, November 3, 1982.

3. Philip J. Cook, "The Great American Gun War: Notes from Four Decades in the Trenches," *Crime and Justice* 42, 1 (August 2013): 27.

4. "History of Brady," Brady, accessed November 6, 2022, https://www.bradyunited .org/history.

5. Herb Block Foundation, "Gun Control Cartoons," *Herblock*, accessed November 6, 2022, https://www.herbblockfoundation.org/gun-control-cartoons.

6. Kristin A. Goss, *Disarmed: The Missing Movement for Gun Control in America* (Princeton, NJ: Princeton University Press, 2008).

7. Gallup Poll, "Guns," Gallup, accessed November 7, 2022, https://news.gallup.com /poll/1645/guns.aspx; James Geehan and Ted Warmbold, "Overview of Gun Control," *Sun-Telegram* (San Bernardino, CA), July 17, 1975.

8. Edward S. Corwin, Harold W. Chase, and Craig R. Ducat, *Edward S. Corwin's Constitution and What It Means Today* (Princeton, NJ: Princeton University Press, 1978), 340–341.

9. John E. Nowak, Ronald D. Rotunda, and J. Nelson Young, *Handbook on Constitutional Law* (St. Paul, MN: West Publishing, 1978); Laurence Tribe, *American Constitutional Law* (New York: Foundation Press, 1978).

10. Robert A. Sprecher, "The Lost Amendment," *American Bar Association Journal* 51, 7 (1965): 554–557.

11. *The Right to Keep and Bear Arms: Report of the Subcomm. on the Constitution of the S. Committee on the Judiciary,* 97th Cong., 2nd sess. (January 20, 1982), 12.

12. Edwin Meese, "The American Bar Association, 7/9/85," accessed November 6, 2022, https://www.justice.gov/sites/default/files/ag/legacy/2011/08/23/07–09–1985 .pdf.

13. *The Right to Keep and Bear Arms: Report of the Subcomm. on the Constitution of the S. Committee on the Judiciary,"* 97th Cong., 2nd sess. (January 20, 1982), 12; "About Us: David T. Hardy," Of Arms and the Law, accessed November 6, 2022, https://arms andthelaw.com/aboutus.php.

14. Stephen P. Halbrook, "The Jurisprudence of the Second and Fourteenth Amendments," *George Mason Law Review* 4, 1 (1981): 1–69.

15. Stephen P. Halbrook, *That Every Man Be Armed,* rev. ed. (Albuquerque: University of New Mexico Press, 2013).

16. *Firearms Owners' Protection Act of 1986, Public Law 99–308, U.S. Statutes at Large* 100 (1986): 451.

17. John B. Salter Jr. and Don. B. Kates Jr., eds., *Restricting Handguns: The Liberal Skeptics Speak Out* (Croton-on-Hudson, NY: North River Press, 1979).

18. Salter and Kates, *Restricting Handguns.*

19. David T. Hardy, "Armed Citizens, Citizen Armies: Toward a Jurisprudence of the Second Amendment," *Harvard Journal of Law and Public Policy* 9, 3 (1986): 559–638.

20. Halbrook, *That Every Man Be Armed.*

21. Charles Debenedetti, "American Historians and Armaments: The View from Twentieth-Century Textbooks," *Diplomatic Affairs* 6, 4 (Fall 1982): 323–337.

22. Paul Murphy, "Time to Reclaim: The Current Challenge of American Constitutional History," *American Historical Review* 69, 1 (October 1963): 64–79.

23. Robert Shalhope, "The Ideological Origins of the Second Amendment," *Journal of American History* 69, 3 (December 1982): 599–614.

24. Lawrence Delbert Cress, "An Armed Community: The Origins and Meaning of the Right to Bear Arms," *Journal of American History* 71, 1 (June 1984): 22–42.

25. Joyce Malcolm, "The Right of the People to Keep and Bear Arms: The Common Law Tradition," *Hastings Constitutional Law Quarterly* 10, 2 (1983): 285–314.

26. "Self-Defense Gun Use," Violence Policy Center, accessed November 6, 2022, http://vpc.org/revealing-the-impacts-of-gun-violence/self-defense-gun-use/.

27. Kathleen Daly, Peter H. Rossi, and James D. Wright, *Under the Gun: Weapons, Crime and Violence in America* (Chicago: Aldine Publishing, 1983).

28. Daly, Rossi, and Wright, *Under the Gun.*

29. Daly, Rossi, and Wright, *Under the Gun.*

30. Peter H. Rossi and James D. Wright, *Armed and Considered Dangerous: A Survey of Felons and Their Firearms* (Chicago: Aldine Publishing, 1986).

31. Gary Kleck and Marc Gertz, "Armed Resistance to Crime: The Prevalence and Nature of Self-Defense with a Gun," *Journal of Criminal Law and Criminology* 86, 1 (1995):

150–187; John Lott, *The War on Guns: Arming Yourself against Gun Control Lies* (Washington, DC: Regnery Publishing, 2016).

32. *Apodaca v. Oregon*, 406 U.S. 404 (1972); *Johnson v. Louisiana*, 406 U.S. 356 (1972).

33. Meese, "The American Bar Association, 7/9/85."

34. Raoul Berger, *Government by Judiciary: The Transformation of the Fourteenth Amendment*, 2nd ed. (Indianapolis: Liberty Fund, 1997).

35. Michael Curtis, *No State Shall Abridge: The Fourteenth Amendment and the Bill of Rights* (Durham, NC: Duke University Press Books, 1990).

36. Laurence Tribe, *American Constitutional Law*, 2nd ed. (New York: Foundation Press, 1988); Don. B. Kates Jr., "Handgun Prohibition and the Original Meaning of the Second Amendment," *Michigan Law Review* 82, 204 (1983): 204–273.

37. Warren E. Burger, "The Right to Bear Arms: A Distinguished Citizen Takes a Stand on One of the Most Controversial Issues in the Nation," *Parade Magazine*, January 14, 1990, https://guncite.com/burger.html.

38. Nelson Lund, "The Second Amendment: Political Liberty and the Right to Self-Preservation," *Alabama Law Review* 39, 1 (1987): 103.

39. *Official Transcript: Proceedings before the Supreme Court of the United States* (Washington, DC: Alderson Reporting, 1989), 16.

40. *United States v. Verdugo-Urquidez*, 494 U.S. 259, 265 (1990).

41. *Perpich v. U.S. Dep't Def.*, 496 U.S. 334 (1990).

42. *Government and Setting Priorities of Federal Programs: Hearings before the Subcomms. of the H. Comm. on Appropriations*, 104th Cong., 1st sess. (January 19, 1995) (statement of James H. Warner, Assistant General Counsel, National Rifle Association), 983–987.

43. Sanford Levinson, "The Embarrassing Second Amendment," *Yale Law Journal* 99, 3 (December 1989): 6.

44. Robert J. Cottrol and Raymond T. Diamond, "The Second Amendment: Toward an Afro-Americanist Reconsideration," *Georgetown Law Journal* 80, 2 (1991): 309–362; William Van Alstyne, "The Second Amendment and the Personal Right to Arms," *Duke Law Journal* 43, 6 (1994): 1236–1255; Joyce Malcolm, *To Keep and Bear Arms: The Origins of An Anglo-American Right* (Cambridge, MA: Harvard University Press, 1996).

45. Akhil Reed Amar, "Putting the Second Amendment Second: Reframing the Constitutional Debate over Gun Control," *Slate*, March 17, 2008, https://slate.com/news-and-politics/2008/03/reframing-the-constitutional-debate-over-gun-control.html.

46. Michael Kinsley, "Slicing Up the Second Amendment," *Washington Post*, February 8, 1990.

## CHAPTER 6: ONE CASE, MANY CONTROVERSIES

1. Josh Sugarmann, *Assault Weapons in America* (Washington, DC: Firearms Policy Project of the Violence Policy Center, 1988), conclusion.

2. Jay Barmann, "Regarding the 1989 School Yard Shooting that Prompted California to Ban Assault Weapons," *SF News*, July 30, 2019, https://sfist.com/2019/07/30/regarding-the-1989-schoolyard-shooting-that-prompted-california-to-ban-assault-weapons/.

3. Gary Kleck, *Targeting Guns: Firearms and Their Control* (New York: Aldine de Gruyter, 1997), 41–42, 112–117, 141–143. FBI statistics also indicate the relatively rare use of rifles in homicides. In 1994, the year the assault weapons ban was enacted, handguns were used in 13,510, or nearly 83 percent, of all homicides. All other types of firearms including shotguns and rifles, of which assault-style rifles are a subset, were used in 2,830, or some 17 percent, of homicides. In 2004, the year the ban expired, handguns were used in 8,330, or 78 percent, of homicides. In that year shotguns and rifles were used in 2,350, or 22 percent, of homicides. US Department of Justice, Office of Justice Programs Statistics, *Special Report on Firearms Violence, 1993–2011*, May 2013.

4. William J. Vizzard, "The Current and Future State of Gun Policy in the United States," *Journal of Law and Criminology* 104, 4 (Fall 2014): 879–904, 884–885.

5. Carl Bogus, "The Second Amendment: Symposium on the Second Amendment: Fresh Looks," *Chicago-Kent Law Review* 76, 1, (2000): 3–26.

6. See, inter alia., Clayton Cramer, "Gun Scarcity in the Early Republic, http://www.claytoncramer.com/gunscarcity.pdf; Robert H. Churchill, "Gun Ownership in Early America: A Survey of Manuscript Militia Returns," *William and Mary Quarterly* 60, 3 (July 2003): 615–642; James Lindgren, "Book Review: Fall from Grace, *Arming America* and the Bellesiles Scandal," *Yale Law Journal* 111 (2002): 2195–2249.

7. *First Monday*, episode "Showdown," aired April 22, 2002.

8. Whether the Second Amendment Secures an Individual Right, 28 Op. O.L.C. 126 (2004).

9. 18 U.S.C. § 922 (g)(8); *United States v. Emerson*, 270 F.3d 203 (5th Cir. 2001), *cert. denied* 536 U.S. 907 (2002); Nelson Lund, "The Ends of Second Amendment Jurisprudence: Firearms Disabilities and Domestic Violence Restraining Orders," *Texas Journal of Law and Politics* 4 (1999): 157, 159–162.

10. *United States v. Emerson*, 46 F. Supp. 2d 598, 610–611, 611 (N.D. Tex. 1999), *rev'd* 270 F.3d 203 (5th Cir. 2001).

11. *Emerson*, 270 F.3d at 264–265.

12. *SCOTUS Blog: Supreme Court Procedure*, 536 U.S. 907 (2002).

13. *Emerson*, 270 F.3d at 264–265.

14. *Silveira v. Lockyer*, 312 F.3d 1052 (9th Cir. 2003).

15. Adam Winkler, *Gunfight: The Battle over the Right to Bear Arms in America* (New York: W. W. Norton, 2011), 45–52.

16. William H. Rehnquist, *The Supreme Court* (New York: Knopf, 2001), 232–233; Winkler, *Gunfight*, 52.

17. Winkler, 52–54; Cato Institute, website pages for Clark Neily and Robert Levy.

18. Winkler, 54–55; Halbrook's resume shows that he argued three cases before the Supreme Court before his encounter with Neily and Levy in 2003: *Castillo v. United States*, 530 U.S. 120 (2000); *Printz v. United States* 521 U.S. 898 (1997); and *United States v.*

*Thompson/Center Arms Co.* 504 U.S. 505 (1992) See Halbrook's resume at www.stephen halbrook.com.

19. Winkler, 55–56.

20. Winkler, 56–57.

21. Winkler, 43, 60; Complaint, *Parker v. District of Columbia,* 311 F. Supp. 2d 103 (D.D.C. 2004) (No. CIV.A.03–0213 EGS).

22. Complaint, *Seegars v. Ashcroft,* 297 F. Supp. 2d 201 (D.D.C. 2004) (No. CIV.A.03–834(RBW)).

23. Complaint, *Seegars v. Ashcroft.*

24. Winkler, *Gunfight,* 60–61.

25. Complaint, *Seegars v. Ashcroft,* 297 F. Supp. 2d 201 (D.D.C. 2004) (No. CIV.A.03–834(RBW)).

26. Complaint, *Seegars v. Ashcroft.*

27. Complaint, *Seegars v. Ashcroft.*

28. *Parker v. District of Columbia,* 311 F. Supp. 2d 103 (D.D.C. 2004).

29. 396 F 3rd 1248 (2005);413 F. 3rd 1 (2005); 126 S.Ct. 1187 (2006).

30. 478 F.3rd 370 (2007): Winkler, *Gunfight,* 118–119.

31. Winkler, 91–92.

32. *Parker,* 478 F.3d at 395.

33. *Parker,* 478 F.3d at 397–400 ("Just as the District may not flatly ban the keeping of a handgun in the home, obviously it may not prevent it from being moved throughout one's house. Such a restriction would negate the lawful use upon which the right was premised—*i.e.,* self-defense.").

34. *Parker,* 478 F.3d at 401.

35. *Parker,* 478 F.3d at 405–409 (Henderson, C.J., dissenting).

36. Antonin Scalia, *A Matter of Interpretation: Federal Courts and the Law* (Princeton, NJ: Princeton University Press, 1997).

37. *Printz v. United States,* 521 U.S. 898, 935–941.

38. Confirmation Hearing on the Nomination of John G. Roberts, Jr. to be Chief Justice of the United States Before the S. Comm. on the Judiciary, 109th Cong. 55 (2005).

39. Confirmation Hearing on the Nomination of John G. Roberts, Jr., 126–127; Historical Society of the District of Columbia Circuit, Oral History of Alan Morrison: Eleventh Interview—June 27, 2008; 552 U.S. 1035 (2007).

40. Winkler, *Gunfight,* 92; Mark Obie, "He Won the Supreme Court Case that Transformed Gun Rights. But Dick Heller Is a Hard Man to Please," *The Trace,* March 20, 2016, https://www.thetrace.org/2016/03/dick-heller-second-amendment-hero-abolish-gun -regulation/; 328 F.3d 567, 569–570 (9th Cir. 2003) (Kozinski, J., dissenting) (dissenting from denial of rehearing en banc). Judge Kozinski dissenting from denial of rehearing en banc, esp. at 569–570.

41. Winkler, 145–148.

42. Dellinger scored a partial victory in this case. On the issue of punitive damages, the Court held that the award was excessive and should be limited to the amount of

compensatory damages, which amounted to $507.5 million, or roughly 20 percent of the original verdict. *Exxon Shipping Co. v. Baker*, 554 U.S. 471, 515 (2008).

43. George Mason University Moot Court, March 6, 2008. Record kept by Stephen P. Halbrook. Copy in possession of authors.

44. Alan Gura, "Briefing the Second Amendment before the Supreme Court," *Duquesne Law Review* 47, 2 (2009): 225–279, 235.

45. Brief for Petitioner, at *8–*11, *District of Columbia v. Heller*, 554 U.S. 570 (2008) (No. 07–290), 2008 WL 102223.

46. Brief for Respondent, at *5, *52, *65, *District of Columbia v. Heller*, 554 U.S. 570 (2008) (No. 07–290), 2008 WL 102223.

47. Brief for Respondent, at *54–*62. Strict scrutiny is applied in many areas of constitutional doctrine, and there are some variations in its application. See Richard H. Fallon Jr., "Strict Scrutiny," *UCLA Law Review* 54 (2007): 1267.

48. Ilya Shapiro, "Friends of the Second Amendment: A Walk through the Amicus Briefs in *D.C. v. Heller*," *Journal of Firearms and Public Policy* 20 (2008): 15–41.

49. Brief of Professors of Criminal Justice as Amicus Curiae in Support of Petitioners; Brief of Criminologists, Social Scientists, Other Distinguished Scholars and the Claremont Institute as Amicus Curiae in Support of Respondent; Brief for Professors of Linguistics and English Dennis E. Barron, Ph.D., Richard W. Bailey, Ph.D. and Jeffrey P. Kaplan, Ph.D. in Support of Petitioners, *District of Columbia v. Heller*, 554 U.S. 570 (2008) (No. 07–290).

50. Transcript of Oral Argument at 3, *District of Columbia v. Heller*, 554 U.S. 570 (2008) (No. 07–290).

51. Transcript of Oral Argument, at 4–5.

52. Transcript of Oral Argument, at 4–5.

53. Transcript of Oral Argument, at 5, 8.

54. Transcript of Oral Argument, at 7–8.

55. Transcript of Oral Argument, at 10.

56. Article I, § 8, cl. 15–16 gives Congress the power to "provide for calling forth the Militia" for certain purposes and "to provide for organizing, arming, and disciplining, the Militia, and for governing such Part of them as may be employed in the Service of the United States." States retain the power to appoint officers and "the Authority of training the Militia according to the discipline prescribed by Congress."

57. Transcript of Oral Argument, at 10–11, *District of Columbia v. Heller*, 554 U.S. 570 (2008) (No. 07–290).

58. Transcript of Oral Argument, at 14–15.

59. Transcript of Oral Argument, at 16–21.

60. Transcript of Oral Argument, at 21–24.

61. Transcript of Oral Argument, at 21–24.

62. Transcript of Oral Argument, at 24–25.

63. Transcript of Oral Argument, at 24–25.

64. Transcript of Oral Argument, at 25–27.

65. The biographical information is taken from Kevin Sack, "Lawyer Opposing

Health Law Is Familiar Face to the Justices," *New York Times*, October 26, 2011, available at https://www.nytimes.com/2011/10/27/us/politics/paul-d-clements-latest-high-profile -cases.html.

66. Sack, "Lawyer Opposing Health Law Is Familiar Face to the Justices."

67. The information in this paragraph draws on Linda Greenhouse, "Gun Case Causes Bush Administration Rift," *New York Times*, March 17, 2008, https://www.ny times.com/2008/03/17/washington/17scotus.html.

68. Transcript of Oral Argument, at 28, 29, *District of Columbia v. Heller*, 554 U.S. 570 (2008) (No. 07–290).

69. Transcript of Oral Argument, at 28.

70. Transcript of Oral Argument, at 29–30.

71. Transcript of Oral Argument, at 30–31.

72. Transcript of Oral Argument, at 32–35.

73. Transcript of Oral Argument, at 34–35.

74. Transcript of Oral Argument, at 34–35.

75. Transcript of Oral Argument, at 36–38.

76. Transcript of Oral Argument, at 39–40.

77. Transcript of Oral Argument, at 41–42.

78. Transcript of Oral Argument, at 41–43.

79. Transcript of Oral Argument, at 41–43.

80. Transcript of Oral Argument, at 45–46.

81. Transcript of Oral Argument, at 46–47.

82. Transcript of Oral Argument, at 46–50.

83. Transcript of Oral Argument, at 50–51.

84. Transcript of Oral Argument, at 50–53.

85. Transcript of Oral Argument, at 53–54.

86. Transcript of Oral Argument, at 53–55.

87. Transcript of Oral Argument, at 53–55.

88. Transcript of Oral Argument, at 55–56.

89. Transcript of Oral Argument, at 56–58.

90. Transcript of Oral Argument, at 56–58.

91. Transcript of Oral Argument, at 59; Winkler, *Gunfight*, 229–230.

92. Transcript of Oral Argument, at 61.

93. Transcript of Oral Argument, at 62–63.

94. Transcript of Oral Argument, at 63–64.

95. Transcript of Oral Argument, at 64–65.

96. Transcript of Oral Argument, at 66–69.

97. Transcript of Oral Argument, at 71–72.

98. Transcript of Oral Argument, at 73–76.

99. Transcript of Oral Argument, at 76–77.

100. Transcript of Oral Argument, at 76–78.

101. Transcript of Oral Argument, at 76–81.

102. Transcript of Oral Argument, at 82–84.

103. Transcript of Oral Argument, at 85.

104. Transcript of Oral Argument, at 86, 89–90.

## CHAPTER 7: A SILENCE BROKEN

1. William H. Rehnquist, *The Supreme Court* (New York: Knopf, 2001), 252–253, 259–264.

2. See, generally, John Paul Stevens, *The Making of a Justice: Reflections on My First 94 Years* (New York: Little, Brown, 2019).

3. See chapter 3, notes 62–65 and accompanying text.

4. Antonin Scalia, "Originalism: The Lesser Evil," *University of Cincinnati Law Review* 57 (1989): 849, 854.

5. Scalia, "Originalism," 864.

6. *District of Columbia v. Heller*, 554 U.S. 570, 573–576, 577 (2008).

7. *Heller*, 554 U.S. at 577–578.

8. *Heller*, 554 U.S. at 578–588.

9. *Heller*, 554 U.S. at 581.

10. *Heller*, 554 U.S. at 581.

11. *Heller*, 554 U.S. at 582.

12. *Heller*, 554 U.S. at 583–586.

13. *Heller*, 554 U.S. at 589–590.

14. *Heller*, 554 U.S. at 592–594.

15. *Heller*, 554 U.S. at 597–598.

16. *Heller*, 554 U.S. at 598–599.

17. *Heller*, 554 U.S. at 598–599.

18. *Heller*, 554 U.S. at 606–614.

19. *Heller*, 554 U.S. at 614–616.

20. *Heller*, 554 U.S. at 617.

21. *Heller*, 554 U.S. at 619–620.

22. *Heller*, 554 U.S. at 622, 637.

23. *Heller*, 554 U.S. at 625–626.

24. *Heller*, 554 U.S. at 626.

25. *Heller*, 554 U.S. at 626–627.

26. *Heller*, 554 U.S. at 627 n26.

27. *Heller*, 554 U.S. at 627–628.

28. *Heller*, 554 U.S. at 628–629. See especially note 27. In constitutional doctrine, rational basis scrutiny merely requires a law to be "rationally related" to a legitimate governmental interest. It is the lowest level of constitutional scrutiny.

29. *Heller*, 554 U.S. at 634.

30. *Heller*, 554 U.S. at 635.

31. *Heller*, 554 U.S. at 636.

32. *Heller*, 554 U.S. at 637.

33. *Heller,* 554 U.S. at 638.

34. *Heller,* 554 U.S. at 640–643.

35. *Heller,* 554 U.S. at 645–646.

36. *Heller,* 554 U.S. at 646–648.

37. *Heller,* 554 U.S. at 661–662.

38. *Heller,* 554 U.S. at 662–665.

39. *Heller,* 554 U.S. at 666–670.

40. *Heller,* 554 U.S. at 677.

41. *Heller,* 554 U.S. at 679.

42. *Heller,* 554 U.S. at 679.

43. *Heller,* 554 U.S. at 681–689 (Breyer, J., dissenting).

44. *Heller,* 554 U.S. at 689–690.

45. *Heller,* 554 U.S. at 722.

46. Nelson Lund, "The Second Amendment, *Heller,* and Original Jurisprudence," *UCLA Law Review* 56 (2009): 1343–1376.

47. For a discussion of eighteenth-century restrictions, see Saul Cornell, *A Well-Regulated Militia: The Founding Fathers and the Origins of Gun Control in America* (New York: Oxford University Press, 2006), 26–30.

48. *Heller,* 554 U.S. at 582.

49. *Kennedy v. Louisiana,* 554 U.S. 407 (2008).

50. See, e.g., Artemus Ward and David L. Weiden, *Sorcerers' Apprentices: 100 Years of Law Clerks and the United States Supreme Court* (New York: New York University Press, 2006).

51. Stevens, *The Making of a Justice,* 481–486.

52. See chapter 1 and footnotes 3, 4, 7, 43, and 45 and accompanying text.

53. "Lock and Load," *New York Times,* June 27, 2008, A18.

54. "Lock and Load," A18.

55. Erwin Chemerinsky, "The Supreme Court Gun Fight: A Case of Conservative Activism," *Los Angeles Times,* June 27, 2008, A27; Saul Cornell, "Originalism on Trial: The Use and Abuse of History in *District of Columbia v. Heller,*" *Ohio State Law Journal* 69 (2008): 625, 632.

56. Patrick Leahy, "Reaction on Supreme Court Decision in District of Columbia v. Heller," *Office of Patrick Leahy,* June 6, 2008, https://www.leahy.senate.gov/press /reaction-on-supreme-court-decision-in-district-of-columbia-v-heller.

57. Anne Davies, "Cities Targeted as DC Gun Ban Ends," The Age, June 28, 2008, https://www.theage.com.au/world/cities-targeted-as-dc-gun-ban-ends-20080627–2y4a .html.

58. Adam J. White, "Wilkinson and Posner, Dissenting: Two Conservative Judges Challenge Justice Scalia," *Weekly Standard,* December 15, 2008.

59. David Gans and Doug Kendall, "Heller Originalism and the Revival of the Privileges or Immunities Clause," Balkinization, December 11, 2008, https://balkin.blogspot .com/2008/12/heller-originalism-and-revival-of.html.

## CHAPTER 8: *MCDONALD*

1. *McDonald v. Chicago*, 2008 WL 5111112 (N.D. Ill. 2008).

2. "The Second Amendment's Reach," *New York Times*, March 2, 2010, https://www.nytimes.com/2010/03/02/opinion/02tue1.html.

3. "The Second Amendment's Reach."

4. *National Rifle Ass'n of America v. Chicago*, 567 F.3d 856, at 856–859 (7th Cir. 2009), *rev'd sub nom* McDonald v. Chicago, 561 U.S. 742 (2010).

5. *National Rifle Ass'n of America v. Chicago*, 859.

6. *National Rifle Ass'n of America v. Chicago*, 860.

7. Lyle Denniston, "Second Amendment Drama: Act II," SCOTUSblog, February 25, 2010, https://www.scotusblog.com/2010/02/second-amendment-drama-act-ii/.

8. Under Rule 12 of the Court's rules of procedure, "parties interested, jointly, severally, or otherwise in a judgment may petition separately for a writ of certiorari" or may file a joint petition. Sup. Ct. R. 12.4. "When two or more judgments are sought to be reviewed on a writ of certiorari to the same court and involve identical or closely related questions, a single petition for a writ of certiorari covering all the judgments suffices." Ibid. The rule goes on to note that "all parties to the proceeding in the court whose judgment is sought to be reviewed are deemed parties entitled to file documents in this Court. . . . All parties other than the petitioner are considered respondents." Sup. Ct. R. 12.6.

9. Brief for Petitioner at 9–42, *McDonald v. Chicago*, 561 U.S. 742 (2010) (No. 08–1521), 2009 WL 4378912.

10. Brief for Petitioner at 42–72.

11. Brief for Respondents the National Rifle Ass'n of Am. et al. in Support of Petitioners, *McDonald v. Chicago* at 21, 561 U.S. 742 (2010) (No. 08–1521), 2009 WL 3844394.

12. Brief for Respondents in Support of Petitioners, 29.

13. Brief for Respondents in Support of Petitioners, 29.

14. Brief for Respondents in Support of Petitioners, 30.

15. Brief for Respondents in Support of Petitioners, 42–45.

16. Brief for Respondents City of Chicago and Village of Oak Park at 8, *McDonald v. Chicago*, 561 U.S. 742 (2010) (No. 08–1521), 2009 WL 5190478.

17. Brief for Respondents City of Chicago and Village of Oak Park, 31–40.

18. Brief for Respondents City of Chicago and Village of Oak Park, 42–79.

19. Brief of the State of California in Support of Petitioners, 2009 WL 1970176 (2009).

20. Brief of NAACP Legal Defense and Education Fund in Support of Neither Party, 209WL 4074858 (Appellate Brief).

21. Dale E. Ho, "Dodging a Bullet: *McDonald v. City of Chicago* and the Limits of Progressive Originalism," *William and Mary Bill of Rights Journal* 19 (2010): 369–417.

22. Motion of Respondents-Supporting-Petitioners for Dividing Argument, *McDonald v. Chicago*, 561 U.S. 742 (2010) (No. 08–1521). Under the Supreme Court's rules, parties are permitted to request divided argument by filing a motion with the Court that "set[s] out specifically and concisely why more than one attorney [for either side] should

be allowed to argue." Sup. Ct. R. 28.4. It further notes that "divided argument is not favored." Ibid., 1, 2.

23. Opposition to Motion of National Rifle Association, et al. for Divided Argument, *McDonald v. Chicago*, 561 U.S. 742 (2010) (No. 08–1521). (citing Sup. Ct. R. 12.4, 12.6).

24. Opposition to Motion of National Rifle Association, et al. for Divided Argument, 8–9.

25. Opposition to Motion of National Rifle Association, et al. for Divided Argument, 9.

26. Tony Mauro, "NRA Will Argue in Second Amendment Case," *The BLT: The Blog of LegalTimes,* January 25, 2010, https://legaltimes.typepad.com/blt/2010/01/nra-will-argue-in-second-amendment-case.html.

27. Mauro, "NRA Will Argue in Second Amendment Case."

28. Transcript of Oral Argument at 1–5, *McDonald v. Chicago*, 561 U.S. 742 (2010) (No. 08–1521), 2010 WL 710088.

29. Transcript of Oral Argument, 5–6.

30. Transcript of Oral Argument, 6–7.

31. Transcript of Oral Argument, 5–10.

32. Transcript of Oral Argument, 10–11.

33. Transcript of Oral Argument, 12–14.

34. Transcript of Oral Argument, 14–15.

35. Transcript of Oral Argument, 15–17.

36. Transcript of Oral Argument, 18.

37. 367 U.S. 643 (1961).

38. Transcript of Oral Argument at 20, *McDonald v. Chicago*, 561 U.S. 742 (No. 08–1521), 2010 WL 710088.

39. Transcript of Oral Argument, 20.

40. Transcript of Oral Argument, 21.

41. Transcript of Oral Argument, 21.

42. Transcript of Oral Argument, 21–23.

43. Transcript of Oral Argument, 27–28.

44. Transcript of Oral Argument, 29.

45. Transcript of Oral Argument, 29.

46. Transcript of Oral Argument, 30–31.

47. 391 U.S. 145 (1968) (incorporating the right to jury trial in criminal cases).

48. Transcript of Oral Argument at 31–32, *McDonald v. Chicago*, 561 U.S. 742 (No. 08–1521), 2010 WL 710088.

49. Transcript of Oral Argument, 32–33.

50. Transcript of Oral Argument, 35–36.

51. Transcript of Oral Argument, 35–36.

52. Transcript of Oral Argument, 39–40.

53. Transcript of Oral Argument, 40–41.

54. Transcript of Oral Argument, 42–43.

55. Transcript of Oral Argument, 43.

56. Transcript of Oral Argument, 44–46.

57. Transcript of Oral Argument, 52–53.

58. Transcript of Oral Argument, 53.

59. Transcript of Oral Argument, 53–54.

60. Transcript of Oral Argument, 57–58.

61. Transcript of Oral Argument, 58.

62. Transcript of Oral Argument, 60–63.

63. Transcript of Oral Argument, 63–64.

64. Jess Bravin, "Bow Ties Are Back (to Honor Justice Stevens)," *Wall Street Journal,* June 28, 2010, https://www.wsj.com/articles/BL-WB-21401; "A Bow-Tie Goodbye for Justice John Paul Stevens," Associated Press, June 28, 2010.

65. Mark V. Tushnet, *Out of Range: Why the Constitution Can't End the Battle over Guns* (New York: Oxford University Press, 2007), 44.

66. *McDonald v. Chicago,* 561 U.S. 742 (2010).

67. *McDonald v. Chicago,* 754–758.

68. *McDonald v. Chicago,* 754–758.

69. *McDonald v. Chicago,* 759–767.

70. *McDonald v. Chicago,* 768–770.

71. *McDonald v. Chicago,* 770–773.

72. *McDonald v. Chicago,* 775–776.

73. *McDonald v. Chicago,* 778–780.

74. *McDonald v. Chicago,* 778–780.

75. *McDonald v. Chicago,* 780–782.

76. *McDonald v. Chicago,* 781–782.

77. *McDonald v. Chicago,* 782–784.

78. *McDonald v. Chicago,* 784–785 (footnote omitted).

79. *McDonald v. Chicago,* 785–787.

80. *McDonald v. Chicago,* 791 (footnote omitted).

81. *McDonald v. Chicago,* 812.

82. *McDonald v. Chicago,* 805–859 (Thomas, J., concurring).

83. *McDonald v. Chicago,* 912–941 (Breyer, J., dissenting).

84. *McDonald v. Chicago,* 928–929 (Breyer, J., dissenting).

85. *McDonald v. Chicago,* 931–940 (Breyer, J., dissenting).

86. *McDonald v. Chicago,* 941 (Breyer, J., dissenting).

87. *McDonald v. Chicago,* 861 (Stevens, J., dissenting).

88. *McDonald v. Chicago,* 912 (Stevens, J., dissenting).

89. *McDonald v. Chicago,* 798 (Scalia, J., concurring).

90. *McDonald v. Chicago,* 798 (Scalia, J., concurring) (footnote omitted).

91. *McDonald v. Chicago,* 798–799 (Scalia, J., concurring).

92. *Timbs v. Indiana,* 586 U.S.__ (2019).

93. *Ramos v. Louisiana,* 140 S. Ct. 1390 (2020)

94. Glenn Harlan Reynolds, "The Second Amendment as Ordinary Constitutional Law," *Tennessee Law Review* 81 (2014): 407.

95. *Woollard et al v. Gallahger et al*, 712 F. 3rd 865 (2013); *Young v. Hawaii*, 992 F. 3rd 765 (2021).

96. *Moore v. Madigan*, 703 F. 3rd 933 (2012); *Wrenn v. District of Columbia*, 864 F. 3rd 650 (2017).

97. *Kolbe et al vs. Hogan et al*, 849 F. 3rd 114 (2017).

98. *Caetano v. Massachusetts*, 136 S. Ct. 1027 (2016) (per curiam).

99. *New York State Rifle and Pistol Association v. City of New York*, 140 S. Ct. 1525 (2020).

## CHAPTER 9: *BRUEN*, AN UNANTICIPATED EPILOGUE

1. *New York State Rifle and Pistol Association v. Beach* 354 F. Supp. 3rd 143 (2018); Jo Craven McGinty, "The Rich, the Famous and the Armed," *New York Times*, February 20, 2011, section MB, p. 1; Rocco Parascandola and Alison Gendar, "Lifestyles of the Rich and Packin': High-Profile Celebrities Seeking Gun Permits on the Rise," *New York Daily News*, September 27, 2010, https://www.nydailynews.com/new-york /lifestyles-rich-packin-high-profile-celebrities-seeking-guns-permits-rise-article-1.441377.

2. *Libertarian Party of Erie Co. v. Cuomo*, 970 F.3d 106, 127–29 (2nd Cir. 2020), *cert. denied* 141 S. Ct. 2797 (2021); *Kachalsky v. Westchester Co.*, 701 F.3d 81, 101 (2nd Cir. 2012), *cert. denied sub nom*; *Kachalsky v. Cacace*, 133 S. Ct. 1806 (2013).

3. *New York State Rifle & Pistol Ass'n, Inc. v. Beach*, 818 Fed App'x 99 (2nd Cir. 2020), *cert. granted sub nom*, *New York State Rifle & Pistol Ass'n, Inc. v. Corlett*, 141 S. Ct. 2566 (2021).

4. Brief for Petitioner, *New York Rifle & Pistol Ass'n, Inc. v. Bruen* (No. 20–843), 35.

5. Brief for Petitioner, *New York Rifle & Pistol Ass'n, Inc. v. Bruen*, 28–39.

6. Brief for Petitioner, *New York Rifle & Pistol Ass'n, Inc. v. Bruen*, 42.

7. Brief for Petitioner, *New York Rifle & Pistol Ass'n, Inc. v. Bruen*, 48.

8. Brief for Petitioner, *New York Rifle & Pistol Ass'n, Inc. v. Bruen*, 48.

9. Brief for Respondent, *New York Rifle & Pistol Ass'n, Inc. v. Bruen* (No. 20–843) at 20–31.

10. Brief for Respondent, *New York Rifle & Pistol Ass'n, Inc. v. Bruen*, 32, 36.

11. Brief for Respondent, *New York Rifle & Pistol Ass'n, Inc. v. Bruen*, 39–40.

12. Brief for Respondent, *New York Rifle & Pistol Ass'n, Inc. v. Bruen*, 43–45.

13. Brief for the United State as Amicus Curiae Supporting Respondents, *New York Rifle & Pistol Ass'n, Inc. v. Bruen* (No. 20–843).

14. Brief for the United State as Amicus Curiae Supporting Respondents, 28.

15. Reply Brief for Petitioner at 3–14, *New York Rifle & Pistol Ass'n, Inc. v. Bruen* (No. 20–843), at 3–14, 18–21.

16. *Brief of the Black Attorneys of Legal Aid, The Bronx Defenders, Brooklyn Defender Service et. al. as Amici Curiae in Support of Petitioners, New York State Rifle and Pistol Ass'n v. Bruen* (July 20, 2021) (No. 20–843) at 5.

17. Transcript of Oral Argument, *New York Rifle & Pistol Ass'n, Inc. v. Bruen,* (No. 20–843) at 4–6.

18. Transcript of Oral Argument, 7–8.

19. Transcript of Oral Argument, 9–10.

20. Transcript of Oral Argument, 11–13.

21. Transcript of Oral Argument, 15–17.

22. Transcript of Oral Argument, 17–23.

23. Transcript of Oral Argument, 25–27.

24. Transcript of Oral Argument, 27–31.

25. Transcript of Oral Argument, 32–33.

26. Transcript of Oral Argument, 34–35.

27. Transcript of Oral Argument, 38–39.

28. Transcript of Oral Argument, 46–47.

29. Transcript of Oral Argument, 52–55.

30. Transcript of Oral Argument, 59.

31. Transcript of Oral Argument, 61–63.

32. Transcript of Oral Argument, 67–74.

33. Transcript of Oral Argument, 77.

34. Transcript of Oral Argument, 80–85.

35. Transcript of Oral Argument, 86–87.

36. Transcript of Oral Argument, 88–90.

37. Transcript of Oral Argument, 99.

38. Transcript of Oral Argument, 104–107.

39. Transcript of Oral Argument, 108–110.

40. Transcript of Oral Argument, 115.

41. Transcript of Oral Argument, 117.

42. Transcript of Oral Argument, 118–121.

43. Transcript of Oral Argument, 122.

44. *New York Rifle & Pistol Ass'n, Inc. v. Bruen,* 142 S. Ct. 2111, 2130 (2022).

45. *Bruen,* 142 S. Ct. at 2132–2133.

46. *Bruen,* 142 S. Ct. at 2133.

47. *Bruen,* 142 S. Ct. at 2134–2135.

48. "Surety laws" required people thought to present a risk of breaching the peace to post bond in order to carry their weapons in public.

49. *Bruen,* 142 S. Ct. at 2150.

50. *Bruen,* 142 S. Ct. at 2155.

51. *Bruen,* 142 S. Ct. at 2156.

52. *Bruen,* 142 S. Ct. at 2156.

53. *Bruen,* 142 S. Ct. at 2161–2162 (Kavanaugh, J., concurring); ibid., at 2162–2163 (Barrett, J., concurring).

54. *Bruen,* 142 S. Ct. at 2167 (Breyer, J., dissenting).

55. *Bruen,* 142 S. Ct. at 2170–2171 (Breyer, J., dissenting).

56. *Bruen,* 142 S. Ct. at 2172 (Breyer, J., dissenting).

57. *Bruen*, 142 S. Ct. at 2174 (Breyer, J., dissenting) (criticizing the Court for "refus[ing] to consider whether New York has a *compelling* interest in regulating the concealed carriage of handguns or whether New York's law is *narrowly tailored* to achieve that interest.") (emphasis added).

58. *Bruen*, 142 S. Ct. at 2181.

59. *Bruen*, 142 S. Ct. at 2181.

60. *Bruen*, 142 S. Ct. at 2190.

61. Jacob Sullum, "Scotus Vacates 4 Decisions Upholding Gun Control Laws Whose Constitutionality Now Looks Doubtful," *Reason*, July 1, 2022, https//reason.com /2022/07/01.

62. "RE: Public Carry Licensing under Hawai'i Law Following *New York State Rifle and Pistol Association v. Bruen*," State of Hawaii, Department of the Attorney General, July 7, 2022, Op. No. 22–02; "Governor Hogan Directs Maryland State Police to Suspend 'Good and Substantial Reason for Wear and Carry Permits," Office of Governor Larry Hogan, maryland.gov; "Understanding Recent Changes to New York's Gun Laws," New York State Attorney General, https://ag.ny.gov/new-york-gun-laws (accessed March 4, 2023); "Governor Hochul Signs Landmark Legislation to Strengthen Gun Law and Bolster Restrictions on Concealed Carry Weapons in Response to Reckless Supreme Court Decision," July 1, 2022, http://www.governor.ny.gov/news/governor-hochul-signs-land mark legislation-strengthen gun law-and-bolster restrictions.

63. "Attorney General James Files Lawsuit to Dissolve NRA," https://ag.ny.gov /press-release/2020/attorney-general-james-files-lawsuit-dissolve-nra.

64. Christopher Ingraham, "Nobody Knows How Many Members the NRA Has, but Its Tax Returns Offer Some Clues," *Washington Post*, February 26, 2018; Dave Gilson, "New Data Shows That the NRA's Trump Bump Has Evaporated," *Mother Jones*, January 24, 2021, https://www.motherjones.com/politics/2021/01/national-rifle-associa tion-membership-magazines/; "NRA to Defend against NY Attorney General in Manhattan, Drops Own Law Suit," CNBC, June 4, 2021, https://www.cnbc.com/2021/06/04 /nra-drops-lawsuit-against-ny-attorney-general-to-pursue-claims-in-manhattan.html.

# Bibliography

## PRIMARY SOURCES

*Court Cases*

*Andrews v. State,* 50 Tenn. 165 (Tenn. 1871).
*Aymette v. State,* 21 Tenn. (2 Hum.) 154 (Tenn. 1840).
*Barron v. Baltimore,* 32 U.S. 243 (1833).
*Caetano v. Massachusetts,* 136 S. Ct. 1027 (2016) (per curiam).
*Cases v. United States,* 131 F.2d 916 (1942).
*City of Salina v. Blaksley,* 72 Kan. 230 (1905).
*Civil Rights Cases,* 109 U.S. 3 (1883).
*District of Columbia v. Heller,* 552 U.S. 1035 (2007) (granting certiorari).
*District of Columbia v. Heller,* 554 U.S. 570 (2008).
*Dr. Bonham's Case,* 8 Co. Rep. 114 (1610).
*Dred Scott v. Sanford,* 60 U.S. (19 How.) 393 (1857).
*Duncan v. Louisiana,* 391 U.S. 145 (1968).
*Exxon Shipping Co. v. Baker,* 554 U.S. 471 (2008).
*Giles v. Harris,* 189 U.S. 475 (1903).
*Haney v. United States,* 536 U.S. 907 (2002) (denying certiorari).
*Kachalsky v. Westchester Co.* 701 F.3d 81, 101 (2nd Cir. 2012), *cert. denied sub nom Kachalsky v. Cacace,* 133 S. Ct. 1806 (2013).
*Kennedy v. Louisiana,* 554 U.S. 407 (2008).
*Kolbe et al vs. Hogan et al,* 849 F. 3rd 114 (2017).
*Libertarian Party of Erie Co. v. Cuomo,* 970 F.3d 106, 127–29 (2nd Cir. 2020), *cert. denied.* 141 S. Ct. 2797 (2021).
*Mapp v. Ohio,* 367 U.S. 643 (1961).
*McDonald v. Chicago,* 2008 WL 5111112 (N.D. Ill. 2008).
*McDonald v. City of Chicago,* 130 S.Ct. 320 (2010).
*Moore v. Madigan,* 703 F. 3rd 933 (2012).
*Muller v. Oregon,* 208 U.S. 412 (1908).
*National Rifle Ass'n of America v. Chicago,* 567 F.3d 856 (7th Cir. 2009), *rev'd sub nom* McDonald v. Chicago, 561 U.S. 742 (2010).
*New York State Rifle and Pistol Association v. Beach,* 354 F. Supp. 3rd 143 (2018).
*New York State Rifle & Pistol Ass'n, Inc. v. Beach,* 818 Fed App'x 99 (2nd Cir. 2020), *cert. granted sub nom. New York State Rifle & Pistol Ass'n, Inc. v. Corlett,* 141 S. Ct. 2566 (2021).
*New York State Rifle & Pistol Ass'n, Inc. v. Bruen,* 142. S.Ct. 2111, 2126 (June 23, 2022).
*New York State Rifle and Pistol Association v. City of New York,* 140 S. Ct. 1525 (2020).
*Nunn v. Georgia,* 1 Georgia (Kelly) 243 (Ga. 1846).

*Parker v. District of Columbia*, 311 F. Supp. 2d 103 (D.D.C. 2004).

*Parker v. District of Columbia*, 478 F.3d 370 (D.C. Cir., 2007).

*Perpich, et. al., v. Dept. of Defense, et. al.*, 496 U.S. 334 (1990).

*Presser v. Illinois*, 116 U.S. 252, 265–266 (1886).

*Printz v. United States*, 521 U.S. 898 (1997).

*Ramos v. Louisiana*, 140 S.Ct. 1390 (2020).

*Seegars v. Gonzales*, 396 F 3rd 1248 (D.C. Cir., 2005).

*Seegars v. Gonzales*, 413 F. 3rd 1 (D.C. Cir., 2005) (denying petition for rehearing *en banc*).

*Seegars v. Gonzales*, 126 S.Ct. 1187 (2006).

*Silveira v. Lockyer*, 312 F.3d 1052 (9th Cir. 2003).

*Silveira v. Lockyer*, 328 F.3d 567 (9th Cir. 2003) (denying petition for rehearing *en banc*).

*Slaughter-House Cases* (83 U.S.[16 Wall.]) 36.

*State v. Buzzard*, 4 Ark. (Pike) 18 (Ark. 1842).

*Timbs v. Indiana*, 586 U.S.__ (2019).

*United States v. Cruikshank*, 92 U.S. 542 (1875).

*United States v. Emerson*, 46 F. Supp. 2d 598, 610–11, 611 (N.D. Tex. 1999), *rev'd* 270 F.3d 203 (5th Cir. 2001).

*United States v. Emerson*, 270 F.3d 203 (5th Cir. 2001), *cert. denied* 536 U.S. 907 (2002).

*United States v. Miller*, 307 U.S. 174 (1939).

*United States v. Tot*, 131 F.2d 261 (1942).

*Watson v. Stone*, 148 Fla. 516 (1941).

*Wickard v. Filburn*, 315 U.S. 110 (1942).

*Woollard et al v. Gallagher et al.*, 712 F. 3rd 865 (2013).

*Wrenn v. District of Columbia*, 864 F. 3rd 650 (2017).

*Young v. Hawaii*, 992 F. 3rd 765 (2021).

Court Briefs, Motions, and Oral Arguments

Brandeis, Louis. *Brief for the State of Oregon in Muller v. Oregon* (1907).

Brief of the Black Attorneys of Legal Aid, The Bronx Defenders, Brooklyn Defender Service et. al. as Amici Curiae in Support of Petitioners at 5, *New York State Rifle and Pistol Ass'n v. Bruen* (July 20, 2021) (No. 20–843).

Brief of Criminologists, Social Scientists, Other Distinguished Scholars and the Claremont Institute as Amicus Curiae in Support of Respondent, *District of Columbia v. Heller*, 554 U.S. 570 (2008) (No. 07–290).

Brief of NAACP Legal Defense and Education Fund in Support of Neither Party, 2009 WL 4074858 (Appellate Brief).

Brief for Petitioner, *District of Columbia v. Heller*, 554 U.S. 570 (2008) (No. 07–290), 2008 WL 102223.

Brief for Petitioner, *McDonald v. Chicago*, 561 U.S. 742 (2010) (No. 08–1521), 2009 WL 4378912.

Brief for Petitioner, *Tot v. United* States, 319 U.S. 463 (1943) (No. 569).

Brief of Professors of Criminal Justice as Amicus Curiae in Support of Petitioners, *District of Columbia v. Heller*, 554 U.S. 570 (2008) (No. 07–290).

Brief for Professors of Linguistics and English Dennis E. Barron, PhD, Richard W. Bailey, PhD, and Jeffrey P. Kaplan, PhD, in Support of Petitioners, *District of Columbia v. Heller*, 554 U.S. 570 (2008) (No. 07–290).

Brief for Respondent, *District of Columbia v. Heller*, 554 U.S. 570 (2008) (No. 07–290), 2008 WL 102223.

Brief for Respondent, *New York Rifle & Pistol Ass'n, Inc. v. Bruen* (No. 20–843).

Brief for Respondents City of Chicago and Village of Oak Park at 8, *McDonald v. Chicago*, 561 U.S. 742 (2010) (No. 08–1521), 2009 WL 5190478.

Brief for Respondents the National Rifle Association of America, et al. in Support of Petitioners, (No. 08–1521), 2009 WL 3844394 (Appellate Petition, Motion and Filing).

Brief of the State of California in Support of Petitioners, *McDonald v. Chicago*, 561 U.S. 742 (2010) 2009 WL 1970176 (2009).

Brief for the United States, *United States v. Miller*, 307 U.S. 174 (No. 696) (1939).

Brief for the United State as Amicus Curiae Supporting Respondents, *New York Rifle & Pistol Ass'n, Inc. v. Bruen* (No. 20–843).

Complaint, *Parker v. District of Columbia*, 311 F. Supp. 2d 103 (D.D.C. 2004) (No. CIV.A.03–0213 EGS).

Complaint, *Seegars v. Ashcroft*, 297 F. Supp. 2d 201 (D.D.C. 2004) (No. CIV.A.03–834(RBW)).

Motion of Respondents-Supporting-Petitioners for Dividing Argument, *McDonald v. Chicago*, 561 U.S. 742 (2010) (No. 08–1521).

Opposition to Motion of National Rifle Association, et al. for Divided Argument, *McDonald v. Chicago*, 561 U.S. 742 (2010) (No. 08–1521) (citing Sup. Ct. R. 12.4, 12.6).

Reply Brief for Petitioner at 3–14, 18–21, *New York Rifle & Pistol Ass'n, Inc. v. Bruen* (No. 20–843).

Transcript of Oral Argument at 3, *District of Columbia v. Heller*, 554 U.S. 570 (2008) (No. 07–290).

Transcript of Oral Argument, *McDonald v. Chicago*, 561 U.S. 742 (2010) (No. 08–1521), 2010 WL 710088.

Transcript of Oral Argument, *New York Rifle & Pistol Ass'n, Inc. v. Bruen*, (No. 20–843).

*Supreme Court Rules of Procedure*

12.4, 12.6, *Review on Certiorari: How Sought; Parties.*

28.4, *Oral Argument.*

*British Government Documents*

An Act Declaring the Rights and Liberties of the Subject and Settling the Succession of the Crown (English Bill of Rights of 1689). The Avalon Project: Documents in

Law History and Diplomacy, http://Avalon.law.yale.edu/17th_century/England
.asp.

*Congressional Hearing Testimonies*

*Hearings Before a Subcommittee of the Committee on Commerce, United States Senate,
Seventy Third Congress, Second Session on S.885, S.2258 (Bills to Regulate Commerce in
Firearms and S. 3680)*, May 28 and 29, 1934 (Washington, DC, 1934).
*H.R. 9066: Hearing Before the Committee on Ways and Means*, 73rd Cong. (1934) (state-
ment of J. Weston Allen, Chairman, National Crime Commission).
*H.R. 9066: Hearing Before the Committee on Ways and Means*, 73rd Cong. (1934) (state-
ment of Homer Cummings, Attorney General of the United States).
*H.R. 9066: Hearing Before the Committee on Ways and Means*, 73rd Cong. (1934) (state-
ment of Karl T. Frederick, President, National Rifle Association of America).
*H.R. 9066: Hearing Before the Committee on Ways and Means*, 73rd Cong. (1934) (state-
ment of Charles Imlay, representing the National Conference on Uniform Law).
*H.R. 9066: Hearing Before the Committee on Ways and Means*, 73rd Cong. (1934) (state-
ment of Joseph Keenan, Assistant Attorney General of the United States).
*H.R. 9066: Hearing Before the Committee on Ways and Means*, 73rd Cong. (1934) (state-
ment of Milton A. Reckord, Adjutant General of the State of Maryland, Executive
Vice President of the National Rifle Association).
S. Hrg. 109–158, *Confirmation Hearing on the Nomination of John G. Roberts, Jr. to be Chief
Justice of the United States Before the S. Comm. on the Judiciary*, 109th Cong. 55 (2005).

*Federal Government Documents*

Bureau of the Census, U.S. Department of Commerce. Statistical History of the United
States from Colonial Times to the Present (1976).
Centers for Disease Control and Prevention, National Center for Health Statistics.
"Compressed Mortality File 1968–1978. CDC WONDER Online Database, compiled
from Compressed Mortality File CMF 1968–1988, Series 20, No. 2A, 2000, accessed
November 7, 2022, http://wonder.cdc.gov/cmf-icd8.html.
"Chapter 10: Control of Firearms." In *The Challenge of Crime in a Free Society: A Report
by the President's Commission on Law Enforcement and the Administration of Justice*,
239–244. Washington, DC: Government Printing Office, 1967.
*The Congressional Globe: Containing the First Session of the Thirty-Ninth Congress.* F & J
Rives, ed. (Washington, DC, 1866), 1839.
*Congressional Record (Senate)*
Doyle, Vincent. *The Second Amendment as a Limitation on Federal Firearms Legislation.*
Washington, DC: Library of Congress Legislative Reference Service, 1968.
H. Rep. No. 1780 (1934).

Leahy, Patrick. "Reaction on Supreme Court Decision in District of Columbia v. Heller." Office of Patrick Leahy, June 6, 2008, https://www.leahy.senate.gov/press /reaction-on-supreme-court-decision-in-district-of-columbia-v-heller.

Official Transcript: Proceedings before the Supreme Court of the United States. Washington, DC: Alderson Reporting Co., 1989.

*Report of the National Advisory Commission on Civil Disorders.* Washington, DC: Government Printing Office, 1968.

Report of the President's Commission on the Assassination of President John F. Kennedy. Washington, D.C.: Government Printing Office, 1964.

United States Coast Guard. The Coast Guard at War: The Temporary Component of the Coast Guard Reserve. Washington, DC: Coast Guard Public Information Division, 1948.

United States Constitution. Article 1, Section 8, §§ 15–16.

US Census Bureau. 1920 Census, "Urban and Rural Population Metropolitan Districts and Center of Population," http://www2.census.gov/prod2/decennial/docu ments/16440598v2cho2.pdf.

US Congress. *Congressional Record* 87, pt. 6. 77th Cong., 1st sess., 1941.

US Department of the Army. "Operator and Organizational Maintenance Manual Including Repair Parts and Special Tools List: M-1 Garand," March 17, 1969.

US Department of Justice. "Whether the Second Amendment Secures an Individual Right." 28 Op. O.L.C. 126 (2004).

US Department of Justice, Office of Justice Programs Statistics. *Special Report on Firearms Violence, 1993–2011.* Washington, DC, May 2013.

US Department of Veterans Affairs. "America's Wars." Accessed November 6, 2022, https://www.va.gov/opa/publications/factsheets/fs_americas_wars.pdf.

US Department of War. *Basic Field Manual: U.S. Carbine, Caliber .30, M1.* Washington, DC: Government Printing Office, 1942.

*Congressional Acts*

1. Stat. 271 (1792) ("An Act more effectually to provide for the National Defence by establishing "an Uniform Militia throughout the United States").

Enforcement Act of 1870, 16 Stat. 140 (1870).

Firearms Owners' Protection Act of 1986, Public Law 99–308, U.S. Statutes at Large 100 (1986): 449–461.

*Gun Control Act of 1968*, Public Law 90–618, *U.S. Statutes at Large* 82 (1968): 1213–1236.

Violence Against Women Act, 18 U.S.C. § 922 (g)(8).

*State Government Documents and Administrative Materials*

Arkansas State Constitution, ratified 1836 (http://ahc.digital-ar.org/cdm/ref/collection /p16790coll1/id/8).

"Attorney General James Files Lawsuit to Dissolve NRA." Released August 6, 2020, https://ag.ny.gov/press-release/2020/attorney-general-james-files-lawsuit-dissolve-nra.

*Certain Offenses of Freedmen. Laws of Mississippi.* 1, 165 (November 29, 1865).

"Governor Hochul Signs Landmark Legislation to Strengthen Gun Law and Bolster Restrictions on Concealed Carry Weapons in Response to Reckless Supreme Court Decision." July 1, 2022, http://www.governor.ny.gov/news/governor-hochul-signs-landmark legislation-strengthen gun law-and-bolster restrictions.

"Governor Hogan Directs Maryland State Police to Suspend 'Good and Substantial Reason for Wear and Carry Permits." Office of Governor Larry Hogan, maryland.gov.

"Public Carry Licensing under Hawai'i Law Following *New York State Rifle and Pistol Association v. Bruen.*" State of Hawaii, Department of the Attorney General, July 7, 2022, Op. No. 22–02.

Tennessee State Constitution, Article I, Section XXVI, http://tngenweb.org/law/constitution1835.html.

"Understanding Recent Changes to New York's Gun Laws." New York State Attorney General, https://ag.ny.gov/new-york-gunlaws.

*Letters*

Frank C. Daniel to John F. Kennedy, letter, April 19, 1961. Papers of John F. Kennedy, John F. Kennedy Presidential Library. Accessed November 6, 2022, https://www.jfklibrary.org/asset-viewer/archives/JFKPOF/131/JFKPOF-131-001.

*Newspapers, Magazines, and Military Periodicals*

*Baltimore Sun*
*Chicago Tribune*
*Guns* (magazine)
*Los Angeles Times*
*New York Daily News*
*New York Times*
*Parade Magazine*
*SF News*
*Sun-Telegram* (San Bernardino, CA)
*Wall Street Journal*
*Washington Post*
*Weekly Standard*

*Newspaper and Magazine Articles*

"Bargains in Guns at the Pawnshops." *New York Times*, August 30, 1911.

Barker, Karlyn, and Paul W. Valentine. "Effort to Kill D.C. Gun Law Hits Snag." *Washington Post*, September 18, 1976.

Barmann, Jay. "Regarding the 1989 School Yard Shooting that Prompted California to Ban Assault Weapons." *SF News*, July 30, 2019, https://sfist.com/2019/07/30/regarding-the-1989-schoolyard-shooting-that-prompted-california-to-ban-assault-weapons/.

Benjamin, Philip. "New Group Urges Laws to Curb Sale of Firearms." *New York Times*, December 4, 1963.

Berghole, Richard. "Reagan Will Fight for Gun Ownership: Opposes Firearms Ban, Says Issue Not Involved in Texas Shootings." *Los Angeles Times*, August 3, 1966, 3.

"Bob Kennedy Blames Rifle Group for Deaths." *Los Angeles Times*, August 25, 1967, 4.

"A Bow-Tie Goodbye for Justice John Paul Stevens." Associated Press, June 28, 2010.

Brevin, Jess, "Bow Ties Are Back (to Honor Justice Stevens)." *Wall Street Journal*, June 28, 2010, https://www.wsj.com/articles/BL-WB-21401.

Burger, Warren E. "The Right to Bear Arms: A Distinguished Citizen Takes a Stand on One of the Most Controversial Issues in the Nation." *Parade Magazine*, January 14, 1990.

Chemerinsky, Erwin. "The Supreme Court Gun Fight: A Case of Conservative Activism," *Los Angeles Times*, June 27, 2008, A27.

"Chicago Council Votes Ban on New Handguns." *New York Times*, March 20, 1982.

"City Wide Raid on Concealed Weapons." *New York Times*, February 14, 1911.

Crewdson, John M. "Levi Says U.S. Is Studying Ways to Curb Pistols in Urban Areas." *New York Times*, April 7, 1975.

Dembart, Lee, and Kevin Roderick. "Voters Overwhelmingly Reject Handgun Law." *Los Angeles Times*, November 3, 1982.

"Dodd Will Tighten Bill on Gun Sales." *New York Times*, November 28, 1963, 20.

"Edward Kennedy Presses for Speed on Gun Controls." *New York Times*, August 17, 1966, 34.

Gallup, George. "The Gallup: A Majority for Permit to Buy Gun." *Washington Post*, January 16, 1964, A15.

Gans, David, and Doug Kendall. "*Heller* Originalism and the Revival of the Privileges or Immunities Clause." *Balkinization*, December 11, 2008, https://balkin.blogspot.com/2008/12/heller-originalism-and-revival-of.html.

Geehan, James, and Ted Warmbold. "Overview of Gun Control." *Sun-Telegram* (San Bernardino, CA), July 17, 1975.

Germania, Ramon. "Buying Rifle Is Easy: Legislation Sidetracked, Guns Bought Abroad." *Washington Post*, November 25, 1963, A9.

Getlin, Josh. "No Constitutional Right to Ownership: Powell Calls for Stricter Control on Handguns." *Los Angeles Times*, August 8, 1988.

Greenhouse, Linda. "Gun Case Causes Bush Administration Rift." *New York Times*, March 17, 2008, https://www.nytimes.com/2008/03/17/washington/17scotus.html.

Gouls, Jack. "The Firearms Issue: 'C.B.S. Reports' Presents a Provocative Examination of a National Problem." *New York Times*, June 11, 1964.

"Gun Aversion Laid to Death of Kennedy." *Washington Post*, March 14, 1964, A5.

"The Gun Culture." *New York Times*, September 24, 1975.

Ingraham, Christopher. "Nobody Knows How Many Members the NRA Has, but Its Tax Returns Offer Some Clues." *Washington Post*, February 26, 2018.

"Johnson's Gun Control Plan Opposed by CORE Official." *New York Times*, July 15, 1968, 18.

Kinsley, Michael. "Slicing Up the Second Amendment." *Washington Post*, February 8, 1990.

"Know Your Lawmakers." *Guns*, April 1960, 4.

Lardner, George, Jr. "McNamara Deplores Lack of Firearms Control Law." *Washington Post*, July 2, 1967, A3.

Leonnig, Carol D. "Gun Ban Ruling Has Fenty on the Spot, Pursuing Case Would Be Risky." *Washington Post*, May 17, 2007, Metro section.

"Lock and Load." *New York Times*, June 27, 2008, A18.

McGinty, Jo Craven. "The Rich, the Famous and the Armed." *New York Times*, February 20, 2011.

"Nelson Shields 3d, 69, Gun-Control Advocate." *New York Times*, January 27, 1993.

Oppenheimer, Reuben. "Gun Control and the Second Amendment." *Baltimore Sun*, September 22, 1968, K3.

Parascandola, Rocco, and Alison Gendar. "Lifestyles of the Rich and Packin': High-Profile Celebrities Seeking Gun Permits on the Rise." *New York Daily News*, September 27, 2010.

"The Right to Bear Arms." *New York Times*, August 31, 1911.

Sack, Kevin. "Lawyer Opposing Health Law Is Familiar Face to the Justices." *New York Times*, October 26, 2011, https://www.nytimes.com/2011/10/27/us/politics/paul-d-cle ments-latest-high-profile-cases.html.

"San Francisco to Appeal Ruling on Gun Ordinance." *New York Times*, October 15, 1982.

Saxon, Wolfgang. "Carl Bakal, 86: Offered a Warning on Firearms." *New York Times*, April 3, 2004.

"The Second Amendment's Reach." *New York Times*, March 2, 2010, https://www.ny times.com/2010/03/02/opinion/02tue1.html.

Valentine, Paul W. "Rush of Paperwork." *Washington Post*, September 24, 1976.

White, Adam J. "Wilkinson and Posner, Dissenting: Two Conservative Judges Challenge Justice Scalia." *Weekly Standard*, December 15, 2008.

Will, George F. "GOP Can Transform Politics with African-American Vote." *Tampa Bay Times*, September 27, 2005.

Young, Robert. "Johnson Signs Gun Bill, Asks Tighter Curbs." *Chicago Tribune*, October 23, 1968, A4.

Zorn, Eric. "Morton Grove Gun Ban Quietly Turns 5." *Chicago Tribune*, June 15, 1986.

*Internet Resources*

Amar, Akhil Reed. "Putting the Second Amendment Second: Reframing the Constitutional Debate over Gun Control." *Slate*, March 17, 2008, https://slate.com/news
-and-politics/2008/03/reframing-the-constitutional-debate-over-gun-control.html.

Cato Institute. "Clark Neily," https://www.cato.org/people/clark-neily.

———. "Robert Levy," https://www.cato.org/people/robert-levy.

Cramer, Clayton. "Gun Scarcity in the Early Republic." Firearms Owners Against Crime,
2000, https://foac-pac.org/uploads/Cramer-GunScarcity%20in%20early%20Amer
ica.pdf.

Davies, Anne. "Cities Targeted as DC Gun Ban Ends." *The Age*, June 28, 2008, https://
www.theage.com.au/world/cities-targeted-as-dc-gun-ban-ends-20080627–2y4a
.html.

Denniston, Lyle. "Second Amendment Drama: Act II." *SCOTUSblog*, February 25, 2010,
https://www.scotusblog.com/2010/02/second-amendment-drama-act-ii/.

Gallup Poll. "Guns." Gallup. Accessed November 7, 2022, https://news.gallup.com/poll
/1645/guns.aspx.

Gilson, Dave. "New Data Shows That the NRA's Trump Bump Has Evaporated." Mother
Jones, January 24, 2021.

"Glenn Miller." Arlington National Cemetery. Accessed November 5, 2022, http:/www
.arlingtoncemetery.mil/Explore/Notable-Graves/Other-Prominent-Figures/Glenn
Miller.

Mauro, Tony. "NRA Will Argue in Second Amendment Case." *The BLT: The Blog of
LegalTimes*, January 25, 2010, https://legaltimes.typepad.com/blt/2010/01/nra-will
-argue-in-second-amendment-case.html.

"NRA to Defend against NY Attorney General in Manhattan, Drops Own Lawsuit."
CNBC, June 4, 2021, https://www.cnbc.com/2021/06/04/nra-drops-lawsuit-against
-ny-attorney-general-to-pursue-claims-in-manhattan.html.

Obie, Mark. "He Won the Supreme Court Case that Transformed Gun Rights. But Dick
Heller Is a Hard Man to Please." *The Trace*, March 20, 2016, https://www.thetrace
.org/2016/03/dick-heller-second-amendment-hero-abolish-gun-regulation/.

"Self-Defense Gun Use." Violence Policy Center. Accessed November 6, 2022, http://vpc
.org/revealing-the-impacts-of-gun-violence/self-defense-gun-use/.

"Seven Ways to Compute the Relative Value of a U.S. Dollar Amount, 1774 to the Present," MeasuringWorth, 2015, http://www.measuringworth.com/uscompare.

"Stephen P. Halbrook, Ph.D.: Attorney at Law—Specializing in Constitutional Cases."
Accessed December 20, 2022, https://stephenhalbrook.com/.

Sullum, Jacob. "Scotus Vacates 4 Decisions Upholding Gun Control Laws Whose Constitutionality Now Looks Doubtful." *Reason*, July 1, 2022, https://reason.com/2022/07/01
/scotus-vacates-4-decisions-upholding-gun-control-laws-whose-constitutionality
-now-looks-doubtful/.

"Supreme Court Procedure." *SCOTUSblog*, https://www.scotusblog.com/supreme-court
-procedure/.

Williamson, Samuel H. "Seven Ways to Compute the Relative Value of a U.S. Dollar Amount, 1774 to the Present." MeasuringWorth, 2015, http://www.measuringworth.

*Unpublished Materials*

George Mason University Law School Moot Court. Moot Oral Argument of District of Columbia v. Heller, March 6, 2008 (on file with Stephen P. Halbrook).

*Books*

Cogan, Neil H., ed. *The Complete Bill of Rights: The Drafts, Debates, Sources and Origins.* New York: Oxford University Press, 1997.
Cooley, Thomas M. *The General Principles of Constitutional Law.* Boston: Little, Brown, 1898.
Corwin, Edwin S. *The Constitution and What It Means Today.* Princeton, NJ, Princeton University Press, 1924.
———, Harold W. Chase, and Craig R. Ducat. *Edward S. Corwin's Constitution and What It Means Today.* Princeton, NJ: Princeton University Press, 1978.
Daly, Kathleen, Peter H. Rossi, and James D. Wright. *Under the Gun: Weapons, Crime and Violence in America.* Chicago: Aldine Publishing, 1983.
Hamilton, Alexander, James Madison, and John Jay. *The Federalist.* Edited, with Introduction and Historical Commentary, by J. R. Pole. Indianapolis, IN: Hackett Publishing, 2005.
Hardy, David T. *The Papers of Justice Harry Blackmun: Insights into the Supreme Court and the Second Amendment.* In the authors' possession.
Kenyon, Cecelia M., ed. *The Anti-Federalists.* Indianapolis, IN: Bobbs-Merrill, 1966.
Lott, John. *The War on Guns: Arming Yourself against Gun Control Lies.* Washington, DC: Regnery Publishing, 2016.
Malcolm, Joyce. *To Keep and Bear Arms: The Origins of An Anglo-American Right.* Cambridge, MA: Harvard University Press, 1996.
Nowak, John E., Ronald D. Rotunda, and J. Nelson Young. *Handbook on Constitutional Law.* St. Paul, MN: West Publishing, 1978.
Pound, Roscoe. *The Development of Constitutional Guarantees of Liberty.* New Haven, CT: Yale University Press, 1957.
Roberts, Joseph B., Jr., ed. *The American Rifleman Goes to War: The Guns, Troops and Training of World War II as Reported in the NRA's Magazine.* Fairfax, VA: National Rifle Association, 1992.
Rossi, Peter H., and James D. Wright. *Armed and Considered Dangerous: A Survey of Felons and Their Firearms.* Chicago: Aldine Publishing, 1986.
Salter, John B., Jr., and Don. B. Kates Jr., eds. *Restricting Handguns: The Liberal Skeptics Speak Out.* Croton-on-Hudson, NY: North River Press, 1979.

Scalia, Antonin. *A Matter of Interpretation: Federal Courts and the Law*. Princeton, NJ: Princeton University Press, 1997.

Stevens, John Paul. *The Making of a Justice: Reflections on My First 94 Years*. New York: Little, Brown, 2019.

Story, Joseph. *Commentaries on the Constitution of the United States*. Edited by H. Jefferson Powell. Durham, NC: Carolina Academic Press, 1987.

Tribe, Laurence. *American Constitutional Law*. New York: Foundation Press, 1978.

———. *American Constitutional Law*, 2nd ed. New York: Foundation Press, 1988.

Tucker, St. George, ed. *Blackstone's Commentaries with Notes of Reference to the Constitution and Laws of the United States and of the Commonwealth of Virginia in Five Volumes* (Orig. pub., Philadelphia: William Young Birch and Abraham Small, 1803). Edited with an Introduction by Paul Finkelman and David Cobin. Union, NJ: Lawbook Exchange, 1996.

Tushnet, Mark V. *Out of Range: Why the Constitution Can't End the Battle over Guns*. New York: Oxford University Press, 2007.

Weber, Max. *Economy and Society: An Outline of Interpretive Sociology*. Edited by Guenther Roth and Claus Wittich. Berkeley: University of California Press, 1978.

Wilson, James. *Works of James Wilson*, vol. II. Edited by Kermit Hall and Mark David Hall. Indianapolis, IN: Liberty Fund, 2007.

*Articles, Book Chapters, and Reports*

Alviani, Joseph D., and William R. Drake. "Handgun Control: Issues and Alternatives." United States Conference of Mayors, Handgun Control Project, Washington, DC, 1975.

Bogus, Carl. "The History and Politics of Second Amendment Scholarship: A Primer." Symposium on the Second Amendment: Fresh Looks, *Chicago-Kent Law Review* 76, 1 (2000): 3–26.

Churchill, Robert H. "Gun Ownership in Early America: A Survey of Manuscript Militia Returns." *William and Mary Quarterly* 60, 3 (July 2003): 615–642.

Cooley, Thomas M. "Constitutional Limitations on Firearms Regulation." *Duke Law Journal* 1969, 4 (1969): 773–802.

Cornell, Saul. "Originalism on Trial: The Use and Abuse of History in *District of Columbia v. Heller*." *Ohio State Law Journal* 69, 4 (2008): 625–640.

Cress, Lawrence Delbert. "An Armed Community: The Origins and Meaning of the Right to Bear Arms." *Journal of American History* 71, 1 (June 1984): 22–42.

Cunningham, John W. "The Tin Star." *Collier's Magazine*, December 6, 1947.

Debenedetti, Charles. "American Historians and Armaments: The View from Twentieth-Century Textbooks." *Diplomatic Affairs* 6, 4 (Fall 1982): 323–337.

Emery, Lucillius A. "The Constitution Right to Keep and Bear Arms," *Harvard Law Review* 28, 5 (1915): 473–477.

Fairman, Charles. "Does the Fourteenth Amendment Incorporate the Bill of Rights?" *Stanford Law Review* 2, 1 (December 1949): 5–139.

Frankfurter, Felix. "Memorandum on 'Incorporation' of the Bill of Rights into the Due Process Clause of the Fourteenth Amendment." *Harvard Law Review* 78, 4 (February 1965): 746–783.

Gura, Alan. "Briefing the Second Amendment before the Supreme Court." *Duquesne Law Review* 47, 2 (2009): 225–279.

Halbrook, Stephen P. "The Jurisprudence of the Second and Fourteenth Amendments." *George Mason Law Review* 4, 1 (1981): 1–69.

Hardy, David T. "Armed Citizens, Citizen Armies: Toward a Jurisprudence of the Second Amendment." *Harvard Journal of Law and Public Policy* 9, 3 (1986): 559–638.

Harris, Richard. "A Reporter at Large: Handguns." *New Yorker*, July 26, 1976.

Ho, Dale E. "Dodging a Bullet: McDonald v. City of Chicago and the Limits of Progressive Originalism." *William and Mary Bill of Rights Journal* 19, 2 (2010): 369–417.

Imlay, Charles V. "The Uniform Firearms Act." *American Bar Association Journal* 12, 11 (November 1926): 767–769.

Kates, Don B. Jr. "Handgun Prohibition and the Original Meaning of the Second Amendment." *Michigan Law Review* 82, 204 (1983): 204–273.

Kleck, Gary, and Marc Gertz. "Armed Resistance to Crime: The Prevalence and Nature of Self-Defense with a Gun." *Journal of Criminal Law and Criminology* 86, 1 (1995): 150–187.

Levinson, Sanford. "The Embarrassing Second Amendment." *Yale Law Journal* 99, 3 (December 1989): 637–659.

Lindgren, James. "Book Review: Fall from Grace, Arming America and the Bellesiles Scandal." *Yale Law Journal* 111 (2002): 2195–2249.

Lund, Nelson. "The Second Amendment: Political Liberty and the Right to Self-Preservation." *Alabama Law Review* 39, 1 (1987): 103–130.

Malcolm, Joyce. "The Right of the People to Keep and Bear Arms: The Common Law Tradition." *Hastings Constitutional Law Quarterly* 10, 2 (1983): 285–314.

Orwell, George. "Don't Let Colonel Blimp Ruin the Home Guard." In *The Complete Works of George Orwell*, vol. 12, ed. Peter Davison, 362–365. London: Seeker & Warburg, 1998.

Plucknett, Theodore F. T. "Bonham's Case and Judicial Review." *Harvard Law Review* 40 (1926): 30–70.

Rau, Charles G. "Those Distinguished Awards." *American Rifleman Magazine* 102, 2 (February 1954): 28–30.

Reynolds, Glenn Harlan. "The Second Amendment as Ordinary Constitutional Law." *Tennessee Law Review* 81 (2014): 407–416.

Scalia, Antonin. "Originalism: The Lesser Evil." *University of Cincinnati Law Review* 57, 3 (1989): 849–866.

Shalhope, Robert. "The Ideological Origins of the Second Amendment." *Journal of American History* 69, 3 (December 1982): 599–614.

Shapiro, Ilya. "Friends of the Second Amendment: A Walk through the Amicus Briefs in D.C. v. Heller." *Journal of Firearms and Public Policy* 20 (2008): 15–41.

Sprecher, Robert A. "The Lost Amendment." *American Bar Association Journal* 51, 7 (1965): 665–669.

Sugarmann, Josh. *Assault Weapons in America.* Washington, DC: Firearms Policy Project of the Violence Policy Center, 1988.

Van Alstyne, William. "The Second Amendment and the Personal Right to Arms." *Duke Law Journal* 43, 6 (1994): 1236–1255.

Vizzard, William J. "The Current and Future State of Gun Policy in the United States." *Journal of Law and Criminology* 104, 4 (Fall 2014): 879–904.

Warner, Sam B. "The Uniform Pistol Act." *Journal of Criminal Law and Criminology* 29, 4 (Nov./Dec. 1938): 529–554.

Yeager, Matthew G., Joseph D. Alviani, and Nancy Loving. "How Well Does the Handgun Protect You and Your Family?: Technical Report 2." United States Conference of Mayors, Washington, DC, January 1, 1976.

*Films and Video Media*

Burger, Warren. *PBS NewsHour.* By Charlayne Hunter-Gault. Public Broadcasting Service, 1991.

Campbell, Norman, dir. *All in the Family.* Season 3, episode 1. "Archie and the Editorial." Aired September 16, 1972, on NBC.

*First Monday.* Episode: "Showdown," aired April 22, 2002.

*Friendly Persuasion.* Allied Artists, 1956.

Hibbs, Jesse, dir. *To Hell and Back.* Universal, 1955.

Houston, John, dir. *The Red Badge of Courage.* Metro-Goldwyn Mayer, 1951.

Jarvis, Lucy, producer. *A Shooting Gallery Called America.* Aired April 29, 1975, on NBC.

MacDonnell, Norman, producer. *Gunsmoke.* CBS Studios.

*Little Caesar.* Warner Bros., 1931.

Nolan, Christopher, dir. *Dunkirk.* Warner Bros., 2017.

Pirosh, Robert, dir. *Go for Broke.* Metro-Goldwyn Mayer, 1951.

*The Public Enemy.* Warner Bros. 1931.

*Scarface.* Warner Bros, 1932.

Wellman, William A., dir. Battleground. Metro-Goldwyn Mayer, 1949.

Zinneman, Fred, dir. *High Noon.* Stanley Kramer Productions, 1952.

*Miscellaneous*

Catalog No. 124, Sears, Roebuck and Co., Chicago, 1912, 906–909.

*Guns,* January 1959.

*Guns,* April 1960.

*Guns,* January 1961.

SECONDARY SOURCES

*Books*

Amar, Akhil Reed. *The Bill of Rights: Creation and Reconstruction.* New Haven, CT: Yale University Press, 1998.

Anderson, Jervis. *A. Philip Randolph: A Biographical Portrait.* New York: Harcourt, 1972.

Bailey, Thomas A., and Paul B. Ryan. *Hitler vs. Roosevelt: The Undeclared Naval War.* New York: Free Press, 1979.

Bakal, Carl. *The Right to Bear Arms.* New York: McGraw-Hill, 1966.

Berger, Raoul. *The Fourteenth Amendment and the Bill of Rights.* Norman: University of Oklahoma Press, 1989.

————. *Government by Judiciary: The Transformation of the Fourteenth Amendment,* 2nd ed. Indianapolis, IN: Liberty Fund, 1997.

Bugliosi, Vincent. *Four Days in November: The Assassination of President John F. Kennedy.* New York: W. W. Norton, 2007.

Clark, Alan. *Barbarossa: The Russian German Conflict, 1941–1945.* New York: Quill, 1965.

Clark, Ramsey. *Crime in America: Observations on its Nature, Causes, Prevention and Control.* New York: Simon & Schuster, 1970.

Cobb, Charles E., Jr. *This Nonviolent Stuff'll Get You Killed: How Guns Made the Civil Rights Movement Possible.* New York: Basic Books, 2014.

Coke, Edward. *The Third Part of the Institutes of the Laws of England.* Buffalo, NY: William S. Hein, 1986.

Cornell, Saul. *A Well-Regulated Militia: The Founding Fathers and the Origins of Gun Control in America.* New York: Oxford University Press, 2006.

Cottrol, Robert J. *The Afro-Yankees: Providence's Black Community in the Antebellum Era.* Westport, CT: Greenwood Press, 1982.

————. *The Long, Lingering Shadow: Slavery, Race and the Law in the American Hemisphere.* Athens. University of Georgia Press, 2013.

Curtis, Michael Kent. *No State Shall Abridge: The Fourteenth Amendment and the Bill of Rights.* Durham, NC: Duke University Press, 1986.

De Conde, Alexander. *Gun Violence in America: The Struggle for Control.* Boston: Northeastern University Press, 2001.

Dewey, Donald. *James Stewart: A Biography.* Atlanta: Turner Publishing, 1996.

Du Bois, W. E. B. *Black Reconstruction in America, 1860–1880.* New York: Meridian Books, 1968.

Engs, Ruth. *The Eugenics Movement: An Encyclopedia.* Westport, CT: Greenwood Press, 2005.

Foner, Eric. *Reconstruction: America's Unfinished Revolution, 1863–1877,* updated ed. New York: Harper, 2014.

Friedman, Lawrence M. *A History of American Law,* 3rd ed. New York: Simon & Schuster, 2005.

Gannon, Michael. *Operation Drumbeat: The Dramatic True Story of Germany's First*

*U-Boat Attacks along the American Coast in World War II.* New York: HarperPerennial, 1991.

Gentry, Curt. J. *Edgar Hoover: The Man and the Secrets.* New York: W. W. Norton, 1991.

Gillette, William. *The Right to Vote: Politics and the Passage of the Fifteenth Amendment.* Baltimore: Johns Hopkins University Press, 1965.

Goodrich, Frances. Albert Hackett, Frank Capra and Jo Swerling. *It's a Wonderful Life: From the 1946 Liberty Film.* New York: St. Martin's Press, 1986.

Goss, Kristin A. *Disarmed: The Missing Movement for Gun Control in America.* Princeton, NJ: Princeton University Press, 2008.

Graham, Don. *No Name on the Bullet: A Biography of Audie Murphy.* New York: Viking Press, 1989.

Halbrook, Stephen P. *The Founders' Second Amendment: Origins of the Right to Bear Arms.* Chicago: Ivan R. Dee, 2008.

———. *Freedmen, the Fourteenth Amendment and the Right to Bear Arms, 1866–1876.* Westport, CT: Praeger, 1998.

———. *That Every Man Be Armed,* rev. ed. Albuquerque: University of New Mexico Press, 2013.

Hall, Kermit, and Peter Karsten. *The Magic Mirror: Law in American History,* 2nd ed. New York: Oxford University Press, 2009.

Harman, Nicholas. *Dunkirk: The Patriotic Myth.* New York: Simon & Schuster, 1980.

Hill, Lance. *The Deacons for Defense: Armed Resistance and the Civil Rights Movement.* Chapel Hill: University of North Carolina Press, 2004.

Hodges, Robert, Jr. *The Browning Automatic Rifle.* Oxford: Osprey Publishing, 2012.

Hyman, Harold, and William M. Wiecek. *Equal Justice under Law: Constitutional Development, 1835–1875.* New York: Harper & Row, 1982.

Johnson, Nicholas. *Negroes and the Gun: The Black Tradition of Arms.* Amherst, NY: Prometheus Books, 2004.

Jones, Martha S. *Birthright Citizens: A History of Race and Rights in Antebellum America.* New York: Cambridge University Press, 2018.

Keith, LeeAnna. *The Colfax Massacre: The Untold Story of Black Power, White Terror, and the Death of Reconstruction.* New York: Oxford University Press, 2009.

Kennett, Lee, and James La Verne Anderson. *The Gun in America: The Origins of a National Dilemma.* Westport, CT: Greenwood Press, 1975.

Kleck, Gary. *Point Blank: Guns and Violence in America.* New York: De Gruyter, 1991.

———. *Targeting Guns: Firearms and Their Control.* Hawthorne, NY: Aldine de Gruyter, 1997.

Kopel, David. *The Samurai, the Mountie and the Cowboy: Should America Adopt the Gun Controls of Other Democracies?* Buffalo, NY: Prometheus Books, 1992.

Lane, Charles. *The Day Freedom Died: The Colfax Massacre, the Supreme Court, and the Betrayal of Reconstruction.* New York: Holt, 2009.

Levy, Leonard W. *Origins of the Bill of Rights.* New Haven, CT: Yale University Press, 1999.

Loewen, James W. *Sundown Towns: A Hidden Dimension of American Racism.* New York: New Press, 2005.

Lord, Walter. *The Miracle of Dunkirk*. New York: Viking Press, 1982.

Malcolm, Joyce Lee. *To Keep and Bear Arms: The Origins of an Anglo-American Right*. Cambridge, MA: Harvard University Press, 1994.

Middlekauff, Robert. *The Glorious Cause: The American Revolution, 1763–1789*. New York: Oxford University Press, 1982, 2005.

Patrick, Brian Anse. *The National Rifle Association and the Media: The Motivating Force of Negative Coverage*. London: Arktos, 2013.

Rawle, William. *A View of the Constitution of the United States of America*, 2nd ed. Durham, NC: Carolina Academic Press, 2009.

Rehnquist, William H. *The Supreme Court*. New York: Knopf, 2001.

Schwoerer, Lois. *The Declaration of Rights*. Baltimore: Johns Hopkins University Press, 1981.

Shields, Pete, and John Greenya. *Guns Don't Die—People Do*. New York: Arbor House, 1981.

Smith, Abbot E. *Colonists in Bondage: White Servitude and Convict Labor in America, 1607–1776*. New York: Norton, 1971.

Smith, David A. *The Price of Valor: The Life of Audie Murphy, America's Most Decorated Hero of World War II*. Washington, DC: Regnery, 2015.

Spector, Ronald H. *Eagle against the Sun: The American War with Japan*. New York: Vintage Books, 1985.

Tucker, William. *The Science and Politics of Racial Research*. Chicago: University of Illinois Press, 1994.

Urofsky, Melvin I., and Paul Finkelman. *A March of Liberty: A Constitutional History of the United States, Vol. II, From 1898 to the Present*. New York: Oxford University Press, 2011.

Ward, Artemus, and David L. Weiden. *Sorcerers' Apprentices: 100 Years of Law Clerks and the United States Supreme Court*. New York: New York University Press, 2006.

Wheeler, Leslie. *Jimmy Who?: An Examination of Presidential Candidate Jimmy Carter—The Man, His Career, His Stands on the Issues*. Woodbury, NY: Barron's Educational Series, 1976.

Winkler, Adam. *Gunfight: The Battle over the Right to Bear Arms in America*. New York: W. W. Norton, 2011.

Wood, Gordon S. *Empire of Liberty: A History of the Early Republic, 1789–1815*. New York: Oxford University Press, 2009.

Wright, James D., Peter H. Rossi, and Kathleen Daly. *Under the Gun: Weapons, Crime and Violence in America*. New York: Aldine de Gruyter, 1983.

Yelton, David K. *Hitler's Volkssturm: The Nazi Militia and the Fall of Germany, 1944–1945*. Lawrence: University Press of Kansas, 2002.

*Articles, Book Chapters, and Encyclopedia Entries*

Boskin, Joseph. "The Revolt of the Urban Ghettoes, 1964–1967." *Annals of the American Academy of Political Science* 382 (March 1969): 1–14.

Bovarnick, Jeff. "Perpich v. United States Department of Defense: Who's in Charge of the National Guard?" *New England Law Review* 26 (Winter 1991): 453–494.

Briggs, B. Bruce. "The Great American Gun War." *Public Interest* 45 (Fall 1976): 37–62.

Brandwein, Pamela. "Dueling Histories: Charles Fairman and William Crosskey Reconstruct 'Original Understanding.'" *Law and Society Review* 30, 2 (1996): 289–334.

Calloway, Carolyn R. "Group Cohesiveness in the Black Panther Party." *Journal of Black Studies* 8, 1 (September 1977): 55–74.

Cantor, Louis. "Elihu Root and the National Guard: Friend or Foe?" *Military Affairs* 33, 3 (December 1969): 361–373.

Caplan, David I. "Restoring the Balance: The Second Amendment Revisited," *Fordham Urban Law Journal* 5, 1 (1976): 31–53.

Capozzola, Christopher. "The Only Badge Needed Is Your Patriotic Fervor: Vigilance, Coercion, and the Law in World War I America." *Journal of American History* 88, 4 (March 2002): 1354–1382.

Churchill, Robert H. "Gun Ownership in Early America: A Survey of Manuscript Militia Returns." *William and Mary Quarterly* 60, 3 (July 2003): 615–642.

Clark, David S. "Comparative Law in Colonial British America." *American Journal of Comparative Law* 59, 3 (Summer 2011): 637–674.

Collins, Michael G. "October Term 1896: Embracing Due Process." *American Journal of Legal History* 45, 1 (January 2001): 71–97.

Cook, Philip J. "The Great American Gun War: Notes from Four Decades in the Trenches." *Crime and Justice* 42, 1 (August 2013): 19–73.

Cornell, Saul. "A New Paradigm for the Second Amendment." *Law and History Review* 22, 1 (2004): 161–168.

Cottrol, Robert J., and Raymond T. Diamond. "'Never Intended to Be Applied to the White Population': Firearms Regulation and Racial Disparity—the Redeemed South's Legacy to a National Jurisprudence?" *Chicago Kent Law Review* 70, 3 (1995): 1307–1335.

———. The Second Amendment: Toward an Afro-Americanist Reconsideration." *Georgetown Law Journal* 80, 2 (December 1991): 309–362.

Crosskey, William W. "Charles Fairman, Legislative History and the Constitutional Limits on State Authority." *University of Chicago Law Review* 22, 1 (Autumn 1954): 1–143.

Denning, Brannon P. "Can the Simple Cite Be Trusted? Lower Court Interpretations of United States v. Miller and the Second Amendment." *Cumberland Law Review* 26, 3 (1995–1996): 961–1004.

Dowlut, Robert. "The Right to Arms: Does the Constitution or the Predilection of Judges Reign?" *Oklahoma Law Review* 36, 1 (Winter 1983): 65–106.

Elinson, Gregory. "Judicial Partisanship and the Slaughterhouse Cases: Investigating the Relationship between Courts and Parties." *Studies in American Political Development* 31, 1 (April 2017): 24–46.

Fallon, Richard H., Jr. "Strict Scrutiny." *UCLA Law Review* 54, 5 (June 2007): 1267–1338.

Fernbach, David. "Tom Wintringham and Socialist Defense Strategy." *History Workshop* 14, 1 (Autumn 1982): 63–91.

Finkelman, Paul. "James Madison and the Bill of Rights: A Reluctant Paternity." *Supreme Court Review* (1990), 301–347.

———. "Prelude to the Fourteenth Amendment: Black Legal Rights in the Antebellum North." *Rutgers Law Journal* 17 (Spring and Summer 1986): 415–448.

———. "A Well-Regulated Militia: The Second Amendment in Historical Perspective." *Chicago Kent Law Review* 76, 1 (2000), 195–236.

Fisher, Charles R. "The Maryland State Guard in World War II." *Military Affairs* 47, 1 (February 1983): 1–14.

Frye, Brian L. "The Peculiar Story of United States v. Miller." *NYU Journal of Law and Liberty* 3, 48 (2008): 48–82.

Goldstein, Robert J. "The Anarchist Scare of 1908: A Sign of Tensions in the Progressive Era." *American Studies* 15, 2 (Fall 1974): 55–78.

Goss, Kristin A. "Policy, Politics, and Paradox: The Institutional Origins of the Great American Gun War." *Fordham Law Review* 73, 2 (2004): 681–714.

Gunn, Steven. "Archery Practice in Tudor England." *Past and Present* 209, 1 (2010): 53–81.

Halliburton, Rudia, Jr. "The Tulsa Race War of 1921." *Journal of Black Studies* 2, 3 (March 1972): 333–357.

Havens, Thomas R. H. "Women and War in Japan, 1937–1945." *American Historical Review* 80, 4 (October 1975): 65–86.

Higgins, Billy. "Peter Caulder: A Free Black Soldier and Pioneer in Antebellum Arkansas." *Arkansas Historical Quarterly* 57, 1 (1999): 80–99.

Hocket, Jeffrey D. "Justices Frankfurter and Black: Social Theory and Constitutional Interpretation." *Political Science Quarterly* 107, 3 (Autumn 1992): 477–479.

Holmberg, Judith Vandell, and Michael Clancy. *People vs. Handguns: The Campaign to Ban Handguns in Massachusetts.* Washington, DC: United States Conference of Mayors, 1977.

Hulsebosch, Daniel J. "The Ancient Constitution and the Expanding Empire: Sir Edward Coke's British Jurisprudence." *Law and History Review* 21, 3 (Autumn 2003): 439–482.

Jackson, Maynard Holbrook, Jr. "Handgun Control: Constitutional and Critically Needed." *North Carolina Central Law Journal* 8, 2 (Spring 1977): 189–198.

Kates, Don B., Jr. "The Necessity of Access to Firearms by Dissenters and Minorities Whom Government Is Unwilling or Unable to Protect." In *Restricting Handguns: The Liberal Skeptics Speak Out*, eds. John B. Salter Jr. and Don B. Kates Jr., 185–193. Croton-on-Hudson, NY: North River Press, 1979.

———. "The Value of Civilian Arms Possession as a Deterrent to Crime or Defense against Crime." *American Journal of Criminal Law* 18, 2 (1991): 113–167.

Kopel, David B. "The Great Gun Control War of the Twentieth Century—and Its Lessons for Gun Laws Today." *Fordham Urban Law Journal* 39, 5 (2012): 1527–1616.

Lackenbauer, P. Whitney. "Guerrillas in Our Midst: The Pacific Coast Rangers, 1942–1945." *B.C. Studies* 155 (Autumn 2007): 31–67.

Lavender, Abraham D. "United States Ethnic Groups in 1790: Given Names as a Suggestion of Ethnic Identity." *Journal of American Ethnic History* 9, 1 (Fall 1989): 36–66.

Leff, Carol Skalnik, and Mark H. Leff. "The Politics of Ineffectiveness: Federal Firearms Legislation, 1919–38." *Annals of the American Academy of Political and Social Science* 455 (May 1981): 48–62.

Levinson, Sanford. "The Embarrassing Second Amendment." *Yale Law Journal* 99 (1989): 637–659.

Lewis, Thomas Tandy. "The Ironic History of Substantive Due Process: Three Constitutional Revolutions." *International Social Science Review* 76 (2001): 21–35.

Lindgren, James, and Justin L. Heather. "Counting Guns in Early America." *William and Mary Law Review* 43, 5 (2002): 1777–1842.

Lubert, Howard L. "Sovereignty and Liberty in William Blackstone's Commentaries on the Laws of England." *Review of Politics* 72, 2 (Spring 2010): 271–297.

Lund, Nelson. "The Ends of Second Amendment Jurisprudence: Firearms Disabilities and Domestic Violence Restraining Orders." *Texas Journal of Law and Politics* 4, 1 (1999): 157–192.

———. "The Second Amendment, Heller, and Original Jurisprudence." *UCLA Law Review* 56, 5 (June 2009): 1343–1376.

Lux, David S. "Tommy Gun," in *Guns in American Society*, ed. Gregg Lee Carter (Santa Barbara, CA: ABC-CLIO, 2012): 586–587.

Martinez, Ramiro, Jr., and Matthew T. Lee. "On Immigration and Crime." *Nature of Crime: Continuity and Change* 1 (2000): 485–524. Accessed via the National Criminal Justice Reference Service, https://www.ncjrs.gov/criminal_justice2000/vol_1/02j.pdf.

Moehling, Carolyn, and Anne Morrison Piehl. "Immigration, Crime and Incarceration in Early Twentieth Century America." *Demography* 46 (November 2009): 739–763.

Murphy, Paul. "Time to Reclaim: The Current Challenge of American Constitutional History." *American Historical Review* 69, 1 (October 1963): 64–79.

Nelli, Humbert S. "Italians and Crime in Chicago: The Formative Years, 1890–1920." *American Journal of Sociology* 74, 4 (January 1969): 373–391.

Peniston-Bird, Corinna M. "'All in It Together' and 'Backs to the Wall': Relating Patriotism and the People's War in the 21st Century." *Oral History* 40, 2 (Autumn 2012): 69–80.

Purvis, Thomas L. "The European Ancestry of the United States Population, 1790: A Symposium." *William and Mary Quarterly* 41, 1 (January 1984): 85–101.

Sandos, James A. "The Plan of San Diego: War and Diplomacy on the Texas Border, 1915–1916." *Arizona and the West* 14, 1 (Spring 1972): 5–24.

Shalhope, Robert E. "To Keep and Bear Arms in the Early Republic." *Constitutional Commentary* 16 (Summer 1999): 269–281.

Sitzmann, Joseph E. "High-Value, Low-Value, and No-Value Guns: Applying Free Speech Law to the Second Amendment." *University of Chicago Law Review* 86, 7 (2019): 1981–2030.

Spierenburg, Pieter. "Democracy Came Too Early: A Tentative Explanation for the Problem of American Homicide." *American Historical Review* 111, 1 (February 2006): 104–114.

Stanzel, Franz-Karl. "German Prisoners of War in Canada, 1940–1946: An Autobiography-Based Essay." *Canadian Military History* 27, 2 (2018): 1–19.

Tyler, Ronnie C. "The Little Punitive Expedition in the Big Bend." *Southwest Historical Quarterly* 78, 3 (January 1975): 271–291.

Volokh, Eugene. "State Constitutional Rights to Keep and Bear Arms." *Texas Review of Law and Politics* 11 (Fall 2006): 191–217.


*Magazine Articles*

Bourjaily, Phil. "JFK's M1 Garand Goes Up for Auction." *Field & Stream*, August 3, 2015.

Canfield, Bruce. "Thompson Submachine Gun: The Tommy Gun Goes to War." *American Rifleman*, February 15, 2011, http://www.americanrifleman.org/articles/2011/2/15/thompson-submachine-gun-the-tommy-gun-goes-to-war/.

Lee, Jerry. "The Lever-Action Rifle: An American Classic." *American Rifleman*, May 9, 2011.

Malcolm Garcia, J. "German POWs on the American Homefront." *Smithsonian Magazine*, September 15, 2009, https://www.smithsonianmag.com/history/german-pows-on-the-american-homefront-141009996/.

McNab, Chris. "Man-Stopper: Colt M1911." *MHQ: The Quarterly Journal of Military History* 26, 2 (Winter 2014): 17.

Schreier, Philip. "The Guns of U.S. Presidents." *American Rifleman*, February 15, 2016.


*Internet Sources*

"About Us: David T. Hardy." Of Arms and the Law. Accessed November 6, 2022, https://armsandthelaw.com/aboutus.php.

Auto-Ordnance Corp. Pre-World War 2 Advertisements, www.auto-ordnancecorporation.com.

Hall, Michelle. "By the Numbers: End of World War II." CNN, September 2, 2013, https://www.cnn.com/2013/09/02/world/btn-end-of-wwii.

Henry Repeating Rifle, c.1862," https://web.archive.org/web/20151024033210/http://www.ket.org/artstoolkit/statedivided/gallery/resources/henry/henry_more.pdf.

"Henry Rifle," http://www.civilwar.si.edu/weapons_henry.html.

Herb Block Foundation. "Gun Control Cartoons." Herblock. Accessed November 6, 2022, https://www.herbblockfoundation.org/gun-control-cartoons.

"History of Brady." Brady. Accessed November 6, 2022, https://www.bradyunited.org/history.

"History at a Glance: Women in World War II." National World War II Museum. Accessed November 5, 2022, https://www.nationalww2museum.org/students-teachers/student-resources/research-starters/women-wwii.

Meese, Edwin. "The American Bar Association, 7/9/85." Accessed November 6, 2022, https://www.justice.gov/site.

Movie Price Information. Dave Manuel. Accessed July 9, 2015, http://www.davemanuel.com/whatitcost.php.

Woolner, David. "The 'Special Relationship' between Great Britain and the United States Began with FDR." Roosevelt Institute, July 22, 2010, http://www.roosevelt institute.org/new-roosevelt/special-relationship-between-great-britain-and-united -states-began-fdr.

# Index